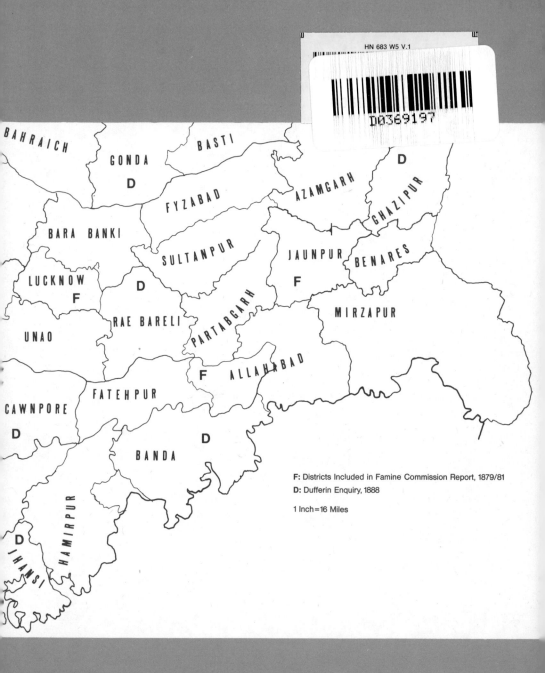

F: Districts Included in Famine Commission Report, 1879/81

D: Dufferin Enquiry, 1888

1 Inch=16 Miles

BAHRAICH

GONDA
D

BASTI

D

FYZABAD

AZAMGARH

GHAZIPUR

BARA BANKI

SULTANPUR

JAUNPUR

BENARES

LUCKNOW
F

D

PARTABGARH

F

MIRZAPUR

RAE BARELI

UNAO

F

ALLAHABAD

CAWNPORE

FATEHPUR

D

D

BANDA

HAMIRPUR

D

JHANSI

The Center for South and Southeast Asia Studies of the University of California is the unifying organization for faculty members and students interested in South and Southeast Asia Studies, bringing together scholars from numerous disciplines. The Center's major aims are the development and support of research and language study. As part of this program the Center sponsors a publication series of books concerned with South and Southeast Asia. Manuscripts are considered from all campuses of the University of California as well as from any other individuals and institutions doing research in these areas.

PUBLICATIONS OF THE CENTER FOR SOUTH AND SOUTHEAST ASIA STUDIES :

Angela S. Burger
Opposition in a Dominant-Party System : A Study of the Jan Sangh, the Praja Socialist Party, and the Socialist Party in Uttar Pradesh, India (1969)

Robert L. Hardgrave, Jr.
Nadars of Tamilnad : The Political Culture of a Community in Change (1969)

Eugene F. Irschick
Politics and Social Conflict in South India : The Non-Brahman Movement and Tamil Separatism, 1916–1929 (1969)

Briton Martin, Jr.
New India, 1885 : British Official Policy and the Emergence of the Indian National Congress (1969)

James T. Siegel
The Rope of God (1969)

Jyotirindra Das Gupta
Language Conflict and National Development : Group Politics and National Language Policy in India (1970)

Richard G. Fox
Kin, Clan, Raja and Rule : State-Hinterland Relations in Preindustrial India (1971)

Robert N. Kearney
Trade Unions and Politics in Ceylon (1971)

David N. Lorenzen
The Kāpālikas and Kālāmukhas : Two Lost Śaivite Sects (1971)

David G. Marr
Vietnamese Anticolonialism, 1885–1925 (1971)

AGRARIAN CONDITIONS IN NORTHERN INDIA

Volume One : The United Provinces under British Rule, 1860–1900

*This volume is sponsored by the
Center for South and Southeast Asia Studies,
University of California, Berkeley*

THE GANGES CANAL IN 1863 by William Simpson

ELIZABETH WHITCOMBE

AGRARIAN CONDITIONS IN NORTHERN INDIA

VOLUME I

THE UNITED PROVINCES UNDER
BRITISH RULE, 1860–1900

UNIVERSITY OF CALIFORNIA PRESS
BERKELEY, LOS ANGELES, LONDON

UNIVERSITY OF CALIFORNIA PRESS
Berkeley and Los Angeles, California
University of California Press, Ltd.
London, England

ISBN: 0-520-01706-4
LC 75-129027

Printed in the United States of America

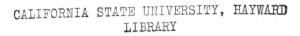

Der ganze Strudel strebt nach oben;
Du glaubst zu schieben, und du wirst geschoben.

FAUST, i, Walpurgisnacht.

PREFACE

As the industrial revolution grew to maturity, Britain's dominance in the West and in the world at large was, by the mid-nineteenth century, an acknowledged fact amply reflected in its factories, its ports, and the increasing number of its colonial possessions abroad. Amongst these, India stood pre-eminent by reason of its vastness, the density of its population, and the seemingly immeasurable extent of its natural wealth. The history of British interests in India had up to this time epitomised an era of commercial aggrandizement—but with one significant difference at least which marked it off from contemporary colonial pursuits of other European powers. The dignity of monopoly by the greatest trading concern of the time, the East India Company, had seen to it that the foundations of formal government by law, according to the dictates of civilized rule, had been securely laid. By the 1850s, however, the Company's narrowness and inefficiency had become an increasingly irksome frustration to the furtherance of the political and economic interests of its supervisor-partner, the Crown, and an obstacle in the way of the expansionist zeal of a wide range of newly formed joint-stock companies with an eye to East India prospects. Events in the last years of that decade followed rapidly in a logical succession : the annexation of Oudh, the "Mutiny" uprising, its suppression by the British Indian army, and the formal substitution of Crown for Company rule as a guarantee henceforth of peace, security, and constructive administration. The experience of the preceding century and, in particular, of the last fifty years was in no way to be jettisoned. It was instead to be consolidated on a grander scale, the range of its achievements widened and the pace of administrative activity intensified by an unprecedented application of "Saxon energy and British capital." In their awareness meanwhile of great temporal power and from a conviction of the rightness of Britain's self-appointed role to create a model amongst empires, spokesmen for Crown Government stressed the responsibility inherent

ix

in the task of enlarging upon its inheritance : not to supplant the existing social order, but to shepherd it firmly towards modernity.

Enterprise under the Crown was, as it had been under the Company, a strictly practical concern. The dominant aim was nowhere to make a desert blossom, but to stimulate the lagging productivity of traditional agriculture into realizing a greater and greater share of its potential wealth, within the shortest space of time and in areas where the investment necessary to achieve this aim might be assured of a generous as well as rapid return. Society, it was assumed with confidence, must inevitably share in the benefits which modernization necessarily implied. The North-Western Provinces and Oudh were drawn by their very geography into the forefront of the grand design. Canals were dug to divert water from the Ganges and Jumna into an irrigation network to expand the productive capacity of the great Doab plains. Railways and roads linked the Ganges valley with the agricultural hinterland, and ensured a passage from Bengal through the Doab to Delhi and Punjab. At the same time, the machinery of Government itself was subject to constant review. The Company's fiscal system, upon which Government and the law which it formulated very largely depended, was revised in accordance with modern standards not merely of equity but also of scientific assessment of the productivity of the land. The radical revision of revenue settlements (fixed, in the Provinces, for a duration of thirty years under Company regulations) which was implemented, district by district, from the mid-1850s brought Government into direct and constant contact with society, the rights and interests of which were redefined, equitably, in terms of quantifiable territorial assets in land. This task was greatly complicated, not merely by the uncooperative nature of the greater part of the available vernacular records and the minute and conflicting complexity of claims but also by the abrupt dislocation which the upper ranks of society—especially in Oudh and the eastern districts of the North-Western Provinces—had undergone following annexation and the "Mutiny" uprising. Their indigenous political figurehead had been removed, the outward expression of their incoherence had been summarily suppressed, and the opportunities for court and military service which the Nawabi and the East India Company militia had regularly offered had suddenly disappeared. Within society, meanwhile, the modernized property laws of landlord and tenant raised new obstructions in the way of the upper classes' exertion of local authority and aided in diverting the force of new economic pressures to which *zamindaris* and *talukdaris* alike were subject on to the lesser elements of society beyond the confines of the law. In the circumstances, Government was powerless to provide significant relief, that is, alternative avenues of employment. The constriction of rural society from top to bottom became in consequence increasingly evident—above all, in the form of a near universal rural indebtedness. The law, which aimed theoretically at the release of proprietary title at least from the encumbrance of debt and its conversion into the desired instrument for secure economic advancement, was hindered by the lawmakers', Government's, need also to observe the cautions dictated by political expediency. Out and out alienation, as a result of the logical working of the debt laws, of the property of large sections (probably the majority) of the zamindari and talukdari classes would have created a social change so revolutionary as to be inconceivable, given the demands of Government's situation. Compromise saw to it that a system of legal reliefs grew up alongside the debt and alienation laws to rescue the indebted proprietor from perdition.

Meanwhile, the development of communications and, from the mid-1870s, the rapid expansion of the export trade in food grains strained further the economic circumstances of agrarian society, whilst untoward physical changes manifested themselves over vast areas of the low-lying tracts of the Doab and the eastern uplands, where deforestation, the obstruction of natural drainage by public works embankments, together with lateral seepage and flush irrigation from canals exacerbated natural geological tendencies towards the accumulation of toxic quantities of alkali salts in the upper layers of the soil. A depressed peasantry laboured in a distorted environment. Government, bound to the inexorable pattern of precedent and hampered continually by the constraints of an increasingly inadequate budget, could do little more than concentrate its available resources on areas (especially to the north-west) which by reason of their superior resources managed to weather most storms and, for the rest, to observe. Official records compiled with dedication and an astonishing attention to detail by generations of overworked European officers presiding over a host of underpaid "native" subordinates constitute collectively a chronicle of what, from month to month and year to year, the great imperial drive for modernization in the late nineteenth century meant in terms of routine administration for the agrarian society and its environment, over which it was so vigorously superimposed. It is this history of transformation allied with preservation which has given

modern agrarian conditions in northern India their peculiar stamp.
From this period, the modern institutional framework—from public
works to the fiscal system, the property law, and the machinery of
justice and local government—derives its immediate origin. It is in
order to clarify the circumstances of that origin and hence the nature
of modern agrarian problems in embryo that this book has been
written.

In their combination of a rare diversity of natural conditions on
the one hand with a recent history of induced ecological distortion on
the other, the North-Western Provinces and Oudh stand as a laboratory
which is perhaps unique in Asia, and the world. Conditions there have
been observed and recorded, frequently with meticulous technical
accuracy, for over one hundred years. This ecological history is
accompanied by a similarly comprehensive documentation of parallel
institutional developments. The elements of innovation, from the
railways, roads, and canals to the enactment of statutes, are readily
distinguishable from the environment into which they were introduced
by their definably foreign origin—an origin known in detail from an
abundant contemporary literature on the engineering techniques and
the political and legal institutions of nineteenth-century Britain.
The initial point of contact may be established with chronological
precision. The story has also its economic counterpart, in the grafting
of new, and datable, economic institutions and incentives onto an
intricate pattern of old, local relationships, once flexible but, by the
mid-nineteenth century, increasingly subject to constriction.

This book can do little more than explore the periphery of such a
wealth of data and provide thus an introduction to further use of the
technical records of Government. In order to achieve this with clarity,
references both to policy and theory which provided the rationali-
zation for much of Government's activity have been cut to a minimum.
Relevant monographs are cited only where it seemed necessary to
draw attention to a major theoretical issue. The emphasis throughout
has been placed on action, and on the routine. Here a caveat must
be added. The excellence of regular nineteenth-century technical
observation, particularly in the natural and mechanical sciences and
in law, is not matched by the official statistical collections. Statistical
methods developed by mathematicians in Britain were seldom put
into routine administrative use. More often than not, quantification
of Government's business was recorded in the monthly and annual
statements compiled in the districts in obedience to directives sent

down from the upper reaches of the Secretariat. The directives themselves paid scant regard to the complexity of local issues— alienations of landed property, for example, where not one but three systems of formal law (revenue, civil. and personal), each with their own internal inconsistencies, conflicted in turn with one another whilst extra-legal complications went unheeded by the processes of registration. Government's need for information backed by at least an estimate of magnitude was such, moreover, as to compel a dis- regard for the difficulties which stood in the way of its collection. As a result, the completed statements—running into hundreds of appendix pages in the annual reports of the provincial revenue administrations—were traceable for the most part to the "village accountant and record-keeper," the *patwari,* and reflected only too often his slender regard for truth, as Government understood it to be. In the course of this book, therefore, figures are given where their source can be analysed—and where the margin of error appears least sensational. Elsewhere, explanations for the lack of precise quanti- fication are offered.

In constructing this account of day-to-day empire from the wide variety of documentation, it has been a guiding principle that com- ments, where they are offered, should be those of the contemporary observers themselves : *dor dor ve'dorashav*—"every generation has its interpreters." This has been done out of respect both for their positive contribution to scientific knowledge and for the refreshing candour of their criticism.

The research for this book was carried out in London from October 1965 to January 1968, financed by scholarships from the School of Oriental and African Studies and from the Institute of Commonwealth Studies, University of London. The examination of technicalities of irrigation and drainage was made possible by a grant for microfilm and photocopying from the University's Central Research Fund. That the book was completed within the scheduled time is due largely to the generosity of Miss H. J. Stocks.

The India Office Library and Records provided the greater part of the research material. My thanks are due to the Librarian and his staff for much assistance. Invidious though it may seem to single out the few for special mention where many have contributed, my appre- ciation to Mr. Charles Flaskett (now deceased) for locating many obscure items should not go unrecorded, nor to Mrs. V. C. Weston who proved both skilful and indefatigable in the pursuit of technicalia, from agricultural implements to the niceties of property law. Mrs. P. Sanders completed the task of reducing the manuscript to professional order admirably and without complaint. I must also thank the editorial staff of the University of California Press for their understanding and, above all, the patience with which they have brought about many improvements on the original presentation.

This book has benefited greatly at various points during its compilation from discussions with specialists. Dr. K. N. Chaudhuri, my supervisor, and Professor W. H. Morris-Jones drew attention on a number of occasions to the need for clarifying details of the argument. Professor R. P. Dore gave a salutary warning of the dangers of lapsing into an unnecessarily Weberian syntax; the obscurities which remain in spite of this testify to a regrettably immutable obstinacy. Meetings at the Centre of South Asian Studies, University of Cambridge, at the School of African and Asian Studies, University of Sussex, and at the South-Asia Institute, University of Heidelberg, proved a great source of stimulus, especially in developing some of the implications inherent in draft chapters on law and government. On economic and political details, discussion with Dr. P. D. Reeves, Professor B. D. Graham, and Mr. P. K. Choudhuri, of the University of Sussex, helped materially. Dr. C. L. Mehrotra, Agricultural Chemist to Government, Uttar Pradesh, and Dr. J. S. Kanwar, Deputy Director-General, Indian Council of Agricultural Research, were kind enough to read through the second chapter. Dr. Dieter Conrad, University of Heidelberg, scrutinized Chapter Five for my benefit. On more general questions of presentation, many friends proved willing and helpful critics. Mr. Yigal Wagner pointed out ambiguities and inadequacies in the original draft; for the defects still present, he is in no way accountable. Mr. Myles Burnyeat and Dr. Nancy Gayer emphasized *inter alia* the need for introductory passages which would summarize the argument.

To Amiya and Jasodhara Bagchi this book owes much, in terms of information, criticism, and an unfailing encouragement first to complete it and then to develop its implications. Daniel and Alice Thorner sifted innumerable outlines and drafts with all warmth and enthusiasm, and enabled some coherence and clarity to emerge step by step from much that was piecemeal and obscure; my debt to their joint interest and their generosity is inevitably beyond expression. It is to Alice, moreover, that I owe the suggestion to confine the study to the United Provinces, which have proved so fruitful an area for exploration. This book has raised many questions, analysed in a few brief passages each. If others will take these up and develop them, something of my debt for this initial suggestion would be repaid in the manner it so well deserves.

The argument on which the book is based grew in the course of discussions with Dr. Solomon Trone. To him I owe the lessons of a lifetime of more than ninety years—the distilled experience of a training in German science at the turn of the century and thereafter of events, encounters, and above all practical action in Russia, America, Europe, and the East. This analysis of agrarian problems of modern India from the standpoint of their immediate past reiterates his most fundamental lesson, which is also India's, that lasting solutions for such problems must be sought in the combination of rigorous technical dissection with a proportionate awareness of the intricacies, and the demands, of social relationships. To his memory and to his wife, whose hospitality and understanding enriched all our discussions, this book is dedicated in gratitude for an incomparable companionship.

ELIZABETH WHITCOMBE
Greve-in-Chianti, Florence

CONTENTS

FIGURES

NOTES

ON THE CAREERS OF PROMINENT OFFICERS
MENTIONED IN THE TEXT[1]

ALEXANDER, ERNEST BRUCE.   Appointed to the civil service, 1869. Served in NWP and Oudh as Assistant Magistrate and Collector, 1871-1874, Assistant Settlement Officer, Settlement Officer, Fatehpur, Moradabad, 1874-1881. Junior Member, Board of Revenue, Joint Magistrate and Deputy Collector, Deputy Commissioner, Magistrate and Collector, 1881-1894. Secretary, Judicial Department, NWP, 1894. Commissioner, Gorakhpur, 1896-1903. Retired, 1903.

BAINES, SIR JERVOIS ATHELSTANE.   Appointed, 1868. Served in Bombay as Assistant Magistrate and Collector, Assistant Political Agent, Deputy Superintendent of Census Operations, 1870-1880. Supervised working of Income Tax Act, 1886. Director of Agriculture, 1886-1889. Census Commissioner, India, 1889-1892. Secretary, Royal Commission on Opium, 1894-1895. Retired, 1895.

BAIRD SMITH, LIEUTENANT-COLONEL RICHARD.   Commissioned, Madras Engineers, 1836. Transferred, Bengal Engineers, 1839. Assistant to P. T. Cautley on Eastern Jumna Canal, 1840-1843; Superintendent of canal, 1843-1845, 1846-1848. Service in First and Second Sikh wars, 1845-1846, 1848-1849. Reported on Italian irrigation systems, 1852; on canal irrigation, Madras, 1853. Deputy Superintendent of Canals, NWP, 1853-1854. Director, Ganges Canal, Superintendent of Canals, NWP, 1854-1857. Distinguished service during "Mutiny," especially at siege of Delhi, 1857-1858. Appointed

[1]For brevity, district level appointments, from the lowest (Assistant Magistrate) to the highest (Magistrate and Collector)—in Oudh, Assistant Commissioner to Deputy Commissioner—together with districts in which these appointments were severally held and dates when held have been listed collectively. Only senior appointments and appointments of special significance for the text have been listed separately.

The sources used in compiling these career notes are as follows: *India Office List,* compiled from Official Records, by Direction of the Secretary of State for India in Council (London, annually from 1876); *Official Quarterly Civil List for the North-Western Provinces* (Allahabad, 1858–1877); *Official Quarterly Civil List for the Provinces of Oudh* (Lucknow, 1866–1877); *Official Quarterly Civil List for the North-Western Provinces and Oudh* (Allahabad, 1878–1901); *Dictionary of National Biography,* ed. Leslie Stephen (London, 1887–1888).

to military charge of Saharunpur, Muzaffarnagar, 1858. Superintendent-General of Irrigation, India, 1858-1859. Secretary, Public Works Department, India, 1859-1861. Reported on famine in NWP, 1860-1861. Died on furlough, 1861.

BENETT, WILLIAM CHARLES.   Appointed, 1865. Served in Oudh as Assistant Commissioner, Settlement Officer, Gonda, 1867-1876. Director, Agriculture and Commerce, NWP and Oudh, 1881-1884. Secretary, Board of Revenue, 1884-1886. Secretary, Revenue and Judicial Departments, NWP and Oudh, 1886-1888. Chief Secretary, 1887, 1889, 1891. Secretary, Revenue and Agriculture Department, India, 1890. Member, Provincial Legislative Council, 1889-1891. Settlement Commissioner, Oudh, 1894-1896. Retired, 1896.

BUCK, SIR EDWARD CHARLES.   Appointed, 1860. Served in NWP as Assistant Magistrate and Collector, Allahabad, Hamirpur, Cawnpore, Assistant Settlement Officer, Settlement Officer, Cawnpore, Farukhabad, 1863-1873. Secretary, Board of Revenue, 1873. Director, Agriculture and Commerce, NWP, 1875-1878, NWP and Oudh, 1878-1882. Commissioner for India, Melbourne Exhibition, 1880. Secretary, Revenue and Agriculture Department, India, 1882-1895. On special duty relating to proposals for agricultural improvements, 1895-1896. Retired, 1896.

BURKITT, WILLIAM ROBERT.   Appointed, 1860. Served in NWP as Assistant Magistrate and Collector, Joint Magistrate and Deputy Collector, District and Sessions Judge, Gorakhpur, Basti, Banda, Cawnpore, Bareilly, Muzaffarnagar, Saharunpur, Etawah, Azamgarh, Muttra, 1862-1891. Judicial Commissioner, Oudh, 1891. Judge, NWP High Court, 1892-1898. Retired, 1898.

BUTTS, HENRY HILL.   Appointed, 1861. Served in Oudh as Extra Assistant Commissioner, Assistant Commissioner, Assistant Settlement Officer, Subordinate Judge, District Judge, Deputy Commissioner, Kheri, Bara Banki, Gonda, Fyzabad, Lucknow, Sitapur, 1863-1893. Retired, 1893.

CADELL, ALAN.   Appointed, 1861. Served in NWP and Oudh as Assistant Magistrate and Collector, Settlement Officer, Magistrate and Collector, Banda, Muzaffarnagar, 1862-1880. Commissioner of Excise and Stamps, Inspector-General of Registration, NWP and Oudh, 1883. Junior Member, Board of Revenue, 1893; Senior Member, 1894. Member, Provincial Legislative Council, 1893. Lieutenant-Governor, NWP and Oudh, 1895. Member, Governor-General's Legislative Council, 1895. Member, Governor-General's Council, 1896. Member, Board of Revenue, India, 1896-1897. Retired, 1897.

CAPPER, WILLIAM COPELAND.   Appointed, 1851. Served in Punjab, Bombay, 1852-1855. Served in Oudh as Deputy Commissioner, Commissioner, Hardoi, Farukhabad, Bara Banki, Rae Bareli, Lucknow, 1856-1869. Financial Commissioner, Oudh, 1869. Judicial Commissioner, Oudh, 1877-1879. Retired, 1879.

CARNEGY, PATRICK. Appointed, 1858. Served in Oudh as Deputy Commissioner, Commissioner, Fyzabad, Rae Bareli, 1861-1874.

CAUTLEY, SIR PROBY THOMAS. Commissioned, Bengal Artillery, 1819. Transferred, Bengal Engineers, 1825. In charge of Doab (Eastern Jumna) Canal construction, 1831-1843. Reported on Ganges Canal project, 1840 (project sanctioned, 1841; construction begun, 1843). Director of Canals, NWP, 1848-1854. (Ganges Canal opened, April 1854.) Left India, May 1854. Died, 1871.

COLVIN, SIR AUCKLAND. Appointed, 1857. Served in NWP as Assistant Magistrate and Collector, Assistant Settlement Officer, Settlement Officer, Magistrate and Collector, Basti, Bijnour, Meerut, Muzaffarnagar, 1858-1864, 1869-1870, 1877. Under-Secretary, Home Department, India, 1864; Foreign Department, 1865. Secretary, Board of Revenue, NWP, 1870. Settlement Officer, Allahabad, 1870-1873. Secretary, NWP, 1873, 1875. Commissioner of Excise and Stamps, Inspector-General of Registration, NWP, 1873-1877. Commissioner, Inland Customs, India, 1877. Transferred to Egypt, Controller of Egyptian Finance, Finance Minister, Egypt, Consul-General, 1879-1883. Financial Member, Governor-General's Council, India, 1883-1887. Lieutenant-Governor, NWP, and Chief Commissioner, Oudh, 1887-1892. Retired, 1892.

CONNELL, CHARLES JAMES. Appointed, 1869. Served in Oudh as Assistant Commissioner, Assistant Settlement Officer, Settlement Officer, Fyzabad, 1871-1877. Under-Secretary, NWP and Oudh, 1878-1879. Assistant Magistrate and Collector, Magistrate and Collector, Budaon, Benares, Lucknow, 1879-1882. Junior Secretary, Board of Revenue, 1883. Retired, 1885.

COTTON, GENERAL SIR ARTHUR THOMAS. Commissioned, Madras Engineers, 1821. Served in Madras, Burma, 1822-1826. In charge of Cauvery irrigation, Madras, 1828, and construction of an irrigation system for Godaveri delta, 1844-1853. Chief Engineer, 1852. Service in Bengal, reporting on water communication between Ganges valley and Calcutta, 1858-1862. Resigned from government service, 1862. Thereafter, employed by Madras Irrigation Company to report on their works on the Ganges Canal and to prepare project for Sone irrigation works, Bihar. Retired from army, 1877.

CROOKE, WILLIAM. Appointed, 1869. Served in NWP and Oudh as Assistant Magistrate and Collector, Joint Magistrate and Deputy Collector, Deputy Commissioner, Magistrate and Collector, Bulandshahr, Gorakhpur, Etah, Muzaffarnagar, Mirzapur, 1871-1896. Retired, 1896.

CROSTHWAITE, SIR CHARLES HAUKES TOD. Appointed, 1857. Served in NWP as Assistant Magistrate and Collector, Joint Magistrate and Deputy Collector, Assistant Settlement Officer, Settlement Officer, Banda, Bareilly, Budaon, Etah, Etawah, Meerut, Moradabad, 1858-1877. Transferred to Central Provinces, 1877-1881. Additional Member, Governor-General's Council, 1881-1883. Chief Commissioner, British Burma, 1883-1884. Chief

Commissioner, Central Provinces, 1885. Member, Public Service Commission, 1886. Chief Commissioner, Burma, 1887-1890. Member, Governor-General's Council, 1890-1891. Lieutenant-Governor, NWP, and Chief Commissioner, Oudh, 1892-1895. Member, Council of India, 1895-1897; Vice-President, 1897-1898. Retired, 1898.

DANIELL, CLARMONT JOHN. Appointed, 1855. Served in NWP as Assistant Magistrate and Collector, Deputy Commissioner, Assistant Settlement Officer, Jhansi, Joint Magistrate and Deputy Collector, 1856-1872. Magistrate and Collector, Cawnpore, 1872-1878. Civil and Sessions Judge, Gorakhpur, 1878-1881. Commissioner, Allahabad, 1881-1883; Agra, 1883-1885. District Judge, Farukhabad, 1885-1886. Retired, 1886.

DAVIES, SIR ROBERT HENRY. Appointed, 1844. Served in NWP and Punjab as Assistant Commissioner, Settlement Officer, Joint Magistrate and Deputy Collector, 1845-1858. Secretary, Punjab, 1859-1864. Financial Commissioner, Oudh, 1864-1869. Chief Commissioner, Oudh, 1869-1871. Lieutenant-Governor, Punjab, 1871-1878. Retired, 1878. Member, Council of India, 1885-1895.

ELLIOTT, SIR CHARLES ALFRED. Appointed, 1856. Served in NWP and Oudh as Assistant Magistrate and Collector, Assistant Commissioner, Joint Magistrate and Deputy Collector, Mirzapur, Unao, Bahraich, Cawnpore, Bijnour, Agra, 1858-1863. Settlement Officer, Central Provinces, 1863-1866. Settlement Officer, Farukhabad, 1866-1870. Secretary, NWP, 1870-1877. Famine Commissioner, Mysore, 1877. Additional Secretary, Famine Branch, India, 1878. Secretary, Famine Commission, 1878. Census Commissioner, Oudh, 1880. Chief Commissioner, Assam, 1881. President, Public Expenditure Committee, 1886. Member, Governor-General's Council, 1887. Lieutenant-Governor, Bengal, 1890-1895. Retired, 1895.

EVANS, HENRY FARRINGTON. Appointed, 1865. Served in NWP as Assistant Magistrate and Collector, Settlement Officer, Joint Magistrate and Deputy Collector, District and Sessions Judge, Farukhabad, Agra, Jhansi, 1867-1890, 1893-1895. On special duty, Madras, Bombay, 1890-1891. Member, Deccan Agriculturists' Relief Commission, 1891-1892. Chief Secretary, NWP and Oudh, 1896-1898. Junior Member, Board of Revenue, 1898-1899. Additional Member, Provincial Legislative Council, 1899; Member, 1900-1902. Retired, 1902.

FORBES, COLONEL JOHN GREENLAW. Commissioned, Royal Engineers, 1854. Served in Public Works Department, Punjab, 1858-1863, NWP, 1863-1867. Superintendent, Irrigation Works, Oudh, 1867-1872. Superintending Engineer, Irrigation Branch, NWP, Punjab, Bengal, 1872-1877. On special duty, Government of India, to revise Sardah canal project, Oudh, 1878. Chief Engineer and Joint Secretary, Public Works Department, Buildings and Roads Branch, NWP and Oudh, 1881, Irrigation Branch, 1881. Secretary, Irrigation Branch, 1887. Inspector-General, Irrigation, and Deputy Secretary, Public Works Department, India, 1889-1892. Retired, 1892.

FORBES, WALTER ERNEST. Appointed, 1860. Served in Oudh as Assistant Commissioner, Assistant Settlement Officer, Settlement Officer, Deputy Commissioner, Commissioner, Pratabgarh, Lucknow, Fyzabad, 1862-1889. Retired, 1889.

FORBES, WILLIAM ARTHUR. Appointed, 1846. Served as Assistant Magistrate and Collector, Assistant Commissioner, NWP and Punjab, 1847-1856. Political Officer, NWP and Oudh, 1857-1858. Magistrate and Collector, Jaunpur, Meerut, 1862-1872. Commissioner, Allahabad, 1872. Junior Member, Board of Revenue, 1872-1875. Retired, 1875.

HALSEY, WILLIAM STIRLING. Appointed, 1854. Served in NWP as Assistant Magistrate and Collector, Ghazipur, Gorakhpur, 1854-1860. Assistant Commissioner of Paper Currency and Private Secretary to Financial Member of Council, India, 1860. Secretary, Civil Finance Commission, NWP, 1860. Joint Magistrate and Deputy Collector, Mirzapur, Magistrate and Collector, Benares, Cawnpore, 1860-1872. Cotton Commissioner, 1872. Civil and Session Judge, Mirzapur, Hamirpur, 1874-1875. Commissioner, Inland Customs, India, 1875-1876. Commissioner of Excise and Stamps, Inspector-General of Registration, NWP, 1875-1876. Retired, 1876.

HARINGTON, ARTHUR HENRY. Appointed, 1862. Served in Oudh as Assistant Commissioner, Bara Banki, Lucknow, 1863-1866. Assistant Secretary, Forest Department, India, 1866. Under-Secretary, Home Department, India, 1867. Junior Secretary to Chief Commissioner, Oudh, Superintendent of Excise and Stamps, Personal Assistant to Financial Commissioner, 1868. Assistant Commissioner, Bara Banki, Hardoi, Lucknow, Kheri, 1869-1872. Deputy Commissioner and Manager of Encumbered Estates, Fyzabad, Gonda, 1872-1878. Assistant Commissioner, Pratabgarh, Rae Bareli; Magistrate and Collector, Saharunpur, 1878-1885. Commissioner, Lucknow, Sitapur, Rae Bareli, Fyzabad, 1886-1887. Commissioner, Allahabad, 1889. Commissioner, Oudh, 1889-1891. Commissioner, Meerut, 1891-1896. Retired, 1896.

HENVEY, FREDERICK. Appointed, 1860. Served in NWP as Assistant Magistrate and Collector, Muttra, Agra, 1862-1865. Under-Secretary, Home Department, India, 1865. Secretary, Board of Revenue, NWP, 1866-1871. On special duty to compile narrative of 1869-1870 famine, 1871. Under-Secretary, Foreign Department, India, 1874. Resident, Nepal, 1877-1878. On special duty, Kashmir, 1878. Resident and Commissioner, Hyderabad Assigned Districts, 1883. Resident, East Rajputana States, 1885. Governor-General's Agent, Central India, 1888-1891. Retired, 1891.

HUME, ALLAN OCTAVIAN. Appointed, 1849. Served in NWP as Assistant Magistrate and Collector, Joint Magistrate and Deputy Collector, Meerut, Saharunpur, Aligarh, Dehra Dun, Mainpuri, Cawnpore, Fategarh, 1850-1858. Magistrate and Collector, Etawah, 1858-1867. Commissioner of Customs, NWP, Punjab, Central Provinces, 1867-1870. Secretary, Home

Department, India, 1870-1871. Secretary, Revenue, Agriculture and Commerce Department, India, 1871-1879. Member, Board of Revenue, NWP, 1879-1882. Retired, 1882.

IRVINE, WILLIAM. Appointed, 1862. Served in NWP as Assistant Magistrate and Collector, Joint Magistrate and Deputy Collector, Settlement Officer, 1864-1881. Magistrate and Collector, Ghazipur, 1881-1888. On special duty to Board of Revenue, 1879. Retired, 1888.

IRWIN, HENRY CROSSLY. Appointed, 1869. Served in NWP and Oudh as Assistant Commissioner, Joint Magistrate and Deputy Collector, Magistrate and Collector, 1871-1889. Secretary, Board of Revenue, NWP, 1893. District Judge, 1895-1896. Retired, 1896.

JENKINSON, SIR EDWARD GEORGE. Appointed, 1856. Served in NWP as Joint Magistrate and Deputy Collector, Benares, Farukhabad, Settlement Officer, Magistrate and Collector, Commissioner, Jhansi, 1858-1878. Commissioner, Oudh, 1878-1880. Retired from India service, 1880. Thereafter, Private Secretary to Lord Lieutenant of Ireland, Assistant Under-Secretary, Police and Crime, Ireland, 1882-1885.

LUMSDEN, JOHN JAMES FOOTE. Appointed, 1857. Served in NWP as Assistant Magistrate and Collector, Mirzapur, Joint Magistrate and Deputy Collector, Gorakhpur, Assistant Settlement Officer, Azamgarh, Joint Magistrate and Deputy Collector, Banda, Magistrate and Collector, Farukhabad, Benares, 1857-1873. Magistrate and Collector, Gorakhpur, 1873-1877, Mirzapur, 1877-1878. Commissioner, Rae Bareli, 1878-1879, Fyzabad, 1879, Gorakhpur, 1879-1889. Senior Member, Board of Revenue, NWP and Oudh, 1889-1891. Member, Provincial Legislative Council, 1891. Retired, 1891.

MACKINTOSH, JAMES SIMON. Appointed, 1867. Served in NWP as Assistant Magistrate and Collector, Benares, Ghazipur, 1867-1868. Assistant Secretary, NWP, 1870-1874. Private Secretary to Lieutenant-Governor, NWP, 1874-1875. Junior Secretary, NWP, 1876. Secretary, Board of Revenue, 1879-1896. Commissioner, Lucknow, 1896. Retired, 1896.

MACONOCHIE, G. B. Appointed, 1860. Served in Oudh as Assistant Commissioner, Assistant Settlement Officer, Settlement Officer, Unao, Lucknow, 1861-1867, Gonda, 1867-1877. Deputy Commissioner, Sultanpur, 1877. (No further appointments listed.)

MARKHAM, ALEXANDER MACAULAY. Appointed, 1863. Served in NWP as Assistant Magistrate and Collector, Assistant Settlement Officer, Settlement Officer, Magistrate and Collector, Bareilly, Bijnour, 1863-1874. Postmaster-General, NWP, 1874. Joint Magistrate and Deputy Collector, Settlement Officer, Allahabad, Joint Magistrate and Deputy Collector, Meerut, Saharunpur, Bijnour, Basti, 1875-1879. Commissioner, Meerut, 1879. Magistrate and Collector, Allahabad, 1880-1887. Commissioner, Allahabad, 1882, 1887. District and Sessions Judge, 1889-1897. Retired, 1897.

MAYNE, FRANCIS OTWAY. Appointed, 1846. Served in NWP as Magistrate and Collector, Banda, Agra, 1855-1864. On deputation to Oudh, 1864. Inspector-General of Police, NWP, 1867-1870. Commissioner, Allahabad, 1870. Junior Member, Board of Revenue, 1871-1872. Retired, 1872.

MCCONAGHEY, MATTHEW ALLEN. Appointed, 1862. Served in NWP as Assistant Magistrate and Collector, Agra, 1863-1865, Assistant Settlement Officer, Joint Magistrate and Deputy Collector, Settlement Officer, Mainpuri, Muttra, 1865-1875, Joint Magistrate and Deputy Collector, Magistrate and Collector, Banda, 1876-1879. President, Census Committee, NWP, 1878. Commissioner, Allahabad, 1878. Commissioner, Meerut, 1879-1880. Retired, 1880.

MESTON, BARON JAMES SCORGIE, OF AGRA AND DUNOTTAR. Appointed, 1883. Served in NWP and Oudh as Assistant Commissioner, Joint Magistrate and Deputy Collector, Settlement Officer, Budaon, 1892-1896, Deputy Commissioner, 1896-1897. Director, Land Records and Agriculture, 1897-1899. Secretary, NWP and Oudh, 1899-1903. Member, Provincial Legislative Council, 1899, 1901. Secretary, Finance Department, India, 1906. Lieutenant-Governor, United Provinces of Agra and Oudh, 1912-1918. Financial Member, Viceroy's Council, 1918-1919. Retired, 1919.

MILLETT, ARTHUR FENNING. Appointed, 1864. Served in NWP as Assistant Magistrate and Collector, Meerut, 1864-1865; in Oudh, as Assistant Commissioner, Unao, Assistant Settlement Officer, Pratabgarh, Bahraich, Sultanpur, Settlement Officer, Fyzabad, 1866-1879. Subordinate Judge, Fyzabad, District Judge, Lucknow, 1879-1883. Civil and Sessions Judge, Saharunpur, 1883-1889. Retired, 1889.

MCMINN, CHARLES WILLIAM. Appointed, 1864. Served in NWP as Assistant Magistrate and Collector, Benares, 1864; in Oudh, as Assistant Commissioner, Lucknow, Assistant Settlement Officer, Hardoi, Sitapur, Pratabgarh, Settlement Officer, Bara Banki, Kheri, 1865-1872. On special duty, Lucknow, for compilation of Oudh gazetteer, 1872-1874. Assistant Commissioner, Lucknow, Unao, Sultanpur, 1874-1877. Joint Magistrate and Deputy Collector, Agra, 1877. Transferred to Central Provinces, 1879. Commissioner, Central Provinces, 1887-1891. Retired, 1891.

MOENS, SEABORNE MAY. Appointed, 1858. Served in NWP as Assistant Magistrate and Collector, Joint Magistrate and Deputy Collector, Assistant Settlement Officer, Bareilly, 1861-1864, 1866-1874, Magistrate, Pilibhit, 1864-1866. Joint Magistrate and Deputy Collector, Allahabad, 1874, Saharunpur, 1874-1875, Jaunpur, 1875-1876. Magistrate and Collector, Gorakhpur, 1877. Died on furlough, 1878.

MONEY, ROWLAND. Appointed, 1831. Served in NWP as Civil and Sessions Judge, Saharunpur, 1858. Judge, Sadr Diwani and Nizamat Adawlat (highest provincial courts), Agra, 1858-1862. Junior Member, Board of Revenue, 1862. (No further appointments listed.)

MORELAND, WILLIAM HARRISON. Appointed, 1886. Served in NWP and

Oudh as Assistant Magistrate and Collector, Joint Magistrate and Deputy Collector, Assistant Settlement Officer, Assistant Commissioner, chiefly at Unao, Lucknow, 1887-1889. Director, Land Records and Agriculture, NWP and Oudh, 1899-1912. Agricultural Advisor, Indore State, 1913-1914. Retired, 1914.

MUIR, SIR WILLIAM. Appointed, 1837. Served in NWP as Settlement Officer, Cawnpore, Jhansi, 1840-1843, Magistrate and Collector, Fatehpur, 1844-1845. Secretary, Board of Revenue, 1847-1852. Secretary, NWP, 1852-1856. Member, Board of Revenue, 1856, 1859-1864. In charge of intelligence, Agra, 1857-1858. Secretary to Viceroy, for NWP, 1858. Member, Governor-General's Legislative Council, 1864-1865. Secretary, Foreign Department, India, 1865-1868. Lieutenant-Governor, NWP, 1868-1874. Financial Member, Governor-General's Council, 1874-1876. Member, Council of Secretary of State, 1876-1885. Retired, 1885. Principal, Edinburgh University, 1885.

NEALE, WALTER ERSKINE. Appointed, 1861. Served in NWP as Assistant Magistrate and Collector, Meerut, Jhansi, Settlement Officer, Farukhabad, Etawah, Hamirpur, 1862-1881. District and Sessions Judge, Allahabad, 1881. Magistrate and Collector, Muttra, Bareilly, 1881-1890. Commissioner, Oudh, 1890-1893. Commissioner, Agra, 1893-1894. Member, Board of Revenue, 1894-1895. Commissioner, Meerut, 1896-1897. Retired, 1897.

OLDHAM, WILTON. Appointed, 1856. Served in NWP as Assistant Magistrate and Collector, Mirzapur, 1857-1862, Joint Magistrate and Deputy Collector, Ghazipur, 1862-1866.

PATTERSON, ALEXANDER BLEAKLEY. Appointed, 1863. Served in NWP as Assistant Magistrate and Collector, Assistant Settlement Officer, Settlement Officer, Joint Magistrate and Deputy Collector, Aligarh, Bulandshahr, Fatehpur, Banda, Allahabad, Agra, 1864-1884. Commissioner, Northern India Salt Revenue, 1884-1889. Retired, 1889.

PITCHER, COLONEL DUNCAN GEORGE. Commissioned in the Royal Marine Light Infantry and Artillery, 1856. Served in Oudh as Assistant Commissioner, Small Cause Court Judge and Registrar, Lucknow, 1868-1882. On deputation to enquire into Forest Department administration, 1876; famine mortality in Rohilkhand and Oudh, 1878; inland emigration, 1882; working of Oudh Rent Acts, 1883. Deputy Director, Agriculture and Commerce, NWP and Oudh, 1882-1887. Director, Land Records and Agriculture, NWP and Oudh, 1887-1889. Director, Land Records, Gwalior State, 1890-1903. Retired, 1903.

PLOWDEN, TREVOR JOHN CHICHELEY. Appointed, 1826. Served in NWP, on settlement duty, Meerut, relating to Begum Sumroo's estate, 1836-1841. Civil and Sessions Judge, Ghazipur, 1851-1856.

PLOWDEN, SIR WILLIAM CHICHELE. Appointed, 1852. Served in NWP as Assistant Magistrate and Collector, Bulandshahr, Meerut, 1854-1855; in

Punjab, 1855-1863. Joint Magistrate and Deputy Collector, Ghazipur, Muttra, Allahabad, 1863-1864. Secretary, Board of Revenue, NWP, 1864-1870. On special duty to compile NWP census report, 1866, and 1872 census results, 1873. Magistrate and Collector, Benares, Meerut, Saharunpur, Civil and Sessions Judge, Moradabad, 1875-1877; Magistrate and Collector, Aligarh, 1877. Commissioner, Allahabad, 1877-1885. Retired, 1885.

REID, HENRY STEWART. Appointed, 1847. Served in NWP as Assistant Magistrate and Collector, Muttra, Saharunpur, 1847-1849, Joint Magistrate and Deputy Collector, Hamirpur, 1849-1850. Visitor-General of Schools (from 1855, designated Director of Public Instruction), NWP, 1850-1857. Secretary and Member, Committee for Framing Rules and Regulations for New Police, 1860. Magistrate and Collector, Meerut, Moradabad, 1864-1865. Civil and Sessions judge, Fyzabad, 1866. Financial Commissioner, Judicial Commissioner, Oudh, 1867. Member, Commission to Enquire into Prospects of Tea Cultivation, Bengal, 1867. Commissioner, Lucknow, 1868. Junior Member, Board of Revenue, NWP, 1868-1871; Senior Member, 1871-1872. Retired, 1872.

REID, JAMES ROBERT. Appointed, 1859. Served in NWP and Oudh as Assistant Magistrate and Collector, Joint Magistrate and Deputy Collector, Benares, Budaun, 1863-1865. Deputy Commissioner, Oudh, 1865-1868. Assistant Settlement Officer, Settlement Officer, Magistrate and Collector, Azamgarh, 1868-1883. Secretary, NWP, 1883-1884. Chief Secretary, NWP and Oudh, 1884-1888. Commissioner, Kumaun, 1888-1890. Member, Board of Revenue, NWP and Oudh, 1890-1891. Member, Provincial Legislative Council, 1891-1894. Retired, 1894.

RICKETTS, GEORGE HENRY MILDMAY. Appointed, 1847. Served in Bengal, Punjab, 1848-1858. Served in NWP as Magistrate and Collector, Civil and Sessions Judge, chiefly at Muttra, Allahabad, 1858-1873. Commissioner, Allahabad, 1873-1878. Junior Member, Board of Revenue, 1878-1879. Retired, 1879.

SMEATON, DONALD MACKENZIE. Appointed, 1867. Served in NWP as Assistant Magistrate and Collector, Allahabad, 1867-1870, Assistant Settlement Officer, Mainpuri, 1870-1873, Assistant Settlement Officer, Settlement Officer, Moradabad, 1873-1879. Settlement Secretary to Chief Commissioner, British Burma, 1879-1882. Secretary, Revenue and Agriculture Department, British Burma, 1882-1886. Director, Agriculture and Commerce, NWP and Oudh, 1886-1887. Remainder of service in Burma.

STOKER, THOMAS. Appointed, 1870. Served in NWP as Assistant Magistrate and Collector, 1872-1878. Deputy Superintendent of family domains of Maharajah of Benares, 1878-1884. Assistant Secretary, Under-Secretary, NWP, 1884-1886. Settlement Officer, Bulandshahr, 1886-1891. Commissioner of Excise and Stamps, Inspector-General of Registration, NWP and Oudh, 1891. Secretary, Scarcity Department, NWP and Oudh, 1897-1899. Retired, 1899.

TREMENHEERE, LIEUTENANT-GENERAL CHARLES WILLIAM. Commissioned, Bombay Engineers, 1829. Service at Dharwar, Surat, Broach, Gujerat, Sind, Poona, and Aden, 1829-1857. Superintending Engineer, Southern Provinces, Bombay Presidency, 1860-1862. Chief Engineer, Sind, 1862-1866; Bombay Presidency, 1866-1870. Political Resident, Aden, 1870-1874. Retired, 1874.

WRIGHT, FRANCIS NELSON. Appointed, 1863. Served in NWP as Assistant Magistrate and Collector, Assistant Settlement Officer, Settlement Officer, Joint Magistrate and Deputy Collector, Mainpuri, Cawnpore, 1864-1879. On special duty in connection with construction of state wells, Cawnpore, 1879. Joint Magistrate and Deputy Collector, Jaunpur, Meerut; Magistrate and Collector, Unao, Cawnpore, Rae Bareli, Benares, 1879-1891. Commissioner, Allahabad, 1891. Opium Agent, Benares, 1894-1896. Retired, 1896.

INTRODUCTION

The violent moment of the "Mutiny" uprising, in highlighting the formal transition from Company to Crown authority which marked its close, obscured the underlying continuity of British rule. The uprising itself had come as the climax to a political fragmentation which the dwindling power of the Nawabi of Oudh in its last decades had accentuated. The disparate forces of the several *talukdars* and *zamindars* which contributed to it found for an instant a single focus for their essentially disunited attack in the East India Company's increasing control of the north. Control meanwhile over British–Indian affairs, once the Company's preserve, had been passing steadily to the Crown : the establishment of joint control by the Charter Act of 1833 had already marked the beginning of the last phase which culminated, in 1858, in the Crown's assertion of its undisputed supremacy. The public outcry over "Mutiny" atrocities, and the demand it had generated for a government for British India which must be seen to be secure, provided the Crown with an unassailable motive for sweeping aside the last remnants of Company autonomy and reconstituting the established structure of government under its supreme authority. Government servants, whose administrative zeal was vastly stimulated by the manifest fact of unrivalled power and impelled further by an unquestioning belief in the rightness of a cause backed by the principles of equity and political economy, pressed ahead with the business of modernization.

Crown achievement, in the succeeding, dominant years of Pax Britannica, from 1860 to 1900, followed, as befitted a government so openly dedicated to the rule of law, on the lines of precedent—Company precedent. The essential consistency in administrative action in the last decades of Company rule and the first of the Crown is striking. Sir John and General Sir Richard Strachey, R. E., both the epitome of imperial vigour, personified it, for they themselves had begun their careers as Company servants, following the family tradition. By the 1880s, with long years of conspicuous achievement

I

securely behind them, they could survey four decades in the great design of planting the incidents of civilization in India with consummate satisfaction—and without reference to the brief and distasteful disruption of the "Mutiny" or to the formal change in British rule which had followed it:

The magnitude of the work that has been accomplished is extraordinary. The England of Queen Anne was hardly more different from the England of to-day, than the India of Lord Ellenborough from the India of Lord Ripon. The country has been covered with roads, her almost impassable rivers have been bridged, 9,000 miles of railway and 20,000 miles of telegraphs have been constructed, 8,000,000 acres of land have been irrigated and we have spent on these works in little more than twenty years, some 150,000,000 £. Our soldiers' barracks are beyond comparison the finest in the world. ... The improvement in the jails and in the health of the prisoners has been hardly less remarkable. The cities and towns are totally different places from what they were. Simultaneously with the progress of all these and a thousand other material improvements, with the increase of trade, the creation of new industries, and a vast development of wealth, there has gone on an equally remarkable change in every branch of the public administration. The laws have been codified, and improved, and simplified, until they have become the admiration of the world. The courts of justice and the police have been revolutionised, and, however far they may still be from perfection, India has obtained, to a degree unheard of and unthought of before, protection for life and property, and an honest administration of justice. ... It is needless to continue this catalogue of changes that have taken place; but it is not the least remarkable part of the story that the accomplishment of all this work, and the expenditure of all this money, which have increased to an extent absolutely incalculable the wealth and comfort of the people of India, have added nothing to the actual burden of taxation.[1]

Few were better qualified to speak on Government's behalf. The Stracheys' joint contribution to Indian administration could by no means be described as insignificant, except, as Sir John had rightly observed, "by a false affectation of humility. There is hardly a great office of the State," he remarked, "from that of Lieutenant-Governor or Member of Council downwards, which one or other of us has not held, and there is hardly a great department of the administration for the management of which, at some time, one or other of us has not

[1] J. and R. Strachey, *The Finances and Public Works of India,* pp. 7–8. Lord Ellenborough took office in February 1842 and resigned in June 1844. Lord Ripon took office in July 1880 and resigned in December 1884.

been responsible. If we have not gained wisdom, we have at least had rare opportunities for obtaining knowledge and experience. [2]

The opportunities had been provided initially and in large measure by service in the North-Western Provinces and Oudh. The acquisition of the province of Benares, as an adjunct to Bengal, had secured for the Company in 1793 its first foothold in Northern India. In 1801, the king of Oudh was persuaded to cede, in addition to the area north of Benares, the Central Doab and Rohilkhand. The Upper Doab fell to the Company by conquest in 1803, and Bundelkhand, the tongue of territory stretching south from the Jumna into Central India, in 1817. Strung out along the great communication line of the Ganges valley from Bengal to the edge of the plains of Punjab, these "Ceded and Conquered Provinces" were renamed the "North-Western Provinces" in 1835. Control of the Ganges–Jumna region opened up prospects of tapping its vast agricultural resources. The Nawabi of Oudh, sandwiched between Company possessions to the east, then to the south and finally to the west as well, and hemmed in to the north by the mountain kingdom of Nepal, tottered on the brink of decadence in the fifty years following the conquest and cession of 1801–1803. Internal dissension robbed it of any remaining substance with which to resist the Company's logical next move, the formal annexation of Oudh itself in 1856. The political chaos of the Nawabi was inevitably bequeathed to the Company. Its latest and most concentrated manifestation, in the uprising of 1857–1858, was brief and summarily dealt with. From then on, the Crown administrations of the North-Western Provinces and of Oudh functioned peacefully side by side; they were amalgamated under a single head in 1877, and the territories were renamed the United Provinces of Agra and Oudh in 1901.

Company rule meanwhile had seen to it that the groundwork of modern Government had been laid in the North-Western Provinces. It had supervised the construction of roads, railways, and the first great canal systems of the Doab. It had developed a fiscal system on which the structure of routine administration, based on the district collectorates, depended. The law of its revenue regulations was the nucleus of a formal machinery of social control. The collective administrative achievement in all these fields was taken as the model for Oudh. The history of its development in the forty years following the establishment of Pax Britannica exhibits more clearly, perhaps, than did any other province of Her Majesty's Indian Empire the complexity of Government's self-appointed tasks.

[2] *Ibid.*, Preface, p. vii.

In area, the North-Western Provinces alone covered some 80,707 square miles, "nearly equal to England, Wales and Ireland together, while in numbers the census of 1865 estimated its total population at no less than 31,110,000 persons. They surpass Great Britain and Ireland, and approach within a few thousand of the population of the United States. This vast province, which would be an empire in Europe, ... [is] ruled by a Lieutenant-Governor, under the Governor-General of India."[3] If such rule was authoritarian, it was nonetheless creative: the continued development of institutions on modern British lines was vigorously implemented. The aim was not, however, to replace the existing social order. The immediate memory of the horrors of the uprising bolstered Government in its essential resolve not to exert direct power over its subjects beyond the extent appropriate to a supreme and benevolent superintendent of modernization. Rather it sought to superimpose a framework of the incidents of civilized society, as they were understood to be, upon the world over which it ruled; its purpose was not to provoke the chaos of a social revolution but to bestow upon society a new and highly desirable coherence.

Conditions in this "little empire" were not such, however, as permitted Government to pursue these aims unimpeded. The task of overhauling the Company's administration for a start—reforming its fiscal principles and practice, codifying and amending its laws, systematizing the range of duties of its various offices—was in itself formidable. Nor was it a task undertaken in vacuum. There were not only restrictions dictated by precedent. Fundamental and far-reaching limitations were inherent in the environment itself—social and ecological—upon which the whole edifice of modernity was constructed. The society which was to be thus improved was long-established and hierarchical; its minute pattern of localized rights to which its small-scale pattern of cultivation had given rise was overlaid by a patchy, disintegrating structure of superior powers.

Modernization, moreover, was not merely confined to legal and administrative reforms for the repair of the outer casing of local society. A thorough remedy was earnestly sought for the perilous state of agriculture, dependent on the caprices of the annual monsoon,

[3]C. H. T. Crosthwaite, *Notes on the North-Western Provinces of India*, p. 2. The total area of Oudh was 23,930 squares miles; see W. C. Benett, ed., *Gazetteer of the Province of Oudh*, Introduction, p. i. Benett gives the population of Oudh as 11,174,287 with a density of 474 persons per square mile; see *ibid.*, p. xiii, and p. 29 below, n. 26.

in large-scale development of agricultural resources and facilities for more efficient distribution of the augmented product through the latest techniques of canal-, road-, and railway-building. Since local society, and its rulers, depended overwhelmingly on the land as the prime source of wealth, Government, in its capacity as overseer of the greatest public works programme in a century celebrated for its world-wide contributions in this field, was necessarily brought into direct contact with local society and the circumstances in which it lived.

Marked regional disparity—in the climate and the condition of the soil—between the Doab and Bundelkhand, Oudh and the eastern North-West Provinces, characterized this environment. Centuries of persistent agricultural settlement had made their mark on land patterns formed by the geomorphic processes of ages; decades of rapid and extensive deforestation, most noticeable in the Doab from the beginning of the nineteenth century, bared vast tracts to the sweeping monsoon rains and the months of scorching summer sun which preceded them.

The power of the monsoon over the life and death of the land, and the powerlessness of the peasantry to change its course, illustrated India's benighted condition to Western observers. The fickleness with which monsoon irregularities disrupted cultivation could only accentuate this impression. Riding through the area covered by the *tehsils* (sub-divisions) of Khair, Chandaus, and Tappal of Aligarh district during the drought of 1860-61, Colonel Richard Baird Smith was struck by "the forlorn dreariness of its appearance. Usually it is in parts a fertile country, but when I traversed it in March 1861, a few scattered plots of culture represented the broad fields one was accustomed to ride through. The country seemed denuded of inhabitants and the emigration had been extensive."[4] Eight months later, the landscape had been transformed. Abundant and, more important, timely rainfall had replaced the bare patches and stunted crops with the rich vegetation of a promising *rabi* (spring) harvest.[5]

Prolonged exposure to the unaccountable vagaries of this environment had bred a wide array of protective devices : cropping patterns fitted to the specific properties of a given patch of soil; rotation by

[4]R. Baird Smith, "Report," p. 301.
[5]H. B. Webster, Officiating Collector, Aligarh, to Government, NWP, November 19, 1861, in NWP, "Revenue Proceedings," December 14, 1861, Index No. 22, Proceeding No. 19.

mixing and by fallowing cycles; manuring of the safest and most lucrative crops. Similarly, minute—but controllable by comparison with the vastness of the monsoon capriciousness—supplementary sources of water supply were found in streams, *jhils* (surface depressions, filled by summer rains), tanks, and, above all, wells, the maximum irrigating capacity of which could rarely have exceeded one and one-half acres. By 1860-61, between 3,000,000 and 4,000,000 acres were irrigated by earthern, shallow-draught wells and, to a lesser extent, by deeper masonry structures (in areas of predominantly sandy soil with a water table below approximately twenty feet)—in all, about one-seventh of the total cultivated area.

Whilst soil and water conditions and the availability of artificial supplements determined the productivity of a given area, production was controlled by the distribution of superior and inferior rights over the land. Every service on which cultivators drew, voluntarily or inescapably, ranging from the supply of implements by local artisans to protection by the headman or zamindar (the *malik* or dominant figure in local society), was requited according to the terms of a traditionally appointed specific right which stipulated a charge on each cultivator's yield at each harvest. The zamindar, appointed by the Mughal Government from amongst local maliks to superintend the collection of land revenue, exercised the widest range of rights: these included not only charges from cultivators but fees levied on all dealings transacted within the range of his jurisdiction—the area guaranteed him by Government as his *mahal*. Practical restrictions on a zamindar's power lay essentially in his capacity to realize the limits beyond which charges due from the majority of cultivators should not be driven, in the interests of an assured level of production. A privileged minority, tied to the zamindar by reason of kinship or service, were subject to minimal liabilities.

Theoretically, the zamindars stood as the focal point for the local accumulation of capital in cash and kind. Skilful employment of such income, as, for example, on the Begam Sumroo's Meerut estate where a system of tied loans from the revenues controlled for the Begum the production of the most lucrative crops of cotton and sugar cane, seems—pending more detailed examination of contemporary zamindari accounts—to have been something of a rarity. The explanation for this would seem to lie in the dissipation, both necessary and frivolous, of zamindari resources virtually at the point of their accumulation. The regular charges levied by the maintenance of a household of generations of dependents, by the Government's revenue demand, and by the costs of armies of retainers which rose in direct proportion to the disintegration of political order, and the interminable ad hoc expenditure on conspicuous consumption—all this would have left, in most cases, an understandably small margin for the expenses of agricultural management.

Practical obstructions to systematic investment arose also from the fluctuating nature of charges on the zamindar and the inhabitants of his mahal. The precariousness of the environment, both ecological and political, eroded any rigid formality in the structure of rights. The legal complexity of the mahals themselves contributed further complications in the pattern according to which wealth was locally distributed. Title to dominant rights in mahals and in parts of mahals passed to shareholders by death, debt, and alienation. Weaker elements were absorbed by stronger through out-and-out acquisition; bargaining from a position of strength, powerful families and clans could prevent the passage of legal title to beyond their ranks with the law of pre-emption. Nevertheless, the zamindari retained a certain coherence as a unit of wealth : there was, apparently, little physical, as distinct from legal, disintegration amongst communities. The established patterns of upper-class migrancy into government service seems to have effectively prevented it. The court of the Nawabi, and the regiments of the East India Company's militia, provided employment for hundreds of thousands of members and dependents of zamindari and talukdari families. Service perquisites swelled the income of mahals and the pressure of converging, and conflicting, zamindari interests was relieved. Yet for all the ties in terms of service between the bureaucracy at Lucknow and the dominant groups in local agrarian society, the complexity and impermanence of relationships and the sheer weight of numbers blurred any direct lines of communication between the Nawab's government and the *mofussil* (rural hinterland) beyond. The administration of the crucial matter of land revenue showed up an instability that was fundamental. Contracts for collection, awarded or more often auctioned to the highest bidder for a period of one, two, or three years in the main, hardly made for practical continuity. The pressure which government could exert through its revenue officers, its principal administrative agency, was at best indirect, unsystematic, and arbitrary.

The Crown Government was committed from the outset to a systematic policy of remedying the deficiencies of its inheritance in Oudh, which was thus drawn into an overall design, common to the two provinces' administrations, of securing conditions sufficient to develop and distribute agricultural wealth on a scale hitherto unparalleled. The vulnerability of indigenous agriculture, cowering beneath the monsoon, had occupied the greater part of the revenue administration's attention since the famine of 1837-38 and its heavy toll of relief, remissions, and suspensions had pointed out the need for remedial action. The minute patterns of cultivation and the crudity of peasant techniques seemed only too clear an explanation for the plight of a vast rural population. Massive assistance was believed to be the solution, through the application of the latest principles of British civil engineering to tap the neglected resources of the Ganges and Jumna for a gigantic network of canals to irrigate the thirsty soil of the traditionally highly productive Doab and provide navigation channels for the speedier distribution of its greatly increased produce. In a little over twenty years from the opening of the pioneer Ganges Canal in 1854, the second and largest canal system in India and the world, some 5,601 miles of main lines and distributaries had been constructed, commanding an estimated irrigated area, in 1877-78, of nearly 1,500,000 acres in the western districts, at a capital cost of nearly 4,500,000 pounds sterling. The relative simplicity of motive behind the construction of the canals, and the underlying assumption that from investment of such magnitude a great and overall increase in wealth must necessarily result, contrasted sharply with the consequences. Whilst the expansion in irrigated area seems to have been general, the increase in acreage under the various crops was highly selective. The *kharif* (autumn) crops of millets and the pulses on which the overwhelming majority of the population depended for its staple food grains and fodder were not adapted to artificial irrigation. Wheat, however, increasingly important as an export staple from the mid-1870s, benefited consistently, as did other "valuable" crops— most notably sugar cane and cotton, indigo and opium. The immediate impact on ecological conditions was more disturbing. The burden on the land through persistent heavy-cropping under the stimulus to cultivate the "valuable" produce increased the threat of deterioration in fertility noticeable earlier in the century wherever the intensification of agriculture, particularly in mid-Doab regions, had brought over-cropping in its wake. Most serious of all, however, was the effect of the canals on the delicate mechanism of the hydrological cycle.

Deforestation in the Doab, especially marked by the beginning of the century, had led to a sharp increase in the rate of evaporation of moisture from the soil, intensifying capillary action in the sub-surface layers. Alkali salts, which owed their original presence in the soil to its geological composition, were brought up in solution nearer to the surface by increased capillarity. During the long, dry months following the summer rains, evaporation transformed them into a grey-white crystalline efflorescence, inimical, in the patches of its greater intensity, to plant growth. Prior to the introduction of the canals, however, the quantity of moisture in the surface layers of the soil and, more important, the distance from surface of the spring level, was chiefly a function of the annual monsoon : a fluctuation in rise and fall of up to ten feet was commonly recorded between the monsoon and the winter months. Well irrigation could neither bring about a significant rise in the spring level on its own account nor, at the maximum irrigating capacity of one-and-one-half acres per well, result in an excessive application of water at surface. From the mid-nineteenth century on, however, this seemingly inefficient but at the same time readily controllable system of irrigation was largely superseded in the Doab by the canals. In the vast low-lying tracts south and east from Meerut, where the bed level of the canals was necessarily pitched higher than the surrounding country to ensure gravity flow of the maximum available discharge, percolation through the earthen walls of the channels increased the moisture content of the soil sharply, in some cases so rapidly as to lead within a few years to sub-soil saturation. Flush irrigation, which the Canal Department offered at lower rates, in place of lift, in order to open the widest market possible for its water sales, led inevitably to an abandonment of the old caution in applying water which the labour of peasants and bullocks in working their well lifts had dictated : serious problems arose where the head of water poured thus on to the whole field was of insufficient quantity in itself to irrigate the area and penetrate the soil to an adequate depth ; it served only to exacerbate the effects of increased evaporation. Further complications arose where the embankments, of roads and railways in addition to canals, insufficiently supplied with the expensive devices of culverts, obstructed surface runoff and led to the progressive formation or intensification of swamps. Age-old tracts of grey balding earth, known as *usar* (from the Sanskrit *ushtra,* "barren"), and of the white saline efflorescence, *reh,* increased in area, whilst new patches appeared in former cultivated land.

Local reaction to the intrusion of the canals symbolized their benefits,

and their threats. At least one folk poem, still current a few decades
ago in Aligarh district, raised Sir Proby Cautley, the master designer
of the Ganges system, to divine status in a variant on the myth of
Bhagirathi. The story was told of how the peasants had initially
opposed all interference with the sacred river, but turned to heaping
praises on Cautley's head as he led the waters of the Ganges down
into the parched fields of their neighbourhood.[6] Similar but more
generalized elevations were ironical. It was common usage along the
West Jumna Canal in nearby Punjab, for example, to refer to the
subordinate, local official of the canal administration who followed
inevitably, and less gloriously, in the engineers' wake as Naib-Khuda
or Deputy God.[7] The superimposition of the canals on the peasant's
world had meant, *inter alia,* the provision of the new service of water
supply calculated according to an old mode of account, at double
the cost: the cultivator had to pay Government its fixed acreage
water rate—and pay the canal official his illegal, but by no means
irregular, commission for securing the service. Servants had always
charged for their services. If the cultivator's water bill was formidable,
the unsatisfactory nature of supply—its irregularity and seemingly
chronic insufficiency—was also a frequent cause for complaint.
Moreover, following the halcyon days of the first two or three years'
conspicuous rise in productivity stimulated by the canals, patches of
less than top-grade soil composition tended to show a decline in
fertility status, through over-cultivation. Whilst this land was sown
season after season beyond its optimal limits, its cultivators and their
bullock teams were laid off. Released from the arduous, lengthy
rhythms of the well lifts, they had no alternative employment to
offset this disruption of their work pattern and were necessarily
condemned to periodic idleness. Meanwhile the outward signs of
excessive accumulation of alkali salts in the soil were found in the
creeping patches of reh.

Local complaints were assiduously collected and largely corroborated by detailed reports of superior canal and revenue officers. The
reh problem was early a concern of Government; it was the subject
of a special inquiry in 1877-78, by which time correspondence on the
subject was rightly said to have been such as would fill a Government

[6]This information was given by Dr. C. L. Mehrotra, Agricultural Chemist to
Government, Uttar Pradesh, India.

[7]Denzil Ibbetson, "Note [on *Reh*]," para 10, in NWP and Oudh, "Revenue
Proceedings," June 1879, Index No. 116, December 28, 1878, Proceeding No. 53.

Blue Book. As regards remedial action, however, the Canal Department's dilemma was acute : warned against the evils of continuing the
unsound practice of flush irrigation, it found itself unable to recommend an alternative since the substitution of lift, at a necessarily
higher cost, would infringe the sound economic principle of widening
the water market to its greatest feasible limits, upon which principle
the budget of this highly important revenue-earning department was
squarely based. Protection against sub-soil infiltration by canal water
was a similar impracticability—it was possible neither to line the
canals nor to fulfil more than a modicum of the original drainage
prescriptions designed as an integral part of the first canal systems.
It was, of course, impossible to rectify the damage caused by the
stripping-off of forest cover—impossible, in fact, owing to the constraints which the revenue budget and an acute concern for caution
engendered, to do more than pursue a course of tentative, peripheral,
and largely inconclusive experimentation. While the available data
on the nature, origins, and theoretical amendment of saline-alkali
soil grew increasingly voluminous, the threat of seeing the north-
western plains of India, as the superintendent of the Geological Survey
put it in 1877, converted into a "howling wilderness" accorded more
and more, in vast expanses, with reality. By 1891, the first agricultural
chemist to report on overall conditions in Indian agriculture estimated
the extent of agricultural land significantly affected by salinity at
between 4,000 and 5,000 square miles, with "valuable" crops isolated
in clumps upon its surface.

The cumulative effects of the piecemeal construction of roads and
railways, again, like the canals, on lines laid down under Company
rule, were a similar story of expansion and induced imbalance.
By 1880, the North-Western Provinces and Oudh together accounted
for one-ninth of the total railway mileage in British India, and metalled
roads fanned out from the great Grand Trunk to connect it with the
district towns of the Doab and central Oudh. The consequent expansion in trade was gradual but voluminous; the export trade, chiefly
in food grains, took pride of place. The systematic movement of
foodstuffs to markets and ports outside the provinces was only temporarily offset when on occasion severe scarcity demanded that the
railways be used to bring in relief supplies. Whilst the funds, the
specialized materials, and the most skilled workers to build the
railways had been found in Britain, the humbler elements of construction necessarily came from the surrounding countryside : *kankar*

(calcareous rubble) ballast for the tracks and above all timber for
sleepers and in many cases for fuel. As the lines and their feeders
spread out north beyond the Ganges valley, concomitant deforestation
exacerbated imbalances established by earlier agricultural expansion.
Great embankments cut across natural drainage lines, and the lack
of culverts (together with the tendency in many which were constructed to silt-up rapidly with the summer rains) impeded surface
runoff (which itself was greatly increased by deforestation) and led to
more swamps, more usar, more reh.

The giant public works dominated Government's concern with the
agricultural environment. Small-scale improvements were co-ordi-
nated neither within the framework of public works nor amongst
themselves, for such co-ordination implied a concept alien to the
conduct of practical affairs and insufficiently developed even in
contemporary theory. Added to this was a chronic lack of agency
and of means. By way of a concrete realization of the prime need to
pay attention to agrarian conditions, a pioneering Department of
Agriculture was set up in 1874. But constraints were built into its
foundation. Its European staff numbered no more than the director
and his assistant. Its budget was in the region of one-five-hundredth
of the average annual land revenue collections of the provinces.
Control of the public water supply for agriculture, the canal system,
lay with the Canal Department, and control of the Agriculture
Department itself, in effect, lay with Revenue and Commerce. What
remained within its purview was mostly the supervision of experiments—with exotic varieties of crops and expensive and in some
cases quaint machinery ill-adapted in essence to the local environment
and well beyond the majority of cultivators' means. Even where
experiments in crop production—chiefly, for necessary reasons of
security, in guaranteed export staples—proved successful, the problem
of their diffusion remained, for there was little or no provision for
an agency of instruction to the farmers. Officers in the field—chiefly
the district staff of the revenue department—expostulated against the
irrelevance of such practices when the crying need was to encourage
supplementary well irrigation by developing the old Mughal institution
of *takavi* loans. The necessary official, and legislative, sanctions were
given but the convolutions of procedure which the overriding concern
for security necessitated effectively obstructed wide-scale dissemination
of takavi and ensured that its distribution was restricted to those
members of local society, the "respectable men," most accessible to

the local administration. In time of severe scarcity, this procedure was relaxed—but the lack of funds on takavi account meant little more than the most summary contribution to relief.

In view of the strides made by modernization, Government found it necessary to reform the crucial elements of its fiscal system which formalized its interest in agricultural wealth. The assumption of a broad division of society into the legal categories of "landlord" and "tenant" had been introduced, with provisions for sub-divisional classification, by the earliest revenue regulations. Settlements under these had proved consistently unsatisfactory. By 1855, a revision of the settlements under Regulation IX of 1833 fell due. The fundamental principle was that the landlord held title to an estate; as yet, even in English property law of the period, the estate was a legal entity only vaguely defined by way of its incidents. This title gave him command over its gross rental. The principle was to remain, as was the corollary that Government, as supreme landlord, was to share at the rate of a fixed proportion in that gross rental. By the 1855 revision of settlement rules, this proportion was reduced from $66\frac{2}{3}$ percent to 50 percent. Meanwhile, the assessment, now operative over a greatly increased area, was more rigorously defined by the introduction of scientific principles based on qualitative estimates of fertility according to soil classification. Estimates of gross rental were henceforth to be tied to estimates of productivity, the net result of such procedure being the establishment of a new standard, a "rent rate," as a point of reference for given units of like soil composition. The revenue demand thus assessed on the estimated capacity of the soil had then to be distributed, according to liability to payment, in society. The revenue-paying ranks of society meanwhile had undergone a sudden and, in many cases, severe dislocation: the abrupt fact of the annexation of Oudh, followed two years later by the cessation of officer service in British-Indian regiments, had thrown hundreds of thousands of uncles, brothers, cousins, and younger sons of talukdari and zamindari families out of their customary avenues of employment. As the multitude of family and clan interests converged now in earnest on the nuclear source of wealth, the settlement officers set out to define those interests in accordance with strict adherence to equity which demanded that liability for payment should be related in the first instance to quantifiable territorial assets. In addition to the persistent legal problems of fragmentation of mahals amongst several zamindaris, multiple status (combined "landlord-tenancies"), and a seemingly interminable variety of leases, this conflict of real interests added a new dimension. The theoretical sublimity of equitable quantification reached in practice the absurd, yet logical, stage of adjudicating territorial claims to one-nine-hundredth of an acre as legally valid.

In view of the complexity, and the labour, of the task of revising the revenue settlements, the records were necessarily compiled on the basis of estimated rather than precisely measured "actual" phenomena. Once assessed, however, and officially sanctioned, the demand was collected with a rigour which contrasted strongly with the arbitrary, sometimes moderate, and unquestionably elastic "system" of Moghul times. When production fell below the norm expected of it by the assessments, remission and suspension of revenue remained the only course open for relief—one which was taken infrequently since it was obstructed by procedural difficulties. Pressures meanwhile on the zamindari were matched by an increase in tension within the mahal. Moves to increase the zamindari income by encroaching on traditional "free preserves" by raising their charges brought forth vigorous opposition amongst privileged cultivator groups who, after 1859, were armed with the powerful legal weapon of occupancy right. Rural conflicts in the shape of litigiousness increased markedly. The net result, in many cases, was for the zamindars to deflect the pressure on to the more vulnerable sections of the community. The tenants-at-will, through the operation of accepted principles of the times, had no legal weapons with which to oppose the zamindars.

Where the land of his cultivators could not meet a zamindar's demands—or where it was expedient not to exhaust it beyond redemption—it had always been possible to take a loan. In addition to the pressures created by the regular exaction of the new assessments, the timing of collections, similarly rigorously enforced with due regard for security and in most cases before the cutting of the crops, necessitated interim borrowing between the due date for the demand and the sale of each harvest's produce. Traditional sources of credit came into their own : zamindars borrowed from bankers and moneylenders, and they loaned, like bankers and moneylenders and rich peasants, to privileged and unprivileged debt-ridden cultivators. There were no regular "rates" of interest : charges, inevitably high since the creditor invested his capital in the loan and profited from the interest payments, were calculated according to the relationship between debtor and creditor. The expansion of agriculture under the stimulus of the public works was inevitably, in an agrarian society where the vast majority borrowed for their livelihood, financed to a great extent by local creditors. The expansion was most marked in "valuable" crops and it was these—especially indigo, sugar cane, and cotton—which were grown almost exclusively on advances. The timing of the revenue and hence of rent payments added a new incentive to cultivate these crops since loans for their production coincided, conveniently, with the collection dates. The steadiest rate of expansion was found in the "valuable" grains, above all in wheat which had long been a crop sold off at harvest by the bulk of the cultivators to meet their charges, amongst which "rent" and "debt" were frequently indistinguishable. Exporting agencies entered the field in greater measure from the mid 1870s, but they remained essentially at the top of a regional dealing network which reached down, spiral like, through the local dealers to the mostly indebted producers. This old network of distribution had long been geared to a seasonal movement: the pattern of trade followed in the wake of the monsoon, which moved up through the provinces from south-east to north-west. Whilst the internal public works developments in the provinces were stimulating the production of "valuable" grains, external conditions had already distorted the old seasonal balance in the trading pattern between the provinces and their neighbours to the south. J. P. Stratton, the British Resident stationed at Nowgong just across the border from Bundelkhand, watched the grain carts passing annually through the town after the rabi harvests of March and April. Until 1862, they came up from Saugor, Jubbulpore, and the Narbadda region and went on to the British districts to the north. Stratton noticed, however, that from 1862 the direction had been completely reversed: the grain carts creaking through Nowgong came now from Banda, Hamirpur, and even Cawnpore, and went on south. The explanation lay in the attraction of better markets in the Deccan; these were created by the sudden contraction in area under food grains which was a direct consequence of the rush to grow cotton in response to the sudden demand by Manchester on the closure of its regular American supply owing to the Civil War. This suddenly induced upset in the traditional direction of the grain trade was steadily stabilized into a norm. As a corollary, the larger road and rail junctions of the provinces' plains districts became accumulation points, sucking grain from the hinterland, holding it according to the prospects offered by the market, and discharging it, at profitable opportunities, into the network of the export trade.

Estimates both of the volume of the grain trade and the rise in prices which accompanied the development of communications in the latter half of the nineteenth century are, owing to the rudimentary nature of trade records of the period and the official distaste and caution of Government in making detailed enquiries into the matter, lamentably vague. The qualitative assertion of conspicuous increase in regional market-town prices, to the extent of 40 to 50 percent between the 1833 settlements and their revision thirty years later, seems plausible. If this was in fact an index of dawning prosperity, as was widely assumed in official circles at the time, it was a highly selective one. For between the benefits of higher prices for produce and the majority of producers stood the ubiquitous creditor in his many forms—zamindar, rich peasant, headman, dealer, moneylender. Meanwhile, the cost of necessities also rose. The problem of rural indebtedness persisted, while its extent could only be conjectured. An estimate of 1869 suggested that all-purpose borrowing in the North-Western Provinces ran into some £10,000,000 per year. What was Government to do? It could not buy the creditors out, not even that more readily detectable segment which went by the public trade name of Bania moneylender. The recurrent scarcities, threatening on the average several divisions every four to five years, only pushed prices higher. Abundance, ironically, did little to relieve the situation since the sudden fall in prices following the inevitable glut of local markets exceeded, in its effect, the profits from the temporarily increased yields of a good harvest. The most securely productive areas, within a few miles of the trading points, benefited. Throughout the greater part of the provinces, however, the disparity between these oases and larger tracts bearing the brunt of a variety of internal and external pressures widened.

Overall, the Government demand of 50 percent on the rental was for the most part met. The zamindar's 50 percent seems frequently to have been more theoretical than real. Cultivators' difficulties, whether genuine or obstructionist, in finding their rent payments could be met only partially by legal coercion—or even physical force—in a society so constricted by its increasing numbers and increasing dependence on the land (its sole source of wealth) that little or no physical displacement could take place. As pressures on the zamindars intensified, legal developments meanwhile harassed the debtors amongst them. The civil creditor's right to attachment and sale after a fixed period of limitation was codified in 1859. The indebted zamindar, the landlord, was liable to have his property attached and sold in the civil courts for his debts and in the courts of the revenue juris-diction for arrears in meeting his assessment. Such measures, developed over decades, were in full accordance with the modernizing principle to rid land of debt, an encumbrance which so clearly obstructed the path to full utilization of its resources. But they conflicted, in essence, with a fundamental caveat of British rule, which was to avoid moves leading to a disruption of the traditional order of local society. Actual displacement of insolvent zamindars would have meant nothing short of a social revolution. The legal machinery of debt and transfer was therefore counteracted, in part, by the legal machinery of debt relief for encumbered estates. Government showed deep understanding of the embarrassed proprietor's predicament. "It is hard for any man placed in the position of a talukdar," wrote Lord Lawrence himself, "to be just and generous where he has difficulties in his own home."[8] By the end of the century, debt was neatly divided. The bulk of the cultivators simply remained indebted, perpetually. So also did their ultimate superiors in effect, except that the condition in their case was cyclical. For them the duration of each debt was limited by law. Indebtedness, at a given stage, passed legally into insolvency, which led legally to compulsory sale. Thereupon, the insolvent proprietor applied to government for relief in the form of temporary government management or for out-and-out extrication from the processes of sale. His, or rather his family's, effective reinstatement led to bewildering deviations from the strict progression, in theory, of the modern property law of British India.

Indigo entrepreneurs, frustrated by the unsatisfactory nature of protection which the law of the Company's courts gave to their enterprise, had long advocated the import of Draconian remedies. With the accession of Crown Government, however, the cautious combination of the precedent of regulations law with modern princi-ples triumphed over the demands for summary decisions in courts of civil jurisdiction, and found its most creative expression in the great property statutes enacted between 1859 and 1882 : the Code of Civil Procedure and the Registration, Negotiable Instruments, Trusts, and Transfer of Property Acts. Parallel developments in rent and revenue law saw to the codification and amendment of the existing law relating

---

[8]This speech of Lord Lawrence, one of his last as Viceroy, on the occasion of the enactment of the Oudh Estates Act, I of 1869, is quoted in part by C. B. Lal, *The Taluqdari Law of Oudh*, p. 244.

to tenancy in the provinces. From the outset, however, conflicts inherent in the structure and substance of the law manifested themselves. The revenue and civil jurisdictions were two distinct arms of the civil administration but, since the overriding concern of each was property law, they frequently overlapped. The result was that decisions given under the one head could be played against the other; appeals, earlier exhausted in the revenue courts, where the commissioner of each division was the final authority, could then be transferred to the civil courts in the form of a newly instituted suit involving, with perhaps minor mutations, the same parties. Within both revenue and civil jurisdictions, decisions on points of law might differ from court to court and bench to bench. Further, provisions in the statutes conflicted with the personal laws assiduously administered under the civil jurisdiction. Lastly and overall, the meeting points of the law with local politics added fuel to the flames of litigiousness. The award of the creditor's rights of foreclosure and sale had already exacerbated conflicts between debtors possessing a title to land and their creditors who coveted it. For all the pressures upon it, the zamindari was to remain the focus for the collection of local income from the combined sources of rents and loans.

The repeal of the usury laws, following the most modern English developments, sharpened the conflict between a zamindar and his rivals still further as the outbursts of highly articulate petitioning on the subject showed. Meanwhile, confusions arose as personal laws were subjected to quasi-modernization in the interests of a uniform set of provisions governing debt and alienations. The Hindu law especially, thus reinterpreted, proved a fertile field for inventive litigation; the joint Hindu family, hedged about with procedural restrictions on the power of its members to do away with property, came into its own as a powerful weapon for defeating an unwelcome creditor whose usefulness had been called into question by his untoward insistence on foreclosure.

The vigorous business of the courts (from which the profits of the profession could not but increase) was recorded in official statistics. The most vital set of these, however, the statistics of alienation, disguised certain fundamental distinctions in the variety of processes going under the name of transfer. Only in a few cases were records kept to show whether the legal title was transferred within the kinship group, whilst legal transfer itself was rarely synonymous with out-and-out sale, which a wide range of devices—fictional purchasers, for example, and notional purchase prices—helped to circumvent. Even where out-and-out sale occurred, it seems frequently to have been followed by failure, or inability, on the part of the alienee to substantiate his legal right by taking physical possession. Legal displacement entailed a priori no physical dispossession; this was a gap in the law that was enhanced by the confusions stemming from the proprietors' debt-relief statutes.

As supreme landlord, Government was some stage removed from such mundane insecurity. The reconstitution of its office, chiefly the revenue administration, which in some of its incidents resembled the management of an estate, fused the old authority of the Company over the collecting of taxes and the keeping of the peace with new powers to safeguard the principles of modern government. The district collectorate was the repository of local power; the collector's staff, European only to the extent of the tiny complement of two or three officers who controlled the fiscal and judicial administration of the district, reached down through the subordinate establishments at tehsil level to the mahals and villages which, with their 1,000,000 or so inhabitants, made up his jurisdiction. The combination of duties, which multiplied in proportion to the increase in the pace of modernization, and the simultaneous importation of the principle, laudable in abstract, of public accountability marooned the collector for the greater part of his working year in his office, attesting literally to the conduct of business.

If in this regard the collectorate preserved a certain static quality in its appearance, sharp constrasts were to be found in the mobility to which the collector's career (as distinct from the careers of his Indian subordinates) was open, in terms of promotion to the higher reaches of service, and in the generous provision of furlough in answer to the acknowledged strains of office. If the subordinate staff in this period rarely moved upwards, cases of movement in a horizontal direction—transfers from one department of government to another—were a frequent cause of concern to overworked collectors, particularly in canal districts where the rival claims of the Revenue and the Canal departments over the scarce commodity of clerically trained staff erupted into anguished memoranda. Subordinate staff in posts at the tehsil level and below irritated their superiors in no uncertain fashion by a seemingly widespread refusal to conform to the standards which Government had marked out for them. In this, they revealed a great and fundamental dilemma inherent in the whole structure of British rule—the consequence of the creation of institutions over society, on a pattern abstracted from contemporary British enlightenment, in which a handful of European civil servants were to hold full executive responsibility, delegating the greater part of routine executive function to petty officials who meanwhile played an active role in their immediate social context. The unhappy coalition of dual service was plain, for example, in the case of the *lambardars* who were generally acknowledged to be useless from the point of view of efficient administration but were retained in service to avoid violating what was understood to be the "village community." It appeared with blatant consistency, however, in connection with the *patwari*. Precedent from time immemorial bequeathed him to Government as the keeper of the records, meaning those records which were in fact kept, being mostly zamindars' tax records. Modernization sought to make out of him, the kingpin of the administration in effect, a disinterested public servant in accordance with the importance of his office. A salary to match, however, was never forthcoming : the patwari persisted in his work on a stipend of some Rs. 80 per year and, not surprisingly, maintained a wide variety of local interests. His services were eminently purchasable, provided—as in the case of a strong zamindari—the sale was sanctioned.

Records in such circumstances left much to be desired, but they remained, *faute de mieux*, the basis of administrative decision in the sphere of property law. Technical amendments also fell short of the ideal, largely through the impossibility of recording by survey the intricate minuteness of the agricultural scene over such a vast area subject to such continual change in patterns of land use. The world of the peasantry defied systematic record. Little could be done by the institution of special enquiries to remedy the gaping defects in administrative information. Such enquiries tended rather to produce a revealing chronicle of the lack of recording agencies adequate to the task, the lack of time to discharge their mandate, and the overwhelming disadvantage in working from the side of Government in an environment where the air was charged with suspicion. The finest records were, and have remained, those of the technical services and the settlement officers' observations on the condition of their environment. In the following pages those records are used to clarify the problems of innovation in the world in which these officers worked.

Chapter I

POINTS OF DEPARTURE

The Pattern of Agriculture

Throughout the provinces, the *fasli* (agricultural) year began with the month of Asarh (June–July).[1] On soil moistened by the first falls of the annual monsoon rains, farmers sowed their kharif (autumn) crops: first, early *dhan* (paddy), where the land was low-lying and the water supply abundant, and on drier, more elevated tracts, small millets and maize.[2] Later in the month, the longer-maturing staples were sown. These were chiefly the millets *jowar* and *bajra,* the pulses urd, mash, and mung, and, in "wet" tracts, *jarhan* (transplanted paddy). These late kharif crops provided the staple food supply for the bulk of the population. In addition to these food grains, later kharif sowings also included cotton and indigo, which required intensive cultivation. The harvesting of the kharif spread over the months of Bhadon, Kuar, and Kartik (September–October). Where no serious climatic disorder disturbed the agricultural cycle, the timing of the harvest was fixed at the beginning of the season by the coming of the rains. Generally, harvests in eastern districts preceded those in the west by some three or even four weeks. Farmers in south-western districts harvested their crops before those to the north by approximately the same amount of time. Where the monsoon was delayed, or when heavy falls of rain in late July or August hindered the ripening of the kharif, harvests were protracted in consequence. In eastern districts, for example, such climatic disorders could mean the delay of harvesting until early in Aghan (November).

[1]The official computation of time in *fasli* years (*fasl* means literally "section," thence "section of the [agricultural] year," "harvest"), the method used for dating all public orders and regulations, originated with Akbar. The date of the fasli year plus 649 gives the Samvat (Hindu luni-solar year); the date of the fasli year plus 592-93 gives the date of the Christian era (thus 1272 Fasli = A.D. 1864–65). For details on the mode of calculation, see H. H. Wilson, *Glossary*, under *fasl*. For the months of the fasli year, with their equivalents in the English calendar, see Appendix 1.

[2]For a list of the chief staple crops of the NWP and Oudh, see Appendix 2.

Where soils were rich enough to stand intensive cultivation without risk of exhaustion, the crops of the second harvest of the year—the rabi (spring) harvest—were sown on plots cleared of the previous kharif. Such rich *dofasli* (double-cropped) land was by its nature confined to a small proportion of the cultivated area of each district. Rabi crops were commonly sown on plots set aside for that harvest and prepared whilst the kharif ripened. The chief rabi staples—wheat, barley, peas, and gram—were usually sown in mixtures of two to three crops per plot. They needed light rains during Kuar (September–October) for their germination, and further showers during Aghan and Pus (December–January) brought them to maturity. The very best rabi was raised on irrigated land, watered two to three times during the season. Shelter for the growing kharif and rabi grains was commonly provided by the staple pulse *arahar*, which was sown together with the later kharif and harvested with the rabi, enriching the soil on which it grew by leaves cast off during its maturity. Rabi harvesting lasted throughout the months of Chait, Baisakh, and Jeth (March–May), the local timing again varying from east to west and south-west to north as for the kharif. The cultivation of sugar cane stretched beyond the confines of a single fasli year. Early in the hot months, from Chait (March–April), land on which the cane was to be planted was ploughed up repeatedly—seven times at least—and left fallow during the rains, after which it was ploughed once more. The canes were planted out on it the following Phagun and Chait (February–March). Irrigated frequently during the subsequent hot season, sugar cane reached its maturity in the following cool months. The long operations of the cutting and crushing of the cane and the boiling of the extracted juice *(ras)* into molasses *(gur)* began in Aghan and lasted well into the following Chait.[3]

Cropping patterns of staples followed the natural conditions of each locality. From an observation reported from Muttra district in 1879—which can be taken as representative in this respect of the provinces as a whole—it is clear how the variety of soils and the extent to which irrigation was readily available determined the basic pattern of agricultural production :

(1) Where water was far from the surface and irrigation conse-

---

[3]For the agricultural cycle of the fasli year in western districts of NWP, see the rural calendar quoted in W. Crooke, *Glossary,* under *barahmasiya ;* for the cycle in Oudh, see *Pratabgarh Settlement Report,* pp. 47–49, and *Unao Settlement Report,* pp. 10–12; for the cycle in eastern districts of NWP, see *Jaunpur Settlement Report,* pp. 119–120.

quently difficult, kharif crops outnumbered the rabi; a small area only was sown with wheat (which required at least two waterings); a (correspondingly) large area was sown with gram.

(2) Where the natural soil conditions were good, jowar (which required merely good soil and little attention) was grown extensively and bajra only nominally, of the staple kharif millets.

(3) Where no jhils (lakes formed by rainfall collecting in hollows in the ground) existed and the climate was generally dry, paddy was not grown.

(4) Where water available for irrigation was brackish, sugar cane was rarely grown.[4]

For the successful exploitation of these various conditions, one fact was paramount: farmers depended on an adequate and timely rainfall to secure a full outturn on the season's sowings. Unevenness in the rains brought sudden and drastic changes: scarcity could follow abundance within the space of a season. H. B. Webster, the Officiating Collector of Aligarh, noted a common phenomenon of the provinces when he reported in 1861 how three tehsils of his district were transformed by the advent of a favourable rainy season from "a barren, burnt-up desert ... to richly fertile and productive fields."[5]

The average rainfall per year of districts west of the Ganges was recorded as some 30 to 36 inches. In Rohilkhand, Oudh, and the eastern districts—the second major meteorological division of the provinces—the annual fall was greater: on the average, between 36 and 40 inches. To the south, the districts of the third region, Bundelkhand, exhibited the widest local variation: whilst the average rainfall for Jaloun was recorded as approximately 25 inches per year, between 30 and 40 inches were registered as annual averages for the neighbouring Jhansi district.[6]

Official figures aimed merely at showing the total rainfall of the

[4] *Muttra Settlement Report*, p. 23.

[5] *Tehsils* Eglas, Khyr (Khair), and Tappal. Officiating Collector, Aligarh, to Government, NWP, November 19, 1861, in NWP, "Revenue Proceedings," December 14, 1861, Index No. 22, Proceeding No. 19.

[6] For the regional incidence of rainfall, see F. Henvey, *Narrative*, pp. 10, 28, 59, 65 (quoting the observations of Colonel Baird Smith, 1860–61). For district rainfall, "average year" contrasted with the famine year 1860–61, see Appendix 3. For meteorological observations in the early 1890s, see the map of average rainfall and temperature, June to October, in J. A. Voelcker, *Report*, frontispiece. For early twentieth-century maps of the monthly distribution of rainfall per annum, see J. Eliot, *Climatological Atlas*.

fasli year, as recorded at the *sadr* station (the chief town of the district) and possibly two to three additional stations at tehsils. More important than the adequacy or inadequacy of the aggregate annual fall was its precise distribution over the rain months—a fact which the rainfall figures concealed. As the Board of Revenue, NWP, observed early in the 1880s, "A small amount of light and frequent drizzle, which gently and safely permeates the soil and freshens crops, is far more useful than many times the amount coming down in heavy and rapid showers, in which the water runs away without doing any good. In many recent discussions it seems to be taken for granted that the agricultural prosperity of a tract or season is in exact proportion to the amount of rain which falls. This is a complete delusion. As a rule, the distribution of rain is more important than its amount."[7]

The consequences to the crops of imbalances in the seasonal distribution of rainfall were dramatic. Frederick Henvey tabulated them in 1871 as follows:

if the rains fail during July and August, the coarse grains composing the food of the poorer classes perish [drought preventing the farmers from sowing the kharif];

if there are no showers in September and October, the rabi cannot be sown, except on lands irrigated by canals and wells;

if there is no rain towards the end of December, only the irrigated portion of the rabi can be brought to maturity;

if, as is often the case, there is heavy rain in March and April, the ripening rabi is exposed to destruction.[8]

The so-called irregularity of seasonal imbalance was, however, the norm. Between the two extremes of severe floods and severe drought, climatic conditions fluctuated so considerably from season to season that statistics which claimed to represent an average year were rendered meaningless. A survey of the condition of the harvests for each of the revenue divisions of the provinces from 1864-65 to 1884-85 shows the degree and frequency of disorder.[9] Further, within each division—an administrative agglomerate of widely disparate conditions—divergences were often extreme, not only between the districts which made up a division, but also between the *parganas*

[7]*NWP Revenue Administration Report*, 1882–83, p. 2. For a modern analysis of the concept of "agriculturally relevant rainfall," see H. H. Mann, *Rainfall and Famine*.

[8]Henvey, *Narrative*, p. 1. For a summary of climatic problems, see Voelcker, *Report*, pp. 25–33. For the extent of irrigation in 1860–61, see p. 31 below.

[9]For the condition of the harvests, 1864–65 to 1884–85, tabulated by divisions, see Figure 1.

(sub-divisions of a tehsil) within a district, between the mahals (revenue estates) within a pargana, and even between the *mauzas* (villages) of a mahal. In 1884, the assistant collector of Muttra noted as a common feature the marked disparity in the circumstances of different "properties" within a single village owing to the extreme variation in rainfall over so small an area.[10] J. R. Reid's comment apropos of the seasonal vagaries with which the Azamgarh cultivators had to deal may be quoted as typical for the provinces as a whole : "A favourable year all round is rare. Most seasons are as faulty in respect to some crops, and some seasons are as nearly altogether unfavourable for all produce, as others are altogether auspicious. Probably 25 percent of the estimated full produce would not be too much to set against the vicissitudes of season."[11]

How did farmers cope with the problems constantly posed by this degree of seasonal uncertainty, as well as with the wide divergences in productivity of soils and facilities for irrigation? As the most comprehensive means of safeguarding against total loss, two, three, or even four crops each season were commonly sown together within a single plot. J. S. Porter noted the Benares cultivators' aversion "to putting all their eggs, so to speak, in one basket. They think if one crop is injured or fails, they can fall back on the other"[12]—an observation which applied to the provinces generally. A typical cultivating holding was composed of a number of plots of a few *bighas* each[13] dotted over tracts containing a variety of soils in areas adjacent to one or more mauzas. In his holding, a cultivator in the eastern districts might grow, by way of kharif crops, early (sown) or late (transplanted) paddy, small millets (*kakun, sawan,* and so forth), staple millets (jowar, bajra), a variety of pulses (urd, mung, or mash), and oilseeds *(til)*. In western districts, where little paddy was grown, staple millets would occupy a larger proportion of a cultivator's kharif area. The varieties of staple rabi crops were again common to all regions; where good soils and good facilities for irrigation existed, a large area of a holding could be sown with wheat and barley, whilst a preponderance of gram indicated poorer soils and an absence of

[10] E. B. Alexander, Assistant Collector, Muttra, December 10, 1884, in NWP and Oudh, "Revenue Proceedings," December 1885, Proceeding No. 19, File No. 18, Serial No. 21.

[11] *Azamgarh Settlement Report,* p. 141.

[12] *Benares Settlement Report,* p. 20.

[13] For indigenous measures of area and English equivalents, see Appendix 4.

irrigation facilities. Colonel William Sleeman remarked on the picture presented by the annual rabi cultivation near Biswa, in Oudh, in February 1850: the wheat was beginning to change colour as it approached maturity, and the fields were "covered with mixed crops of peas, gram, alsi, teora, sarson [oilseeds], mustard—all in flower, glittering like so many rich parterres," and in amongst these, "patches here and there of the dark-green arhar and yellow sugar-cane."[14]

Investigations in selected districts for the official enquiry instituted by Lord Dufferin into the condition of the cultivating population[15] provided detailed examples of cropping patterns of family farms reported to be typical of their localities. Munna, a Jat cultivator of Muttra district with a family of three, farmed some twenty *kachha* bighas at the time of the enquiry. For his kharif crops, he sowed jowar and mung in ten of these, bajra in another four, and cotton in three. For his rabi that year, he sowed gram in three bighas only.[16] Tunda, a cultivator who lived in another village in the same pargana with his family of five (their caste is not given), held fourteen *pakka* bighas that year. In the kharif, he sowed cotton in one bigha three *biswas*, *chari* (gram) in one bigha seventeen biswas, bajra in another patch of the same size, and jowar together with urd in a further two bighas sixteen biswas. The following rabi, he sowed two crops: barley in five bighas four biswas, and *bejhar* in one bigha eleven biswas.[17] In the neighbouring district of Etah, William Crooke estimated from data collected on the Awa estate under the management of the Court of Wards that a typical crop pattern within a "small tenant holding"—a prosperous one, it is clear—of some ten pakka bighas would be as

---

[14]W. A. Sleeman, *Journey*, II, 220 : February 16, 1850, eighteen miles east of Biswa. According to Sleeman, the common *rabi* crops of Oudh were wheat, barley, *arahar* (two kinds), *masur* (pulse), *alsi* (linseed), *sarson* (oilseed : fine mustard), mung, peas (three kinds), sugar cane (six kinds), *kusum* (safflower), opium, palma christi; see *ibid.*, II, 63–64. Sugar cane is included in the rabi, though it spans *kharif* and rabi seasons (see above, p. 00) and is commonly grouped with the kharif.

[15]For the full text of the Dufferin Enquiry, see "Reports on the Condition of the Lower Classes of the Population in India," Government of India, "Famine Proceedings," December 1888, Proceedings Nos. 1–24. For the section on the NWP and Oudh, see Enclosures to Director of Land Records and Agriculture, NWP and Oudh, No. T-83A, June 8, 1888, *ibid.*, Proceeding No. 18, Serial No. 32. Reports from this section are cited hereafter under Dufferin Enquiry (Enclosures, NWP and Oudh); pagination is that of the Enclosures. For the districts covered by the enquiry, see the endpaper map.

[16]Muttra, *pargana* Kosi, *mauza* Kamar. Dufferin Enquiry (Enclosures, NWP and Oudh), p. 9.

[17]Muttra, pargana Kosi, mauza Gauhari. *Ibid.*, p. 12.

follows. In the kharif, cotton might occupy some one and a half bighas, maize and jowar a bigha each, and millet fodder a further half-bigha. Castor oilseed would be planted round the sides of the kharif fields. In the following rabi season, wheat might occupy two and a half bighas and bejhar the same, both interspersed with mustard. A further bigha might be planted out with sugar cane.[18] A more extensive and at the same time obviously prosperous holding permitted not merely larger proportions of the finer crops to be grown but a greater uniformity of cropping pattern overall. Ram Kishn, a Lodha (low-caste) cultivator of Pilibhit district with a family of six, was reported to hold some thirty-eight bighas in one mauza and sixty more in another. In the first of these holdings, the kharif crops occupied some eighteen bighas in all—ten under mung, eight under dhan—and the following rabi crops occupied twenty—all under wheat. In the second, sixty-bigha tract, the kharif covered thirty-nine bighas—thirty under dhan, nine under *kodon* (small millet)—and the rabi covered sixteen—again, all under wheat. Lastly, sixteen bighas were planted with sugar cane.[19]

The proportions of a single holding sown with kharif and with rabi fluctuated from year to year, as did the proportions of the types of crops within these categories, in accordance with current climatic conditions. At the beginning of each season, a farmer had to decide which crop as principal and which as secondary would provide him with a better overall yield.

The common practice of mixing crops in one plot was not merely to reduce risk; it also provided a means of crop rotation which permitted the soil to be cultivated fairly constantly without being overburdened. District officers frequently ignored the practice, listing the various crops singly in their *jinswar* (distribution of crops) statements for each fasli year.[20] In some cases they were also unaware of the essential relief to the land which it provided.[21]

Rotation cycles, in which seasons of heavy and lighter crops were interspersed with fallowing periods, were also common. Farmers tilled their ordinary *harjins* (food grains) land in Azamgarh, for

[18]*Ibid.*, p. 21.

[19]Pilibhit, pargana Puranpur, mauza Mathena Zabti and tehsil Pilibhit, mauza Jangrauli. *Ibid.*, p. 110. For further examples of diverse crop patterns in "typical" holdings, see "Report of the Indian Famine Commission, 1879," *P.P.*, 1881, 71, Pt. III, Ch. I, Question 9, pp. 248–290 *passim;* for districts covered by this report, see the endpaper map.

[20]E. B. Alexander, Settlement Officer, Moradabad, cautioned against such errors. See his observation in *Moradabad Settlement Report*, pp. 54–55.

[21]Voelcker, *Report*, p. 233.

example, according to the following basic pattern. Following a light kharif crop, cleared early in the harvest, the land would lie fallow through the subsequent rabi season, at the end of which it would be prepared for sugar cane. The following spring, the canes would be planted out. Land cleared of the mature sugar cane in the following cool season remained untouched until the monsoon. It would then be prepared for barley—sown in October, and cut and threshed the following March and April. In the next fasli year, a fallow period in the kharif followed by barley sowings in the rabi might be the pattern; alternatively, an early kharif crop could be followed by light rabi sowings—peas, for example, or *gojai* (mixed barley and wheat), or even gram.[22]

Additional means of relieving the land by the application of vegetable manures, such as dung and even—but rarely, it seems—bones and wood and stubble ash, were known but were practised mostly by Kachhis and Malis (gardener-cultivators) on small plots of highly productive soils.[23]

In the northernmost districts of Oudh and in parts of Bundelkhand, a form of shifting agriculture was common as late as the last decades of the nineteenth century. Here, relief to the soil was guaranteed by the mobility of cultivation; farming communities moved their fields, and their villages, over the arable area of, say, a pargana when land exhaustion demanded it. "The proper [sic] rotation of crops is not generally observed," T. R. Redfern commented from his experience on settlement in Kheri district in the 1870s; instead, "in parganas where culturable land is abundant, long fallows are the remedy for incipient exhaustion : whole *hars* [tracts] are abandoned after a few years of sowing for fresh soil in some other quarter. In such cases, *merhs* [raised boundaries between fields] are never constructed, except

[22]For Unao, a representative district for southern Oudh and Central Doab practices, the rule in the mid-1860s was as follows : one heavy crop followed by two or three light crops. For example, a field of light soil would be sown in the first year with wheat, in the next year with a light kharif crop (*kakun* or *mendua,* small millet), followed by a light rabi crop (barley or peas). The following year, it would be sown with late kharif only (*jowar,* for example), and in the third year with wheat again. *Unao Settlement Report,* pp. 12–13. For further details of common rotation practices, especially prevalent in eastern NWP, see *Azamgarh Settlement Report,* pp. 118–119, and for the general rotations in North India, see Voelcker, *Report,* pp. 93–134.

[23]Sleeman, *Journey,* II, 329–330; *Unao Settlement Report,* pp. 12–13. For one instance where remedial manuring with ashes was practised, in sandy tracts of pargana Sangrauli, Mirzapur district, see NWP, "Revenue Proceedings," May 2, 1868, Index No. 6, Proceeding No. 22. On manuring generally in North India, see Voelcker, *Report,* pp. 93–134.

to arrest the ebb of water." A comparison of maps drawn at the first settlement survey of the district with those of some ten years later showed the extent of this local mobility: "Scarcely anything remains the same except the village boundaries, and generally, but not always, the village site; the old fields can no longer be recognized."[24] C. W. McMinn's observation that "the system is in full force" whereby agricultural communities abandon village sites to establish new settlements in healthier, more fertile areas[25] must refer only to the northern districts. The relative density of population per square mile in Oudh according to the census of 1869 suggests strongly that only in the far north was the ratio of persons to land still sufficiently low to allow such regular mobility.[26]

For irrigation, where such was practicable, farmers relied on tanks, streams, jhils (the shallow lakes formed by the summer rains in hollows in the ground), and above all on wells. Where the water table was high and soils ranged from compact to heavy loam, kachha or simple earthen wells, lined with thick cables of straw and twigs, could be constructed readily and at little cost for materials: Sleeman estimated that an outlay on such wells, assuming the materials were paid for, would run between Rs. 5 and 10.[27] Where the soil was heavy and rainfall was so distributed over the monsoon season, in particular, as to avoid floods, these kachha wells might last many years. Elsewhere, lighter soils and the damaging effect of heavy rain on earthen wells necessitated their frequent renewal. A seventeenth-century Dutch observer noted that in the region round Agra, where light soils predominated, wells were commonly renewed each rabi season.[28] In the *bhur* (sandy) tracts of upland areas, where water lay

[24]*Kheri Settlement Report*, pp. 19–20.

[25]C. W. McMinn, *Introduction*, p. 122.

[26]According to the Oudh census of 1869, the average density (in persons per square mile) for the province was 474 (as against the NWP figure of 361, according to the 1865 census). Figures for population density for the northern districts fall well below this average—with Bahraich, for example, at 347 and Kheri at 311—whereas the figure for Fyzabad is 614 (630, if Fyzabad city is included) and that for Lucknow is 696 (which includes Lucknow city).

[27]Sleeman, *Journey*, II, 3–4. Sleeman's calculations in rupees are misleading, since the peasant's source of materials was most frequently local groves, over which he had rights to meet his needs of cultivation. Therefore, he seldom purchased materials outright. For details of rights over groves, see p. 37 below. On the question of monetary calculation of peasants' "budgets," see pp. 269–270 below.

[28]Willem Pelsaert, *Remonstrantie* (ca. 1626), cited by I. Habib, *Agrarian System*, p. 28, n. 23. The practice was common in such areas two centuries later—in parts of Shahjahanpur, for example; see *Shahjahanpur Settlement Report*, pp. iv–v.

deeper below the surface, kachha wells were largely impracticable.[29]
Only the more substantial pakka wells, lined with burnt bricks or
with bricks and cement and demanding a much larger outlay in
time and materials, could be constructed. The distribution of wells
per cultivated area was therefore far greater in low-lying lands,
and greatest of all in the Doab regions. The majority of wells—both
pakka and kachha—were worked by one, or less commonly two,
pair of bullocks harnessed to a *charrus,* or leather buckets drawing
some fifteen to twenty gallons of water at a time. Where water lay
very close to the surface, and particularly in the *khadir* or river-valley
lands, *dekhlis* or manually operated levers were used to draw the
water. The amount of land a farmer could irrigate per day varied
according to his source and his equipment. The following information
from Unao district may be taken as typical of irrigated areas throughout the provinces :

| Water | Area (in Biswas) Irrigated per Day | |
Lifted	By Pakka Well	By Kachha Well
1. By manual labour (dekhlis)	5–10	2–3
2. By one pair bullocks	8	8

Irrigation from streams and tanks, where teams of two or four cultivators
lifted the water manually in *behris* (shallow baskets) on cords into *guls*
(channels leading into the fields), was both inefficient and expensive :
a relatively smaller area was irrigated with a greater amount of labour
expended.[30]

Prior to the nineteenth-century developments in public works,
canal irrigation was a rarity even in the Doab region. The Western
Jumna Canal, reported to have been dug by Firuz Shah and re-
excavated in the mid-seventeenth century by Shahjahan, was said
to have "conferred benefit upon the cultivation of many parganas
and irrigated gardens near the Capital [Delhi],"[31] but the proportion
of the area it may have irrigated relative to that served by wells,
let alone to the total cultivated area, can safely be regarded as mini-

[29]In Kheri, for example, the ordinary lifting machinery of simple wells could not
be supported on *bhur* soils; see *Kheri Settlement Report,* pp. 19–22.

[30]*Unao Settlement Report,* pp. 8–10. For similarly common methods of irrigation
from wells, tanks, *jhils,* and streams in other districts, see *Fyzabad Settlement Report,*
pp. 54–59; *Lucknow Settlement Report,* pp. 63–65; *Kheri Settlement Report,* pp. 19–22;
Muttra Settlement Report, pp. 15–18.

[31]Habib, *Agrarian System,* p. 32, n. 46. The actual origin of the canal dates back
many centuries before Firuz Shah; *ibid.,* p. 31, n. 41.

mal.[32] In 1860-61, Colonel Baird Smith estimated that of a total cultivated area throughout the NWP of some 24,000,000 acres (approximately one-half of the total geographical area), probably not less than 3,000,000 to 4,000,000 acres were watered by wells. By that date, the canal system in the provinces, already vastly superior in extent to the canals of the Mughal administration, irrigated an area of barely 1,000,000 acres.[33]

Which crops required or benefited from irrigation? Not, it must be emphasized, the kharif food grains which supplied the staple food of the majority of the population and which depended overwhelmingly on the rainfall for their cultivation. Of the kharif crops, it was cotton, tobacco, vegetables, and indigo which needed supplementary watering. Sugar cane required extensive irrigation. Similarly, in the rabi season it was not the coarse, common gram but the finer grains, wheat and barley, which needed to be watered artificially to supplement the insufficient supply of moisture from the light rains of the cooler months. When the rains failed, it is true that farmers could look only to irrigation to save something of their harvest, but generally that part which was recoverable customarily depended on irrigation and did not supply the farmers with staple foods.

In an agricultural milieu composed of such disparate and fluctuating conditions, standards of cultivation were, predictably, far from uniform. The varying extent to which different areas could readily be brought under cultivation was matched by differences in the relative intensity with which local groups and castes of cultivators worked such land as was available to them. Foreign observers, impressed by the industriousness and opulent yields of cultivators in regions which were naturally highly productive, could on occasion mistake others' subtle if apparently crude skills in dealing with a harsher environment for simple backwardness. They assumed that the superior techniques practised in the most fertile areas were, a priori, universally applicable and that only ignorance or refusal to progress prevented their being more commonly applied.[34] Within the range of this restricted concept

---

[32]For a summary of the state of irrigation prior to the nineteenth century, see I. Habib, "Wittfogel's Theory," *Enquiry*, Old Series, No. 6. (Delhi, n.d. [1962], pp. 54–73. Techniques of large-scale canal irrigation were, as might be expected, unfamiliar also in Oudh. Nasr-ud-din Haider's canal in Unao district was notorious for its poor engineering, which made it virtually useless; *Unao Settlement Report*, pp. 3–4.

[33]R. Baird Smith, "Report," p. 81.

[34]In defining areas where improvement in existing methods of cultivation seemed

of efficiency, it was impossible for observers to distinguish which peasants in the provinces were either absolutely or relatively inefficient farmers. The scale of efficient cultivation as conventionally drawn by field officers of the British administration was simple : it ranged from those who produced the most the best—following the contemporary criteria of what was good for agriculture—to those who produced the least in circumstances of visible discomfort. At the top of this scale came the prototype of the all-round proficient farmer, the Jat cultivator of the best-endowed Doab districts : most notably of parganas Mat and Noh Jhil of Muttra district,[35] and the four parganas of Meerut (Kotanah, Barote, Burnawa, and Sirdhana) which, with pargana Burhanah of Muzaffarnagar district, had constituted the prize estate of the Begam Sumroo early in the century.[36] The prosperous holdings of Jat farmers showed that favourable conditions for intensive farming were readily exploited : irrigation was common; a sizeable area of land was double-cropped; much of each holding was sown with the finer varieties of cereals and with cotton, sugar cane, and indigo.[37] The Jats maintained their reputation throughout the century. The frontispiece to W. Crooke's *North-West Provinces,* published in 1897,[38] depicted a Jat cultivator and his plough, with the caption "The Pillar of the State."

If these Jats were pre-eminent as all-round farmers, it was the Kachhis and Malis who excelled in raising the specialist heavy crops of tobacco, vegetables, and opium. The conditions under which such cultivation flourished were exemplified in the three trans-Gangetic parganas of Farukhabad—Imratpur, Khakatmau, and Paramnagar.

---

a practical prospect, Voelcker classified disparities in terms of differences (1) inherent to the people themselves as cultivators (e.g., caste and race distinctions); (2) arising from external surroundings (e.g., climate and soil conditions, facilities for water, manure, wood, grazing); and (3) arising directly from want of knowledge (i.e., diversities in agricultural practice). *Report,* pp. 10–19 (Abstract, p. vi). It is probable that (1) and (3) of this classification are in practice generally subsidiary to (2).

[35] *Muttra Settlement Report,* p. 244.

[36] The Begum Sumroo's estate was celebrated for its prosperity, and for the amount of revenue it produced consistently for its controller, chiefly based on the production of sugar cane and cotton, which were marketed both locally and further afield in Delhi. For details of this estate, see the settlement reports of T. C. Plowden in NWP, "Revenue Proceedings," May 24, 1838, Proceeding No. 170, Enclosure; and, in greater detail, *ibid.,* February 22, 1841, Proceeding No. 174, Enclosure.

[37] *Muttra Settlement Report,* pp. 137–138. Jats predominated in the eastern parganas of the district. Parganas Muttra and Chhata to the west made a striking contrast, being poor overall except for small pockets of Jat cultivation.

[38] W Crooke, *The North-West Provinces,* frontispiece.

Water was never more than two to three feet below the surface, yet the low-lying position of the land did not in these areas entail the constant danger of diluvion and floods. As a result, farmers could exploit the richness of the soil without interruption. The proximity of water to the surface meant that irrigation was practicable only by means of manually operated dekhlis, which could irrigate land only at the rate of approximately one acre per month. Cultivation had therefore to be confined to very small plots. In these parganas, large numbers of Kachhis had, as C. A. Elliott remarked in 1870, achieved great success with "their peculiar system of cultivation." By occupying very small areas and manuring and watering them thoroughly, they managed "to turn out really wonderful crops of opium and market vegetables" which they carried for sale to Farukhabad city.[39]

Judged by the standards of excellence persistently achieved by Doab Jats and Kachhis, Bundelkhand cultivators—in Banda district for example—seemed the epitome of slovenliness. Their circumstances were certainly not propitious. Poor, light soils predominated, and consequently crops which were considered most valuable in districts to the north-west (such as sugar cane, indigo, and opium) were noticeably absent in Bundelkhand, whilst large areas were sown with coarse crops little known in the Doab. There was next to no sign of uniformity in crop patterns : mixed crops were universal. The harshness of a naturally dry climate was all the more apparent through the general absence of irrigation to supplement the meagre supply of moisture. Population was sparse and clearly insufficient for more intensive cultivation. (The question was not asked whether, considering the sparseness of population, such intensive cultivation was in fact needed in these areas.) Given these conditions, it was hardly to be wondered at that settlements of the "more industrious castes" were not as a rule to be found in Banda. These indices of "poor agriculture" stood out sharply to the eye of a settlement officer experienced in assessing to revenue the developed and densely populated canal tract of Muzaffarnagar.[40]

In most districts, a mixture of "standards" of cultivation was common. Whilst the Kachhis of the trans-Gangetic parganas of Farukhabad triumphed with their market gardens in low-lying areas, the other principal cultivators, the high-caste Rajputs and Brahmans,

[39]*Farukhabad Settlement Report*, p. 145.
[40]*Banda Settlement Report*, pp. 48–49.

farmed extensive upland tracts. Their "larger area of occupancy," manured and irrigated little in the course of the agricultural year, made up, in Elliott's view, for the "inferior style of their cultivation" as contrasted with the laborious practices of the Kachhis.[41] Those plots of a holding which lay close to the farmer's home and which were called his *khudkasht* land were invariably cultivated with greater care than his *pahikasht* land—fields which lay at some distance from his village. It was common practice in the provinces for farmers to enrich this khudkasht land with "the sweepings, refuse and dung of the village," as Redfern observed in Kheri district,[42] whilst the labour and cost of transporting manure to plots further afield left them necessarily less well cared for by comparison.

By the mid-nineteenth century, the areas of the most intensive cultivation were undoubtedly found in the western and north-western districts of the NWP, particularly the Upper Doab. The frequency of such areas diminished on moving out of the great river valleys towards the east, with the sparsest and most mobile patterns of settlement being found in the far north of Oudh and to the south of the provinces, in Bundelkhand. The contrast in intensity between the north-west of the British provinces and the neighbouring districts of the Nawabi of Oudh posed interesting questions of relative productivity. In 1850, Sleeman interviewed Brahmans of two villages of Mahamdi (in north-west Oudh) on precisely this point, *inter alia*. The (Brahman) zamindars of the villages had had recent experience of life in the district of Shahjahanpur, to which they had fled, temporarily, from the rapacities of the local revenue contractor appointed the previous year by the Nawab's administration. Nothing, they told Sleeman, could be better than the administration of Shahjahanpur under its present collector and magistrate, who was loved and respected by all classes; the entire surface of the country was under cultivation, the poorest had as much protection as the richest, the whole district was indeed a garden. Then came the crucial question: "But the returns, are they equal to those from your lands in Oudh?" "Nothing like it, sir; they are not half as good; nor can the cultivator afford to pay half the rate that we pay when left to fill our lands in peace." Why was this? Because the depredations of the revenue administrators of Oudh drove cultivators and zamindars into exile on occasion, and consequently the land was left waste to recover

[41]*Farukhabad Settlement Report*, p. 145.
[42]*Kheri Settlement Report*, pp. 19–22.

its powers.[43] The British law and order which protected Shahjahanpur from the evils of such lawlessness deprived it at the same time of the benefits : the land was given no rest. By 1850, it was facing obvious deterioration from constant over-cropping unaccompanied by adequate reliefs.

The Structure of Rural Society

Whatever the precise nature of his environment, a farmer in the provinces worked his holding with a few common implements of the simplest description. He needed a *hal*, or light plough, which aired the soil by turning up a shallow furrow without digging so deeply that sub-soil moisture escaped. He needed a *surraon*, or harrow, to scratch up the surface of his field, and a *dholna*, or club, to break up obstinate clods. He needed a *gainti*, or pick-ax, for digging ditches for irrigation and drainage. A *kurpa* or trowel was required for planting and a *kudali* (hoe) for weeding. To irrigate his fields, he needed a charrus or *pur* (bucket) for his well; if he drew the water manually from a ditch or stream, a behri, or shallow, dish-like water basket, sufficed.[44] Implements had to be readily portable, for use on outlying plots as well as those nearer home. In addition, a farmer needed a pair of bullocks to draw his plough, work the lifting gear of a well, and pull his cart to and from the local markets. Most farmers kept draught beasts on their holdings, feeding them on chaff and fodder crops and such grazing land as was available on nearby waste and fallow fields. The poorest farmers had to borrow or hire bullocks when required from more well-to-do neighbours.

As well as implements and a bullock team, farmers needed a regular supply of grain sufficient for both seed and food requirements. The general precariousness of their circumstances owing to the frequency of climatic disorder, the small size of holdings and plots, and the

[43]Sleeman, *Journey*, II, 65–69. Earlier, Sleeman had had similar conversations with Thakur farmers in Agra district. The Thakurs attributed the acknowledged deterioration of their land to their having to grow "exhausting crops" in order to feed their increasing numbers and to pay the "Government rents"; see W. A. Sleeman, *Rambles and Recollections*, II, 48–58. On the increasing pressure of "proprietary brotherhoods" on the land, following 1857–58 and coincident with the revision of settlements, see pp. 137 ff. below.

[44]For a list of common implements, see *Unao Settlement Report*, p. 10. For detailed descriptions of implements, with illustrations, see *Azamgarh Settlement Report*, Ch. II, and Crooke, *Glossary*, under the names given in the text above (Crooke also lists local and dialectal variants)

diversity of cropping patterns within them left most farmers little opportunity to accumulate reserves from one harvest to the next. Their meagre stocks were further depleted by the demands of various members of the local community which, as we shall see, had to be met from the outturn of each harvest. A common resource, therefore, was to take *bijkhad* (literally, seed and food) loans from those who held sufficient stores of grain : from *mahajans* and Banias, whose profession was dealing in produce and local wares; from farmers whose more promising holdings, greater efficiency, or chance success with a season's bumper crop put them in a position to lend out a portion of their outturn for the next harvest; or from the most powerful members of the community, in whose interest it was to increase their local prestige by making numbers of small farmers dependent on them for the regular satisfaction of basic needs.

These facilities fulfilled routine requirements, except where large-scale—particularly seasonal—disorders drained local stores of their supplies which the farmers could not replenish from the scorched or flooded land. Access to such facilities was open to the farmers as members of a local community and was by no means necessarily restricted to a single village. They had certain *haqs* (rights),[45] which established them as cultivators in a given area and set the number and precise limits of the fields they cultivated, which changed from season to season in accordance with the local agricultural cycle and with the individual's position in local society—particularly vis-a-vis his relation to his superiors. In addition to this overall right of cultivating occupancy—*haq-i-raiya*—farmers had certain privileges which enabled them to work their holdings : rights of way across land cultivated by other members of the community who might or might not reside in the same village; rights of access to such water sources as could be used for irrigation; grazing rights for cattle.

By the mid-nineteenth century, rights of cultivating occupancy were largely hereditary in the majority of districts—excluding those areas to the far north of Oudh and in Bundelkhand newly reclaimed

[45]The term *haq* covers all rights, fees, and perquisites held by members of a given community according to established custom within that community—within the family, clan, or caste, for example, within any Hindu or Mohammedan religious group—or, alternatively, within a given geographical region or by an official grant of Government. For the comprehensiveness of the term, ranging from family rights to perquisites of Government office, see the examples listed in Wilson, *Glossary*, under *hakk*. For a comparative description of common haqs of rural communities in northern areas of Central India, see Raja Dinker Rao of Gwalior's *Memorandum . . . on the Administration of India*, p. 8, cited by W. N. Lees, *Land and Labour*, pp. 99–105.

from jungle.[46] It must not be supposed that these hereditary rights were equally distributed within a community. The outline which follows below of claims to shares in the outturn of the harvest shows the marked disparity between privileged and under-privileged farmers. The legal rights of the latter amounted in effect to an hereditary status of subordination to the former.

Rights over local groves were similarly differentiated : the dominant members of a local community granted subordinate rights of access to farmers beneath them on the social scale.[47] Rights over groves were essential to every farmer, whatever his status, since the groves supplied him with the bulk of the materials required for his implements and his house. Furthermore, they guaranteed him except in seasons of extreme drought a supplementary food supply in the form of the fruits of mango and *mahwah* to cover the thin period preceding the kharif harvest when grain stocks were low.[48] Together with rights of cultivating occupancy, rights of access to groves constituted a farmer's strongest local tie. They lapsed on his departure from the neighbourhood.[49]

Each member of a local community who met the farmers' needs by providing certain services or by guaranteeing their rights over the land also had his specific haq, his right to share in his clients' or his dependants' produce. The following examples from Bareilly district[50] illustrate the range of local *chungi* haqs, or service dues, which farmers in most parts of the provinces would be liable to pay. From materials which they themselves supplied—usually from the groves to which they had guaranteed rights of access—farmers had their implements built and kept in repair by a local *barhai*, or carpenter. His payment for this service ranged from some 7.5 to 12 pakka *seers*[51]

[46]This suggests an answer to the problem which frequently taxed British revenue officers—that is, whether an hereditary right of cultivating occupancy had existed or had been recognized by Government prior to British rule. It seems probable that such a right was known, but that it was confined to those areas where agricultural settlement had been established over generations and was not known in those parts where shifting cultivation, to a greater or less degree, was the norm, as, for example, in the north of Fyzabad district as late as the 1860s and 1870s; see P. Carnegy, *Note on Land Tenures*, pp. 39–67.

[47]*Unao Settlement Report*, pp. 75–76; *Lucknow Settlement Report*, p. 95.

[48]Sleeman, *Journey*, II, 31–32; *Partabgarh Settlement Report*, p. 9.

[49]Sleeman, *Journey*, I, 169–171, 254–255.

[50]*Bareilly Settlement Report*, pp. 79–80.

[51]One *pakka* seer is equivalent to two-and-one-half *kachha* seers or to approximately two pounds avoirdupois. For indigenous measures of weight and capacity with their English equivalents, see Appendix 4.

of the coarser grains at each harvest for each plough. In addition, he claimed a few smaller perquisites—2.5 seers, or a sheaf of unthreshed grain—recognized by specific names (*phiri, niboni,* and so forth) and again charged on each plough.[52] For each *kolhu* (sugar press) he constructed or repaired, a barhai was entitled to claim 2 sheaves of corn, 2 seers of gur (molasses), and a few canes from each field; he also shared in the juice parted out among the workers at each press during the cane-crushing season. A local *lohar* (blacksmith) had much the same chungi haqs as a barhai; in small communities, a single craftsman performed both services, as was reported to be often the case in Azamgarh in the 1870s.[53] Farmers had also to pay fees to their *nai* (barber) and *dhobi* (washerman) besides the barhai and lohar—amounting to some 8 to 10 seers of grain per plough per harvest. The *chaukidar,* or watchman, took a further 5 pakka seers per plough for his services in guarding the crops. *Chamars,* or low-caste labouring men, might take a further 12.5 seers on each 100 maunds of grain per harvest[54]—the same fee which a local weighing-man was entitled to claim. Whilst offerings to the local priests were usually of fixed proportions and constituted regular chungi haqs, religious dues to gurus, pandits, and itinerant holy men varied "according to the giver's superstition or liberality"—or so S. M. Moens observed apropos of Bareilly practice.[55] A servant's clientele might be limited to all or part of a single local community, depending on its size and on the range of specific services he performed, or his work might take him on a regular circuit of several neighbouring hamlets. Outside the ordinary daily routine, certain servants—notably the nai and dhobi—performed special ritual services at local festivals and family ceremonies such as births and weddings. For these, they received presents from their clients in addition to their chungi haqs.

Payment for services did not end with these. Charges levied on bijkhad loans or on such cash sum as a farmer may have borrowed to marry a daughter or a son with appropriate ceremonial had also

[52]In Azamgarh, *barhais* took additional perquisites, termed variously *sali, lahna, barva,* and *kharihani* and totalling an estimated five annas per plough in value; *Azamgarh Settlement Report,* p. 145.

[53]*Ibid.*

[54]This was the practice, for example, in mauza Baheri; *Bareilly Settlement Report,* p. 78.

[55]*Ibid.,* p. 80. In Lucknow, the regular practice seems to have been for the local *purohit* (priest to high-caste households) and the fakir (holy man) to take each an *anjli* (an offering of two handfuls of grain) from the grain heap of each cultivator; *Lucknow Settlement Report,* pp. 75–76.

to be met from the season's outturn. The amount of each charge was fixed by the lender at so many seers per maund or annas in the rupee in agreement—theoretically, at least—with each of his clients. Charges generally ranged between 25 and 37.5 percent, but the amount of interest charged (which in the vast majority of reported cases fluctuated only between high and higher percentages of the loan) is explained by the conventions of local moneylending. The lenders' concern was not so much to try to regain their capital but rather to create a regular source of income by pitching the charge high enough to make repayment of the total loan difficult, if not impossible, for most borrowers particularly in view of the frequency of indifferent harvests. As a result, cumulative debts would regularly be carried over from season to season and from generation to generation.[56] Though no example is known to the present writer of the use of the term "haq" in this context in the provinces—one instance is reported from the Bombay Deccan in 1822[57]—the claims of professional lenders (mahajans and Banias) to their charges amounted virtually to a recognized service haq. The lien established by the numerous non-professional lenders over their debtors' produce was less formally recorded.

The heaviest obligation most farmers had to meet was the payment of dues in return for the recognition and maintenance of cultivating rights—collectively, *haq kashtkari*—levied on each harvest by their malik, or master.[58] These maliks were the dominant members of a local community whose power derived from the sources of wealth and the degree of prestige they commanded, measured ultimately in terms of the number of their dependants. The greater proportion of arable land was also subject to such power as the Government wielded over the countryside from time to time : it was termed officially as *khalsa,* liable to be assessed for revenue. In view of its interests in securing revenue and in view of the non-existence of a bureaucracy staffed by agents who might collect it unimpeded by dependence on the power of local revenue-paying communities, Government enlisted the maliks, who controlled local wealth, as its servants by formally

[56]For a detailed account of "rural credit" in the later nineteenth century, see pp. 161–170 below.

[57]W. Chaplin, *Report,* p. 22.

[58]A *malik* was literally one who possessed a *milk* or *milkiat,* variously translated as "possession," "mastership," "proprietary right." On the range of the term, see Wilson, *Glossary,* under *milk.* The term is used by the present writer to cover the whole range of dominant members of local communities; specific distinctions (between' for example, *mokuddam*-maliks and zamindar maliks) are made in their appropriate context.

recognizing their haqs and adding grants of specific office tenures graded according to the relative power of a malik and consequently determining the position he should be accorded in the official hierarchy. From the lowest to the highest, each office stood—formally—to guarantee the passage of revenue from the place of its production to the Government treasury. The maliks themselves—or the representative appointed by the family or clan where the dominant group was numerous—were familiar to contemporary observers by their additional, "superimposed" status, by their official titles of *mokuddam*, zamindar, or talukdar.[59]

The lowest in official ranking were the mokuddams, or headmen, who represented the powerful elements amongst the local cultivating community; they were the first link in the chain which bound the rural communities—theoretically—to the superstructure of Government. Even within a single district their status in relation to their local superiors could vary. In Bahraich for example, some mokuddams held power amounting to little less than an unobstructed dominance over the community for which they stood surety. This seems to have been especially the case where the titular supervising agency of district Government officials appointed by the Nawabi had either lapsed or was subject to frequent change. Others, the majority, acted as agents for a nearby superior and were removable from office at his pleasure[60]—provided he could summon up the force required to get rid of them. Mostly the mokuddams were privileged farmers: the most "respectable" men of the community. In return for their service in guaranteeing the payment to their superiors of a specified amount in charges due by cultivators subordinate to their authority as maliks, their own produce was made liable to less rigorous exaction.[61] They appeared to settlement officers not only respectable but also "thrifty and industrious."[62]

Above the mokuddams came the zamindars. By virtue of their position as the most powerful authority over a local community, they contracted for responsibility to supply Government with a stipulated amount of revenue and supplied the agency for its collection. The area which a zamindar's revenue assignment covered was termed officially as his mahal, or estate, and was based on the nucleus of *sir*

[59]For a summary of these office tenures, see G. Campbell, "The Privileges over Land," *Indian Economist*, December 31, 1874, at p. 120, col. 1.

[60]*Bahraich Settlement Report*, pp. 107–108.

[61]*Ibid.*, p. 112.

[62]*Ibid.*, p. 107.

land over which he himself held unobstructed rights of cultivation.[63] All farmers living or cultivating within the limits of his mahal were subordinate to the zamindar's authority in some degree and liable to his exactions. This authority of the zamindars was itself restricted where more powerful superiors existed who could control it. Whilst in the majority of NWP districts by the mid-nineteenth century it was the zamindars who tended to dominate local affairs, the situation was different in Oudh, where zamindars were largely subject to the supremacy of talukdars, whose talukas comprised several mahals. These talukas were assignments of Government. The Oudh talukdars were grantees, assigned certain authority over specified areas to perform a variety of services officially approved by Government. Some held grants to extend cultivation over waste lands. Some held commissions to perform duties of administration; originally made coterminous with the lifetime of the grantee, such office and its accompanying privileges tended to become hereditary, especially in the distant and wild areas of northern Oudh where Government surveillance was least in evidence. Others held Government grants entitling them to specific percentages on the revenue collections of the taluka. Talukdars could be appointed from amongst the members of a local clan controlling a mahal or series of mahals, in which case the relation of the superior talukdar to his inferior zamindar(s) would be one of kinship. Elsewhere, talukdars were appointees super-imposed—by force or agreement—over the existing local authority as Government saw fit. The appointments were made in return for service to Government—military (as in the case of the warrior Rajput talukdars), financial (as in the case of bankers—Brahmans and Kayasths—who stood surety for large sums of revenue), and adminis-trative.[64]

Charges due by the cultivators to the "mokuddam-maliks" amount-ed to a small commission—a few seers in the *maund* or annas in the rupee—on the payments of grain or cash for which the mokuddams stood surety to their superiors. It was those payments, exacted regularly by these superiors under the officially recognized authority of a *haq zamindari* or *haq talukdari*, which constituted the heaviest charges

[63]*Ibid.*, pp. 101–102. For a detailed discussion of the legal problems of defining *sir* land and its incidents, see the reports of the conference of settlement officers, 1867, in NWP, "Revenue Proceedings," December 21, 1867. Index Nos. 17–22, Proceedings Nos. 16–21.

[64]Carnegy, *Note on Land Tenures*, Ch. IV; *Bahraich Settlement Report*, pp. 86–91; McMinn, *Introduction*, pp. 116 ff.; H. C. Irwin, *Garden of India*, pp. 8–10.

on farmers' produce. As far as the bulk of the cultivating population
was concerned, it made little difference whether a zamindar or
talukdar made the exactions. Broadly speaking, the difference was
one of distinct regional authorities : a zamindar's haq in districts of
the NWP covered a similar range of sources of wealth, although the
accumulated income varied widely from mahal to mahal, as a talukdar's local haq in Oudh excluding in both cases the additional perquisites of Government office. An analysis, therefore, of the charges a
zamindar was entitled to levy by reason of his haq will exemplify the
liabilities of subordinate farmers to a "zamindar-" or "talukdar-
malik."

A zamindar's exactions varied from locality to locality. His direct
charges on the outturn of each harvest were realized in cash equivalents of the proportion due to him, or by an actual amount of grain
taken by *batai,* a physical division on the threshing floor, or by *kankut,*
an estimate of the standing crops made during tours of inspection of
the mahal by the zamindar or, more commonly, by his *karindas*
(agents). An example of batai from Bahraich, where this form of
exaction was still common in the late nineteenth century, shows
typical proportions claimed as zamindars' shares, translated in most
other areas by this date into cash equivalents. The settlement officers
recorded four different "systems" of division within this district
alone : where the terms were most favourable to the cultivator, a
zamindar might take some $7/24$; where they were less so, his share
came to some $10/24$; the most usual proportion was near to one-half
or $19/40$; finally, where terms were "very stringent," he was entitled
to some $21/40$. This disposed of the threshed grain. The chaff, estimated at 20 percent of the gross produce, was then haggled over by
the zamindar, or his karindas, and the farmers. Ordinarily, the
farmers did better in this round with the result that a zamindar
seldom took more than one-fifth of the chaff. In all, his share would
amount usually to some $21/50$ of the gross produce.[65] On top of this,
however, came his claim to further charges recognized as part of his
haq and known collectively as his *sawai* and his *gaon kharch,* or "village
expenses." From these individual payments per cultivator of perhaps
a tenth of a maund of grain or an anna in the rupee, a zamindar paid
his servants. Of these, the patwari (accountant) was the most important. His service consisted of keeping records of transactions between

[65]*Bahraich Settlement Report,* pp. 152–156. For details of the division of produce
within each pargana, see *ibid.,* Appendix C.

his master, the zamindar, and the cultivators under his master's aegis—records, that is, of all claims, arrears, advances, and debts in which the zamindar's interests were involved. The patwari's post was generally hereditary, leaving to the zamindar a titular right to dispense with his servant should he prove unsatisfactory. Effective supervision of the patwari by the zamindar depended upon the size of a zamindar's mahal and his energy in pursuing his interests and upon the distance of the patwari's place of residence from his master's. In addition to the patwaris, chaukidars or watchmen-cum-policemen held posts of importance. They too depended on their master's collection of gaon kharch for their pay.[66] Not infrequently, they were also assigned small *jagirs,* or plots of land, the produce of which was theirs free of charges. In Lucknow, for example, chaukidars (who were universally of the Pasi caste of professional watchmen) commonly held jagirs of some two to three acres each.[67]

Zamindar's charges on the produce of cultivators were subject to some potential restrictions. A zamindar's ultimate resource for collecting his dues was to use force, but this was of limited usefulness where culturable land was readily available or where a number of zamindars competed for cultivators and were able to hold out offers of protection to a farmer harassed by his malik. Excessive coercion by zamindars in these circumstances would merely drive cultivators to abscond, straightway diminishing the source of wealth at the zamindar's disposal. It was the growing political instability in Oudh towards the end of the Nawabi which incited talukdars and zamindars to disregard these rational limits and take as much from the farmers as possible while their brief period of uncontested power lasted. In the majority of districts of the NWP the margin of uncultivated land had shrunk to negligible proportions and asylum was consequently not as readily available to farmers anxious to escape from maliks' extortions. A brake here, however, might be applied by the zamindars' own interests. Theoretically, it suited a zamindar better to stop short of exacting the maximum in dues on the harvests, to allow cultivators a small margin to cover some basic needs and for the rest to keep them in a state of dependence on him; this way, his income and prestige were assured.

Within a mahal, too, there were restrictions on a zamindar's

[66]For details of *sawai* and *gaon kharch,* see *Bareilly Settlement Report,* pp. 79–80; *Cawnpore Settlement Report,* p. 102; *Lucknow Settlement Report,* pp. 74–75.

[67]*Lucknow Settlement Report,* pp. 55–56. Compare the Pasi *chaukidars* and their *jagirs,* near Daryabad, whom Sleeman encountered; *Journey,* II, 253.

unlimited exercise of power. Not all cultivators were equally liable
to exactions. As Moens noted of Bareilly district—and his observation
is valid for the provinces as a whole—the amount zamindars levied
varied according to local custom. Fundamentally, "local custom"
was a trial of strength : a zamindar realized as much as it was in his
interests to take where cultivators had not the power to oppose him.
Charges in fact were regulated specifically according to the terms on
which cultivators of the various strata of a community stood vis-a-vis
their superiors.[68] The top strata—the minority—were linked to the
maliks by ties of kinship, religious duties (as in the case of Brahman
priests who served Rajput households), and retainer service. In
consideration of their position and as a return for their services, the
total amount of charges payable by these upper-class farmers was
reduced below that of the cultivators beneath them. In two parganas
of Kheri district (Dhaurahra and Firozabad), privileged cultivators
were especially noticeable and exemplify the power of privilege
generally to withstand exactions by maliks. A community known as
Amnaeks, who had been professional warriors to the Raja of Dhaurahra
under native rule, held their cultivating rights at low charges and
steadily refused to pay more when talukdars attempted to make
them do so. Their strength lay in the fact that they were high-caste
cultivators of the same ilk—Brahmans and Kshatris (warriors)—as
their superiors, and the relative ease with which arable land in Kheri
district could still be broken in made their position even more unassailable.[69] Further south, H. H. Butts drew attention to the way in
which privileged cultivators of Lucknow district benefited from a
certain relaxation of charges on their produce. The "cesses" a zamindar charged in addition to his bulk share—his sawai and gaon kharch—
were, says Butts, never taken from a Brahman or Thakur, from the
bhala manas, the respectable man. His total payment was therefore
always less than that of the "common cultivator."[70] These examples
refer to high-caste privileged cultivators, and they may therefore
disguise the important point : privilege of this kind derived not from
the caste ranking per se of these cultivators, but from their blood or
service relationship with the maliks above them. Thus in Lucknow,
as Butts noted, the charges to which a Brahman cultivator was liable
might well be less overall than those of the majority of his neighbours,

[68]*Bareilly Settlement Report*, pp. 78–79.
[69]*Kheri Settlement Report*, p. 16.
[70]*Lucknow Settlement Report*, pp. 74–75.

but they varied nonetheless "with the varying histories of, and the moral influence and status of the Brahmans in the different parganas."[71]

The obstructions a zamindar might meet with in the form of opposition by the privileged strata of local cultivators to uniformly rigorous exactions were to some degree offset by the fact that a haq zamindari was not confined to the dues which the cultivators paid : it entitled its holder to claim income from every taxable source contained within his mahal. Every resident as well as every activity in the villages or small townships under a strong zamindar's protection was subject to fiscal control. The confiscation of the rights of fractious zamindars over certain bazar towns in Gorakhpur district, as reported in 1867, revealed to the British administration of the provinces the extent of the yield from such a source. One such bazar, Captaingunge, brought in an annual income, for 1866-67, of Rs. 510, itemized as follows (in rupees and annas) :

Source of Revenue	Rs.	as.	Source of Revenue	Rs.	as.
Salt sellers	38	8	Duria (grain weighers)	36	0
Tobacco-leaf sellers	38	8	Cotton sellers	5	0
Grain sellers	15	0	Putchra	5	0
Gur sellers	15	0	Shoe sellers	10	0
Haldi (turmeric) sellers	12	0	Tobacco sellers	5	0
Linseed sellers	13	0	Tumallee	5	0
Cloth sellers	15	0	Blacksmiths	2	0
Shroffs (money changers)	10	0	Shovel sellers	10	0
Spice sellers	8	0	Confectioners	5	0
Thuthaia	10	0	Wholesale-grain dealers	125	0
Busati (pedlars)	5	0			
Vegetable sellers	16	0	TOTAL	429	0
Oil sellers	10	0	Plus rent of houses	81	0
Brokers	15	0			
			GRAND TOTAL	510	0[72]

This was far from the highest yield : another in this small group of confiscated bazars brought in an estimated annual income, from a comparable range of dues, of some Rs. 2,000.[73] Nor was this a phenomenon confined to the wilder districts of the north. In Moradabad,

[71]*Ibid.*

[72]Collector, Gorakhpur, to Commissioner, Benares Division, March 30, 1867, in NWP, "Revenue Proceedings," July 27, 1867, Index Nos. 40, 41 (Memorandum), Proceedings Nos. 12, 13.

[73]Barhalganj, Gorakhpur district, in NWP, "Revenue Proceedings," July 27, 1867, Index Nos. 37, 38 (Schedule), Proceedings Nos. 9, 10.

for example, a survey of zamindars' takings from a few villages as recorded at the revision of revenue settlements in the 1870s showed them to run from some Rs. 60-70 per year for a small village to Rs. 250-300 per year; in one case—Bilari village—the income was stated to be measurable in "hundreds if not thousands" of rupees. In addition to these sums came perquisites in kind : blankets, hides, pairs of shoes, and so forth, supplied as dues by local craftsmen.[74] Residents were not merely taxed on their occupation of a house, but a charge had to be paid to the zamindar on any materials used in building or in alterations.[75] It was not uncommon for him also to claim his *haq chaharam,* or the right to a quarter of the proceeds from the transfer of such right of occupancy.[76] The fiscal power wielded by a zamindar could, as in the case of Powayn town which the Raja of Powayn regarded as his "private domain," effectively prevent a town from growing into the "larger, more flourishing" centre which the settlement officer believed it could become in the natural course of things.[77]

Most of the inhabitants of these villages and townships were local farmers or tradesmen and craftsmen who cultivated small plots part-time. The range of charges which had to be met each season ate so deeply into a family's income as to leave little or nothing to carry over into the next season, even from holdings of a considerable size. Take the case of Dewan Singh, a Jat cultivator of Muzaffarnagar district, reported in 1878 to the Famine Commission. His family consisted of eleven persons, all dependent on the family holding of 31 pakka bighas. His cultivation certainly was not of the poor class : 10 bighas for example were sown with wheat that season, yielding some 45 maunds at an estimated value of Rs. 72, whilst his 3 bighas of sugar cane, yielding 39 maunds 30 seers (presumably of gur), were reported to bring him in an additional Rs. 139. 6. 0. The total estimated value of his outturn for the fasli year 1877-78 came to Rs. 269. 14. 0. From this, Rs. 55. 12. 0 had to be deducted for the value of the fodder crops he used for his cattle. From the remaining

[74]*Moradabad Settlement Report*, p. 65.

[75]As, for example, the *chapparbandi* or "residence" charges levied by the zamindar of Agori Barhar mahal, Mirzapur district; see NWP, "Revenue Proceedings," May 15, 1875, Index No. 57, Proceeding No. 21.

[76]For examples of *haq chaharam* from mauza Barhalganj, Gorakhpur district, see the reference cited in n. 73 above, and as exercised in Shahjahanpur district by the Raja of Powayn, see *Shahjahanpur Settlement Report*, p. 99. For a discussion of this haq in British Indian law, see *Heera Ram* v. *Raja Deo Narain Singh* (1867), *NWP High Court Reports—Full Bench Rulings*, January–June 1867, 63.

[77]*Shahjahanpur Settlement Report*, p. 99.

Rs. 214. 2. 0., an apparently considerable sum, he had to make over Rs. 64 *bilmokta* (in a lump sum) to the zamindar for his share in the outturn. After this, he had to meet the service charges of field labourers and artisans such as the potter, blacksmith, and carpenter, estimated in aggregate at another Rs. 56. 13. 6. Other charges for the purchase of necessities, such as a water bucket, bullocks, household utensils, cloth, salt, and spices, came to Rs. 46. 8. 0, leaving him with Rs. 46. 13. 6. The sale of *ghi,* clarified butter made from the milk of his cattle, brought in another Rs. 20, but this was cancelled out by the charge due to his mokuddam-malik of Rs. 20. Even the Rs. 46 or, more precisely, the grain valued at that amount, could not be kept by the family, since Dewan Singh had been in debt over the last seven or eight years. Originally, he had borrowed Rs. 45 for the purchase of a cow and other necessities. By 1877-78, he owed Rs. 400, of which Rs. 250 had been borrowed in the previous and current years. As a result, the family kept back from the entire outturn of their sizeable holding sufficient grain for one or two months only, making over the rest to the "village banker." There were 164 cultivators in Dewan Singh's village; only one was not in debt.[78] These circumstances were typical of the majority of cultivators unconnected by ties of service and privilege to their superiors in both the NWP and Oudh.[79] Let us suppose that a small residue remained after all obligations were met and that with it a cultivator attempted to make some small improvements to his house or holding. For these, he needed local materials, the use of which was conditional on paying zamindar's charges—which meant the contraction of fresh obligations. His residue would vanish in no time, a formidable disincentive to expansion on the part of the bulk of the population. As against the regular drain on a family's resources, ceremonial expenditure could hardly account more than minimally for the often-observed inability of farmers to accumulate reserves. Occasions for such expense—"extravagance"—arose comparatively seldom; and, in the case of marriages at least, the expenses paid represented an investment for the benefit of the bride or bridegroom. H. C. Irwin placed these realities of ceremonial expenditure by the majority of the rural population of Oudh firmly in perspective and quoted the findings of the Deccan

[78]"Report of the Indian Famine Commission, 1879," *P.P.* 1881, 71, Ch. I, pp. 248–249.

[79]For a summary discussion of the condition of Oudh cultivators in the early years of the revenue settlement, see Irwin, *Garden of India,* pp. 38–39.

Riots Commission of 1875 to emphasize the point that to attribute peasant indebtedness to the outlay local festivals cost him was nothing short of misrepresentation : " '... probably in a course of years the total sum spent in this way by any ryot [farmer] is not larger than a man in his position is justified in spending on social and domestic pleasures.' This remark is as applicable to the north as it is to the south of the Jamna."[80]

Much of the cultivator's loss was the malik's, especially the zamindar's, gain. From stocks accumulated by the regular exercise of his haq, a zamindar could make periodic loans to cultivators—by which he ensured that a sizeable proportion of his debtors' produce passed each season into his stores or, in the form of its cash equivalent, into his treasury. Sleeman somewhat euphemistically reported that such loans were a practice of "benevolent proprietors" in Oudh as exemplified by the powerful family of Darsan Singh, maliks of Shahganj district.[81] In Jhansi, typical of Bundelkhand conditions generally, bijkhad loans by local zamindars were commonplace.[82] Such loans by maliks were termed officially—in view of their official status in the revenue-collecting hierarchy—as takavi, or advances to cultivators from official funds. The finest example of the use of takavi loans to obtain maximum yields in cultivators' output and a zamindar's income is provided by the history of the *ilaqah,* or estate, held in Meerut district by the Begam Sumroo. A remarkable lady by any mode of reckoning, the Begam was Mohammedan by birth and married to the soldier-adventurer, Walter Reinhard, nicknamed "Sombre" (hence "Sumroo"). Some three years after his death at Agra in 1778, his widow the Begam was baptized, under the name of Joanna, and received into the Roman Catholic Church. During the rest of her by no means uneventful life,[83] she ruled her Meerut ilaqah with consummate skill. T. C. Plowden, appointed to assess the ilaqah revenue when it lapsed to the British government of the provinces in 1836, two years after the Begam's death, managed to obtain accounts for the ilaqah for the last twenty years of her life, from 1221 to 1241 Fasli (A.D. 1813-14 to 1833-34). During those years, the five parganas which made up the ilaqah yielded the Begam net collections of

[80]*Ibid.,* pp. 6–7.

[81]Sleeman, *Journey,* I, 162–165; cf. *ibid.,* II, 77–78.

[82]C. J. Daniell, Collector, to G. M. Lloyd, Commissioner, March 31, 1863, in *Jhansi Settlement Report,* p. 33.

[83]For details of the career of the Begum Sumroo, see Sleeman, *Rambles and Recollections,* II, 267–289.

Rs. 567,211 per year on an average; the arrears as recorded for the entire period came to a mere Rs. 19,439.[84] This, said Plowden, was the utmost that could be exacted "and sustained by the fictitious aids with which it was propt up."[85] These "fictitious aids" were none other than takavi loans and forced labour which together, according to Plowden, prevented the ilaqah from breaking down and cultivation from diminishing. It was all very systematic : "The greater part of the sugar-cane which is a staple of these Pergunnahs, was cultivated on Tuccavee advances and if a man's bullock died or he required the usual implements of husbandry, Tuccavee was advanced to him with which he was compelled to supply his agricultural wants and to sow a quantity of land proportional to his means ... These Tuccavee advances were always recovered either at the close of the Fasl [harvest] or of the year, with 25% interest."[86] Meanwhile, the revenue demand was carefully adjusted each year according to specific crops, and regular inspections were made by the Begam's agents. Under such effective control the ilaqah became a by-word for agricultural prosperity, although the enjoyment of its fruits was confined to the Begam and her circle. To Plowden, such prosperity based on such extortion could not be other than superficial : "within was rottenness and misery," to be revealed when the commanding presence of the Begam was withdrawn. Her heir, whose avarice and impatience seem to have induced him to forego her ingenuity, abandoned the old system of annual assessments linked to takavi advances. He fixed the annual demand (for a three-year period) at more than Rs. 100,000 in excess of the average demand of the preceding twenty years, abandoning both takavi and the practice of making allowances for bad seasons. This withdrawal of assistance coinciding with the increase in the fiscal burden brought ruin, which was remedied only when the assessments were reduced under the summary British settlement to Rs. 523,186 for the revenue year 1837.[87] The "prop" of takavi, however, was not restored.[88]

[84]T. C. Plowden's report, March 16, 1840, in NWP, "Revenue Proceedings," February 22, 1841, Proceeding No. 174, Enclosure, para. 10.

[85]Ibid., para. 12.

[86]Ibid., paras. 19–20.

[87]Ibid., para. 31. For the amount of the summary assessment (including relevant calculations), see Plowden's earlier, shorter report in NWP, "Revenue Proceedings," May 24, 1838, Proceeding No. 170, Enclosure, para. 5. For a brief, overall account of the Begum Sumroo's ilaqah (estate), see Meerut Settlement Report, pp. 8–10, 15–17, 40.

[88]A detailed discussion of takavi in the context of British administration follows on pp. 110–118 below.

To suggest that the stocks accumulated through the power of maliks' haqs were reserved for the enjoyment of the maliks themselves would be misleading. They too were liable to pay routine service charges to local barbers, washermen, carpenters, blacksmiths, and the rest, although the means available to them for doing so were appreciably greater than those of the majority of the servants' cultivator clients. However, among the maliks, zamindars and talukdars in particular had also to cope with the claims for maintenance of near and often numerous relatives and of the dependants who supported them in their authority: their retainers. They had to pay their agents for inspecting mahals and talukas and for assisting in the collection of payments from their subjects. Their prestigious position had to be kept up constantly by a conspicuous degree of expenditure on ceremonial and festivities. Above all, they had to meet such demands for revenue as Government could impose.

Broadly speaking, the position of zamindars prior to British rule was "one of moderate comfort," as W. C. Benett remarked apropos of Gonda district, "tempered by the liability to occasional ruinous exactions." From the zamindars' point of view, pre-British revenue assessments had certain conspicuous advantages where they remained between formal limits and fell short of "ruinous exactions"; the demand varied with almost every year, accommodated, as Benett noted, by good Nazims (ministers of the Nawab of Oudh) to the state of the harvests.[89] This apparently common feature of indigenous revenue assessments—their elasticity—was emphasized by officers in other districts: by Alan Cadell in Banda, for example,[90] and by E. G. Jenkinson in his notes on Jhansi district under the Mahrattas.[91] The contracts on which the demand was based were fixed locally between ministers and local maliks—usually zamindars and talukdars—who applied for specific engagements as revenue farmers or were appointed to that position by ministers of Government. A zamindar contracted to pay a sum specifically itemized in the contract[92] which would leave him sufficient of the actual collections made from his mahal. It was of no concern to Government as to what the zamindar did within his mahal to make ends meet. Provided his relations with

[89]*Gonda Settlement Report*, p. 36.
[90]*Banda Settlement Report*, pp. 95–96. See below, p. 146.
[91]E. G. Jenkinson's notes of 1867 are included in *Jhansi Settlement Report*, pp. 81–82.
[92]For essential details of these local revenue contracts, in which charges were specified according to classes of land and types of crops, see *Unao Settlement Report*, pp. 57–58.

Government were cordial—provided, that is, he paid in his revenue—
or provided Government was too distant, or too weak, to make its
authority felt in the case of defiance, a zamindar was subject only
to the local restrictions we have examined above.

It was customary for Government ministers, in adjusting their
demand to local circumstances, to give formal recognition to the
haqs of local maliks on whom, after all, they depended for the realization of their revenue. The mode of this adjustment can be seen
clearly in the case of a number of *ubaridars* of Lalitpur district. These
ubaridars were minor, local chiefs, each with his specific haq. Their
territory was fought over, in the early nineteenth century, by certain
Rajas of Bundelkhand. Conflicts, at least in the armed version, were
resolved in 1830 by the signing of the Treaty of Buttota, by which
the superior rights over the ubaridars' region were parted up between
the Raja of Gwalior and Raja Morperlad of Chanderi in the proportion of two to one respectively. For the present purposes, Raja Morperlad's acquisitions are the more interesting. Assignments of revenue
now declared due to him were drawn up on the basis of the estimated
yield of each chieftain's mahal. Where this yield did not exceed the
amount of the haq recognized by the new ruler as due to each subordinate chieftain and listed in the treaty in terms of its cash valuation,
that chieftain's tenure was confirmed as a jagir free of any superior
charge. Where, on the other hand, the estimated yield of a mahal
exceeded the limits of its chieftain's recognized haq, he was required
to pay the difference to the Raja as *ubari*. Hence the official denomi-
nation of this group of chiefs as ubaridars.[93]

Beneath the ubaridars, the ramifications of service tenures spread
out as before, undisturbed by the adjustments of administration
vis-a-vis the superior rights. Families of Chaudhuris continued to
provide their chiefs with *gomashtas,* or stewards, who acted as *kanungos,*
or record-keepers and accountants, and conducted commercial
transactions. These kanungos depended on the Chaudhuris for their
pay, amounting to some Rs. 58 per month for each kanungo—an
aggregate charge of Rs. 696 per year. The Chaudhuris paid the
kanungos by assigning to them the revenues of villages and numerous
small parts of villages, which were held *muafi* or tax-free in return
for their service.[94]

[93] G. M. Lloyd, Commissioner, Jhansi Division, to Board of Revenue, NWP,
June 30, 1864 : "Report on the Oobaree Tenures of Lullutpore" (Lalitpur) in NWP,
"Revenue Proceedings," September 10, 1864, Index No. 15, Proceeding No. 13.
[94] W. B. Tyler, Settlement Officer, Lalitpur, to G. M. Lloyd, Commissioner, Jhansi

At each level, the rights of maliks were recognized. All holders of official tenures were entitled to the produce of their sir land, that area over which they held direct rights of cultivation, free of revenue charges. They were granted rights to stipulated percentages on the revenue collections. These perquisites were commonly termed *malik-ana,* and varied in amount even within a single tehsil.[95] In Oudh, perquisites known as *nankar* which amounted to 10, 20 or even 100 percent of the revenue of a mahal, were recognized in the public accounts, the amount varying according to whether "the holder [of the claim to nankar] happens to be an object of fear, or favour, or otherwise."[96] In the north of Bundelkhand, a group of local maliks known as Mundlooes were entitled to a variety of perquisites of office : percentages on "land rent" (revenue), on opium sales, and on the "rent" of ground where melons were grown, the *jama* (revenue) of so many measures of land, and the entire proceeds from charges due on a village.[97] This principle of maintenance and recognition through additional perquisites of existing local rights was not—in theory, at least—violated when grants over defined areas of land were made by the highest ranking individual in the administration as, in the case of Oudh, by the Nawab : "The bestowal of an estate in jagir [permanent grant of rights] or farm [temporary grant of rights of revenue collection] ought not to interfere with the right of the proprietors [maliks] of the lands comprised in it," commented Sleeman, "as the sovereign merely transfers his own territorial rights, not theirs."[98]

The neat stratification of this formal structure of rights was subject to distortions in practice as the processes of sub-division went to work. To secure services or increase his income, a zamindar could use his extensive power of sub-division. He could divert to chosen servants a proportion of the produce due to himself by issuing *pattis,* or leases of

Division, August 13, 1864, in NWP, "Revenue Proceedings," December 3, 1864, Index No. 2, Proceeding No. 3.

[95] As, for example, in certain *malikana* villages in tahsil Roorkee, Saharunpur district, on which see Board of Revenue, NWP, to Government, NWP, June 30, 1863, in NWP, "Revenue Proceedings," November 14, 1864, Index No. 26, Proceeding No. 54. For the entire correspondence relating to zamindars' malikana in Saharunpur, see *ibid.,* Index Nos. 26–48, Proceedings Nos. 54–74.

[96] Sleeman, *Journey,* II, 23–26. For recognized "cesses" levied by talukdars and zamindars on regular revenue, see *Bahraich Settlement Report,* pp. 183–184.

[97] NWP, "Revenue Proceedings," July 27, 1861, Index Nos. 156–174, Proceedings Nos. 88–93.

[98] Sleeman, *Journey,* I, 151–153.

cultivating rights, and *thoks* entitling the holder access to revenues they were appointed to collect. He could lease out rights by *zar-i-peshgi,* which gave the *zar-i-peshgidar* in return for his assistance in lending money to the zamindar a local right of occupancy and usufruct, which was somewhat similar in principle to a "mortgage with posession." Pattis, thoks, and zar-i-peshgi leases did not disturb subordinate cultivating rights already established. By granting certain servants jagirs, or rights over plots of land, he attempted to secure their continued performance of important local functions—the patwari's keeping of the records of a part of his mahal, for example, or the chaukidar's watching of the crops of a specified number of fields. The wider the range of his authority and the greater his need for servants to maintain it and for increased income to maintain them, the more necessary it became for him to multiply the number of his agents and, consequently, to make specific sub-divisions of his rights. This growing multiplicity increased necessarily the lack of co-ordination between the local maliks and their superiors, the officials of regional and central administrations. The picture was complicated still further by inheritance and partition, which gave rise to the celebrated "mixed mahals."[99] The patterns of rights which could emerge after a generation or two is illustrated by the following example, from Fyzabad district :

... say that A is a landowner, owning 44 villages [that is, holding the dominant haqs therein], and he has four sons, B, C, D, and E. On A's death, each son takes, as his share of the paternal estate, an entire village and one-fourth of the remaining 40; as generation succeeds generation, the various off-shoots of each family increase in number, and subdivide the lands formerly the estate of B, C, D and E. We will say that B's family branches off into five families having independent estates; we shall then find the one village taken by B now divided into five, and each of the five families descended from B will own the whole, or a portion of each of the 40 villages which fell to B's share; in the same way C, D and E will have expanded into a fewer or larger number of families. The intricate subdivision of villages amongst different estates has been rendered more complicated by the disruption of some of the estates and their absorption by the remainder ...[100]

[99]For examples of "mixed mahals," see NWP and Oudh, "Revenue Proceedings," February 1884, Proceeding No. 111, File No. 160, Serial Nos. 6, 8, 9.

[100]McMinn, *Introduction,* pp. 112–113, quoting from a report by the settlement officer, Fyzabad. For further examples of complex mahals see Sleeman, *Journey,* I, 285–286, 293–294.

Distortions in the structure of rights also came about through violent disruptions of formally established patterns. The absence of homogeneity in agrarian society was matched by a conspicuous lack of harmony. From the complicated and often self-contradictory awards of grants and leases, resulting in an increasing multiplicity of rights, an ill-co-ordinated network of agencies grew up between grantor, grantee, and the grant itself, which made the use or threat of force indispensable in establishing any claim.

Subordinate rights were theoretically protected by the *haq shufa*, which gave clansmen the power of pre-emption, in the case of a transfer made by a member of the community, in order to prevent the control of their rights from passing out of their hands.[101] Where both superior and inferior rights—of talukdar and zamindar, or of zamindar and mokuddam—were held by fellow-clansmen, the lesser social connections of the greater power were simply his dependants who held haqs amounting to no more than maintenance grants and who thus intercepted, to the extent that more powerful relative might permit, a part of the income from the various sources which made up the talukdari estate. But where the talukdar was a "foreigner," unrelated by kinship ties to the upper strata of local society, his relations with them "depended on agreements which could be binding only so long as neither party had the power to infringe them," which was the position, for example, of the powerful talukdar Maharajah Man Singh of Fyzabad district.[102] Where on the other hand local, subordinate groups constituted an actual or potential threat to the authority of their superior, or too great an obstruction to the realization of revenue, and where means were available to unseat them, mere pre-emptive restriction or tenuous agreements could offer little by way of substantial resistance to encroachments from above. Few overlords seem to have resisted opportunities to acquire "by fraud, violence and collusion" local rights, as vested in hereditary titles of access, to the products of mahals. Usurpation was so common an occurrence in Oudh in the mid-nineteenth century that if lords were to be made liable to moral condemnation on this account, scarcely any of good repute could be said to exist.[103] Meanwhile, across the

[101]For a definition of *haq shufa* and its incidents, see, for example, *Unao Settlement Report*, p. 29. For the juridical history of this haq, see *Gobind Dayal* v. *Inayatullah, Indian Law Reports*, (1885), 7 Allahabad 775 (FB) (Mahmood, J.).

[102]*Fyzabad Settlement Report*, pp. 449–453.

[103]For an example of a typical voracious talukdar-malik, see Sleeman's account of Rana Beni Madho of Rae Bareli; *Journey*, I, 244–246.

border in the British districts of Upper India, the same sources of conflict persisted, but found their outlet less frequently in armed battles than in the systematic and ruinous exploitation of the amenities provided by the judicial procedure of the civil courts.[104]

The spread of conflict amongst warring clansmen over their respective shares in the fruits of local power was checked by the "safety valve" provided by opportunities for service under the Nawabi or the neighbouring British administrative establishments, or in British Indian regiments. Younger brothers and cousins enlisted, and left their families to the protection of an elder brother who managed the family estate and to whom they fed back the greater part of their pay. The size of these native-staffed establishments, and the effectiveness of the consequent drain of potential warriors from areas of local conflict, should not be under-estimated. Thousands of courtiers alone thronged the seat of Government at Lucknow, and hundreds more resided in the *qasbahs*, the regional "capitals," all claiming their perquisites of office. Sleeman reported that from the single district of Baiswara in Oudh some 16,000 men were said to be in service in the British army and other establishments, and that there were another 15,000 from the adjacent district of Bunoda to the east.[105]

Connections between the "overgrown aristocracy" of Government officials, concentrated in residence in Lucknow, and the mofussil areas which ultimately provided them with their incomes under the Government system of revenue contracts were as insecure as they were tortuous. The city gentlemen of Lucknow, remote from the rural world beyond its walls, knew nothing of matters of agriculture except how to squeeze money out of those who practised it : "One of these city gentlemen," Raja Bukhtawar Singh of Shahabad told Sleeman, "when sent out as a revenue collector in Saadut Ali's time, was asked by his assistants what they were to do with a crop of sugar-cane which had been attached for balances and was becoming too ripe. [He] replied, 'Cut it down, to be sure, and have it stacked!' He did not know that sugar cane must, as soon as cut, be taken to the mill or it spoils." One and all, the gentlemen revenue contractors were branded by the local lords as "the aristocracy of towns and cities, ... learned enough in books and court ceremonies and intrigues, but

[104]*Ibid.*, I, 167–169.

[105]*Ibid.*, I, 169–170. Irwin estimated the military strength of the Nawab to be some 60,000 troops; *Garden of India*, p. 159. On the numbers employed in court, civil, and military service, see also p. 138 below.

utterly ignorant of country life, rural economy and agricultural industry.[106]

Unless the gentlemen from Lucknow specifically held offices in the mofussil, and, more important, were equipped with a powerful force of troops, residence outside the city was a dangerous impracticality. The situation led more and more to the deputation of authority by means of subordinate agencies created for the (grossly inefficient) conduct of business beyond the sphere of the seat of Government. The concentration of official aristocracy in Lucknow city towards the end of the Nawabi, and the show of pomp and circumstance which accompanied it—the multitudes of retainers, the spectacle of flaunted wealth, and above all the supreme frivolity of the court—all this seemed to symbolize, for sober European observers, the splendour and impotence of an oriental despot's rule.[107]

The incoherence of central and local authorities also made a system of regular financial accounts impossible. The central administration nominated, or estimated, according to specific localities, sums for the collection of which it offered contracts to selected servants. The *kubz* or revenue contract was usually offered for one to two years, and it was up to the contractor to realize what he could. Meanwhile, the local powers themselves kept their own records. In the complicated, tripartite system of accounts, discrepancies in charges current could never be narrowed. Arrears were fixed at sums that were as arbitrary as the demands and collections. Officials were unable to control the sources of their revenues or even to make assessments by measurement and enquiry within mahals owing to local hostility which compelled them to employ an agent who was forever prepared to compromise.[108] In addition, the capriciousness of climatic conditions led to inevitable seasonal fluctuations in the amount of revenue available,[109] for revenue was overwhelmingly derived from the products of the peasantry.

Collections of current demands and outstanding balances depended on force, and the maintenance of troops thus became an essential perquisite. No "coercive process" other than physical force could be adopted by the administration against a recalcitrant contractor,

---

[106]Sleeman, *Journey*, II, 49–50.

[107]*Ibid.*, I, 273–275. Sleeman was frequently moved in the course of his narrative to deplore vehemently the "vitiated tastes of the overgrown metropolis."

[108]*Ibid.*, II, 1–2.

[109]Sleeman to Lord Dalhousie, May 8, 1849 (*inter alia*, on the relation between deficient kharif outturns and reduced revenue collections), *ibid.*, I, liv (Introduction).

and the same means were all that lay open to a contractor against local maliks who obstructed him.[110] The troops, also, had to be paid. The common practice, since talukdars and contractors were unable to collect revenues in any other way, was for them to assign to the troops revenues due to themselves. The commander then settled in with his soldiers in the locality prescribed in the assignment and, disregarding local haqs, appropriated such produce as lay before him — this in addition to daily depredations for forage and food supply.[111]

By 1849 most of the great maliks of Oudh were in open opposition to the fragments of Government which subsisted under the title of the Nawab's administration.[112] If they chose to evade revenue payments outright, it was open for them to take up residence in neighbouring British districts. The absentee Oudh talukdars who resided in Gorakhpur and conducted their Oudh affairs through agents were to Sleeman mere tax-evaders. He condemned the practice as a glaring abuse of the privilege of sanctuary.[113] Open resistance was, however, more common. For this to be effective, large bodies of retainers had to be kept in regular service, and the retainers had both to ensure the collection of income and prevent its disbursement to recipients other than their malik. The indispensable retainers (a single armed force might consist of some 4,000 men)[114] could be kept on by permitting them to make exactions from all available sources, often tantamount to plunder.

Given the uncertainties inherent in the conditions within which he operated, a malik could apply no systematic pressure on the cultivating body. For the extension of his income, he was compelled to range over a wider territorial area, or increase the demands within his immediate sphere of influence. A third source often was available : like the rest of rural society, he could resort to regular borrowing to maintain his costly establishment. His creditor, whom British officials called an "agricultural capitalist," was a banker usually resident in town (for purposes of security), the holder of a government office, and commonly the owner of rights in a number of mahals. He took care of the maliks' needs from the revenues of his office and from his income

[110]*Ibid.*, I, 194; II, 225-226.
[111]On the assignment of revenues to troops in lieu of direct payment, see *ibid.*, I, 139–141. On forage raids, see *ibid.*, I, 196–197; II, 13–14, 99–100.
[112]*Ibid.*, I, lx–lxix (Introduction).
[113]*Ibid.*, I, 33.
[114]As in the case of Raja Gorbuksh's establishment; see *ibid.*, I, 24–25.

from trading transactions. His position was both lucrative and dangerous, exposed as he was to threats from desperate clients or rapacious
ministers. Ramdut Pande, for example, a Brahman, and one of the
most substantial—and "respectable"—of this class, made his money
by standing surety for lords' revenue payments, rating his risks and
his percentages according to his estimation of their character and
capability. Ultimately, his power courted the envy of the Nawab's
Nazim, who had him murdered.[115]

Disorder and extortion frequently turned the lives of the peasantry
into a nightmare of instability. The upper strata, allied necessarily
to one party or other in the frequent struggles through their ties of
kinship and obligatory service, received protection only as long as
their superiors remained dominant and were thus able to provide it.
Subordinate cultivators were subject to continued and even increasing
exactions, or were forced by oppression to flee from one malik to
another. The ultimate asylum was the Oudh *terai*, resorted to only
in desperation since few were known to return from its malaria-ridden
jungles. But the constant violence brought relief to the land itself
by forcing the cultivators into exile and cultivation to come to a stand-
still. During breaks in hostilities, the cultivators would return to their
refreshed land and resume production without any need to intensify
efforts to replenish the soil's productivity.[116] No law of abandonment
and no boundary marks denoting fixity of possession existed in territory where such mobility had become an acknowledged way of life.
Whilst the specialist garden cultivation typical of Kachhis and Malis,
which required prolonged and intensive care, could make little
headway in most districts, the benefits of enforced fallowing were
attested in yields of food grains that were believed superior to those in
the intensely cultivated, peaceful districts of neighbouring NWP
where Pax Britannica and the increase in population dependent on
the land were bringing, by 1850, serious problems of over-cropping.[117]

Whilst this mobility guaranteed productivity without the need to
improve techniques of production, at the same time output over a
period of years fluctuated so violently that no stable trading pattern
of a comprehensive order could be widely built up. The exploitation

[115]*Ibid.*, I, 252–254. See also the story of Chandan Lal, a prominent "agricultural
capitalist" indispensable to Government, landholders, and cultivators, in *ibid.*,
I, 280–281, and similarly of Subsukh Rai and his urban clientele of Pathans, in *ibid.*,
II, 46–47.

[116]*Unao Settlement Report*, p. 13.

[117]Sleeman, *Journey*, II, 41–43, 45. See also above, pp. 34–35.

of permanent lines of communication was also hampered by climatic disorder and the roving presence of armed bands. In Sleeman's time, the only road to carry any appreciable traffic in Oudh was the new highway from Cawnpore to Lucknow, built by a British military engineer and metalled throughout. The flow of such grain trade as existed was dictated primarily by the seasons. Whereas the usual current of grain was from north-east Oudh down to the already great grain mart of Cawnpore, from 1848 to 1850 the direction was completely reversed in response to shortfalls caused by bad harvests throughout Oudh; Sleeman reported vast quantities going up from Cawnpore by road and river.[118] Similarly, the southern districts of the Doab, for example, where harvests ripened appreciably earlier than in those to the north, supplied their northern neighbours according to seasonal demands. Local violence could distort this seasonally set pattern. As a result of the tyranny of Raghubar Singh, for example, who held a revenue contract for the districts of Gonda and Bahraich in the 1840s, these areas which had formerly supplied Lucknow were forced in their impoverishment to draw grain from it, and from as far distant a source as Cawnpore.[119]

The persistent sparring of revenue contractors and talukdars and the inevitable collapse of the vacuous authority of the Nawabi did more than disrupt local trade. Provoked finally by the hard fact of the Company's annexation of Oudh, local conflicts burst out into a brief, concerted explosion which convulsed the northern provinces : the "Mutiny" uprising of 1857-1858. For the Company, the task of suppressing this political disorder was a relatively straightforward one : proof of its superior military power was the more readily established through the disunity of its opponents. A task of infinitely greater complexity, dwarfing the difficulties of coping with post-"Mutiny" devastation and the great famine which followed it in 1860-1861, was taken up with vigour by the Crown government. The new administration set itself publicly to promote the modernization, on a vast scale, of the agricultural world over which it ruled, which meant the development of the resources of a densely populated environment where small-scale cultivation was inextricably entwined with a minute and highly flexible pattern of local rights. Government's standards for the task were awesome, a fact which went far to disguise

[118]*Ibid.*, II, 279–315.
[119]*Ibid.*, I, 66.

their conflicting nature. On the one hand, its criteria for sweeping efficiency owed their inspiration to the successes of contemporary British capitalism. On the other hand, the guiding principle of routine administration, to avoid direct and wilful interference with local society, symbolized the paternalistic conservatism of newly constituted British rule, having proper regard to the lessons of 1857-1858. Inherent constraints were also of a dimension proportionate to the problem : an abiding commitment to safeguard all investment by seeking adequate security and the inescapable reality of a budget encumbered a priori with external charges and increasingly incapable of providing the means which modernization demanded of it.

Chapter II

THE DEVELOPMENT OF AGRICULTURAL RESOURCES

The cries of triumph which heralded, in British circles, the suppression of the "Mutiny" disorders and the formal transfer in 1858 of the last vestiges of the East India Company's government to the British Crown might lead one at first to assume that these events in themselves brought a sudden and radical transformation in the British presence in India. The corrupt, lethargic, and despotic rule of the Company in its last days was now to be replaced by an administration representing the greatest and most energetic industrial power in the world. It was confidently expected that Government, having tamed the native barbarism recently manifested during the disturbances of 1857 and 1858, would, as a matter of course, lead its Indian subjects towards a civilized modernity, in whose undoubted benefits they, as well as their rulers, would ultimately participate.

There was nothing intrinsically new in this belief. It was merely the latest manifestation of a long-familiar spirit which accompanied the rise to supremacy of British industry and commerce. Public assertions by eminent promoters of Britain's trade abroad to the effect that prosperity must necessarily attend those of the hitherto backward peoples of the Orient fortunate enough to receive bounty in the form of British manufactures were already familiar :

What a satisfaction it is to every man going from the West to the East, when he clambers up Mount Lebanon to find one of the ancient Druses clothed in garments with which our industrious countrymen provided him! What a delight it is in going to the Holy City to stop with the caravan at Nazareth—to see four thousand individuals, and scarcely be able to fix upon one to whom your country has not presented some comfort or decoration! Peace and industry have been doing this and much more; for be assured that while this country is diffusing blessings, she is creating an interest, she is erecting in the minds of those she serves an affection towards her, and that commerce is a communication of good and a dispensing of [benefits] which were never enjoyed before . . .[1]

What the events of 1857-1858 did signify was that India was Britain's, at least for the foreseeable future. Meanwhile, old restraints on expansionist activity had now been removed. The Company, and its exclusive monopoly, had been increasingly regarded as a prime cause of India's retardment "in her agricultural and commercial pursuits."[2] Now it had gone, taking with it the last impediments placed by an outdated mercantilism in the path of large-scale investment of British capital in India.[3] The establishment beyond doubt of Pax Britannica completed the picture for the eager bystanders in London and the Midlands: the opportunity for vigorous action by Government, entrepreneurs, bankers, and a technical army of engineers to achieve a degree of expansion hitherto unheard of had arisen. "India has been given to Britain, that the blessings of Christianity may overspread the land," Alderman Baynes of Blackburn announced, on behalf of the cotton interest; "and our exigencies, sooner or later, will compel us to develop its resources."[4]

The prospect of these resources was not uninspiring. The *Bankers' Magazine*, one amongst many hard-headed business journals, was moved to lyricism on account of the "unexplored mine" that India represented, "the wealth of which we have not yet even begun to enjoy."[5] That wealth was to be tapped by the application of European enterprise and science, "to produce results which shall place the great Asiatic peninsula as high above the rest of the world for affluence in modern as it was in ancient times."[6]

The attractiveness of the prospects of development was enhanced by the fact that India appeared to lack very nearly everything which, according to contemporary capitalist criteria, was required in order to tap her vast wealth—or alternatively, to progress to a state of civilization. After the troubles of 1857, wrote Sir John Strachey, "ten thousand things were demanded which India had not got, but

[1]From the speech of John Bowring, Manchester, at the founding of the Anti-Corn Law League; quoted in N. McCord, *The Anti-Corn Law League*, p. 23. For further examples of entrepreneurial fervour, see *ibid.*, pp. 24–25. For Bowring's speech in full, see A. Somerville, *Free Trade and the League*.

[2]C. N. Cooke, *Banking in India*, p. 69.

[3]Radicalism and laissez faire demanded the East India Company, in Jenks's words, "as a propitiatory sacrifice" and were satisfied; see L. H. Jenks, *Migration*, p. 207.

[4]A. Baynes, *The Cotton Trade*, p. 3.

[5]"India," *Bankers' Magazine*, CLXXIX (June 1858), 430–431.

[6]"India's Financial Position," *Bankers' Magazine*, CLXXX (March 1859), 145–148.

which it was felt must be provided. The country must be covered with railways and telegraphs, and roads and bridges. Irrigation canals must be made to preserve the people from starvation. Barracks must be built for a great European army ... In fact the whole paraphernalia of a great civilized administration, according to the modern notions of what that means, had to be provided."[7]

The means were certainly to hand—in Britain. The international finance system could now provide for the ready movement of capital abroad for large-scale construction under contract by means of the joint-stock discount houses, the British development on the lines of the *credit mobilier*.[8] Engineers with considerable experience of railways and, to a lesser extent, of canals were readily available. The whole question of investment in India was given unparalleled publicity: Parliament appointed a Select Committee, outstanding entrepreneurs with a sprinkling of distinguished administrators experienced in Indian affairs, to enquire exhaustively into the practicability of the "colonization and settlement" of India.[9] The *Economist* scrutinized the problems confronting the British investor and found that however formidable the obstacles dwelt upon by witnesses before the Select Committee might appear, they were largely confined—as far as experience showed—to indigo planting; the way seemed open for the investment of capital in public works. Nothing in fact looked more promising than the prospects for development in terms of mines, railways, canals, steam-boats ...[10]

The post-"Mutiny" zeal, sufficient in its belief in the universal efficacy of "Saxon energy and British capital" to reclaim not one but a number of deserts, disguised two points of considerable significance. First, whatever attempts might be made to avoid direct contact with "Agriculture," after the unhappy experiences of indigo planters in Bengal, some such entanglement was inevitable in an environment where the land was the prime source of wealth : on this

[7]J. and R. Strachey, *Finances and Public Works*, p. 2. For a similar exposition of India's backwardness, from a viewpoint common to administrators and capitalists, see Cooke, *Banking in India*, pp. 66–67.

[8]Jenks, *Migration*, pp. 248 ff. On the "financial revolution" of the early to mid-nineteenth century, see D. S. Landes, "Vieille banque et banque nouvelle," *Revue d'histoire moderne et contemporaine*, New Series, III (1956), 204–222. On the elaborate linkage between European merchant banks and Oriental trade and finance networks, see D. S. Landes, *Bankers and Pashas*, p. 16.

[9]"Reports of the Select Committee on Colonization and Settlement in India."

[10]"Why is Not British Capital More Largely Invested in India?," *Economist*, October 9, 1858, pp. 1121–1122.

the people depended overwhelmingly for their livelihood, the Government for its revenue, and the investors for their dividends. Second, as far as the major area for investment was concerned, that is, the public works—roads, railways, and canals—the activity after 1858 merely continued along lines laid down twenty to thirty years before. The post-"Mutiny" investors were not so much pioneers as heirs to an inheritance.

The NWP and Oudh were the provinces most intensely involved in the "Mutiny" struggles; large areas, notably the poorer parts of Jhansi and the less opulent regions of Doab districts, had suffered severely from devastation. Their geographical features—particularly as regards the Doab districts—had already rendered them liable to large-scale developments, designed to exploit the resources of the river valleys for increased production and increased distribution through trade. With the pacification of the provinces, public works activity intensified.

The Public Works and Agriculture

The great nineteenth-century developments in canal engineering were concentrated largely in the Doab.[11] They began early, in the 1820s, with the building of the East Jumna Canal. This system, a radical re-development of an old Mughal canal line, was opened in 1830. It irrigated tracts in the Saharanpur, Muzaffarnagar, and Meerut districts. By 1878, its main and branch channels, together with distributaries, totalled 748 miles and irrigated 206,732 acres (as against the average of the preceding five years, 188,648). The cost of the works, excluding interest, came to £261,235. One of the most remunerative canals of British India, it paid nearly 23 percent on the capital expended on it by Government.[12]

Irrigation in the grand manner began, however, with the Ganges Canal. The works were begun under Government order of May 1847, water was admitted into the canal in 1854, and irrigation commenced the following year.[13] In 1861-62, the area irrigated by the canal was officially set at 372,000 acres; in 1864-65, it was set at 350,000 acres (the area under canal irrigation had contracted in comparison with

[11]For the extent of the main lines and distributaries of the NWP canals, as constructed up to 1900, see endpaper map.

[12]R. B. Buckley, *Irrigation Works*, pp. 93–95, and table, p. 92.

[13]For a summary of the history of the Ganges Canal construction to 1854, see *ibid.*, pp. 95–101.

the figures for 1861-62 as a result of good seasons and adequate rainfall). By 1864-65, the canal works as completed comprised its main line (181 miles); the Fategarh Branch (82.5 miles); the Bulandshahr Branch (45 miles); the Cawnpore Branch (170 miles); and the Etawah Branch (170 miles)—a total length of 648.5 miles with 2,266 miles of distributaries. The total capital outlay thus far was £2,155,997[14]— by 1866, capital expended on the canal stood at more than 88 percent of total expenditure of British capital in the NWP since 1858.[15] So far, only Upper Doab districts were served by the canal. In 1868, on the proposal of General (later Sir) Richard Strachey, the construction of a Lower Ganges Canal began, together with modifications in the completed channels. By 1877-78, the area actually irrigated by the whole complex was set at 1,045,013 acres (as against the average of preceding five years: 906,036). Some 593 miles of main and branch lines had been completed by then in the Upper and Central Doab. With another 3,417 miles of distributaries, the total length of the channels constructed ran into 4,010 miles, and the cost, excluding interest, stood at £3,055,015.[16]

In 1868, the first works—sanctioned for the purposes of famine relief—began on the Agra Canal. In March 1874, the canal was formally opened and irrigation began the following rabi season. By 1877-78, it commanded an area of 375,800 acres altogether— 114,200 acres in Muttra district and a further 113,100 acres in Agra made up the proportion irrigated in the NWP.[17] Smaller works in Bijnour, fed by a stream in Moradabad district, covered an area of 4,000 to 5,000 acres. On a capital cost of £6,996, the Bijnour Canal paid 11 to 12 percent: "it has always been a remunerative little work," was R. B. Buckley's comment.[18] In Bareilly, a further group of some four channels, totalling 256 miles in length and known collectively as the Rohilkhand Canals, irrigated a belt of country along the terai where rice was grown extensively. The capital cost was £148,207,

[14]"Resolution Relative to the Canals of the North-Western Provinces," *P.P.*, 1865, 39 (343), pp. 1–2.
[15]C. Thornhill, Senior Member, Board of Revenue, "Note on the Connection Between the Water-Rate and the Enhancement of Land Revenue," November 3, 1866, in NWP, "Revenue Proceedings," August 15, 1868, Index No. 7, May 11, 1867, Proceeding No. 2.
[16]On the alterations to the canal, to 1877–78, see Buckley, *Irrigation Works*, pp. 105–112. On the Lower Ganges Canal, see *ibid.*, pp. 121–127.
[17]On the Agra Canal, see *ibid.*, pp. 112–118. The net profit on the whole system by 1877–78 was estimated at £90,000.
[18]*Ibid.*, p. 120.

on which only a small percentage had been realized by the end of 1870s. A series of small watercourses in the Dun, and south in Bundelkhand, fed by tanks and streams, completed the network of canals in the NWP : some 5,601 miles of channels and distributaries, irrigating in 1877-78 an area of 1,459,938 acres, by which time the cost of their construction, excluding the payment of interest, came to £4,338,384— all of it borrowed in England.[19]

Work continued on the modifications and extensions to the Ganges Canal, as projected. After 1878, further works for the protection of unirrigated tracts specially liable to drought were thenceforward to be closely scrutinized by Government, "in the light of the latest knowledge," with rigorous attention to the "financial liabilities of the execution of works." On these principles, General Richard Strachey, as President of the Famine Commission of 1878-79, recommended immediate and special enquiry into two schemes which had not yet been implemented : the Sardah Canal to be constructed in Oudh and Rohilkhand, an elaborate project first prepared by Major (later Colonel) J. G. Forbes, R. E., in 1871, and a system of canals to be supplied from the rivers Betwa and Ken in Bundelkhand.[20] The Sardah scheme was shelved in the face of opposition by both the talukdars of Oudh and the Chief Commissioner. Work on the Betwa Canal however, owing to pressure to provide relief for famine distress in the conventional form of temporary employment on public works was begun early in the 1880s.[21]

Accurate statistics cannot be given of the overall increase in irrigated area owing to the canals. Acreages fluctuated with the seasons, the irrigated area expanding vastly in the threat of drought to contract again in seasons of adequate rainfall.[22] The question of payment of water rates also affected the area under irrigation during each season. In tracts where the cultivators were dependent on the canals, times in the fasli year when measurements were taken varied from district

[19]*Ibid.*, pp. 120–121.

[20]R. Strachey, "On the Need for Examining Certain Irrigation Projects in the NWP and Oudh," June 7, 1868, Government of India, "Famine Proceedings," June 1878, Proceeding No. 35. The projects for immediate review thus also included a navigation canal in Meerut Division to connect the (East) Jumna and Ganges canals, and a scheme to extend the Lower Ganges Canal as far as Allahabad.

[21]Inspector-General of Irrigation, NWP and Oudh, "Note on Works Projected or in Progress in the NWP and Oudh," in "Report of the Indian Famine Commission, 1879," *P.P.*, 1881, 71, Pt. III, Appendix V.

[22]For the area irrigated by canals in NWP from 1868–69 to 1896–97, according to Canal Department statistics, see Figure 2.

to district, pargana to pargana, and even mauza to mauza, thwarting any attempt at the compilation of a comprehensive statistical record. The period over which the increases in area were to be measured also posed a problem which was insoluble given the recording procedure used. Time limits were fixed according to the dates of revenue records compiled under Regulation IX of 1833 : the period within which measurements were taken varied therefore from district to district, in the order of their settlement. In many cases, no statistics of irrigated area existed prior to the revision of settlements beginning in 1860. Further, both the earlier and revised settlements made no distinction between "irrigable" and "irrigated." In 1884, W. C. Benett noted that an enquiry by the director of Agriculture and Commerce "showed that [in several Doab districts] the settlement statistics are of no use in ascertaining the irrigated area, lands within irrigating distance of a well or tank being included in the actually irrigated area ..."[23] Lastly, the problem of inadequate statistics is complicated by discrepancies in the percentage of increase in irrigated and in cultivated areas given in the various official sources.[24]

Canal development was concentrated in those areas where facilities existed for it—that is, in the western districts of the NWP. Those districts had a long-established and sophisticated pattern of farming, in which well irrigation particularly played a large part.[25] Colonel Baird Smith estimated that in 1848-49 the number of pakka (masonry) wells in the NWP came to some 137,337 of which 72,523 were in the Doab. Devastation during the "Mutiny" brought this latter number down to close to 70,000, with each well having an irrigating capacity of approximately 4.5 acres per season. The corresponding number of the more common kachha (temporary) wells was estimated

[23]W. C. Benett, Officiating Secretary, Board of Revenue, NWP, to Government, NWP and Oudh, December 4, 1884, "Note Regarding the Proposal to Exclude from Canal Irrigation All Lands at Present Assessed as Irrigated from Wells or Other Sources" (referring to *NWP Revenue Administration Report,* 1880–81, p. 58), in NWP and Oudh, "Revenue Proceedings," May 1885, File No. 380, Serial No. 10, Proceeding No. 19.

[24]In settlement reports, for example, figures given in (a) the main report and in (b) pargana (rent-rate) reports generally differ, a fact which is largely explained by the differing times and circumstances of their respective compilation. In an all-NWP table of irrigated area, district by district, 1860–1872, Auckland Colvin gave figures from those main (district) settlement reports available in 1872 and from yet another, incomplete (not from pargana reports) set for which the source is not given. See A. Colvin, *Memorandum,* Appendix III.

[25]See above, pp. 30–31.

at 280,000, each with an irrigating capacity of 1.5 acres per season. From this, Baird Smith concluded that some 1,470,000 acres in the Doab were irrigated by wells in 1860-61.[26] As the number of wells and their relatively low irrigating capacity would suggest, the Doab districts were densely populated by the latter part of the nineteenth century. Table 1 gives the density of population for selected canal-irrigated districts for which figures are available from the settlement reports.

TABLE 1

DENSITY OF POPULATION FOR SELECTED CANAL-IRRIGATED DISTRICTS

Canal	District	Population per Square Mile [a]
Ganges, East Jumna	Muzaffarnagar (1872)[b]	415.9
Ganges	Bulandshahr (1865)	719.5
Ganges	Aligarh (1882)	548.0
Ganges	Etah (1872)	465.0
Ganges	Mainpuri (1872)	452.0
Ganges	Etawah (1872)	395.0
Ganges	Cawnpore[c] (1872)	442.0
Ganges	Fatehpur (1872)	419.0
Ganges	Farukhabad (1871)	534.0

a According to the census of 1872, the average density of population for the NWP was 381.24 per square mile.

b The dates in brackets are those of the various settlement reports used.

c Excluding Cawnpore city.

For its part in supplying this dense population, the well irrigation of the Doab was not regarded by Baird Smith and other official observers trained in engineering as wholly inefficient. He himself noted, significantly, that the effects of wells were "less open to doubt than those of canal-irrigation," whilst the labour required to work the wells ensured the maximum use of water drawn; it was clear

[26]R. Baird Smith, "Report," paras. 98–100.

also that "the produce from land under well-irrigation is generally larger and better than that watered in any other way."[27] The only trouble with the wells was that they did not produce enough. The land had to be induced to produce more, and to achieve that the canal system had to be expanded. Baird Smith confidently anticipated that in time canal irrigation would show results comparable to those of the wells, and that over the enormously increased area opened to irrigation by the canal system, "existing differences in relative value will disappear."[28]

In Meerut, the richest of the Doab districts, irrigation prior to the introduction of canals had "naturally coincided very much with the character of the soils", E. C. Buck noted in 1874 in reviewing the settlement report. As a general conclusion from the pargana reports, it was clear that wells could be dug more easily, and lasted longer, in proportion to their distance from the great natural drainage lines : "the best well tracts were on watersheds." It was precisely these tracts which the new canals covered most extensively—canals being "only serviceable for irrigation along the watersheds of the district." The East Jumna Canal, opened in 1830, supplied the "rich Jat country between the Jumna and Hindun with a close network of distributary channels." The main line of the Ganges Canal, opened in 1855, ran through the centre, level tract between the Hindun and the Kali Nadi, whilst its Anupshahr Branch, opened five years later, fed the comparatively narrow but fertile strip between the Kali Nadi and the Ganges.[29] The division between areas with high proportions of better soils and the poorer tracts intensified : parganas Puth and Gurhmukhtesur, where widespread irrigation by wells was impracticable owing to the predominance of bhur ridges, also lay outside the range of canals and remained unreclaimed, whilst the extension of irrigation through the naturally fertile areas—for example, the central tracts of parganas Jalalabad and Baghpat—was reported by the end of the 1860s to have produced immediate and extraordinary increases in production.[30] Where the soils were of the stiffest compo-

[27]*Ibid.*, para, 85. F. Henvey, *Narrative,* cited Baird Smith on these points, which suggests that the situation in 1868–69 was little improved.

[28]Baird Smith, "Report," para. 85.

[29]E. C. Buck to C. A. Elliott, *Meerut Settlement Report,* pp. 7–10.

[30]*Meerut Settlement Report,* pargana reports by W. A. Forbes : Puth (1866), pp. 12–14; Gurhmukhtesur (1867), pp. 23–24; Baghpat (1868), pp. 60–62; Jalalabad (1867), pp. 37–38.

sition, well construction remained at least theoretically possible alongside the introduction of canals. In pargana Kotanah, to the north-west of the district, channels of the East Jumna Canal covered almost the entire area, yet good wells could still be readily constructed. This was reassuring: "In case of any accident to the canal, there could not possibly be any danger to the imperial revenue, for temporary wells could be dug in every field at trifling expense." The supersession of wells by the canal, which immediately commanded a much greater area was said to have saved Kotanah and neighbouring parganas— the core of the opulent estate of the Begam Sumroo—from the ravages of famine in 1860-61; indeed, "the proprietors" (chiefly Jats) made enormous profits from the grain trade. To the south, pargana Dasnah benefited similarly from the Ganges Canal.[31]

Elsewhere, however, disadvantages and even deleterious effects of the canals were already becoming noticeable by the end of the 1860s. The growing dependence on canal irrigation brought its problems. In 1866, W. A. Forbes noted that in pargana Chaprauli, which he, like Sir Henry Elliot thirty years before, agreed to be the finest in the district, the inroad of canals had left most wells in disuse and that well-sinking was now "almost entirely abandoned. It would be fortunate," he cautioned, "if the people would take further advantage of the natural facilities for well-irrigation, and thus guard against the uncertainties of canal-supply—a precaution some of the enterprizing Jat proprietors in the neighbourhood have already begun to recognize."[32] J. S. Porter noted the advantage the canal brought to pargana Sirdhana in that it enabled "sugar and other more valuable products doubtless to be grown in greater abundance." But against this "is to be placed the uncertainty of the water supply and the utter dependence on the canal to which the people are reduced by the ruin of their wells." Several villages in the pargana had already sustained loss from the canal's (or its distributaries') interference with natural drainage: two had lost their entire kharif owing to flood water which had swamped the fields because its outlets had been obstructed by the canal; a considerable part of another mauza just beneath the canal bank was so swamped by percolation as to be unfit for cultivation.[33] In other areas—parts of Baghpat, for instance—puddling

[31]*Ibid.*, Kotanah (1867), pp. 20–21; Dasnah (n.d.), pp. 27–28.

[32]*Ibid.*, Chaprauli (1866), p. 8.

[33]*Ibid.*, pp. 40–41. Pargana Meerut also showed similar effects of canal irrigation, viz. immense impetus to sugar cane cultivation, accompanied by a marked deleterious effect on both wells and soil; *ibid.* (J. S. Porter's report), pp. 52–53. In pargana

was the inevitable consequence of the volume of water made available from the canal, far exceeding that supplied by wells and distributed by flush irrigation. Problems of soil saturation were imminent. Buck, however, noted with reassurance in 1874 that it was "entirely within the Government's power to alleviate or entirely remove these evils."[34]

Wherever canal irrigation had been introduced, the same—or similar—benefits accrued, as well as the same problems. If the driving principle behind the construction of the canals was the achievement of increase, without which no real prosperity could be envisaged, this aim was certainly satisfied, even if its exact measure remains out of reach. But in which products was this increase realized?

The overwhelming majority of the population—the peasantry—relied on the kharif millets, principally jowar and bajra, and the various pulses for staple food grains. These and fodder for draught beasts were generally grown on the wider areas of middle- and even poor-quality soils dependent for their moisture on periodic rainfall; irrigated land, of better- and top-quality soils, was used for the heavier and more valuable crops which required careful attention and a number of waterings in addition to rainfall for good yields. The expansion of irrigated and irrigable areas through the introduction of canals resulted in the increase in production of these "valuable" crops—principally cotton, indigo, sugar cane, and wheat.[35]

In the trans-Jumna parganas of Muttra district before the building of the Agra Canal, the principal kharif crops were jowar, bajra, and cotton, and the chief rabi staples were barley, gram, and bejhar (mixed barley and gram). The canal was confidently expected to alter this, in favour of the "richer" crops. Whilst the area under cotton would be little affected, the pattern of cereal cultivation would show significant changes—"the substitution of irrigated wheat [encouraged by the relative richness of soils in these parganas], bejhar or barley for either jowar, bajra or unirrigated rabi crops."

Kethore, swamps resulting from the inflow of canal water into the Barh Ganga River were already conspicuous by the mid-1860s; *ibid.* (Porter's report), pp. 50–51.

[34] E. C. Buck to C. A. Elliott, *ibid.*, pp. 7–10.

[35] For the total canal-irrigated area in the NWP and the specific proportions of kharif and of rabi 1868–69 to 1896–97, see Figure 2. For the proportion of total canal-irrigated area under principal crops in the kharif, 1868–69 to 1896–97, see Figure 3. For the proportion of total canal-irrigated area under principal crops in the rabi, 1875–76 to 1896–97 (statistics for rabi crops are not available before 1875–76), see Figure 4. For convenience, no separate figure is given for sugar cane, which has been included under kharif.

The next stage would be the introduction of sugar cane, indigo, and opium—all hitherto almost unknown in the area—and an increase in *kachhiyana* (garden produce); double-cropping would become prevalent. "There will then be not only an improvement in the quantity but also in the quality of the produce," that is, the balance of the crop pattern would turn against the coarse staple food grains.[36] These anticipations were realized. Two or three years later, R. S. Whiteway recorded in the settlement report that sugar cane had in fact been planted extensively along the canal distributaries; the coarser kharif crops, such as jowar, had in fact been "greatly superseded by the more valuable ones," including cotton, and even indigo had been sown in some villages.[37] Of the canal-irrigated area of the parganas, 69.4 percent was recorded under rabi crops in the year of revenue survey as against 26.4 percent under kharif: wheat occupied 26.2 percent, barley 12.3 percent, and bejhar 21 percent, compared with kharif staples of jowar, now only 9.7 percent, and bajra 4.1 percent.[38] Throughout, the valuable crops of cotton, wheat, and barley alone accounted for some 39 percent of the canal-irrigated area; in the cis-Jumna parganas, untouched by the canal, these crops aggregated a mere 23 percent of the total cultivated area.[39] Etah district, too, showed a crop pattern generally characteristic of canal-irrigated areas, which were most extensive in the Meerut and Agra divisions of the NWP: the best districts, supplied now by an abundance of canal water, went over to producing larger quantities of the most saleable crops. In Etah's kharif harvests sugar cane, cotton, and indigo predominated, and in the rabi, it was wheat, barley, and bejhar once again. In pargana Mahrehra—the best in the district—the Cawnpore Branch of the Ganges Canal had brought an immense stimulus to indigo growing: almost every village had its factory.[40]

The distribution of wheat itself became one of the clearest indications of the direction in which the stimulus of canal irrigation was applied. In 1876-77, the total area under wheat throughout the NWP and Oudh was officially estimated at 5,902,770 acres, with 2,257,344 acres in the Ganges–Jumna Doab, as against 2,695,730

[36]M. A. McConaghey, Settlement Officer, Muttra, "Memorandum on the Proposed Water and Owner's Rates to Be Adopted on the New Agra Canal," *NWP Irrigation Revenue Report*, 1873–74, p. civ.

[37]*Muttra Settlement Report*, pp. 12–15.

[38]*Ibid.*, pp. 21–22.

[39]*Ibid.*, p. 3.

[40]*Etah Settlement Report*, pp. 66–67.

in the considerably larger area between the Ganges and Gogra which was barely watered by canals. That year, the acreage under wheat for the whole of Oudh was recorded as some 1,904,798 acres; and in Meerut Division alone, one of the great canal-irrigated regions of the NWP, wheat was said to be grown on no less than 1,371,103 acres.[41] It was well known that wheat was "not the food of the masses. They live either on the millets of the autumn crops or the coarse mixed grains (barley, gram, and peas) of the spring harvest. The urban population undoubtedly do consume a large proportion of wheat for their numbers; and the richer proprietors or tradesmen in the villages also use wheaten flour. But to the millions wheaten flour is a luxury, untasted perhaps from birth to death or only at high festivals and holidays."[42]

Given these conditions, we may ask what sort of protection the canals offered in the event of drought. When the summer rains failed, it was the staple kharif grains and fodder crops which suffered; where the winter rains were insufficient, it was the poorer rabi crops. Canals were used to redress the balance only in dire emergency, and the growing of kharif food grains on canal-irrigated lands was never sustained once the immediate pressure of severe scarcity had eased. The famine years of 1868 and 1869 in the NWP exhibited a pattern which was to reappear whenever the rains failed. At the beginning of the drought, Government issued a circular encouraging the sowing of grain and fodder crops in canal-irrigated areas. This resulted, according to Frederick Henvey, in a considerable increase in areas cultivated with miscellaneous grains, "though cultivators at first were very reluctant to water food-crops at the expense of other more remunerative produce." It was not until August 1868, when the destruction of the kharif harvest was clearly imminent, that a rush for water took place. "The fact is, as has been stated in the Irrigation Report for the year 1868-69, that farmers will only take canal-water to save, not to improve, the coarser grain-crops."[43]

[41] F. N. Wright, "Report on Wheat Cultivation in the NWP and Oudh," June 28, 1878, paras. 6–7, Government of India, *Selections from the Records of Government,* No. CLX, pp. 156–157.

[42] *Ibid.,* para. 25, p. 163.

[43] According to Henvey, *Narrative,* pp. 113–114, in 1868–69 the canal-irrigated area was estimated at 1,441,898 acres (exceeding the highest recorded figure for any single preceding year, viz. 983,390 acres). Of this area, the total acreage under food and fodder crops together was 1,189,925 acres (82 percent). Of this, the total acreage under food grains alone was 1,178,558 acres. Of this, the total acreage under wheat was 597,936, and under barley it was 257,509.

The disastrous failure of the summer rains of 1877 in most districts of Meerut, Agra, Rohilkhand, Sitapur, and Lucknow divisions, and in parts also of Allahabad, Jhansi, and Rae Bareli districts, destroyed the kharif food and fodder crops. The enormous deficiencies in outturn could not be supplemented by canal irrigation, even where such existed, since, "at the sowing season, cultivators could not foresee the terrible drought that was to prevail, and did not avail themselves of canal-water for this class of crop, the canal-irrigated lands being principally devoted to sugar-cane, indigo, and cotton."[44] W. R. Burkitt saw how, in Etawah, sugar cane and indigo were gradually ousting food grains in the canal tracts and why this should give cause for alarm rather than the enthusiasm for increase so commonly expressed amongst his colleagues in the service : "During the late drought [in 1877], when I was out inspecting the condition of the country, it was to me a most melancholy sight to see acre upon acre of magnificent indigo and sugar-cane, while hardly a blade of any food-grain was to be seen. The same remarks apply, though in a very much less degree, to cotton."[45] Crop patterns in canal-irrigated areas persisted with their preponderance of "valuable" crops, as did the consequent lack of any effective remedy for recurrent dry seasons. Again in 1880-81, an official report noted that "highly cultivated crops (sugar, wheat) suffered as might be expected least damage while the drought was felt most by peas and gram and the other pulses ... sown on inferior localities and out of reach of water."[46] The fact was that, except for crops sown before the onset of the monsoon proper, irrigation in the kharif was practically inconsiderable and, as was clearly stated by the highest officers of Government in the provinces, "must always be more or less so." When the rainfall failed entirely or almost entirely, canals and wells could not take its place.[47]

Only in those few areas where canal irrigation combined with excellent soil conditions to make wheat the chief grain staple was

[44]D. G. Pitcher, *Report on the Scarcity*, 1877–1879, p. 10. See also "Report on the Condition and Prospects of the NWP and Oudh," October 4, 1877, in Government of India, "Famine Proceedings," October 1877, Proceeding No. 14.

[45]W. R. Burkitt, Officiating Collector, Etawah, to Board of Revenue, NWP, November 16, 1877, in NWP and Oudh, "Revenue Proceedings," February 1879, Index No. 65, June 9, 1878, Proceeding No. 140.

[46]*NWP Revenue Administration Report*, 1880–81, p. 2.

[47]Lieutenant-Governor, and Senior Member, Board of Revenue, "Observations on Difficulties in the Collection of Land Revenue in the NWP and Oudh, Owing to the Failure of Crops," in Government of India, "Famine Proceedings," October 1877, Proceeding No. 13.

the threat of scarcity least felt. As previously mentioned, the Jat proprietors of pargana Kotana, Meerut district—a by-word for fertility—not only were saved by the East Jumna Canal during the drought and famine of 1860-61 but made enormous profits by supplying grain to stricken districts of the NWP famine tract.[48] Generally speaking, canal irrigation did, and could do, little to decrease the ravages of scarcity by expanding the sources of staple food supply; indeed, its effect tended to be the reverse, to contract them—a process which tended to worsen with the added stimulus of the export trade in grains, particularly wheat, beginning in the late 1870s.[49] In addition, the canals incited the cultivators to load the land with an unrelieved burden of crops year after year, disrupting the regular practices of following. As we have seen, Colonel William Sleeman reported double-cropping and consequent deterioration of the land through exhaustion to be conspicuous in certain Doab districts at least by 1850.[50] A sizeable area of dofasli, or double-cropped, land was generally taken by field officers as a sign of local prosperity. A. B. Patterson however agreed with Sleeman and drew attention to the dangers of gross deterioration from the obvious over-cropping in Fatehpur district, where, he warned, cultivation was increasing in area and intensity with a disregard for the necessary reliefs to the soil. He admitted further to hearing from "men familiar with Oudh" that there the same distressing tendency was now evident also: "the *pox Britannica* [as Patterson's report obligingly states] has worked its natural effect in inducing a dense population to keep as much land as possible constantly under cultivation, and ... the 'Garden of India' has already lost some of its relative superiority in fertility."[51]

This tendency was encouraged by the canals.[52] Auckland Colvin noticed it as early as 1864, in pargana Thana Bhawan in the canal tract of Muzaffarnagar district:

... the chief danger in the canal area is overcropping. The land is rarely allowed to rest. For example, cotton is sown in a field in autumn, and wheat follows as the next crop; chari will be sown the following autumn, succeeded by wheat, then cotton as before and so on. The only crop for which the land

[48]See above, p. 70, n. 31.
[49]For details on the grain trade and its effect on local agriculture, see below, pp. 179 ff.
[50]See above, pp. 34–35.
[51]*Fatehpur Settlement Report*, p. 2.
[52]For the proportion of *dofasli* land to total canal-irrigated area, NWP, 1876–77 to 1896–97, see Figure 2.

is rested is sugar cane, and not for more than one season. In ordinary villages, this system is kept within bounds, not more than 10% of the cultivated area being "do-fuslee" but on the canal, it is carried to excess. The cane is very much deteriorated.[53]

According to Lieutenant-Colonel A. F. Corbett, whose *Climate and Resources of Upper India,* published in 1874, was the first outspoken technical criticism of the Government's zeal in promoting canal irrigation at all costs, over-cropping in itself was only a superficial explanation of the noticeable decline in productivity in certain canal tracts.[54] A more fundamental cause could be found in the increase of irrigated area under the stimulus of the canals. By irrigation, as Corbett explained,

... the whole surface-soil is brought into the condition of sun-dried bricks; the more water that has been applied to the land the harder the soil becomes, and while its powers of absorption and radiation are reduced, those of reflection and retention of heat are increased; and we find also that the power of capillary attraction possessed by the land is increased, and that the soil so compacted will sooner become dried up than soil left loose and open, partly from the fact of the interstices between its particles having been reduced in size, thus increasing its capillarity, and partly from the increased heat of the surface ...[55]

This hardening of the upper soil by irrigation coincided with the consolidation of a "pan" in the sub-soil

by the treading of cattle in ploughing ... This causes shallower ploughing, the roots of plants have less depth of soil in which to search for food, and cannot force their way into the hardened pan; and there is the alternate soaking and drying of the land, during which the natural salts of the earth are gradually brought nearer the surface by capillary attraction.

This process may go on for some years before the land shows any excessive amount of *reh* (saline efflorescence) on the surface; but the soil is steadily being poisoned by its accumulation in the upper soil, which accounts, together with the increased hardness of the soil, for the diminished fertility of lands some time under irrigation.[56]

[53] *Muzaffarnagar Settlement Report,* p. 135.

[54] A. F. Corbett, *Climate and Resources,* pp. 66–67.

[55] *Ibid.,* p. 19.

[56] *Ibid.,* p. 67. For a corroboration of Corbett's analysis of the origin of reh as traceable to increased capillary attraction, see J. A. Voelcker, *Report,* para. 74, pp. 56–58. For a summary discussion of the problems of reh and *usar* (soil salinity and alkalinity) on the basis of observations made from 1858 to the 1890s, see Appendix 5.

Why did this not happen with the large numbers of irrigation wells worked in the Doab districts? C. H. T. Crosthwaite explained the reason for the decline of canal—as against well-irrigated—land as follows :

... wells require a large livestock and great labour. The soil reaps two benefits therefrom : more manure saved from burning, and the tendency to overfarm checked. If a farmer has to work his well, he cannot sow more sugar and wheat than he has time to irrigate but when he is relieved from all well duty he has nothing to keep him within bounds. He sows more of these crops, and has less manure ... The extraordinary large produce of the first years of canal irrigation calls forth all the powers of the soil but if not backed up by a due supply of other food, it leaves exhaustion behind it.[57]

Meanwhile the over-watered, unmanured soil was still ploughed up with bullock teams. Problems of double hardening inevitably followed, and an ominous increase in the barren and frequently reh-infected land known as usar.

Crosthwaite had reported with some alarm the spread of reh in pargana Phapphand, Etawah district—irrigated by the Ganges Canal— as early as 1871. Although reh was as yet by no means widespread, as G. H. M. Ricketts, then Officiating Commissioner of Agra Division, was at pains to point out when commenting on Crosthwaite's report, it was nonetheless an evil "demanding an immediate remedy."[58] Seven years later, and two years after Corbett's careful examination of the reh problem, the condition had become far more obvious— sufficient now to cause serious, if somewhat academic, concern on the part of Government officers. A committee was appointed to investigate the problem thoroughly, on the basis of reports—chiefly from a Mr. David Robarts, a substantial zamindar of pargana Sikandra Rao, Aligarh district—of the disastrous spread of reh in parts of Aligarh, Meerut, and throughout the Kali Nadi valley. In each case some hundreds of acres, which in these populous districts represented thousands of livelihoods, had been put out of cultivation; in each case, the damage was directly attributable to excessive irrigation by canal water. In introducing the final report of the Reh Committee in 1878, Buck, then Director of Agriculture in the provinces, warned that these and similar cases noted elsewhere, brought to light at the last

[57] *Etawah Settlement Report,* pp. 14–19.
[58] Officiating Commissioner, Agra, to Board of Revenue, NWP, December 12, 1871, in NWP, "Revenue Proceedings," June 29, 1872, Index No. 36, Proceeding No. 26.

minute and even sometimes by accidental observation, were "the first and earliest outcome of the introduction of a canal system" (it was now four years since the publication of Corbett's treatise), and that the same disturbing influences might be slowly at work in many areas.[59]

The findings of the Reh Committee amounted, in substance, to little more than a corroboration of Corbett's assertions.[60] Its enquiry was far from adequate. No account, for instance, was given of the extent of usar tracts in the provinces : they were said to cover "immense areas," without details as to acreage. No agricultural chemist was appointed to the committee nor even consulted during the investigations.[61] However, the committee's final report made it clear that the chief cause of the increase in usar had not gone unnoticed : they condemned the "vicious system" (in Buck's words) of swamping the fields for irrigation, which was the direct result of the accessibility of "flush water."[62] The "true remedy" was stated equally categorically : a greater economy in the distribution of water, to be achieved by the raising of rates charged by Government on flush irrigation. This was more than the Canal Department could provide. Since flush rates were already high, an increase would deter farmers altogether with disastrous results for the revenue accruing from canal charges. The committee itself realized that a remedy which it acknowledged to be inferior would have to be applied and recommended accordingly that lift irrigation should be substituted for flush irrigation as far as possible—"a waste of labour for a waste of water," sighed the president. He was encouraged solely by the realization that the waste of water was by far the more serious evil, leading as it so clearly had done to swamping, thence to deterioration of the soil and of the health of the people, thence to a diminution of their income, and ultimately, it was certain, to a reduction in the land revenue.[63] For the rest, the committee recommended that experiments in reclaiming usar tracts

[59]NWP and Oudh, "Revenue Proceedings," June 1879, Index No. 117, December 28, 1878, Proceeding No. 55. For an account of the reh problem in Aligarh, the focal area for official enquiry and experiment, see *ibid.*, May 1880, Index Nos. 100–106, May 22, 1880, Proceedings Nos. 17–23; see also Appendix 5.

[60]For a concise summary of the committee's findings, see Voelcker, *Report*, para. 74, pp. 56–57; see also Appendix 5.

[61]Voelcker, *Report*, para. 78, p. 62.

[62]H. S. Reid, President, "Review of the Proceedings of the Reh Committee," para. 16, in NWP and Oudh, "Revenue Proceedings," June 1879, Index No. 112, December 28, 1878, Proceeding No. 50.

[63]*Ibid.*

which had begun in 1874 under the supervision of the newly created Department of Agriculture should be continued.[64] These consistently showed that usar could be brought back into cultivation only by careful watering accompanied by intensive manuring.[65] Nothing however was done on any significant scale to increase the local supply of manure near these tracts in order to keep pace with the increase in irrigation from the canal. When Dr. J. A. Voelcker, the first agricultural chemist to be appointed by Government to report on Indian agrarian conditions, toured India in 1891, it is hardly surprising that he found "enormous tracts, especially in the plains of Northern India," affected by reh. In the NWP alone, it was estimated to cover between 4,000 and 5,000 square miles. In the midst of this desolated usar land, patches of "valuable" crops—opium, sugar cane, wheat, castor-oil plant, and cotton—stood out "like oases in the salt-covered desert around them."[66]

The contrast between the benefits and drawbacks of canal irrigation was not always so clear to the eye. In Etawah, for example, the indices of prosperity in the form of extensive cultivation of "valuable" crops dominated the scene. The drought of 1868-69 had brought a stimulus to irrigation from the Ganges Canal. The falling-off in the use of the canal water after these dry months was however "chiefly confined to cotton and ordinary kharif crops which would not benefit by irrigation," whilst the area under indigo began rapidly to increase, as did canal-irrigated sugar cane.[67] The rest of the picture was filled in from the complaints of local farmers, recorded in this instance by Crosthwaite, when on settlement work in the district. They complained of corruption by the authorities administering the canal (standards

[64]On the Department of Agriculture, NWP, see pp. 101–102 below. On consultation as regards action to be taken against reh, the Irrigation Branch of the Public Works Department (Canal Department) found itself unable to meet the costs of measures recommended by the committee, viz. the appointment of a permanent agricultural chemist and regular experiments estimated at Rs. 3,000 per annum. It agreed, however, to make an allotment for the Irrigation Branch and Agricultural Department expenses incurred in collecting data in the special (i.e., Sikandra Rao and vicinity) tract; see "On the Deterioration of Land by Reh," in NWP and Oudh, "Irrigation Proceedings," November 1879, Proceeding No. 1. For the annual revenue and expenditure (in the form of regular charges on the revenue) of the Irrigation Branch, 1876–77 to 1899–1900, see Figure 5.

[65]For a summary of experiments carried out on usar tracts to 1891, see Voelcker, *Report*, paras. 75–76, pp. 58–61; see also Appendix 5.

[66]Voelcker, *Report*, para. 73, p. 55.

[67]*Etawah Settlement Report*, pp. 14–19.

seemed to vary with the character of the successive district canal officers). They complained of uncertainty in the supply of canal water and of its inferiority as a fertilizing agent. They complained, as might be expected, of the deposits of silt and reh and the consequent deterioration of the soil. Kachhis, the skilled gardener-cultivators, and even the officers of the Government Opium Department were reported to have a marked preference for wells. But the real disadvantage of the canal was, as "universally asserted in Etawah," that "after the first two to three years, the crops do fall off."[68] Along with all this, the canal disrupted the farmer's former pattern of work. Far from firing him with the much-heralded spirit of industriousness which increase was assumed to bring, canal irrigation required less by way of labour than his well had demanded. As Crosthwaite went on to note,

... the great relief from labour given by the canal probably goes as far as anything else with an ordinary peasant in directing his choice when it is possible for him to choose [between canal and well]. When a man has no sons or male relatives to help him, or when he has to keep more bullocks for irrigation than he wants for his plough, he may realize that he actually saves money by employing the canal. But ordinarily it strikes him the other way. The expenses of well-irrigation disbursed by degrees consists [sic] largely of the consumption of the cultivator's own produce. The canal rate has to be paid in cash, and in a lump sum, and by a stated time, its collection attended by all the annoyance of a tax. To the average cultivator the canal appears an expensive business more costly than his well, but . . . he is swayed by his being saved an infinity of toil, and his ability to irrigate a much larger area of land . . .[69]

It was not always a matter of choice for the farmer. He had to use canal water where the canal had put local wells out of use, especially where it had made well-digging impracticable by the rise in the water table which it had caused. Whiteway made enquiries as to the situation in Muttra in the hot weather of 1878—a difficult season—and discovered that all kachha wells in villages through which the main (Agra) canal passed and from which more than 5,000 acres had previously been irrigated were now useless, owing to the rise in spring

---

[68]*Ibid.* On the corruption of the canal administration, see pp. 88–89 below.

[69]*Etawah Settlement Report*, pp. 14–19. William Young, Collector of Muzaffarnagar in 1880, recorded similar observations (apropos of the East Jumna Canal) made by "an intelligent zamindar of the neighbourhood"; see Young to C. A. Daniell, Commissioner, Meerut, January 28, 1880, in NWP and Oudh, "Irrigation Proceedings," January 1881, Proceeding No. 8, para. 5.

level.[70] He concluded with caution that the canals therefore were, very possibly, a failure as an insurance against famine owing to their indirect effect on indigenous methods of cultivation. The Secretariat noted the following year that Whiteway's remarks were "deserving of attention."[71]

Deleterious effects of canals on wells were by now widely noted. Saturation of the sub-soil was especially common in bhur (sandy tracts) irrigated by the canals, and this in turn caused the sides of kachha wells to fall in and made the continued construction of them to any depth out of the question. In Bulandshahr, according to R. G. Currie, a general rise of some six feet in the water level all over the canal area had resulted in the kachha wells being almost entirely superseded.[72] A similar situation was reported from Mainpuri,[73] and W. H. Moreland later collected further examples of this destruction of kachha wells in canal tracts from Aligarh and Agra.[74] The only remedy was to construct a pakka (masonry) well. Its cost in materials and labour, however, made it inconceivable as a viable alternative for the majority of farmers.

The problems that canals caused or, more often, aggravated were not restricted to over-cropping, salination, and the destruction of wells. Percolation from main channels or *rajbahas* (distributaries) could create swamps. In the Budh Ganga valley area of Etah district, the entire sugar cane crop of 1878-79 was ruined by this. The Canal Department provided the sum of Rs. 4,150 in compensation, but it did not undertake to drain the swamp.[75] More widespread and serious swamping arose from the canals' obstruction of natural drainage lines where an insufficient number of syphons had been built to carry the canals beneath these natural watercourses. The obstruction caused by canal embankments led to swamping, the worst consequence of which was the aggravation of malaria. During the 1870s, the incidence of the disease increased alarmingly throughout the canal-irrigated districts where the saturation from flush irrigation

[70] *Muttra Settlement Report*, pp. 12–15.

[71] *Ibid.*, p. 3.

[72] *Bulandshahr Settlement Report*, p. 10.

[73] *Mainpuri Settlement Report*, p. 9.

[74] I. Habib, *Agrarian System*, p. 28, n. 3, citing W. H. Moreland, *The Agriculture of the United Provinces* (Allahabad, 1910).

[75] *NWP Revenue Administration Report*, 1878–89, p. 3. For details of the swamping of the Budh Ganga valley near Soron by percolation from the Lower Ganges Canal, see NWP and Oudh, "Irrigation Proceedings," August 1879, Proceedings Nos. 1–13.

coincided with the obstruction of natural drainage lines.[76] In spite of a series of minor drainage operations begun by the Irrigation Department, fever continued to be a frequent cause of death and, worse still for a larger number of cultivators, a frequent cause of debilitation, especially in districts with large irrigated areas.[77] According to Alan Cadell, even the climate in Muzaffarnagar had grown worse, in terms of an increasingly unhealthy humidity, "than it was before irrigation from the canal became so general and the cultivation of rice [an export staple] so much extended."[78]

A farmer in a low-lying area irrigated by a canal might therefore have had to face a number of setbacks with which he was hardly equipped to deal. His fields might become salinized. If they lay close to an irrigating channel, he might have had the (often doubtful) benefit of easy access to the water supply or the prospect, alternatively, of swamping from drainage obstructions. Such drainage channels as were built to take excess water off the land ran into the same problem with the natural lines; a farmer might therefore oppose their construction, with reason. The obstruction or inadequacy of drainage facilities increased the dangers from seasonal flooding. Excessive rain in the early kharif would turn his irrigated fields into a lake and drown his "valuable" crops.[79] Meanwhile, his well might have fallen into disuse, leaving him no alternative but the canal for his irrigation. With the expansion of cultivation of "valuable" crops into land formerly occupied in part by staple cereals and with the increase in population, his food supply became more precarious. Not only food, but fuel and fodder were also threatened : "Since the introduction of canal-irrigation on an immense scale in this part of the country, the conditions of agriculture have been almost revolutionized," William Crooke, then manager of the Awa estate in Etah district, declared in reviewing the situation in the Central Doab towards the

[76]For this condition in Saharunpur, see *NWP Revenue Administration Report,* 1870–71, pp. 6–7; in Meerut, *ibid.,* 1871–72, p. 8; in Meerut and Bulandshahr, *ibid.,* 1873–74, p. 8; in Meerut, Bulandshahr, Aligarh, and Etawah, *ibid.,* 1874–75, p. 5.

[77]*Ibid.,* 1875–76, p. 3. For further observations on the problem reported in 1879, see C. Planck, Sanitary Commissioner, NWP, to Government, NWP and Oudh, October 14, 1879, "The Effect of Canal Extensions on the Mortuary Rate of the Etah, Meerut and Bulandshahr Districts," in NWP and Oudh, "Irrigation Proceedings," March 1881, Proceedings Nos. 22–35.

[78]*Muzaffarnagar Settlement Report (Canal Tract),* pp. 4–5, 6.

[79]For an example where this inundation was reported as the "usual occurrence" when such rains occurred early in the kharif, see *NWP Revenue Administration Report,* 1876–77, pp. 1–2.

end of 1881. "A great part of the culturable waste lands has been broken up, and the supply of firewood and grass seriously diminished. The consequences would have been more serious had not the use of canal-water enabled the cultivators to dispense with a large number of their plough cattle." This, however, as Crooke went on to show, was of little genuine assistance for the farmer in dealing with this sudden revolution in his environment, especially since his techniques remained unadapted to the changed circumstances. "The number of cattle now maintained is, in comparison with the area under cultivation, inadequate. This has led to a slovenly system of cultivation, and has greatly reduced the manure supply."[80]

Early in the century, *dhak* jungle (*butea frondosa*, a fine timber tree which also provides excellent charcoal when burned) had covered much of the Doab. With the extension of agricultural settlement, the jungle had been largely stripped away, leaving bare usar patches by the time when Crooke was writing. As a result, forage and firewood for the cultivator had already become scarce and costly—a condition which was now aggravated by the contraction of "waste" areas owing to the expansion stimulated by the canals. Firewood, according to Crooke, cost a rupee for four maunds, assuming it could be bought, and dry grass for cattle was sold at from two to four maunds a rupee.[81] The condition of cattle, especially during the thin period prior to the rains when no fresh fodder was avilable, was "miserable in the extreme."[82] Cattle starvation and concomitant diseases (rinderpest, foot-and-mouth disease, fever) became regular occurrences which were aggravated by, rather than originating in, years of severe drought.

Could this be remedied? Crooke himself advocated a scheme which would combine the reclamation of usar tracts in the Central Doab with the establishment of fuel and fodder reserves. Exhaustive discussions over the next three years by the Revenue Department, however, revealed the "material difficulties" which prevented the implementation of this project and other proposals to buy up waste land and enclose it for emergency reserves : the cost was too great for Government.[83] These same schemes went forward for discussion

[80]W. Crooke, "Note on Fuel and Fodder Reserves in the Central Ganges–Jumna Doab," November 2, 1881, in NWP and Oudh, "Revenue Proceedings," April 1883, Index No. 31, April 8, 1882, Proceeding No. 63.

[81]*Ibid.*

[82]This is an observation on the state of the cattle in pargana Firozabad, Kheri district, in NWP and Oudh, "Revenue Proceedings," May 1880, Index No. 77, May 15, 1880, Proceeding No. 16.

[83]Government, NWP and Oudh, to Board of Revenue, NWP, January 11, 1884,

by the Revenue and Agricultural Department of the Government of India, and were wrecked on the same rocks :

The expense of taking up as reserves even a small proportion of waste lands now used as pastures would be enormous. For example, a reserve of some 6% of the grazing grounds of Bareilly would cost for acquisition alone Rs. $1\frac{1}{2}$ lakhs [Rs. 150,000]. The experiment of acquiring and enclosing 954 acres of usar land in Aligarh is to cost Government more than Rs. 10,000. Without multiplying illustrations, it may be briefly said that in those fully-settled districts, where pressure on the available pasturage is felt, no reserves could, by fencing, planting, and re-foresting waste and usar land, be created which would have an appreciable effect, except at an outlay so enormous as to place the measure at present beyond the means of the Government to undertake ...

... a small experiment in reclaiming and planting usar has been in progress in Cawnpore since 1882. The results so far demonstrate the necessity of great caution in undertaking any large expenditure on the formation of grass preserves in such soil ...[84]

Meanwhile, the contraction of fodder areas in the Doab had a direct effect on the pastoralists who supplied cattle to the agricultural communities. In pargana Lonee, Meerut district, the expansion of cultivation was rapidly converting the traditionally pastoral Gujars into settled agriculturists, a transformation described by the Settlement Officer, Forbes, as in the "spirit of industry."[85] The same transformation was taking place in pargana Dadri, Bulandshahr district, where the Gujars, according to the Settlement Officer, had begun to "recognize the value of property" : they "have benefited considerably," Currie wrote, "by greatly increasing their cotton cultivation in the last two years."[86] But here too there were problems. Most Gujar settlements were situated in the low-lying khadir areas—the river valleys—where the constant threat of inundation meant little regular kharif cultivation could be hazarded, whilst pasture lands were

"Proposals for Experimental Fuel and Fodder Reserves in Certain Localities in the NWP," in NWP and Oudh, "Revenue Proceedings," January 1884, Index No. 31, January 12, 1884, Proceeding No. 41.

[84]Government, NWP and Oudh, to Government, India, October 3, 1885, "Fuel and Fodder Reserves," in Government of India, "Famine Proceedings," May 1891, Proceeding No. 91. For details of relevant enquiries and experiments in NWP, see NWP and Oudh, "Revenue Proceedings," April 1883, Serial No. 74, p. 76; *ibid.*, January 1884, Serial Nos. 28–31, pp. 51–77; *ibid.*, March 1885, Serial Nos. 78–86, pp. 86–101.

[85]*Meerut Settlement Report*, pp. 31–33.

[86]*Bulandshahr Settlement Report*, pp. 107–108.

extensive, with long grass flourishing in the moist soil conditions. Gujars therefore derived their regular livelihood from grazing and from the sale of thatching grass, and their food supply from rabi grains since these were sown when there was no threat of flood. When conditions prevented cultivation, they could resort to cattle thieving. Thus, with the expansion of cultivation into the khadir, the Gujars benefited from rabi cultivation, though the kharif crops were still precarious. But with the conversion of the Gujars into agriculturists, the supply of cattle to the cultivators necessarily contracted; for this reason, cultivators had to rely on their own, often deteriorating, stock. Meanwhile, Gujars in areas outside the range of the canal developments remained obstinately unmoved by the "spirit of industry." In Muzaffarnagar, Auckland Colvin noted in 1864 how the Gujars of pargana Bedauli derived their chief support from cattle. "This," he wrote, "supplies them with a motive for maintaining large tracts of uncultivated land, and materially diminishes their necessity for cultivating land." It was assumed that this regrettable situation could be changed only by the realization of enormous gains from an increase in cultivation. "Nothing, I believe, will outweigh this motive but some agent not only bringing greater profits than cattle-stealing and cattle-breeding, but profits sufficiently great to supplant the old pleasant habits of indolence and theft by the laborious habits of toil and agriculture." Such an agent was to be found in Colvin's view in the form of canal water.[87] Crosthwaite's observations on the labour-saving consequences of the canal[88] lead one to doubt a priori that Colvin's vision would ever be realized.

The awe-inspiring size of the great canals obscured, to those minded to see in them a monument to engineering achievement and administrative virtue, their less direct repercussions and the faults in their construction. The Ganges Canal, for example, was in all senses a great pioneering work—"the most magnificent work of its class in the whole world," wrote W. T. Thornton from the distant vantage point of the India Office, "the value of which will be very inadequately appreciated if it fail to secure for the memory of Sir Proby Cautley, its principal designer and constructor, an Indian immortality."[89] As a pioneering work, the canal had virtually no precedent. Its

[87] *Muzaffarnagar Settlement Report*, pp. 128–129.
[88] See p. 80 above.
[89] W. T. Thornton, *Indian Public Works*, p. 109.

construction was therefore largely experimental, and errors in the design and its implementation could not necessarily have been foreseen, though the consequences would have been less disturbing had the canal been built in an uninhabited wilderness. The controversies amongst engineers which it aroused however centred less on constructional defects than on questions of expenditure. The famous dispute between Sir A. T. Cotton and Cautley, which threatened to rob the latter of some of his claim to immortality, opened with an acrimonious memorandum on the canal compiled by Cotton for the East India Irrigation Company, which financed the project, and published in July 1863. In it, Cotton listed the following as the "greatest fundamental mistakes." The head of the canal had been sited too far up the Ganges with the result that its fall was "very great" whilst it had to be carried across the very heavy drainage from the sub-Himalayan hills and had been cut to carry water below surface level—all of which amounted to a vast amount of unnecessary excavation at considerable cost. All the masonry work was of brick instead of the (cheaper) local stone. All the water carried in the canal was admitted at the head, and some was therefore conveyed 350 miles to the irrigable land when it might have been obtained at from 50 to 100 miles' distance. No permanent dam had been built across the river at the head of the canal to secure a constant supply of water; instead, temporary works were thrown up after every monsoon, adding heavily to the annual maintenance costs. The fourteen "minor mistakes" listed by Cotton were also related chiefly to construction costs.[90]

Cotton's estimate for the required alterations was some £2,725,000. To achieve the maximum expansion of the canal system, by which some 6,500,000 acres could be irrigated—a figure which was never in fact reached prior to 1900—the total expenditure was estimated at £5,000,000. Modifications to the existing canal channels and the extension of the network into the Lower Doab were not begun till 1868, by which time the budget for this alone had swelled to £3,183,390.[91]

The prime aim with which canal irrigation was so ardently promoted, to increase wealth and consequently revenue by expanding the acreage under "valuable" crops to its greatest possible extent, did not change. It was inevitable that a host of minor details should

[90]For a summary of this dispute between Cotton and Cautley, of Cotton's critique, and of the alterations to the canal as finally sanctioned by Government, see Buckley, *Irrigation Works*, pp. 103–105.

[91]*Ibid.*, pp. 104–105.

be overlooked here and there in the rush to construct. The crucial problem of the local distribution of canal water was left to work itself out haphazardly. Muzaffarnagar district provided an illustration. Cadell attributed the exceptional advance of the canal tract in the twenty years prior to 1878—an advance measured largely in terms of the increased acreage of sugar cane—entirely to "this noble work," the Ganges Canal. Almost every village was said to be protected from periodic scarcity. But, he admitted, in "the anxiety to make canal water promptly available and to secure immediate revenue, distributaries had been constructed too hastily and without sufficient care . . ." Serious mistakes were almost certainly owing to the "anxiety for palpable results. It was generally acknowledged that the system of distribution adopted had for its object the prompt collection of water-rates for the largest possible area of the more valuable crops."[92] It was difficult to make more than minor adjustments to the canals. Meanwhile, the aim of increasing the revenue was achieved.[93]

Sound engineering principles were frustrated at the outset by the official policy on the construction of the minor channels of the canal systems. "As a rule," Whiteway remarked apropos of the Agra Canal in Muttra district, "the Government only makes the main distributaries and the zamindars must make the minor ones . . . It is easy for a rich landlord to apply to the Collector to have land taken up in the next village to make his watercourse, but practically impossible for a petty proprietor to incur the odium of an application, not only for land to be taken up from the next village, but from his neighbour's field."[94] The construction of distributaries was also used by powerful maliks as an instrument against each other and against recalcitrant cultivators.[95] Equality of rights to irrigation might well exist on paper. In practice, access was controlled by the distribution of local power in the regions through which the canals ran.

Access was also subject to charges. Water rates were levied by the administration according to "the just claims of the Government to a suitable return on the capital sunk in the works on the one hand,

[92] *Muzaffarnagar Settlement Report (Canal Tract)*, pp. 100–101.

[93] For the canal revenue of the NWP, 1876–77 to 1899–1900, see Figure 5. For details of heads of account, see pp. 134–136 below.

[94] *Muttra Settlement Report*, pp. 12–15.

[95] As, for example, in the (characteristic) dispute between the zamindars of Gowra and Surajpore, Bareilly district, reported in NWP, "Revenue Proceedings," January 11, 1868, Index Nos. 11–16, June 8, 1867, Proceedings Nos. 80 and 81, and November 23, 1867, Proceedings Nos. 60 and 61.

and to the known capabilities of the land on the other."[96] As read-justed by Government order in 1864, the rates were fixed at Rs. 5 per acre for sugar cane and Rs. 2–4 per acre for other crops. "Cultivators refusing to accept these rates," it was firmly stated, "should not obtain any water at all."[97] The rates could legally be raised by the Irrigation Department according to the principles on which they were initially levied. In addition, the Canal Act of 1873 provided for the levy of an "owner's rate" whenever the local Government should see fit to apply it.[98] At the same time, the revenue demand was increased on irrigated lands, recorded in the Irrigation Department accounts as "indirect revenue."[99]

Charges for the use of canal water did not stop at the officially levied rates. To compute the acreage-based charges on each cultivator's irrigated fields of a few bighas in extent, to record the names and numbers of cultivators liable to pay the rates, and to collect the sums due—at each season—the Irrigation Department employed a vast number of local agents : chaukidars, *mohurrirs* (clerks), and *amins* (measuring clerks). Each official of this "subordinate establishment" performed a local service, in this case assisting in the supply of canal water. Consequently, each official claimed his haq from his "clients" who used the water, over and above the Government dues. Cultivators paid their water rates, their share in the increased revenue demand, and *faslana,* a fee exacted per plough at each harvest by the local malik who ruled the access to the canal; they also paid a due to the chaukidar, a fee on the rajbaha (distributary) to its controller and faslana to the sub-overseer or his agent, and the costs of the amin's board and lodging when he came on his measuring round. This last item alone could amount to some Rs. 10 a season. In 1879, A. P. Webb, a zamindar of pargana Baraut, Meerut district, exposed the practices of the subordinate establishment of the East Jumna Canal in a pamphlet entitled "Irrigation Topics."[100] Webb also raised questions concerning the condition of crops watered by wells as against canals,

[96]Government of India (Department of Public Works), August 15, 1864, "Resolution on the Canals of the NWP," in *India Gazette,* Supplement, December 31, 1864, para. 13.

[97]*Ibid.,* para. 13.

[98]Act VIII, 1873, §§ 37–44. For a select list of statutes relating to agrarian conditions in NWP and Oudh, 1859–1900, see Appendix 6.

[99]See p. 000 below. For collections of indirect revenue, 1876–77 to 1899–1900, see Figure 5.

[100]A. P. Webb's text was reprinted verbatim in NWP and Oudh, "Revenue Proceedings," October 1879, Index No. 6, September 6, 1879, Proceedings Nos. 60–61.

and the promotion of well construction. His disclosures, documented from records in canal villages, roused the superior establishment to investigate. On the instructions of W. C. Plowden, then Commissioner of Meerut Division, the officiating collector and the superintending engineer of the First Circle of the Irrigation Works in the district enquired into Webb's "allegations . . . impugning the administration of the Government canals"—and found more than copious corroboration.[101] These officers suggested that further enquiry might be made in Muzaffarnagar and Saharunpur, but this seemed unnecessary to the Commissioner : "I have not a doubt myself that practices similar to those detected in the Meerut district exist in other parts, but I question the advisability of going on with this enquiry."[102] Meanwhile, Webb continued to supply the Collectorate with an abundance of details, including specimens of *malbah* accounts, which were summaries of cash payments on account from a "collective village community" compiled from *rokras,* or daily cash books.[103] His *pièce de résistance* was a series of extracts in the vernacular from some *bahis* (account books) of the village of Suf from 1850 to 1873. These provided

documentary confirmation of the oral statements of various lambardars [now in the collector's possession] . . . , that illegal canal imposts have been extorted ever since the introduction of canal-irrigation, or that they have paid the same, or known them to be paid, ever since they were lamberdars [sic], and that their fathers paid before them.

In fact there is not a Canal *Deputy Magistrate* who did not share in the plunder of the people when *ziladar* [an official heading the local canal administration], and not a *ziladar* who is not concerned in extortion.[104]

By the 1890s, the farmers of the provinces cultivated and irrigated a greater area than their predecessors had in 1860, and grew more of the "valuable" crops. The increase towards which all the piecemeal schemes of public works had been directed, each in its own way, had been achieved. The cost, however, was considerable. Whilst the number of farmers and their dependants had risen—at what rate it

---

[101]NWP and Oudh, "Revenue Proceedings," October 1879, Index No. 54, September 6, 1879, Proceeding No. 52 (summarized in turn by W. C. Plowden, *ibid.,* Index No. 52, Proceeding No. 50).

[102]Plowden, *ibid.*

[103]Webb to Collector, Meerut, *ibid.,* Index No. 70, October 4, 1879, Proceeding No. 37.

[104]*Ibid.,* Index No. 71, October 4, 1879, Proceeding No. 38.

is impossible to say on the basis of available statistics—their food supply had not kept pace with them; nor had they been encouraged to make it do so. The canals did not remedy the growing imbalance, and still less did it protect the people from scarcity and famine, contrary to the retrospective assertions of Sir John Strachey.[105] As we have seen, the canals could not be used to increase the production of kharif food grains, and they were a powerful if not exclusive cause of a noticeable decline in productivity in many long-settled areas; moreover in the most extensively irrigated of the canal tracts, the health of the people as well as the condition of the soil on which they depended for their livelihood deteriorated badly under the effects of swamps. For all this, compensation was not and could not be given. The Northern India Canal and Drainage Act of 1873 provided, *inter alia*, that no compensation should be awarded for any damage caused by stoppage or diminution of percolation, by floods, or by deterioration of climate or soil—the principal areas of trouble created by the engineering works.[106] In such cases where the law provided for the Irrigation Department's liability to compensate, applications for redress had to undergo an elaborate procedure, expensive in time as well as money. In 1872, for example, zamindars and tenants in pargana Kilpuri, Barcilly district, were awarded compensation for flood damage for which the Irrigation Department admitted responsibility. A bureaucratic wrangle then ensued between the Irrigation and Revenue departments as to who should actually pay over the compensation money of Rs. 6,892.9.5. A final ruling was obtained only in 1877, when the matter reached the Financial Department of the Government of India.[107]

Meanwhile, the expansion of cultivation brought a corresponding contraction in waste lands. This disrupted the fallowing cycles, curtailed the farmers' supplies of fuel and fodder, and induced pastoralists in the low-lying Doab tracts to settle in on the land as cultivators, increasing its burdens. Whatever ecological revolution the canals brought or helped to bring, most farmers' techniques were not adapted to deal with such sudden and radical changes. Nor did the canals provide them with a greater degree of control over the means by which they continued to cultivate: local power was paramount,

[105]See p. 63 above.

[106]Act VIII, 1873, § 8.

[107]Superintendent, Tarai district, to Commissioner, Kumaon, November 6, 1879, NWP and Oudh, "Revenue Proceedings," March 1880, Index No. 9, March 13, 1880, Proceeding No. 3.

as the double status of maliks as canal officials so clearly showed. In fact, maliks' haqs were capable of almost indefinite extension.

Government also paid increasingly for the canals, albeit in straightforward terms of account. Maintenance and improvement charges rose from Rs. 626,116 in 1876-77 to Rs. 1,391,159 in 1898-99. Establishment charges, which in 1876-77 were recorded as Rs. 848,040, had increased to Rs. 1,523,248 by 1898-99.[108] The canals proved a costly experiment.

In addition to large-scale irrigation works to spur on production to unheard of heights of prosperity, the practically minded entrepreneurs who viewed India in the late 1850s considered its most pressing need to lie in communications. The urgency to satisfy this need was increased by the seriousness of the deficiency and by the size and diversity of profits envisaged as the fruits of such worthwhile investment. "The state of existing means of travelling in India is sufficient alone to prevent the country and its resources from becoming known to capitalists," Major-General C. W. Tremenheere, R. E., declared in 1857 to the Select Committee on Colonization and Settlement. "The ordinary mode of travelling is either by marching in stages from twelve to fourteen miles a day, or travelling by dawk in a palanquin. Capitalists will not submit to this tardy mode of progress."[109] Carriage was similarly ill-developed. The *rath*, or two-wheeled cart, drawn by a pair of bullocks "whose jog-trot keeps the ruth in a perpetual oscillation," was the commonest form of transport, and had been for centuries. "Rocks have altered, worlds have changed, and nations have worn away," wrote Bholanauth Chunder in 1869 on a journey from Muttra to Brindaban, "but no improvement has taken place in the vehicular architecture of the Hindoo."[110] Throughout the later nineteenth century, carts remained the predominant and indispensable mode of transport serving a widening network of railways and feeder roads.

As in the case of the canals, the construction of roads and railways after 1858 followed well-established precedents.[111] The pioneer

[108]*NWP Irrigation Revenue Reports*, 1876–77, 1898–99. See also Figure 5.

[109]"Reports of the Select Committee on Colonization and Settlement in India"— First Report : *P.P.*, 1857–58, 7, 1 (261), p. 2.

[110]Bh. Chunder, *Travels of Hindoo*, II, 39–40. For an illustration of the typical U.P. cart, see W. Crooke, *Glossary*, under *ghari*.

[111]For developments prior to 1857–58, see D. Thorner, *Investment in Empire*. On the role of the railway contractor, as exemplified by the ubiquitous Mr. Thomas

achievement of all public works in British India, the Grand Trunk Road, metalled throughout, already ran up from Calcutta to Benares, then to Allahabad and Cawnpore, and on through the Doab to Delhi. The commercial linkage of the great marts of the Ganges–Jumna region and the political linkage of the capital centres of administration were accomplished by the East Indian Railway, which bound Delhi, Agra, Cawnpore, and Benares to each other and to Calcutta. Subsequent developments were to extend lines out over all but the least productive districts, where expenditure on communications would hardly be repaid by the amount of traffic which could use them.[112] Branches of the East Indian Railway spanned out through the Doab while the central and eastern regions were tapped by the Oudh and Rohilkhand Railway.[113] District road-building seems to have depended largely on the relevance of each district to the overall scheme and pattern of traffic : areas farthest from the great arterial routes or the feeder lines—eastern parganas of Fyzabad, for example, and most of Bahraich—were poorly supplied with roads.[114]

Whatever intentions of universal expansion supported the promotion of the rail- and road-building schemes, they were thwarted at the outset by the means used to carry out the actual construction. The rapidity of railway-building in British India up to 1875 was, as L. H. Jenks has remarked, greater even than in Great Britain and France, but was not accompanied by a comparably intensive development of subsidiary roads or by a growth in local trade binding markets to metropolitan centres. The capital for the railways was imported from Britain. No industry grew up to provide the materials for their construction; instead, iron and timber were imported—into a country rich in these natural resources. The skilled staffs of the railway were English, paid wages and salaries at English rates. The remittance of two-thirds the railway capital to India in bullion may have contributed to the inflationary effects of the increasing amounts of specie sent in payment for India's increasing exports, with the result that prices rose steeply, especially those of grain in the urban marketing

---

Brassey, see A. Helps, *Life and Labours,* especially as regards Indian railways, at pp. 270–277.

[112]For an outline of the prospective pattern of communications, see the evidence of Major-General Tremenheere in "Reports of the Select Committee on Colonization and Settlement in India"—First Report : *P.P.,* 1857–58, 7, 1 (261), pp. 28–29, 37–38, and Baird Smith, "Report," pp. 105–108.

[113]See endpaper map. For sections of lines, with dates of construction, see Appendix 7.

[114]*Fyzabad Settlement Report,* pp. 15–16; *Bahraich Settlement Report,* p. 61.

centres. The inevitable consequence was a "highly precarious" prosperity, disruptive of traditional arrangements and benefiting only those in a position to manipulate the new machinery of commerce.[115]

The construction of the railways also brought its measure of physical disturbances; as in the case of the canals, there was trouble over the natural drainage lines. In the Ramganga valley area of Bareilly, for example, landowners complained of damage done to crops and lands owing to the obstruction by the embankment of the Oudh and Rohilkhand Railway of the natural drainage of floods during the period 1870-1873. The company was finally called upon (in 1875-76) to pay the Government assessed compensation of Rs. 5,242 and to provide a remedy. Landowners in the Ganges khadir of Unao district (north of Cawnpore) complained of similar floods in 1870, 1871, 1872, and 1874, with the last of such severity that an enquiry was held into the extent of the losses. Ten years later, floods occurred in Budaon; a great part of the damage was reported as owing to the same cause— the Oudh and Rohilkhand Railway line.[116]

The new lines of communication cut across old lines of local supply. Compensation for land taken up for works did not allow for this. In Cawnpore, an investigation into the case of the insolvent Raja Dhiraj Singh of Gangaganj revealed the extent to which arrears of revenue accumulating on the lands under his charge was owing to heavy assessments combined with an inability to recoup losses attributed to deteriorations from public works. One village commanding a total area of 2,191 acres was assessed at Rs. 3.10.0 on each of its 965 cultivated acres, a rate admitted to be high even in "this highly assessed part of Cawnpore," and it was all the more so since the soils were light and of under- rather than above-average quality. By 1873, this village had been "much cut up" by roads and canals. The compensation for land taken up by the works themselves was said to have been given at a fair rate as far as the land itself was concerned because it was founded on the revenue rate;[117] "but the village has suffered much damage in consequence of the interference with its communi-

[115]Jenks, *Migration*, pp. 227–230. On local manipulation of the new machinery of commerce in the NWP and Oudh, see pp. 188 ff. below.

[116]Administration of the Guaranteed Railways, *Report on the Oudh and Rohilkhand Railway*, 1874–75, p. 14. For further details on the Bareilly floods, see *NWP Revenue Administration Report*, 1872–73, pp. 6–7. On the Budaon floods, see *ibid.*, 1880–81, p. 6.

[117]For the rules regulating the calculation of compensation payments (based on an estimate of "customary rent" at fair rates) for land acquired by Government for "public purposes" (that is, public works development), see NWP, "Revenue Proceedings," June 29, 1867, Index No. 32, May 25, 1867, Proceeding No. 28.

cations, and of course no compensation has been given for this. For instance, one large tract of valuable land was highly manured before the [East Indian] railway was constructed. Since its construction the railway embankment has completely precluded the transfer of manure from the village site to this tract, and the value of it has fallen quite 50%." Added to this came the swamping of some acres through the interference of the canal's watercourses with natural drainage lines. Elsewhere on the estate, a kachha road had "eaten out the heart of a plot of land devoted to market gardening." Lastly, the shade of trees planted to hold the East Indian Railway's embankment and the side of the Kalpi road was proving very injurious to adjacent cultivation.[118]

Perhaps the most disturbing consequence of the railways—most disturbing because least capable of remedy—was the widespread use of local timber as fuel for the locomotives. Tremenheere had noted the relative scarcity, even in 1857, of wood fuel in the Gangetic valley, and he cited this as an additional reason for the necessity of constructing branch lines into the sub-Himalayan plains and other hilly districts of Central India where wood was to be found in "inexhaustible abundance." Tremenheere suggested that the railways might even make this wood available, at a moderate transport charge, to supply abundant and cheap fuel to the inhabitants of the long exhausted plains.[119]

In practice, the railway companies drew their fuel supply directly—and cheaply—from local timber until the 1880s. As early as 1865, a Government of India Resolution noted the "very considerable deforestation already occurring in the Doab" owing to the railways' requirements, as well as the "absence of any reliable expectation of an early cessation of the demand which gave rise to it." Remedial measures were clearly already required to provide for "the reproduction of trees where the country was most affected by the extraordinary

[118]E. C. Buck, Settlement Officer, Cawnpore, April 19, 1873, "Report on the Case of Dhiraj Singh," an example of one of the many heavily assessed estates in the district disturbed by the public works, in NWP, "Revenue Proceedings," December 1873, Index Nos. 4–5, July 5, 1873, Proceedings Nos. 75–76. The outcome was that Dhiraj Singh received a Government loan to clear his debts (and to provide for a dowry as befitted his station in the event of his marriage, with the express intention that this might serve as a safeguard against further insolvency). The revenue demand on the estate remained unaltered. For examples of legal provisions introduced to restore financially failing zamindaris to solvency, see pp. 203, 231–233 below.

[119]"Reports of the Select Committee on Colonization and Settlement in India"— First Report: P.P., 1857–58, 7, 1 (261), pp. 28–29.

demand for wood-fuel." Remedial measures however lay beyond the means of the Government : its answer was to suggest that the proprietors of land be induced to plant trees.[120] But groves were assessed to revenue, and those who controlled them had every incentive to sell the wood for railway fuel and thus pay the revenue with ease. This situation was illustrated clearly in the case of mahwah groves in the western half of Partabgarh district. The fruit of the mahwah was a valuable source of food for the local peasants, who also used its seed for fuel-oil. W. E. Forbes, the Settlement Officer, noted, however, that it was on the mahwah—as he had already observed two years earlier—that

the axe falls heaviest, and in respect of which the planting does not keep pace with the destruction. A considerable amount of timber has found its way across the Ganges. From one estate alone, a short time since, thousands of trees were purchased by the Manikpur Firm of Moula Dad Khan and Khuda Dad Khan who, I have heard, concluded a most profitable bargain with the East Indian Railway Company. The straight trees were sawn up into planks, while the crooked and gnarled stems were converted into charcoal. Mahwah charcoal is highly esteemed as fuel, and always commands a good price. No doubt the proximity of the Railway has caused a more wholesale destruction of this tree than would otherwise have been the case.

Reforestation of the mahwah was a difficult matter. For one thing, the mahwah, in comparison with the mango, is—as Forbes noted—a slow-growing tree, "and in these days, zamindars cannot afford to wait long years while the land yields no return." For another, the *peri* or mahwah tax, "a universally recognized impost throughout the district, is a deterrent to the cultivator who would plant a 'Mahwah' grove, for he well knows that by and by it will but too surely form the pretext for systematically depriving him of the usufruct."[121]

Deforestation seems to have appeared a regrettable necessity to the railway companies. The Oudh and Rohilkhand Railway Company drew its fuel supply from the country adjoining the line. By the end of the financial year 1872-73, the company already ran a second regular service daily between Lucknow and Cawnpore, and with the rapid extension of its lines over the next years, its demand for local fuel increased accordingly. The company's report of 1872-73

[120]Government of India (Home Department), Resolution No. 3565, April 17, 1865, in NWP, "Revenue Proceedings," May 27, 1865, Index No. 26, Proceeding No. 4. The matter was reported to have been constantly under consideration by the local Government "for the last two years"; *ibid.*, Index No. 27, Proceeding No. 5.

[121]*Partabgarh Settlement Report*, pp. 9–10.

referred to attempts which had already been made to substitute coal,[122] but, as the report of the following year noted concerning similar discussions, the company was "averse to doing this as long as it is dearer than wood." The stumbling block was the charge levied by the East Indian Railway Company on the freight of coal from the nearest source, Bengal: from Giridi to Benares, the rate was Rs. 33 per 100 maunds. The Oudh and Rohilkhand Railway Company could afford to use coal only if the rate were brought down to Rs. 22 per 100 maunds, which would allow a safe margin of return on capital expended over running costs.[123] In 1874-75, the East Indian Railway agreed to give a rebate on all freight charges for coal carried to Benares paid by the Oudh and Rohilkhand Company, on quantities of not less than 6,000 tons freighted per six months. But the coal freight was still subject to a heavy charge owing to the four-mile gap between the stations of the two companies at Benares.[124] The Oudh and Rohilkhand Railway was still being supplied with local timber in the 1880s.

The Public Works Department also competed with the rural population for fuel; their source was even cheaper than that of the railways: dung. In 1879, A. O. Hume drew attention to the contrast between the relatively meagre amount of dung used by the "natives," chiefly for cooking, and its "vast consumption in brick-making. ... The Public Works Department are great sinners. The increase of brick-making, and with it, the consumption of dung as fuel (it being, in most places, cheaper than wood) has been enormous of late years."[125] With the contraction of other fuel supplies from the dwindling waste lands, pressure to use dung increased, which in turn diminished the amount of manure available to nourish the soil.

The overwhelming proportion of "Saxon energy and British capital" introduced into India in the form of public works was concentrated on immediately productive areas. Schemes for the reclamation of wilderness and barren waste were less attractive to contemporary expansionist zeal. Such attempts as were made to bring waste lands in northern Oudh under some sort of cultivation had been frustrated through unfavourable conditions—unhealthiness, scarcity of labour, and the lack of a nearby market for timber and firewood which were

[122]Administration of the Guaranteed Railways, *Report on the Oudh and Rohilkhand Railway*, 1872–73. Enclosure to Despatch No. 243, Railway.
[123]*Ibid.*, 1873–74, pp. 17–18.
[124]*Ibid.*, 1874–75, p. 13.
[125]A. O. Hume, *Agricultural Reform*, footnote to p. 30.

expected to produce the first profits. Out of thirty-three lessees of the Kathna forest grants (an area of some 94,432 acres), the eleven lasting beyond the first round had discontinued their efforts, either because the strain on their capital was too great, or prudence forbade them to expend without hope of an early return.[126] C. W. McMinn cast doubts on the practicality of any scheme for reclamation of the terai "by English gentlemen, allured by the exquisite beauty of the Oudh wilderness." The whole area, from the Ganges at Hardwar to the Koriali at Gola-ghat, some 250 miles by 20 miles in extent and at one time under cultivation, had been turned by Firoz Shah into a hunting ground. Within a few years, the abandoned fields had become dense jungle, and the jungle, catching the rainfall and retarding its flow, became a swamp : "it is doubtful if all the power and wealth of England could now bring back into cultivation the wilderness which Firoz Shah created by a word. A civilized Government cannot send hundreds of thousands of its subjects into a pestilential swamp for each man to cut down a few trees and then dying, hand his axe to another fated for brief toil."[127] Hard-headed enterprise had better avenues for the employment of its resources than to dream of such picturesque impracticalities.

Small-Scale Improvements

As a systematic series of propositions, "economic development" existed only in theories constructed by political economists chiefly of the classical school.[128] In practice, certainly as far as British India was concerned, such "development" as took place was the work of a variety of promoters of "Progress and Civilization"—members of joint-stock companies and the ubiquitous engineers to Government itself, all of whom candidly pursued their aims of increasing wealth. They proceeded with vigour, and achieved much within a surprisingly

[126]*Kheri Settlement Report,* pp. 25–26. For further details on Government's resumption of grants in wastelands, see NWP, "Revenue Proceedings," April 1874, Index Nos. 23–59.

[127]C. W. McMinn, *Introduction,* footnote to pp. 12–13.

[128]For a summary of the "development" theories of classical political economists, see E. McKinley, "The Problem of 'Underdevelopment' in the English Classical School," *Quarterly Journal of Economics,* LXIX (1955), 235–252. For theory as applied to the empirical problem of Ireland (seen as analogous to India in many respects), see R. D. C. Black, *Economic Thought,* especially on "development" at pp. 86–89, and R. D. C. Black, "Economic Policy in Ireland and India in the Time of J. S. Mill," *Economic History Review,* 2nd Series, XXI, 2 (August 1968).

short space of time : "Backward and partially-developed tracts are rare in the NWP," the secretary to the local Government wrote in 1871 to the Board of Revenue.[129] There was, however, little concern as to how the various schemes might match up, one with another The example of the gap between railway stations at Benares is but one of many such instances of the lack of co-ordination. There was even less interest in catering specifically to the needs of those on whose environment the promoters' capital was bestowed. Beneath the weight of public works embellishment, the basic techniques and requirements of the great mass of cultivators in the provinces persisted unchanged.

Robert Knight, who was constantly and publicly at war with the Government of India over its persistent and seemingly foolish obstructions of entrepreneurial ambitions,[130] cried aloud at the neglect of agriculture. In July 1876, his paper, the *Indian Agriculturist,* came out with a review of Corbett's treatise,[131] which stated the case for agricultural modernization in no uncertain terms :

There is great truth in his [Corbett's] assertion that an irrigation cry and a drainage cry, have induced the Government to embark in projects purely engineering and not agricultural, to trust the agricultural education of India solely to engineers and to district officers; the former of whom look upon agricultural projects from a purely engineering point of view, while the latter have little interest in agricultural matters beyond the narrow one of collecting the revenue. In a country which is so largely dependent as India, not only for the subsistence of its vast population but for its political maintenance, upon the productiveness of the earth, the science of agriculture should doubtless be made of the first importance and should have been called in to aid all projects of agricultural improvement ...[132]

The views of district officers on the efficiency of peasant techniques varied according to the relative intimacy of their experience with Indian agriculture.[133] S. M. Moens in Bareilly and J. R. Reid in Azamgarh, to name but two settlement officers who made themselves experts on the peasants' activities in their respective districts, showed

[129]June 28, 1871, in NWP, "Revenue Proceedings," March 1874, Index No. 27, March 7, 1874, Proceeding No. 73.

[130]Knight also voiced his expansionist zeal in the columns of other journals he edited, viz. *Indian Economist* and the daily newspaper *The Statesman.*

[131]See pp. 76–77 above.

[132]*Indian Agriculturist,* July 1, 1876, p. 194.

[133]On contemporary European criteria for Indian agricultural efficiency, see pp. 31–32 above.

clearly in their reports how skilful the cultivators were in the main extracting a varied livelihood from the soil in the face of obstacles posed by their frequently hostile environment. W. A. Forbes and his predecessors, in assessing the best of the Meerut parganas, showed how the much-admired prosperity of the Jat cultivators derived from their own modes of exploiting the excellent natural facilities of the region. Others, deceived by the simplicity of cultivating equipment and the distressing condition of so many of the cultivators, committed the error of a simple attribution of the latter to the former. McMinn, for example, whose juristic turn of mind was better adapted to detecting the subtleties of tenure and the errors of Government policy, was emphatic in his denunciation of the peasants' practices: "Indian modes of agriculture, far from being the ripe result of Indian experience represent the dregs of an old world barbarism, all the main features of which are common to both East and West."[134]

The opinion that modern Europe, evolving from an origin common to that of ancient Indian society, was in agriculture as in all else superior and that owing to this unquestioned superiority the fruits of its enlightenment could be rapidly and successfully transplanted in alien soil, was widespread. District officers, who noted with approval the simple fact of vast acres coming under cultivation owing to the stimulus of the canal, subscribed to it. So did officials in the higher reaches of the Secretariat, where peace and public works were believed a priori to bring the only tangible and therefore secure prosperity.

This opinion, which some might call a prejudice, was not backed by any comprehensive scheme for remedying the lamentable defects in indigenous techniques. Plans for "vertically integrated" agricultural improvement were not—and could not be—developed in the context in which the provinces' administrators found themselves. They had to balance the powerful expediencies of revenue and commerce at every turn; they were buffetted by gusts of disapproval from the Supreme Government in Calcutta or in London; and they were haunted by the nightmare of political upheaval should they disturb unawares the agrarian society whose loyalty was so precariously secured. Hence it is understandable that problems of ecological imbalance were discussed in engineering terms, with no more than piecemeal consideration for

---

[134]McMinn, *Introduction*, p. 192. His attitudes did not change but reappeared in full vehemence in his *Famine Truths*, published thirty years later (1902) and containing, *inter alia*, a spirited denunciation of the assertions of R. C. Dutt to the effect that British rule was a major cause, in its land revenue policy, of India's poverty.

the social issues involved. The question of narrowing the gaps between better and worse cultivation, where attempts at solutions would have involved direct interference by Government in the affairs of the rural population, was seldom raised in administrative circles.

In 1870, after much insistence by the Viceroy, Lord Mayo, a Department of Agriculture was finally set up as part of the central administration of the Government of India at Calcutta. This might at first be taken as clear evidence that Government has serious intentions of coming to grips with the problems of agricultural improvement. Lord Mayo himself, alone of the viceroys of India, boasted of years of practical experience in agricultural affairs : "many the day have I stood the livelong day in the market selling my beasts." Before his appointment, he had indeed been a farmer—of an extensive estate appropriate to the means and the station of a prosperous Irish gentleman.[135] Previous to Lord Mayo's time, "the attention of the Government had been chiefly directed to collecting the revenue, and little had been done to develop agricultural resources; more energy had been applied to shearing the sheep than to feeding him. Lord Mayo, as an expert, understood the fatal consequences of such a policy . . .,"[136] and he had ideas, certainly, as to what might be done by an agricultural department. As Sir John Strachey noted later with pride :

The objects which Lord Mayo had in view were distinctly sketched in the Despatch of 6th April, 1870. The new department [its title is significant : Revenue, Agriculture and Commerce] "was to take cognizance of all matters affecting the practical improvement and development of the agricultural resources of the country," but its operations were not to be confined solely to this object. The administration of the land revenue and cognate matters, the development of mineral resources, of manufacturing industries, and generally of commerce and trade of the country, were to come within its scope, while among its most important functions was to be the collection of agricultural and commercial statistics ... The programme was accepted with little modification by the Secretary of State.[137]

[135]For the career of the Earl of Mayo, see W. W. Hunter, A Life of the Earl of Mayo. On Mayo in the context of classical economics and administrative policy, see Black, "Economic Policy," Economic History Review, 2nd ser., xxi, 2 (August 1968), pp. 321–336.

[136]W. Wedderburn, Hume, p. 27. The creation of the Department of Agriculture could not bring about a reversal of this policy.

[137]J. Strachey, "Minute on the Measures Necessary for Carrying out in the NWP the Objects with Which the Department of Revenue, Agriculture and Commerce Was Organized," para. 1, in NWP, "Revenue Proceedings," December 1874, Index No. 42, December 5, 1874, Proceeding No. 58. For the full text of the "Minute," see Indian Agriculturist, June 1, 1877, pp. 164–166.

What Strachey did not make clear was that substantial modifications had in fact already been agreed to by Mayo, under duress. His original plan had been for a "real working Agricultural Bureau; he was forced to content himself with the miscellaneous department of the Secretariat which was all the India Office would give him."[138] The department was doomed to ineffectiveness from the start, sandwiched between the two massive pillars of Revenue and Commerce. It collapsed finally in 1879 under the combined weight of interminable restrictions on its activity "in the field," insufficiency of funds and lack of staff, and the unremitting pressures applied by the India Office. Its nine-year history of frustrations was chronicled by its first Director, A. O. Hume, in *Agricultural Reform in India,* which was published on his 'retirement' from Government service in 1879.[139]

In 1874, a subsidiary department was set up in the NWP with the same objects in view. Its programme was ambitious :

the collection and organization of agricultural and commercial statistics . . . ; to direct experiments for agricultural improvements in model farms and elsewhere; to watch and report on the progress of trade, and to suggest in what directions it may be developed, or hindrance to its prosperity removed; to investigate facts connected with the condition of the agricultural classes, and generally to be the executive agency by which the local Government may carry into effect, in these provinces, the intentions of the Government of India, when the department was founded.[140]

The provision for staff for the newly created department—a director and his assistant (both European officers), and a number of "native" clerks—could hardly inspire confidence in its capacity to perform the monumental tasks Sir John Strachey's minute envisaged,[141] nor could the size and itemization of the department's annual budgets. In 1887, for example, when the department had been in operation for thirteen years, the total "agricultural expenditure" for the NWP for that year was accounted at Rs. 101,400. Of this, the cost in salaries and wages for the director and his subordinate staff came to Rs. 62,000; experimental farms took a further Rs. 12,400; well-sinking—through-

[138]Wedderburn, *Hume,* pp. 27–32.

[139]For details of the career of A. O. Hume, Bengal Civil Service, advocate of the introduction of capitalist farming in India and founder of the Indian National Congress, see Wedderburn, *Hume.*

[140]Strachey, "Minute" (cited above, n. 137), para. 3.

[141]Compare the relatively grandiose revenue establishments for each district—and the burden of work assigned to them; see pp. 235 ff. below.

out the provinces—took some Rs. 7,000; and reh experiments, chiefly in Aligarh, took Rs. 20,000.[142] That year, 1886-87, the land revenue receipts stood at Rs. 42,587,917—99.4 percent of the demand.[143]

With such authority and resources as Government allowed it, the department could do little other than follow meekly in the steps of precedent as far as agricultural improvements were concerned. But precedent was obviously deficient, as Knight's *Indian Agriculturist* announced with its usual candour :

Where or when has any systematic attempt been earnestly made under British rule to insure good husbandry; or indeed improvements of any kind in the way of obtaining supplies of food? It is true that some measures have been taken with reference to cotton-growing; but these seemed framed more for benefitting the foreigner than the native; or in other words, more for furthering the growth of the article of commerce in preference to that of the food needed for the support of the actual cultivator and producer of it.[144]

Such experiments with agricultural staples—for export—as had been made prior to the department's coming into being had not been conspicuously successful. The distribution of New Orleans cotton seed amongst zamindars in Banda district in 1861 to coax them into bigger and better production was an unqualified failure.[145] All experiments with foreign cottons tended to meet more or less the same fate.[146] The cultivation of indigenous strains also ran up against difficulties which prevented the vast increase in cotton production from developing as officials and entrepreneurs had once hoped. Apart from the vulnerability of the plant to disorders which hardier crops might survive, the chief restrictions on the spread of cultivation on a par with, say, sugar cane was the extreme fluctuation in demand—both in India and abroad. The enormous impetus to cotton-growing created in 1860-61 by the American Civil War ceased as abruptly as it had developed.[147]

[142]Finance Department, *Report of the Finance Commissioner*, 1887, pp. 581–583.

[143]*NWP Revenue Administration Report*, 1886–87, pp. 5–6. For the land revenue, demand, collections, and balances, NWP· and Oudh, 1864–65 to 1884–85, and 1885–86 to 1899–1900, see Figures 7, 8, and 9.

[144]*Indian Agriculturist*, April 1, 1876, pp. 100–101, at p. 100.

[145]NWP, "Revenue Proceedings," August 10, 1861, Index No. 56, Proceeding No. 37.

[146]For a summary of cotton experiments in British India, see S. Leacock and D.G. Mandelbaum, "A Nineteenth Century Development Project," *Economic Development and Cultural Change*, III (July 4, 1955), 334–351.

[147]For a concise account of the Indian cotton boom, see Landes, *Bankers and Pashas*, pp. 69–74. For further details on the cotton boom and NWP agriculture, see pp. 178–179 below.

Meanwhile, the complications arising from the distribution of Manchester yarn and piece goods created a norm of instability on the home market.[148]

Experiments with imported varieties of food grains—again for export—fared little better. For example, in 1869 Carolina rice seed was distributed to zamindars in certain districts of the NWP selected on grounds of prosperity and influence (Rohilkhand and Jhansi divisions alone were not represented); this, the most extensive experiment of its kind yet tried in the provinces, was a total failure.[149] Nonetheless, Government persisted, and in 1872-73 the same experiment was repeated, with nothing more than poor results obtained in any area and failure in the majority of samples.[150] The same was the case with wheat experiments. Rs. 100 worth of the "best white" wheat from Jubbulpore—some 122 maunds—was imported by the department in 1876. The experiments ran into difficulties because the seeds had not been thoroughly cleaned (part of the wheat had been grown mixed with peas and barley in Jubbulpore) and because the rabi season was unusually damp. The seed proved, in addition, to be ill-adapted to canal-irrigated land. The result, in sum, was failure once again.[151] The next year's experiments in improving the quality of wheat failed likewise.[152]

The failures were not confined to those samples distributed to zamindars. Attempts at the improvement of agricultural staples of this kind were also made on model farms established for this purpose in the districts of Allahabad, Cawnpore, and Bulandshahr.[153] They met with a similar fate. Even Sir John Strachey was compelled to express a measure of disappointment: "There can ... be no doubt that the farms have hitherto [up to 1874] failed to effect much good, in consequence of the absence of any responsible controlling authority."[154] The chronicle of the model farms is for the most part a gloomy

[148]For an outline history of Manchester cotton interests in India, see A. W. Silver, *Manchester Men*.

[149]NWP, "Revenue Proceedings," April 2, 1870, Index No. 3, Proceeding No. 19.

[150]*Ibid.*, September 1873, Index No. 20, September 13, 1873, Proceeding No. 3.

[151]F. N. Wright, Officiating Director of Agriculture and Commerce, NWP and Oudh, to Board of Revenue, NWP, May 31, 1878, in Government of India, *Selections from the Records of Government*, No. CLX, pp. 182–183.

[152]*Ibid.*, pp. 190–193.

[153]For a discussion on the advisability of the establishment of model farms to promote agricultural improvements, see Government of India, "Famine Proceedings," December 1873, Appendix A, pp. 1–17.

[154]Strachey, "Minute" (cited above, n. 137), para. 7.

record of wasted and irrelevant expenditure. The current working expenses of the Cawnpore farm for 1873, for example, came to Rs. 5,982. This did not include the superintendent's pay nor make any allowances for interest, or wear and tear of machinery (which totalled an additional Rs. 820 on Rs. 8,286 worth of fixed capital). Receipts from the sale of the farm's produce came to Rs. 2,384. Ricketts, then Commissioner of Allahabad Division, demolished the pretention that the farm was a useful institution and pressed for its abolition. The area on which this expenditure was concentrated was seventeen acres of garden, not farm land. Moreover, the farm represented a departure from other forms of rural expenditure by the administration in that the procedures practised there lay beyond the reach even of the prosperous :

No native farmer, however well off he may be, or however enterprising, can hope in his own land to attain anything like the success that has been attained occasionally in experiments conducted under this farm. He sees at a glance that the conditions of the farm and his own fields are so different, that the results attained in the farm are beyond his reach. He sees there . . . an unlimited supply of water, manure, costly implements, machinery, labour and supervision, and capital—that, in fact, field produce is treated as garden produce and he knows that this cannot be done on a large scale; he sees through the experiments at once, and resolves not to imitate what he has seen.[155]

Peasant conservatism. Government's orders were, however, that the farm was to be maintained, but not on a large or expensive scale; the larger part of the land was to be devoted to the cultivation of shrubs and flowers, and a good native gardener was to be employed.[156]

By 1886-87, as we have seen, some Rs. 12,000 was budgeted for expenditure on experimental farms thus modified and, by this time, largely confined to Cawnpore; the farm in Bulandshahr had been abolished in the mid-1870s, and experiments at Allahabad were even more restricted than those at Cawnpore owing to the absence of irrigation.[157]

A wider area for judicious experiment lay, theoretically, in the

[155]G.H.M. Ricketts to Government, NWP, September 30, 1873, in NWP, "Revenue Proceedings," November 1873, Index No. 38, November 15, 1873, Proceeding No. 24. For the report on the Cawnpore experimental farm by the Collector (C. J. Daniell), see ibid., Index No. 39, November 15, 1873, Proceeding No. 25.

[156]Government Order, NWP, ibid., Index No. 37, September 27, 1873, Proceeding No. 85

[157]"Report on the Administration of the Department of Agriculture and Commerce,

estates of insolvent proprietary families which came under the hard-bargaining management of the Court of Wards.[158] The prospect for developments within the estates was not exactly unlimited. The management's priorities were to work the estate back into revenue-paying health and at the same time to keep relations between the proprietor (and his "agent"—the Government manager) and culti-vators as near to the status quo as possible during the period of tem-porary caretakership, which ensured that any improvements intro-duced would be of the peripheral variety. Nonetheless, the temporarily captive Court-of-Wards estates presented Government with its clearest opportunity to state the official view on "the role of the State as regards agriculture" :

We cannot, it is true, *force* civilization, or any of her handmaids, on any people; but it is possible, by patience and tact, if we do ourselves possess the knowledge, so to put before all we deal with, good and evil in any matter, that many shall inevitably choose the good : and this is all that our supposed State intervention in agriculture has ever aimed at. We advocate no system of State agriculture, we do not propose to cultivate the poeple's land for them, but only by careful study of local conditions, and by the application, with suitable modifications, of methods thoroughly approved elsewhere, to evolve improvements in the indigenous practice; and so put these before all interested in such questions that they may realize their full scope and verify them for themselves ...

If this be not an appropriate and legitimate undertaking for the more enlightened rulers of a less enlightened nation, we must abandon all scientific conceptions of the functions of a Government thus situated.[159]

What better area for the application of enlightenment could be found than the Awa estate? Although in size it was but "a scarcely perceptible speck on our vast empire ..., it is none the less fairly typical as regards soil, climate, population and agricultural condition, generally, of more than half of the NWP (to say nothing of other parts of the country). Tentative measures now (and hereafter, as experience is gained, *to be*) proposed for Awa, will be equally applicable to enor-mous tracts yielding a land revenue of several millions sterling..."[160]

NWP and Outh," 1877–78, in *India Gazette,* Supplement, May 3, 1879, pp. 436–437, 439.

[158]Strachey, "Minute" (cited above, n. 137), para. 8.

[159]Junior Member, Board of Revenue, NWP, "Remarks on E. C. Buck's Proposals Regarding the Improvement of Agriculture in the Awagarh Estate," paras. 15–16, in NWP and Oudh, "Revenue Proceedings," March 1880, Index No. 4, February 28, 1880, Proceeding No. 24.

[160]*Ibid.,* para, 10.

Awa had an additional feature to recommend it as an area for experiment. It was situated in part of an enormous reh-infested tract, not far from pargana Sikandra Rao in the neighbouring district of Aligarh where the Agricultural Department's reh statistics were to be collected under Government instructions.[161] The director's proposals for using this wealth of opportunity were approved by the Board of Revenue and the Lieutenant-Governor of the provinces as showing due practicality and foresight with the required amount of caution. Expenditure was budgeted in two parts. The estate administration would cope with charges amounting to approximately Rs. 14,000 for arboriculture, survey, drainage operations, wells, and the purchase of cattle. Expenditure by the Agricultural Department was to be of the order of Rs. 5,000. This was to include the cost of improved implements (ploughs and sugar mills) and cattle, the collection of village statistics, and, most important, the improvement of staple produce.[162] But which staples? The director's listing may be summarized as follows:

Wheat?   Doubtful if it will live in competition with the American trade in ordinary years; may be rejected as one of the principal crops for experiment.

Indigo?   Has received almost all the improvement possible by indigo planters.

Linseed?   For flax? Cultivation too empirical as yet to attempt to try it except at the Government's experimental farm.

Safflower?   Trade declining; not worth attention.

Rice?   Can never form a large NWP export.

"We are therefore almost confined," Buck concluded, "to cotton and sugar."[163]

Small wonder that the Court-of-Wards estates proved only marginally superior as experimental grounds to the model farms. Year after year, the estates' managers reported on their improvements: the installation and repair of tanks and indigo vats; experiments with staples—chiefly cotton and wheat; cattle-breeding; experiments of almost academic interest with costly implements and installations such as elaborate masonry wells. The question of the applicability

[161]E. C. Buck, Director of Agriculture and Commerce, NWP, "Note on Measures Proposed for the Improvement of Agriculture in the Awa Estate," para. 8, in NWP and Oudh, "Revenue Proceedings," March 1880, Index No. 2, February 28, 1880, Proceeding No. 22.

[162]*Ibid.*, para. 43.

[163]*Ibid.*, Appendix A, paras. 2–3, Index No. 3, Proceeding No. 23.

of the experiments to their environment was asked afterwards more often than before. All the while the managers were enjoined to bear in mind the necessity of caution in introducing new staples or novel methods, "recognizing the suspicious nature of the people."[164] Small wonder that in 1880, Sir George Couper reiterated familiar statements of the pioneering 1860s : "Barely on the threshold, as we still are, of the great work of improving native agriculture, it would be idle to suppose that we can as yet fully appreciate all that is required, or that our designs—however carefully conceived—will always be successful. The most that is possible is to feel our way cautiously, collecting and classifying facts, and making modest attempts to advance whenever openings appear to present themselves."[165]

Even in the (relatively rare) cases where Government-sponsored experiments in improved agriculture were successful, problems arose as regards their diffusion amongst the rural population. Cultivators were indeed persuaded by a variety of incentives to produce "valuable" crops, and lamentable though this might be when viewing the declining production of coarse food grains, it was certainly desirable that the better methods of production of "valuable" crops should be encouraged. How could this be done, practically speaking, over so vast an area with such limited resources for encouragement? There were even obstructions by other aspects of Government, aside from its caution in promoting improvements wholesale. Chief among these was the fiscal system itself. Once more the *Indian Agriculturist* lost no time in clarifying this issue :

The Indian Government, by placing the three most valuable and powerful mineral manures so largely extant in this great empire under the lock and key of the excise (namely, salt, nitrate of potash and nitrate of soda) has virtually rendered improvements in agriculture, and the production of large crops of grain of the best quality, an impossibility. Hence as nitrate of potash, or saltpetre or nitrate of soda may not be freely manufactured from saline soils, for fear of illicit culinary salt being made on the sly, we have to look to England, Europe and Egypt to supply our wants ...[166]

Transport costs alone on such bulky imports made a regular supply of mineral manures out of the question.

[164]For accounts of the experiments on the estates, see *NWP Court of Wards Reports*, annually, from 1879–80, Appendix C or D (Improvements).

[165]NWP and Oudh, "Revenue Proceedings," March 1880, Index No. 5, February 28, 1880, Proceeding No. 25.

[166]*Indian Agriculturist*, March 1, 1876, pp. 61–63, at p. 62.

The lack of adequate means for widespread improvement was paralleled by the lack of any agency for instruction. Who could inform the peasants of the provinces of newly developed techniques? The overworked revenue officers did not act as agricultural advisers. The Department of Agriculture itself could do little beyond collating data at its Allahabad office from such sources as the revenue administration made available. In 1886, D. M. Smeaton, then the Director, formed an Agricultural Association of eighty-six selected influential zamindars, who were appointed his honorary assistants. As with the extension of irrigation by minor distributaries, the encouragement to re-plant tracts stripped of trees, and the dispensation of special experimental seeds, now the "diffusion of agricultural science" was entrusted to the detectably powerful among the zamindars of the provinces.[167]

This at least was in accordance with the improvements themselves, which were to remain firmly in the luxury class. Hume had already noted the apparent poverty of indigenous technology and the disproportionately grandiose nature of European-imported machinery that was suggested as the corrective.

Improvements ... are urgently called for, but they have yet to be created, and this not by the bodily importation of the results achieved by science in Europe, but by the application of the principles on which those results are based to the widely different conditions and requirements of this country. Of these, the people who pester the Government to purchase grand combined steam ploughing, reaping and threshing machines for the ryots here, seem to have about as accurate a conception as a certain Maharajah, who was with difficulty dissuaded from sending home an elephant to an old pensioner at Bayswater (who complained of being no longer able to get about on foot and being too poor to keep a conveyance) had of those of our London suburbs.[168]

Experiment with complex machinery, however, proved irresistible. Yearly, from 1882-83, the Government of India published a list of agricultural implements tested, and found useful, on the experimental farms. Most items were of labour-saving design and high initial capital cost; many were for use on large farms; a few were of some direct practicality—such as light-weight ironshare ploughs—but the problems of distributing them among the peasants put a prior restriction on the number produced. Some were frankly absurd, such as the Kewani

---

[167]On the formation of the Agricultural Association, NWP, in 1886, and its first meeting, at Cawnpore, on April 15, see NWP and Oudh, "Revenue Proceedings," May 1886, File No. 941, Proceeding No. 3, Serial No. 4.

[168]Hume, *Agricultural Reform*, pp. 52–53.

windmill, which was procurable in the U.S.A. at a cost of Rs. 299.4.3. Its special advantages were said to be its continuous action without requiring attention and its dependence on the wind for motor power. The report went on to state, however, that its action was in fact known to be irregular; it might perhaps be worked from a reservoir, but it could not apparently stand the rush of a dust storm and "may not be working when water is most required."[169] Most notable of all was the Banda steam plough "affair" of 1882. The spread of *kans* grass, a seasonal phenomenon that was aggravated by long periods of drought, could not be dealt with by indigenous implements; the cultivators were accustomed to abandoning kans land, to return after a few seasons as the kans withered. The regular revenue demand under the revised settlement put an end to this sporadic mode of cultivation; if the land was made liable to pay according to each season's fixed assessment, it had to be cultivated each season. The appearance of kans, however, made cultivation literally impossible— and therefore necessitated remissions of the revenue demand. The loss to Government account, and the intractability of the kans grass (its roots were sometimes all of forty feet in length and were supplied with a complex water-storage system enabling the plant to grow undetected in the subsoil over long periods) seemed to call for a mechanized remedy—the subject of a long and detailed correspondence in the "Revenue Proceedings." A steam plough, the latest development in English agricultural machinery, was imported for the purpose of getting rid of the kans. Its capital cost, to the Government, was Rs. 42,304.12.3. To this was added the cost of maintenance, amounting by the end of 1881 to Rs. 9,220.11.6. The cost of further maintenance would, it was estimated, come to another Rs. 6,000 if wood were used for fuel, or Rs. 9,000 if coal were used. There were additional problems : where the plough was located, wood was very scarce; and there was proved to be no superiority in a steam as against a bullock-drawn, "native" plough for newly broken-up land, which deprived the new machine a priori of any subsequent use. Access to fuel was difficult, and the bill disturbing. Meanwhile, when the plough reached Banda, the kans had disappeared. Government had no alternative but to order the machinery, the cost of which had already amounted to approximately Rs. 51,500 (equal to nearly

[169]See Revenue and Agriculture Department, *List of Agricultural Implements*, 1882–83. No catalogue seems to exist of machines tested and judged inefficient.

one-half of the annual budget for the Agricultural Department), to be broken up for sale as spare parts.[170]

Nowhere was the irrelevance of improvements on which Government chose to spend with such comparative lavishness more clearly demonstrated than in the case of the Agricultural Shows. These were held from time to time (chiefly at Bulandshahr and Allahabad) in the best traditions of English capitalist farming. Ricketts, Collector of Allahabad in 1865, described how the shows were promoted by Government "to induce the Natives to attempt to improve their ancient methods of cultivation and to breed superior stock." In the same note, he also described the reaction of "an intelligent and observing Native" to the Government's efforts:

What does he see? English machinery of most costly kinds; steam-ploughs and threshing-machines, which will be of no use here until the plough-bullock rises in price to £40, or the cooly's wages rise to 14s. a week, and corn at English prices—English ploughs which his cattle cannot draw, and which break when used (as at Lucknow) in this hard soil, and which he cannot mend—and weeding machines which he can never want, for he has cheap and abundant weeding power in the women and children of his village; and in cattle he sees the pampered favourites of some amateur or Native Chief, which have cost ten times their value to feed, and which he sees at once are no use to a poor man, for he cannot feed them—and he retires to his village and says, these English do not understand his great want; he will dispense with all their machinery if they will simply give him help to make wells, and place the water within his reach . . .[171]

In Ricketts' view, such assistance was now needed more urgently than before: deforestation of the Lower Doab plains, he asserted, was contributing to a conspicuous increase in the occurrence of droughts and unfavourable seasons. But by what means could "these English" (that is, Government) help the cultivator to keep the soil supplied with the requisite moisture? Ricketts pressed for takavi loans (advances from public funds) to cope with the problem—he was, in his own words, "advocating what, though in reality is an old

[170]For the correspondence relating to the Banda steam plough, see NWP and Oudh, "Revenue Proceedings," April 1882, Index Nos. 10–20, pp. 41–57. For a description of such a steam plough, a prize-winning machine manufactured by John Fowler—Fowler's Patent Steam-Ploughing Apparatus—see M. Partridge, *Early Agricultural Machinery*, pp. 21–24 (illustration, p. 24).

[171]G. H. M. Ricketts to Commissioner, Allahabad, January 9, 1865, in NWP, "Revenue Proceedings," May 6, 1865, Index No. 8, February 18, 1865, Proceeding No. 23.

system, is new to most of those in Government employ in these Provinces, where it seems to have grown obsolete." Only one of Ricketts' staff had any practical acquaintance with the takavi system, and his knowledge was very limited.[172]

Takavi loans were indeed an "old system," dating back to pre-Mughal times. Revenue officials' advances of cash from the treasury or their own resources to cultivators for the purchase of seed and plough cattle and the digging of wells were first recorded in the fourteenth century. By Mughal times (the sixteenth and seventeenth centuries), takavi had become commonplace.[173] It constituted a regular means of supply for cultivators and a regular means by which the lenders could increase their claim to the produce of each harvest (official dues plus repayment charges) and their control over the producers. Takavi was in fact an integral part of revenue administration.[174] We have already seen how the Begam Sumroo utilized it over a twenty-year period, greatly to her advantage.[175]

The early years of British rule in the NWP saw the principle of takavi officially recognized in revenue regulations of 1793, 1795, 1803, and 1805.[176] Rules for the administration of the loans were later drawn up and included in the official manual, *Directions for Collectors of Land Revenue*.[177] There is evidence that in at least one district in the first three decades of the century, takavi loans were in fact made extensively: Moradabad was said to have been prospering rapidly as early as the 1820s, and much of its sudden rise (its state at the time of the British conquest was one of abject poverty) was attributed to lavish amounts of takavi.[178] "Advances seem to have been made with a liberality which is unknown now," E. B. Alexander noted wistfully fifty years later, at the time of settlement revision, "large sums, amounting in some cases to as much as a lakh

---

[172]*Ibid.*

[173]I. Habib, "Usury in Medieval India," *Comparative Studies in Society and History,* VI (1963), 396–397. See also Habib, *Agrarian System,* pp. 253–255.

[174]For a late nineteenth-century summary account of this "State action in India in ... assisting the supply of agricultural capital," see A. H. Harington, "Economic Reform in Rural India," *Calcutta Review,* LXXVI (1883), 153–181.

[175]See pp. 48–49 above.

[176]Bengal Regulation XXXIII 1793, extended to Benares Province by Regulation XLVI, 1795, to the Ceded Provinces by Regulation XXIV, 1803, and to the Conquered Provinces by Regulation VIII, 1805.

[177]*Directions for Collectors of Land Revenue,* paras. 46–47; Appendix V, paras. 245–249.

[178]*Moradabad Settlement Report,* p. 16.

[Rs. 100,000] being spent in encouraging sugar-cane or in purchasing seed and cattle for distressed cultivators."[179]

Such liberality vanished with the growing concern of officialdom for security and the consequent increase in elaborate procedure to protect it in its dealings with the rural populace. As early as 1861, it was clearly recognized that advances were restricted to the construction and repair of "works of permanent utility," such as the more expensive types of well, and to renovations to tank *bunds* (embankments). A period of three, four, or five years maximum was stipulated for repayment; if the work for which the advance was specifically made were not completed by the date officially stipulated, the whole advance with 12 percent interest was to be recovered forthwith.[180] Even in its truncated form, takavi remained the only official source from which agriculturists might seek assistance for improvements. Efforts were persistently made by district officers to widen the range of takavi grants—witness the strenuous pleadings of Ricketts—but these were frustrated with equal persistence by procedural obstacles. The shortcomings of Government policy as regards takavi were most conspicuous in poorly endowed districts. From Jhansi, E. G. Jenkinson urged Government to increase takavi loans for the repair of old and the construction of new works to develop local irrigation by wells and tanks—targets within the limited range of official sanction for the loans. Some Rs. 17,492 had been distributed among eighty-one villages between 1864 and 1866, but "Much more might be done and many old bunds which zamindars are most anxious to repair might be repaired," Jenkinson wrote, "if Government would consent to relax the rule regarding the term of years within which takavi advances are repayable." In the NWP, no provision for takavi advances was made in the Budget. It was therefore thought inadvisable to grant advances which are repayable by instalments extending over a longer period than five years.[181] Yet, by the same token, it was surely unwise to allow a "mere question of procedure to retard the improvement of a district and prevent the construction of so many useful works" : the term for repayment should be extended[182]—but it remained unchanged.

[179] *Ibid.*, p. 15.

[180] Board's Circular No. IV, cited in correspondence regarding takavi advances of Rs. 200 to certain zamindars of Etawah district. See Board of Revenue, NWP, to Government, NWP, November 27, 1861, in NWP, "Revenue Proceedings," December 21, 1861, Index No. 78, Proceeding No. 26.

[181] *Jhansi Settlement Report*, p. 72.

[182] *Ibid.*, p. 73.

Advances for the purchase of seed were restricted to times of scarcity, and district officials were instructed to disburse them with great caution. In July 1868, a confidential circular was issued to magistrates and collectors, drawing attention to cases of "hardship and distress demanding Government interposition" : where fields had been extensively sown but the seed had failed to germinate owing to the drought, high prices for seed corn were making it difficult for cultivators to find a second supply. "To supply seed under such circumstances," the circular warned, "is a duty in the first instance devolving on the landlord; and ordinarily it may be safely left in his hands." Government might intervene only where the zamindars were poor and, more especially, where the cultivators of an estate were the "proprietary community" of zamindars themselves. Even in these cases, the matter was hedged about with procedural restrictions. The magistrate and collector of the district was required to submit an application for the exact amount of takavi estimated necessary to the Board of Revenue in Allahabad. Where distress was reported to be general, he could apply further to the board for a lump sum based on an approximate estimate. Only where it had become clear that the harvest could be saved by immediate action could the magistrate and collector bypass the board's office for the time being and make the necessary advance, "in anticipation of sanction."[183]

Such advances as were made went to those in a position and with the time and money to apply for them : powerful local maliks, or Government acting on their behalf in the case of Court-of-Wards estates. In 1870, the officiating collector of Allahabad announced proudly that large takavi advances had been made in his district: some Rs. 28,044.8.0. All of it went to "principal landholders, that aid might be afforded to the poorer classes on their estates" through the construction of irrigation works : Rs. 19,845 to the Raja of Manda's estates under Court-of-Wards management by the collector; Rs. 3,150 to the Raja of Dhya; Rs. 1,000 to the talukdar of Burokhur ...[184]

Reviewing the takavi situation in 1870, the Governor-General—Lord Mayo himself—made it plain that for some time past he had been "satisfied that measures might be taken with great advantage, in many parts of India, for extending and improving the system of giving

[183]Circular 8 A (Confidential), July 14, 1868, in NWP, "Revenue Proceedings," August 8, 1868, Index No. 13, July 18, 1868, Proceeding No. 62.
[184]Officiating Collector, Allahabad, to Government, NWP, January 15, 1870, in NWP, "Revenue Proceedings," February 5, 1870, Index No. 4, Proceeding No. 24.

assistance to proprietors of land for the construction of permanent works of agricultural improvement ... The Government has always, if not by extensive practice, at least by its legislation, recognized the duty which, in this country, devolves upon it of giving advances of public money for the promotion of agricultural improvements ..."[185] This duty appealed to the Governor-General. Security was watertight since the land on which the improvement was to be made was declared by law to be liable for the repayment of advances ("they may be recovered by the same processes as are applicable to the recovery of land revenue arrears"). What was more, the takavi system was in principle "identical with that which has been carried out in the United Kingdom, with admirable results, by means of the Land Improvement Acts." What was needed for India's agriculture, therefore, was to consolidate and amend the law on takavi, to bring the system into line with present-day circumstances :

No sounder or more useful principle could be acted upon by a Government which desires to make the resources of the State available for the promotion of wealth or improvement of the people. There is perhaps no country in the world in which the State has so immediate and direct a need in such questions. The Government of India is not only a Government, but the chief landlord. The land revenue, which yields 20 millions of our annual income, is derived from that portion of the rent which belongs to the State and not to individual proprietors. There can be no doubt that throughout the greater part of India, every measure which can be taken for the improvement of the land, and for increasing its productive powers, immediately enhances the value of property of the State and adds ultimately to the public resources without the imposition of any fresh burden on any class of the community ...[186]

The following year, a bill embodying these principles was made law : the Land Improvement Act, XXVI of 1871, "to consolidate and amend the law relating to advances of money by the Government for agricultural improvements." But the gap between principle and practice was not closed, as became clear with the re-appearance of the scarcity spectre. In 1874, an alarm of famine went up in Jaunpur on the failure of the chief staple food grain, rice. Failure of the crop was matched by near-failure of the takavi machinery to provide assistance. "The Board permitted small takavi advances to be given,"

[185]Government of India (Home Department), to Government, NWP, June 2, 1870, in NWP, "Revenue Proceedings," December 3, 1870, Index No. 1, June 18, 1870, Proceeding No. 56.
[186]Ibid.,

Ricketts commented, "but the grant was, on the whole, quite homeo-pathic, and it was homeopathically administered, for some advances were as low as four annas."[187] The codification of takavi regulations had perpetuated rather than relaxed restrictions on their use. In 1873, the official rules for the administration of loans under the Land Improvement Act had been published by the lieutenant-governor of the provinces, with the previous sanction of the governor-general.[188] Government was well-protected from any danger of over-hasty expenditure. Applications for takavi were to be made by landlords, or by tenants with the consent of the landlord. They were to be written, and on stamped paper. They were to be presented in open court by the applicant in person, or another authorized by him. Each appli-cation was to include, besides the applicant's name, profession, parentage, tribe or caste, and residence, the exact amount applied for and whether it was to supplement any private capital and, if so, to what extent; a description of the proposed work and an estimate of its cost were to be attached, together with details of the position, character, and area of the land and the village and revenue sub-division in which it was situated. Applicants were required to state the advantages expected to result from the work and its anticipated effect on adjacent or other lands. The nature of the applicant's rights or interests in the land or in any other land offered as security for repayment had to be made plain. The amount and number of instal-ments for repayment, and the security offered, were also to be stipu-lated.[189] Where the advance exceeded Rs. 500, a rough plan and estimate were to be submitted with the application; where the advance exceeded Rs. 5,000, an accurate plan, with specifications and estimates, was required.[190] This was merely the beginning. A local enquiry was to be held into every application, conducted by the revenue officials on their tours and, in the case of applications for more than Rs. 500, by the chief revenue officer of the district. Officers were required to publish notice of the proposed work and the proposed date of the

[187]*NWP Revenue Administration Report*, 1873–74, p. 6. Though rumours of a wide-spread "famine" proved unfounded, the loss of the rice crop remained an established fact.

[188]Government, NWP, "Notification," June 18, 1873, in NWP, "Revenue Pro-ceedings," September 1873, Index No. 7, June 21, 1873, Proceedings Nos. 59, 60. For the Oudh rules, separate but in all essentials identical to the NWP set, see NWP, "Revenue Proceedings," August 1874, Index No. 35, August 22, 1874, Proceeding No. 55.

[189]"Notification" (cited above, n. 188), § iv.

[190]*Ibid.*, § v.

enquiry; the notice had to be read by the principal inhabitants of the village, and a copy was to be signed by the village headman, an accountant, a policeman, "or other local officials or respectable inhabitants."[191] The remaining rules (there were thirty in all) stipulated the procedure for investigation and for certification of such works as the local enquiry proved bona fide and allowed to proceed. A seven-year period was fixed for repayment, unless special sanction of Government were obtained, for advances not exceeding Rs. 500. The period for advances above this sum was twelve years (the larger the work, the farther it was removed from the needs of cultivators but the more generous were the terms of assistance). In case of any proposed period for repayment exceeding twenty years, the Government of India's sanction had to be obtained. Lastly, the interest charged on advances was 6.25 percent, to be altered as Government saw fit.[192]

Subsequent notifications made no fundamental alterations in these rules, with the result that the procedural obstacles to widespread use of takavi remained in full force. In the course of an official enquiry into the working of the Land Improvement Act made during 1875, R. M. Lind, then Commissioner of Meerut Division, pointed out that the act had done nothing to solve the basic problem : the need for assistance remained undeniably greater amongst those classes of the peasantry designated as "tenants" than amongst their masters, the landlords,[193] but tenants were in no position to ask Government for advances for the construction of such works as the act contemplated. Their wants were seed and plough bullocks : where could assistance be found to provide these under the provisions of the act, which could serve the interests only of the landlords?[194] Statistical statements compiled for the enquiry proved this to be the case. Of Rs. 26,322.12.0, the total sum advanced under the act to date, Rs. 24,293.8.0 went to landlords. The remaining Rs. 2,029.4.0 was distributed to some fifty-two tenant applicants throughout the provinces.[195] In its con-

[191]*Ibid.*, § ix.

[192]*Ibid.*, §§ xxiv, xxx.

[193]For details of tenancy categories in the later nineteenth century, see pp. 152 ff. below and Appendix 8.

[194]R. M. Lind to Board of Revenue, NWP, May 5, 1874, para. 8, in NWP, "Revenue Proceedings," July 1875, Index No. 39, July 10, 1875, Proceeding No. 55.

[195]Board of Revenue, NWP, to Government, NWP, June 9, 1875, "Report on the Working of the Land Improvement Act ... from Its Introduction to the End of the Official Year 1874–75," Statements II and III, in NWP, "Revenue Proceedings," July 1875, Index No. 27, July 10, 1875, Proceeding No. 43.

clusions on the evidence of the enquiry, the Board of Revenue could not but agree that "the class who have most availed themselves of the Act are the landlords"—a conclusion to which they were themselves resigned : "This is only what was to be expected."[196]

The takavi situation changed little throughout the last quarter of the century. Later enactments—the Northern India Takavi Act, X of 1879, repealed by the Agriculturalists' Loans Act, XII of 1884— did extend the scope for Government loans, but the old rules remained in force, effectively barring access to the majority of cultivators. For "smallholders," the qualification for assistance was still "distress." Advances for seed and cattle were made only during scarcity years; all were of course recoverable with interest.[197] In 1891, Voelcker noted the wisdom of Government proposals to make loans available locally for well-digging :

The plan is an excellent one; but its success depends entirely upon how it is worked, and how nearly it is brought home to the people, and is adapted to their means. What is still requisite is, to make it clear to the cultivators that the system is one that will benefit them, one that will enable them to benefit themselves. If this idea could be once thoroughly grasped, the advantages not alone to the people, but to the Government, in the form of an increased revenue from the land, would be very great.[198]

This was precisely the situation as Mayo had seen it, twenty years before.

It is hardly surprising, therefore, that throughout the period takavi loans should have borne the small proportion to the collections of land revenue year by year which the official statistics indicate. "If what has been done be compared with what might be done [by way of takavi], the discrepancy is startling," commented the anonymous contributor of the series of papers "Oudh and Optimism" to Knight's *Indian Economist* in 1874.[199] Oudh figures were typical for the provinces as a whole. In 1868-69, Rs. 115,867 had been advanced under the pressure of the severe drought of that year for "improvements,"

[196]*Ibid.*, board's review of commissioners' reports.

[197]See, for example, "Report on the Scarcity and Relief Operations, NWP and Oudh, 1877–78, 1879," p. 12, in NWP and Oudh, "Revenue Proceedings," December 1880, Index Nos. 2–3, November 6, 1880, Proceeding No. 11; *ibid.*, December 4, Proceeding No. 2. See also Government of India, "Famine Proceedings," September 1880, Proceeding No. 1; *ibid.*, October 1880, Proceeding No. 2. Loans to small holders were approved in principle, provided "adequate security" was offered.

[198]Voelcker, *Report*, para. 107, p. 85.

[199]"Oudh and Optimism," *Indian Economist*, October 31, 1874, pp. 61–64.

which represented barely 1/111 of the land revenue of the year. It fell steadily during the succeeding years until it reached the "contemptible sum" in 1872-73 of Rs. 16,523. In 1874, whilst the land-revenue demand had risen by the equivalent in rupees of £200,000, a little more than 1/900 of the total collection was returned as takavi advances.[200]

In all, who could benefit from this piecemeal "development" of the provinces? In densely populated districts where the canal and railway companies had been most active, the land itself had paid a heavy price for the expansion in cultivation and communications which the public works had stimulated. Cultivators in canal-irrigated areas paid charges for the new facilities twice each season : water rates to Government and illegal dues to the subordinate canal establishment appointed by Government to record and collect its rates ; zamindars paid, in addition to their owner's rates (from 1873), indirect charges in the form of an increased revenue demand. Where railways cut through arable land, cultivators and zamindars had to face *inter alia* the consequences of increasing deforestation. Remedial action by Government was consistently frustrated by its unwillingness to expend on projects promising little or nothing by way of immediate returns. Government's attempts at technical improvements on a small scale, in line with the best of contemporary farming practice in Britain, were too far removed from the millions of small cultivators and their needs to be in any sense efficacious. Meanwhile, the small cultivators' notorious lack of resources persisted. Their own means and methods proved consistently inadequate to increase the productivity of their holdings to the extent desired by Government. Charges levied by their social superiors and the increasing cost even of necessities such as fuel and fodder deprived them of opportunities to lay up reserves over the seasons. Lastly, they could find little assistance from the only source remaining beyond the malik or the money-lender : Government. The history of takavi outlined above exhibits in itself the insoluble problems which confronted Government from the introduction of improvement schemes which, although with the means to hand, could not be adequately adapted to the physical, let alone the

[200]*Ibid.*, at p. 63. For the amount of takavi advanced annually in the NWP and Oudh, 1871–72 to 1899–1900, see Figure 6 (statistics before 1871–72 are not available). Compare the revenue demand, collections, and balances, 1864–65 to 1884–85 (by divisions), Figures 7 and 8, and 1885–86 to 1899–1900 (provincial aggregates), Figure 9.

social, environment of the provinces. Only that minority of the rural population already in a position of prosperity and sufficient power to maintain some independence of action had access to the benefits of innovation.

Chapter III

THE REVISED
REVENUE SETTLEMENTS

The share of Government in the wealth which India produced or was judged capable of producing had necessarily to be fixed at a sizeable proportion. "The whole paraphernalia of a great civilized administration"[1] was installed and maintained at vast expense and transcended the immediate needs of India itself, as they were officially interpreted. In addition to the actual costs of the governments of the several provinces and the supreme establishment at Calcutta, a wide variety of expenses incidental to imperial power at home and abroad were met from the Indian revenues :

The costs of the Mutiny, the price of the transfer of the Company's rights to the Crown, the expenses of simultaneous wars in China and Abyssinia, every governmental item in London that remotely related to India down to the fees of the charwomen in the India Office and the expenses of ships that sailed but did not participate in hostilities and the cost of Indian regiments for six months' training at home before they sailed,—all were charged to the account of the unrepresented ryot. The sultan of Turkey visited London in 1868 in state, and his official ball was arranged for at the India Office and the bill charged to India. A lunatic asylum in Ealing, gifts to members of a Zanzibar mission, the consular and diplomatic establishments of Great Britain in China and in Persia, part of the permanent expenses of the Mediterranean fleet and the entire cost of a line of telegraph from England to India had been charged before 1870 to the Indian Treasury. . . .[2]

That official policy and practice as regards the agricultural world of India should have been dominated throughout by a concern for the land revenue is understandable : it constituted by far the largest portion of Government's income and, with the expansion of agriculture

[1]See pp. 62–63 above.

[2]L. H. Jenks, *Migration*, pp. 223–224, and references there cited. The revenues of British India during the first thirteen years of Crown administration rose from £33,000,000 per year to £52,000,000 per year. Deficits accruing in the period 1866 to 1870 alone amounted to some £11,500,000 whilst the Home Debt accruing in the period 1857 to 1860 amounted to some £30,000,000.

so zealously promoted in the later nineteenth century, it could not but increase.

For the assessment and collection of the revenue, the Company had bequeathed to its successor precedents which, as in the case of public works, were to be preserved in essentials whilst the application of modern principles enlarged their scope and improved upon their admitted deficiencies. The thirty-year district settlements of the NWP initiated by Regulation IX of 1833 had been completed at various dates in the 1830s and 1840s and came up for renewal during the first decades of Crown Government.[3] The new administration of the NWP was therefore faced with the immediate necessity of re-defining its revenue claims which it set about doing by an extensive but far from radical revision of the existing settlements. This occupied the greater part of the administration—the revenue establishments—for nearly three decades, from the mid-1850s to 1880. Meanwhile, the first regular settlement of Oudh since annexation in 1856 was also completed, district by district, on principles of assessment identical in all essential respects to those followed by field staff in the NWP.

Where significant changes had occurred was in the social and the physical environment. Annexation, in bringing the Nawabi to an end, told heavily on the talukdari and zamindari families of Oudh and the eastern districts of the NWP. Suddenly, they ceased to be the suppliers of hundreds and thousands of court servants and ceased as suddenly to enjoy the perquisites of office. Younger sons and cousins, in the majority of cases, could now look little further for their income than to the limits of the family's haq which the senior member now managed unassisted by their contributions from service outside the

[3]The dates of the expiration of settlements of districts included in the NWP on May 1, 1846 are as follows:

Agra	1872	Bulandshahr	1859	Mainpuri	1870
Aligarh	1868	Budaon	1866	Meerut	1865
Allahabad	1869	Cawnpore	1870	Moradabad	1872
Azamgarh	1867	Etawah	1871	Muttra	1871
Banda	1874	Farukhabad	1865	Muzaffarnagar	1861
Bareilly	1867	Fatehpur	1870	Saharunpur	1857
Bijnour	1866	Gorakhpur	1859	Shahjahanpur	1868

Source: Act VIII, 1846 ("An Act for Determining the Duration of the Existing Settlement of the NWP"), § 1. Excluded are (1) districts constituted after 1846, (2) districts of Benares Division which were permanently settled, and (3) Oudh districts (annexed, 1856). For the dates of publication of reports compiled at the completion of the revised settlements, see the Bibliography (in which the reports are listed in alphabetical order by district).

taluka or mahal. More widespread and in some cases equally sudden changes were taking place in the productivity of the land, especially under the stimulus of public works. The new revenue assessments represented established precedent revised in the light of principles of equity and political economy widely accepted as sound. How far was the revision adapted to these changes?

The Assessment of the Demand

The immediate task which confronted the Company's revenue officers early in the century was to find in the uppermost levels of the rural society of the provinces figures who might validly be entitled "proprietors" (or "landlords"), on whom the obligation to meet the Government demand for land tax would rest. A proprietor, when found, would be recognized as holding a legal right to definable territorial assets in the form of an estate. His share in the produce of that estate taken annually from the cultivators, with whom he contracted to guarantee their rights so long as they paid the stipulated amount, would be defined as his rent. The Government demand would be calculated on the aggregate rents of a given revenue subdivision and so fixed as to allow Government to take its full measure and at the same time leave to each proprietor an adequate residue to cover costs of cultivation as well as a margin of profit. The conditions on which proprietorial rights were recognized and maintained by Government were the recognition and fulfilment by the proprietors of their revenue obligations. Government's security was the proprietor's estate. On default of payment, Government reserved the right to sell up a proprietor's rights and realize its claim to revenue from the sale proceeds. With the yardstick of the contemporary economic and juristic concept of "property" in hand, the settlement officers set out to identify the proprietor. This involved the classification of rights into two broad categories—those of the proprietor who received rent and those of the tenant subordinate to him who paid it.

The earliest revenue regulations of the NWP, of 1795, 1803, and 1805, had established the first precedents (a modified version of Bengal practice) for the definition of tenurial categories in the first summary settlements. Who else could be recognized as proprietors but those local maliks who had held office as zamindars prior to British rule? Beneath them came a bewildering series of "sub-proprietors," other maliks who could not be squeezed into the tenant categories and who suffered, legally, from a conspicuous lack of precise definition as to what the range of their proprietorial authority might be. The vast mass of the population was classified as "tenants." The first systematic settlement of the NWP under Regulation VII of 1822 used these categories, but its cumbersome methods of assessment proved after some ten years' experience, or rather experiment, to be unworkable. Refinements were introduced by the thirty-year settlements made under Regulation IX of 1833, which was the first to be based on local records of rights compiled under the supervision of the settlement authorities by patwaris, the accountants who held hereditary office under the zamindars. These records were held to establish the recognized proprietary right of the zamindars, and the "rents" recorded in them as payable to the zamindar by the cultivators of his mahal were the basis of assessment, fixed at the equitable proportion of $66\frac{2}{3}$ percent. Two categories of rent-paying tenantry were recognized by the revenue law : *maurusi*, or tenants with hereditary right of occupancy, and *ghair-maurusi*, tenants cultivating fields within the mahal but resident outside it.[4]

While the tenurial categories remained as before, a major development in procedure was introduced by the beginning of the revision of the 1833 settlements in the last days of the Company's administration. The rules drawn up in 1855 for the settlement of Saharunpur district (due to expire in 1857) established a new principle which became the crux of future assessments. Officers were to ascertain rates for valuation from the aggregate recorded rentals of mahals composing a pargana or "vicinage." The rental as recorded in the accounts for each mahal was to be compared with this deduced "rent rate," which was then to be adjusted if it proved too much in excess of the assets recorded for the majority of mahals. The revised rate was the basis on which the demand was fixed.[5] Zamindars whose recorded rentals from their mahals were below the standard rate were thus provided with an incentive to increase the amount of cultivation under their control. Meanwhile, since the new scientific standard of assessment increased the scope of Government's claim on the "rental assets," the actual proportion taken could be safely reduced

[4]For a summary of the principal features of the first English settlements, see W. H. Moreland, *Revenue Administration*, pp. 31–39. For the main lines of revenue policy from 1801 to 1833, see S. C. Gupta, *Agrarian Relations*. For legislative definitions of the incidents of tenancy, 1859 to 1881, see Appendix 8.

[5]For a summary of the Saharunpur rules, see Moreland, *Revenue Administration*, pp. 42–43.

from 66$\frac{2}{3}$ percent to 50 percent without fear of a loss in revenue.

The revising officers of the Crown administration throughout the provinces adopted the Saharunpur principle. "It was on a basis of rent-rates that the whole of the revision of the revenue assessment in the NWP proceeded," A. F. Millett commented in his Fyzabad report. "A basis of rent-rates was practically commanded by the Oudh Government; a basis of rent-rates was very generally framed by the Settlement Officers of Oudh."[6] Emphasis in settlement directives was placed more than ever before on actuality : the rent rate was to be calculated, according to official instructions, from data amassed by observation and direct enquiry. As William Muir, later (as Sir William Muir) Lieutenant-Governor of the NWP and the author of numerous memoranda on the principles and problems of revenue assessments, stated apropos of Jhansi district in 1863, the *jamabandi* (rent roll) on which the assessment was to be based was "to be framed in accordance with the facts as they exist."[7]

First, the nature of "rent" had to be determined : in any given area, did "rent" adjust itself by competition or by custom? By Muir's time, it has become official doctrine that "customary rents" prevailed throughout the provinces. The second task for the settlement officer was therefore to measure the "customary rents" of his district by the simple expedient of recording the rent he adjudged to be in force "by prescription." In case of local disputes as to the amount of this rent, his third task was to arrive at the "actual" figure by means of enquiry. If the zamindar claimed to be entitled to raise this prescriptive rent (the technical term is "enhance"), or if a maurusi ryot asserted his right to have it lowered, it was the duty of the settlement officer to decide the dispute. In this, he was to apply as his standard the "custom of the pargana or vicinage." Should he decide in favour of the maurusi ryot, instructions as to the next course of action were

[6]*Fyzabad Settlement Report*, p. 385. The Oudh settlements were made with the talukdars, as distinct from the policy in the NWP, where zamindars engaged for the revenue, but the principles on which the assessments were formed were common to both provinces. For the official view of the talukdari policy, see W. C. Benett, ed., *Gazetteer of the Province of Oudh*, Introduction. For the contrary view, critical of the policy, see C. W. McMinn, *Introduction*, which contained trenchant observations *inter alia* on the talukdari settlements and reached no further than the proof-copy stage, to be withdrawn and replaced by Benett's more orthodox appraisal. Criticism of talukdari policy is also to be found in H. C. Irwin, *Garden of India*, pp. 191–296.

[7]*Jhansi Settlement Report*, p. 20, referring to *Directions for Settlement Officers*, p. 149 (Regulation VII, 1822, § ix). Compare W. C. Benett's reiteration, some fifteen years later, of the necessity of placing direct enquiry first, ahead of all statistical calculations; *Gonda Settlement Report*, p. 2.

contained in the Bengal Recovery of Rents Act, X of 1859.[8] The ghair-maurusi ryot lay beyond the pale of the protective clauses of revenue and rent legislation.

This system of assessment envisaged, ideally, the compilation of detailed statements of field-by-field accuracy, defining not only the rental assets of each mahal but also their exact territorial basis. But practical restrictions were imposed from the start by the limited means available to the revenue establishments to carry it out. "It is obvious," Muir declared, again speaking of Jhansi in 1863, "that the attempt to fix the rental of every field in a village, in every village of a district, is beyond the skill and power of any settlement authority, varying as every field ordinarily does from its neighbour, by every shade of difference known in the lapse of time to the people themselves, but not appreciable by a stranger."[9] Since, therefore, "actual" rents eluded all available means of direct enquiry, the settlement officers had to be granted some leeway in forming their assessments. A note of 1864 by Rowland Money, then Junior Member at the Board of Revenue, shows how "estimated" rapidly became an acceptable replacement for "actual" in the compilation of revenue accounts: "The exact assets cannot be ascertained with any certainty. The rule for settlement at one-half assets is not invariable but indicates the general proportion of jama to rent that should be maintained. Much must necessarily be left to the discretion of the Settlement Officer. Mathematical precision is unattainable, and the variations of conditions are so numerous that no invariable rule or formula of assessment can be made generally applicable."[10] Each settlement officer had to cope with the varying conditions of his district as best he could and make his assessments, as Patrick Carnegy remarked, "as moderate as it was possible to make them compatibly with an honest regard to the due interests of the State."[11] Throughout the cold season, year after year, the officers wound their way through the districts with their assistants and amins (field clerks), maps, plane tables, measuring chains, rule books, and discretion, enquiring as to the outturn of last season's harvests from the principal inhabitants of each village and calculating the rent rate pargana by pargana.

[8] *Jhansi Settlement Report,* p. 20.
[9] *Ibid.*
[10] R. Money, "Notes on the Governor-General's Minute on Permanent Settlement," in NWP, "Revenue Proceedings," September 3, 1864, Index No. 3, June 18, 1864, Proceeding No. 35.
[11] *Fyzabad Settlement Report,* p. 338.

S. N. Martin's report on the annual value and distribution of agricultural produce in Muzaffarnagar district for 1272 Fasli (1864-65) shows the typical terms of reference within which the settlement officers worked, however divergent their respective methods were in incidentals. Martin reported that "rent" in his district was of "four well-known kinds" : *zabti*—cash rents for the more valuable class of crops, such as sugar cane, cotton, and Indian corn; *nijkari*—rents in kind for wheat, barley, bajra, and so forth; *tashki* and *surasuri*—leases, so much a bigha, irrespective of crop sown but divided into irrigated and unirrigated tracts; and *bilmokta*—a lump sum for so many fields, without any specification of a bigha rate. Martin then noted the principle of variation :

All these rates [sic] of course vary in amount according to the productive power of the soil in various localities, and contingent in a measure upon the industry or the revenue of the class of cultivators available on the spot. For the purposes of this Report ... it will be sufficient to take an average of prevailing rents throughout a range of circles. It is obvious to remark that in zamindari and pattidari estates the gross amount of this rental is the fund which provides for the Government and Zamindars' shares—the ryots' share is the residue of the entire produce.[12]

For the first years of revision, the establishment of rent rates consisted largely of attempts at correction of *khasra* (field book) entries made by the settlement staff in surveying each village. New refinements in standards of assessment came, however, with the publication in 1868 of C. A. Elliott's "Rent-Rate Report" for pargana Chibramau, Farukhabad district, which brought in the words of his colleague, A. B. Patterson, a "revolution in the most important branch of settlement work : inspection and assumed rates." Elliott's method was to mark off the field maps into hars (tracts), filling in the (assumed) rates and adding notes on the character of soils. The result was a map which was to stand as an index to "the village." Patterson for one claimed that this method "introduced a degree of accuracy and confidence hitherto unknown in the NWP settlements." He dwelt on the cardinal importance of correct measurement of soils—the basis of comparison between different villages—as the "great principle underlying Elliott's ... system."[13]

---

[12]"Reports on the Annual Value and Distribution of Agricultural Produce for 1272 Fasli [1864–65]," in NWP, "Revenue Proceedings," October 6, 1866, Index No. 5, Proceeding No. 19.

[13]*Fatehpur Settlement Report*, p. 53.

Previously, the settlement officer's source for ascertaining the "actual" rental had been the so-called village returns—in reality, the zamindar's *nikasi*, or roll of cultivators, in which each ryot working under the zamindar's guarantee, together with his payment per harvest, was recorded by the zamindar's patwari. The nikasi was a highly diverse document, influenced by fluctuations in local social circumstances and often exceedingly difficult to comprehend within the abstract frame of reference of the revised settlements. Elliott's "revolution" now provided the harassed settlement officer with a basis of estimation of actual conditions—but of a natural, not social, order. Although relatively free from the perennial danger of local manipulation, it was by the same token, devoid of social significance. Though the two sources were joined together in an unnatural coalition for the purposes of settlement procedure, preference went to the relatively precise soil rates. Officers differed only in the order in which they dealt with the two sources.

Take, for example, the assessment of Lucknow district. W. C. Capper's system was to apply certain rates arrived at by experience to the various soils as classified in his amins' returns, then to compare the estimate of assets thus arrived at with the "village returns." G. B. Maconochie, on the other hand, began by deducing rates from average rents—that is, from what he took to be the *actual* rents paid by the *average* class of all cultivators in each village for all the various soils. From these he determined the rate for the average *chak*, or unit of like soils, and for the actual pargana. Thus far the returns furnished by the zamindars formed the basis of his estimate. His next step was to classify the lands according to their soils and holdings according to "tenancies." The holdings he classified as sir, or owner-cultivator land, which was to be assessed at a reduced rate; *muafi*, or tax-free land; and land held by tenants-at-will. The first two classes were to represent the highest rent, the third the lowest rent. Maconochie then deduced rates applicable to these classes by taking as a "village rate" the average rent paid by the tenant-at-will. This, in turn, gave him chak and pargana rent rates. The deduced rates were then checked against an estimate of the capabilities of a village—taking into account its population, its soils, its irrigation, and the proportion of its land that was fully manured (and assumed at maximum productivity). Here, his method was to calculate the percentage of population per 100 acres of cultivation. This, according to Maconochie, made comparisons between villages easier. The very last round of the whole procedure was a visit to the relevant village.[14]

Whereas most settlement officers dutifully checked through the village returns the zamindars provided before, or after, turning to the more amenable, if more laborious, task of estimating natural conditions, Carnegy for one—an officer of much experience—candidly dismissed not only the returns but also "the rental actually received by the proprietors which we may as well not trouble ourselves much about, as it is impossible to ascertain it accurately"—as indeed it was by the official methods. He relied throughout on precedent, on "the assumed rental, which is ascertained by the application of reason, and the best known tests and methods devised by many eminent settlement officers in whose steps we now tread."[15] A confrontation between the estimations of natural capacity and conjectural distribution, the standards of assessment which formed the basis for the "assumed rates," and the "recorded rental," far from providing a measure of corroboration of the former, complicated further the problem of defining the rental assets. It was only logical that a situation should arise where C. H. T. Crosthwaite was prompted to warn, in a report published in 1881, "that the tendency to exact actual proof of the assumed rates, which is a growing tendency, is a dangerous one. Such proof can only be obtained from the recorded rentals, and as the recorded rentals are well known to be more or less fictitious the proof is really worth nothing."[16] The opinion was general. E. B. Alexander wrote of Moradabad district that the patwaris' records "cannot be trusted to furnish accurate statistics of the assets of any one year."[17] H. H. Butts noted with regard to the settlement of Lucknow that both Capper and Maconochie, his predecessors, "saw the impossibility of persuading owners to give you accurate statistics."[18] Butts himself believed zamindars were perpetually minded to defraud but were at a conspicuous disadvantage in achieving this aim when confronted with the superior skills of the British revenue administration. He suggested how

the native [zamindar] little knows, or fails to grasp, the means at our disposal. He has not the powerful weapons of a system to fight with.

[14]*Lucknow Settlement Report*, W. C. Capper's method, pp. 6–9, G. B. Maconochie's method, pp. 9–15. For Maconochie's method applied elsewhere, see *Unao Settlement Report*, pp. 55–56.

[15]*Fyzabad Settlement Report*, pp. 319–320.

[16]*Moradabad Settlement Report*, p. 92.

[17]*Ibid.*, pp. 97–98.

[18]*Lucknow Settlement Report*, p. 7.

He does not comprehend you have mapped out, and classified all his village, that you know the exact area of manured lands near the homestead and the dry hars unapproachable by water on the outskirts, and that your statistics show you whether labour and skill are amply or only poorly applied. He does not know, in a word, that you can almost measure out the amount of money that a village can produce, or he might try and practise a better and more systematic course of deception, but the odds are greatly against him.[19]

The assumption of zamindari duplicity, however, failed to explain the crux of the settlement problem, which was that local records fitted a context radically different from that recognized in the settlements. Indeed, the records applied to a context in which social differentiation was paramount, formulated in terms of dues and claims, where no authoritative system in terms of arithmetical standards could create a recognized "rent rate," and in which the amount exacted depended on the relation of zamindar to cultivator. Butts himself was, he admitted, inclined to think that some idea of "a natural average rate" existed, "a general rate the farmers and landlords would, *prima facie*, apply, and which they could tell you of, which would vary with the nature of the soil or the position of the land in the village . . . ; rent is not a haphazard thing that is guessed at or drawn by lot." Yet he observed on the other hand that in Lucknow district, "all rents are modified chiefly by the caste of the cultivators [that is, by their relation to the zamindar], and the lengths to which the landlords may wish, or dare, to go."[20] In Unao, Maconochie commented flatly, no indigenous rent rate existed, that is, there was no rate per bigha on the different kinds of soil or fields classed by position in the village.[21] When, therefore, Alan Cadell spoke of entries in the records in pargana Shikarpur of Muzaffarnagar district appearing "to have been false and against Government in proportion as the zamindar was rich and powerful,"[22] he was drawing attention to a dilemma which in fact could not be solved by the administration : the amount of the zamindar's charges depended on his wealth, and on his power; where these fluctuated, charges also fluctuated, and where the charges corresponded to the sober arithmetical estimate of the settlement officer, it was largely the work of coincidence. As a consequence it became impossible to detect the true fraud.

[19]*Ibid.*, pp. 14–15.
[20]*Ibid.*, p. 15.
[21]*Unao Settlement Report*, pp. 13–14.
[22]*Muzaffarnagar Settlement Report* (on western, permanently settled parganas), p. 32.

Other problems beset the settlement officers besides the calculation of average "rates" in such highly diverse circumstances and the constant suspicion of fraudulence. In areas where all cultivators' charges taken at the harvest were paid over in kind—by the late nineteenth century, fortunately for the officers, this was the case in only a small minority of areas—assessment was still more complicated than in those mahals where the accounts, such as they were, listed cash sums. "As Government does not and cannot take its revenue in the same way [that is, in kind], but by a fixed cash payment, the problem was at once presented," as Crosthwaite clearly saw, "how to calculate the rate at which this ought to fall."[23] Price lists from local bazars, where such were available, seemed to offer the only solution; these, however, were woefully inadequate as far as any abiding standard of value was concerned.[24]

With these numerous and persistent complications, settlement was understandably a lengthy process, spun out further by transfers of staff, revisions, and delays in the grant of official sanction. Take, for example, the settlement of Muzaffarnagar district. The old settlement was due to expire in 1861. In April 1860, H. G. Keene, as Collector, had been charged with the completion of the new settlement, with Auckland Colvin as Assistant Collector and Rai Nanuck Chand as Deputy Collector. In the cold season of 1862-63, the measurements were completed. In March 1862, Keene left for England on furlough. The charge of the district—much of its assessments being completed— was then made over to S. N. Martin as Collector. In May 1862, a second Assistant Collector, Charles Grant, and a second Deputy Collector were appointed in the Settlement Department. In March 1863, Grant was transferred to Meerut. In January 1864, Colvin was transferred to Bijnour. Martin then carried on the work with his deputy collectors. The divisional commissioner's final report was received by the Board of Revenue in January 1867. In 1868, the Lieutenant-Governor, Muir, reopened the question of the assessments, cancelled Grant's entire work and most of Martin's, and instructed Cadell, newly appointed to the district, to conclude operations for the introduction of a permanent settlement and to revise the assessments of seven parganas. This was still in progress at the end of 1873.[25]

---

[23] *Moradabad Settlement Report*, p. 91. On charges paid traditionally by cultivators in kind, see pp. 37–39 above.

[24] For a discussion of "bazar price rates," see pp. 184–187 below.

[25] A. Colvin to C. A. Elliott, December 12, 1873, *Muzaffarnagar Settlement Report*,

In this light—Muzaffarnagar was a typical case—the claim of the administration to have introduced a new sense of stability through its improved revenue system under the revisions seems at best dubious. F. O. Mayne, Officiating Junior Member at the Board of Revenue in 1871, spoke vehemently of

the great injury inflicted on a people by our system of protracted settlements. We talk of a limitation of demand and of a thirty years' settlement, in order to give a value to property by allowing the proprietors the benefit of improved and extended cultivation, of rise in prices and better Government. It is all nonsense. We go on for years pursuing a system of blood-letting; a process of slow torture, which not only destroys all sense of security and causes depreciation in the value of land, but also entails on the proprietors a succession of marauders in the shape of settlement establishments, which must add little to the profits of the people or to the reputation of Government. .... I look upon the way in which our settlements are allowed to drag their weary length year after year, the manner in which they are tinkered, from time to time, with new orders and revised principles, all more or less having retrospective effect, as an unmitigated evil to the country at large.[26]

Mayne called for more unrestricted authority to be given to the settlement officer to speed up the business of assessment. But the Government could not have acceded to such a request : its security requirements demanded the elaborate procedure of scrutinizing the settlement officer's work.

After the delays which such scrutiny inevitably entailed, the end result could well be the simple expedient of *factum valet*. The Saharunpur assessment reports, compiled over thirteen years (1854-1867), were stated to be "deficient in all qualities which go to make up a good Settlement Report. The lieutenant-governor," his secretary was instructed to remark, "misses in all the reports the mention of many important subjects concerning which information should have

---

pp. 1–2. A. Cadell's report on the canal tract was finally published in 1878. Compare, for example, the longevity of the Kheri settlement. In 1867–68, A. Boulderson assessed pargana Aurangabad. From October 1869 to March 1872, McMinn, with "brief and interrupted assistance of A. Murray and G. R. C. Williams," assessed fourteen parganas. Beginning in 1872, H. R. Clarke revised these assessments, over the following six years, with T. R. Redfern as his assistant from 1875. The final report was published in 1879. The settlement of other districts was even more prolonged. In Jaunpur, for example, T. E. Smith worked on the revision from 1869 to 1877. The final report was submitted by P. C. Wheeler and published in 1886.

[26]F. O. Mayne, March 20, 1871, "Note on Correspondence Regarding the Delay Incurred in the Revision of Bijnour Settlement Work," in NWP, "Revenue Proceedings," September 2, 1871, Index No. 17, July 29, 1871, Proceeding No. 43.

been given." These included a comparison of the present and former state of each tehsil; changes in canal and well irrigation; the effect of canals on crops; mode of cultivation; changes in proprietorship (castes and classes); and changes regarding the area held and the kind of rents paid by different cultivating classes. Above all, the reports were said to be "remarkable for their want of accuracy and precision as to figures." If the Saharunpur reports told the Secretariat little of Saharunpur, nonetheless the assessments—amounts and incidence—as arrived at by the settlement staff, were accepted: they "have been working for seven years actually and have lasted successfully through some bad seasons. Therefore the Lt.-Governor confirms the settlement for thirty years [July 1, 1860 to June 30, 1890]."[27]

Saharunpur raised a fundamental problem. In addition to the tardiness of settlement and the uncertainties of its results—in spite of the pursuit of accuracy through increasing procedural refinements— there was a further source of insecurity: this was the necessity for Government to readjust its demand in accordance with subsequent modifications in the agricultural environment, in terms of developments, so as to secure its due share of the new prosperity. Saharunpur had been settled during a transition period,

when old rates and prices were becoming obsolete but before the effects of a new state of things were generally felt, before the zamindars had thoroughly found out the power of enhancement given them by Act X, 1859,[28] and before confidence was felt in the stability of the higher scale of prices which set in with the cotton famine and the reduced value of silver. The zamindars' receipts had risen with the rise in prices, but there had (as yet) been little or no change in the staples grown or rates of money rents paid by the cultivators.[29]

What were the best means to guarantee continued progress and at the same time safeguard Government's interest in its fruits? The old question of the advisability of a permanent settlement of the land revenue was raised once more. Colonel Baird Smith, an ardent protagonist for permanent settlement for the NWP, had urged its implementation to intensify as well as perpetuate the best aspects (he emphasized security of title and accuracy of record) which he believed

---

[27]*Saharunpur Settlement Report* (Resolution CMLXX of 1874), pp. 14–15. Saharunpur was the district for which the first scientific rules for settlement procedure had been drawn up; see pp. 123–124 above.

[28]For a discussion of rent enhancement, see pp. 152–153 below.

[29]*Saharunpur Settlement Report* (Resolution), pp. 14–15.

the settlements of 1833 to 1845 had achieved. A permanent settlement would, in short, secure the essential prerequisite for economic progress : stability.[30] In his despatch of 9 July 1862, the secretary of state had stipulated that such settlement should or *might* be introduced into those parts of India that fulfilled certain conditions for its reception — primarily where evidence existed that cultivation had reached its limits, or nearly so (based on the common assumption that the optimum level of production was identical to the maximum degree of expansion) — whereupon the revenue demand might remain fixed in perpetuity without fear that it would subsequently be revealed as inadequate in view of new developments. The problem for the late nineteenth-century administration, with its increasing need to augment its finances, was that a permanent settlement whilst undoubtedly supplying a motive for enterprise on the part of the landlord, in leaving him free from the harassment of periodic reassessments, would necessarily mean a surrender of revenue on the (potentially) rising value of crops and increasingly improved cultivation.[31] In 1868, Muir, then Lieutenant-Governor, placed the responsibility for decision regarding the introduction of permanent settlement with the Board of Revenue, which was to determine the question in each case submitted on the evidence of the settlement officer's report.[32] In the end, only the canal tract of Muzaffarnagar district was considered a serious candidate.[33]

Each settlement officer had in fact to consider as a matter of course the essential point raised by the permanent settlement discussions : how much could Government claim of the fruits of the improvement it

[30]R. Baird Smith, "Report," especially pp. 67–68, 70, 78–79.

[31]Viceroy and Governor-General of India, "Minute on the Question of Permanent Settlement in the NWP," in NWP, "Revenue Proceedings," September 3, 1864, Index No. 5, June 18, 1864, Proceeding No. 32. For the bystanders' view of permanent settlement as an incentive to enterprise, see "Sir Charles Wood's Despatch Recommending the Perpetual Settlement of the Land Revenue," *Economist*, September 13, 1862, pp. 1009–1011. See also *Economist*, September 20, 1862, pp. 1038–1040. The *Economist* approved the principle of fixity of settlement — for the non-interference it implied on the part of Government officers.

[32]Sir W. Muir, "Minute on Certain Points Connected with the Permanent Settlement of the Land Revenue," June 6, 1868, in NWP, "Revenue Proceedings," July 11, 1868, Index No. 2, Proceeding No. 51. The standard to be reached before permanent settlement might even be considered was an indication of maximum expansion : cultivation had to cover at least 80 percent of the culturable or *malguzari* (revenue-paying) area.

[33]This tract was settled by Alan Cadell, separately from the remainder of the district. See *Muzaffarnagar Settlement Report, Canal Tract*, 1878, which was published five years after the main district report.

sponsored whilst ensuring at the same time that the landlord retained sufficient to encourage him to intensify his efforts? This point the settlement officer had to consider in every case where he noted the indices of India's mid-nineteenth-century "economical revolution," namely the enormous rise in the prices of agricultural produce and the increase in cultivated and irrigated areas.[34]

The problems of estimating rental assets were multiplied in areas where improvement was manifested in the expansion of cultivated area and in modifications in crop patterns. Like the rent rate, the indices of prosperity might in the abstract be clear. A fair estimate could be reached via the half-asset rules and monetary calculation of the respective claims which ought to accrue to Government and landlord. But whatever the indices of value—prices—signalled, rents, on which the assessment was to be based, could not be seen to rise in proportion, or indeed even in co-ordination, with them. Where a rise in rents was recorded, it was found to be coincidental to price movements.[35] In improved, as in unimproved tracts, rents seemed to remain governed by the relative power of the zamindar. But the settlement officer had nonetheless been directed to base his estimates on the assumption that price rise must induce rent rise. His assessments of the "expanding" areas were therefore calculated on assumed rates enhanced by his estimate of increased capacity.[36] The consequence was that the assessments came to dictate the rise in rents—where the zamindars were in a position to secure it.

In the canal districts, the prototype of modernized Indian agriculture, zamindars paid heavily—in terms of official charges alone—for the increase in irrigation. Canals were important revenue earners to the Government on two main accounts : dues collected by the Irrigation Department, and the increment to the land revenue charged on "enhanced assets" of irrigated areas. The precise amount of this increase could not, General Richard Strachey told the Parliamentary Select Committee on East India Finance in 1872, be separated in a precise way, "but it is not disputed that it would be approximately

[34]See, for example, Government of India (Home Department) to Government, NWP, May 26, 1871, where emphasis is laid on the "great additional value given to the land" by irrigation works, railways, navigation canals, and the opening up of new and profitable markets; NWP, "Revenue Proceedings," February 1872, Index No. 42, June 24, 1871, Proceeding No. 58. No reference is made here to signs of deterioration due to public works.

[35]A. Colvin, *Memorandum*, pp. 97–136.

[36]On the "actual" passed over for the "potential" in assessments, see Moreland, *Revenue Administration*.

about half of what is received as the direct revenue ... Whereas the gross receipts from the Ganges Canal are at the rate of Rs. 2 p. acre on irrigated area, the addition to the land revenue (not appearing on the Canal accounts) is about Re 1 more."[37]

In addition, the Northern India Canal and Drainage Act, VIII of 1873, provided for the assessment of an owners' rate—to be levied at the rate of one-third the existing occupiers' rate.[38] The justification for setting this proportion reflected the conventional method of estimation. M. A. McConaghey, for example, concluded that it was safe to assume that the zamindars of the tracts in Muttra to be commanded by the new Agra Canal "will, within a very short period from the introduction of the system, succeed in realizing from their cultivators, in the shape of enhanced rent, about one-third of the net increase in the value of produce attributable to the canal. Of this enhanced rent, Rs. 2 p. acre on average land, Government is assuredly entitled to its half, Re. 1 p. acre."[39] The rate was duly fixed in accordance with the expected shape of things to come.

By 1876, the fiscal ramification of the canals was as wide-ranging as any medieval lord's charges over his domain—or, for that matter, as wide-ranging as the haqs of a powerful zamindar. Water rates from irrigation; owners' rates on irrigated lands; miscellaneous

[37]Reply to Question 6594, "Report of the Select Committee on East India Finance," *P.P.*, 1872, 8 (327). Compare Strachey's reply to Question 6593: "It is impossible to say in one sentence what, up to the present time, has been the cost of the Ganges Canal to the people of India. The accounts are incomplete." On canal water rates, see p. ooo above. For both the direct and indirect revenue to Government from the canals, NWP, 1876–77 to 1899–1900, see Figure 5.

[38]Act VIII, 1873, §§37–39. For the rules regulating the imposition of owner's rate, see NWP, "Revenue Proceedings," February 1874, Index No. 91, February 14, 1874, Proceeding No. 34; *ibid.*, September 1874, Index No. 28, September 5, 1874, Proceeding No. 53. For the Betwa Canal system in Bundelkhand, completed in the 1880s, the charges were modified. Owner's rate was omitted altogether, and moderate occupier's rates were imposed, "to be gradually raised. As the value of water comes to be appreciated, it is believed the State will best be able to secure the full market price [sic] of its water" by this means; NWP and Oudh, "Revenue Proceedings," December 1885, File No. 210, Serial No. 22, Proceeding No. 1.

[39]M. A. McConaghey, Settlement Officer, Muttra, "Memorandum on the Proposed Water and Owner's Rates to Be Adopted on the New Agra Canal," *NWP Irrigation Revenue Report*, 1873–74, pp. civ, cv–cvi. McConghey calculated the division of increased profits anticipated from irrigation as follows. The gross profits to the cultivator from increased outturn *should* be Rs. 12 on every acre he irrigates. The net benefit to the cultivator after paying for his water and meeting the expenses of distribution (that is, taking only the officially recorded charges into account) *will* be not less than Rs. 6 per acre on an average on land brought within the influence of the canal. (Emphasis supplied.)

receipts from sales of water supplied for purposes other than irrigation and town consumption; water supply for towns; receipts from plantations; receipts from other canal produce (to include proceeds from the sale of wood and grass from canal banks other than registered plantations); water power (to include mill rents and all charges for water applied to turn machinery); navigation receipts (transit dues, transport profits, tolls, hire of boats); rents of buildings; fines (for wastage of water, infringement of canal rules); and, lastly, miscellaneous dues (to include receipts from sale of driftwood, fines on establishment, rents of lands)—each one of these was a recognized head of account.[40]

Throughout the provinces, the 50 percent share of Government of the assumed "net rental assets" (assumed gross assets less the cultivator's residue) was increased indirectly by additional cesses. Table 2 reproduces C. J. Daniell's calculations as to how the total charges which zamindars in Jhansi were regularly liable to pay were to be accounted.[41]

TABLE 2
DISTRIBUTION OF ZAMINDARS' CHARGES IN JHANSI

In Every Rs. 100 of "Rental"	Rupees	Annas	Pies
Government demand	50	0	0
Cesses, road fund, school fund, *dak* (postal cess), moiety	1	2	0
Chaukidar's pay	1	1	11
Bullahar's pay	0	12	4
Patwari's pay[a]	2	5	5
Lambardar's cess (5 percent)[b]	2	8	0
Loss on exchange of local coin into British currency at actual payment of demand	2	8	0
TOTAL	60	5	8

SOURCE: *Jhansi Settlement Report*, pp. 26–27.

a Under the Saharunpur Rules of 1855, § xliii (as cited in *Jhansi Settlement Report*, pp. 26–27), the patwari's pay was to be fixed at a maximum of 3 percent on the average revenue collections for a five-year period.

b This is a diminution *pro tanto* of profits the proprietor would retain were it not levied. On the lambardar and his office, see Chapter VI, pp. 000–000.

[40]NWP and Oudh, "Revenue Proceedings," May 1877, Index No. 33, March 31, 1877, Proceeding No. 59. For additional charges exacted illegally but regularly by the subordinate canal administration appointed by Government, see pp. 88–89 above.

[41]For further details on the imposition of cesses, see W. Muir, Senior Member,

The Distribution of the Revenue Demand

From the first years of British rule, the fundamental problem which faced the administration—having recognized the zamindar as pro-prietor—was how to measure the revenue-paying capacity of the specific territorial assets (the mahal) to which his proprietorial title was held to apply. The summary settlements under the first regulations of 1803 and 1805 answered this crucial question with conjectures, a situation which the first formal settlement under Regulation VII of 1822 only marginally improved. Regulation IX of 1833 brought in the use of vernacular records as a basis for assessment, but experience soon made evident the extent of their defects in this context. The revised settlements provided the only logical answer to the problem of measurement : the absolute standard of the rent rate (by district or pargana) and the general law of the natural capability of the soil were henceforth to be the cardinal principles of revenue procedure. When, consequently, local records were weighed in the settlement officer's balances and were found wanting, they could not but be rejected as invalid. This process of refinement and abstraction meant that the revenue demand, based on estimates obtained with the minimum direct interference in local affairs and calculated in terms of what was assumed to be equitable rather than what was seen to be actual, could take little account of the condition of the revenue-paying classes—zamindars and talukdars. The question of their capacity to meet the demand was not confined to the extent to which the productivity of soils in their mahals corresponded to the settlement officers' assumptions or expectations. It was intimately connected with the relations between zamindars and Government, and with the zamindars' position in local society.

The revision of settlements introduced technical changes in the revenue contracts which can be seen as the culmination of a fifty-year process of definition. This coincided with the culmination of another fifty-year process, the impact of which was felt directly and over a large part of the provinces. The supplanting of "native" rule by an administration which throughout its upper reaches—civil and mili-tary—was solidly staffed by Europeans was complete when Oudh

Board of Revenue, "Note on the Mode of Assessing Cesses at Settlement," April 8, 1863, in NWP, "Revenue Proceedings," October 10, 1863, Index No. 9, April 25, 1863, Proceeding No. 35. See also Board of Revenue, NWP, to Government, NWP, June 10, 1868, in NWP, "Revenue Proceedings," August 8, 1868, Index Nos. 9, 10, July 4, 1868, Proceedings Nos. 43, 44.

had been annexed, the "Mutiny" suppressed, and Crown Government established. This last and most radical phase of the change in administration was registered most clearly in Oudh and in parts of Benares Division—Azamgarh, for example—where relations with the Nawabi had been close.

Prior to annexation, the zamindar's position in, for example, Lucknow district was that of a head man of a group of local maliks, who appointed him for purposes of management. As their representative, he would be summoned to the court of the local *chakladar* (regional revenue official of the Nawab's administration) to take up the revenue contract.[42] His authority was based on that area of his mahal, government-granted or government-guaranteed, in which he lived. To the income from the wide range of sources which made up the mahal, perquisites of office could be added. These were provided by younger and more mobile members of the zamindari group, earned in service to more powerful zamindars and talukdars or at the court of the Nawab himself. Such service regularly absorbed hundreds and thousands of members of the upper strata of society.[43] Each member of a dominant family or coparcenary (as groups of such families were termed by the British revenue authorities)[44] held a claim to the local revenues of the zamindari by reason of his share defined on the basis of his precise relationship within the group. The need to realize this claim seems to have been regularly forestalled in the great majority of instances by the existence of alternative sources of wealth, such as opportunities for civil and military service outside the mahal. Up to 1857-58, the militia of the East India Company had provided these opportunities: according to H. C. Irwin, there were "said to have been sixty thousand Oudh Rajputs and Brahmans, or between two and three, on an average, from every village in the province, in the service of the East India Company."[45]

By 1858, this situation was radically transformed. The overstocked bureaucracy of the Nawabi was disbanded, and European officers replaced the sons and younger brothers of zamindari and talukdari families in British Indian regiments. By 1872, the representation of the upper ranks of society in the civil administration of Oudh was minimal, and incomes from Government employment had contracted drama-

[42]*Lucknow Settlement Report*, p. 89.

[43]See pp. 55–56 above.

[44]This should be distinguished from the joint Hindu family, also termed a "coparcenary" in the Hindu law as administered in British Indian courts.

[45]Irwin, *Garden of India*, p. 48.

tically. C. W. McMinn reported that there were only five "natives" who drew over £600 per year from Government service; forty-one "native" judges on incomes of £300 and over; and forty-nine subordinate judges or *tehsildars* whose annual income was below £300.[46]

The British administration had not been wholly insensitive to the financial problems which reared up for the upper classes on the curtailment of their service perquisites. An award of compensation in the form of malikana, a due to be paid to proprietors at a rate equivalent to their lost profits, was legally prescribed in the first regulations.[47] Under the 1833 settlements, it was fixed at 10 percent on the revenue and was to be paid directly to landowners by the Treasury.[48] The procedure is significant. It was intended to ensure the landowners that their right to this compensatory charge was fully recognized as an obligation to be directly discharged by Government from its land revenue. In 1867, when the Board of Revenue in the NWP recommended that the landowners, with their new legal powers against defaulters (which we shall examine below), could well relieve the revenue administration of the burden of malikana collections and extract the charge themselves, the lieutenant-governor solemnly upheld the Government's duty to safeguard the payments. Referring to a letter of Government to the board in 1844, he noted that it was there clearly shown "that the collection of Malikana by Government and its payment from the Government Treasury to assignees was intended as a boon, bestowed as a portion of compensation given for their exclusion from management." To make any change as proposed—during the term of the current settlements—would, therefore, in the lieutenant-governor's opinion, naturally be regarded as a breach of faith. It could not be sanctioned.[49] The revision of settlements, however, was held to bring an increase in "proprietors' profits" since Government now reduced its demand from 66⅔ percent to 50 percent of the "rental assets." Malikana was promptly reduced in accordance—regardless of the circumstances of

[46]McMinn, *Introduction*, p. 67. According to the Oudh census of 1869, the total population was then 11,174,287. For the composition of the district revenue establishments under the Crown Government, the most comprehensive branch of the British administration, see pp. 235–236 below.

[47]Regulation VIII, 1793, §§ 44, 46, 75, 83; Regulation XXV, 1803, §29; Regulation XXVII, 1803, § 53; Regulation IX, 1805, § 8.

[48]Settlement Circular No. IV, para. 180, in *Directions for Settlement Officers*, para. 113.

[49]Government, NWP, to Board of Revenue, NWP, March 2, 1867 (referring to Government, NWP, to Board, January 17, 1844), in NWP, "Revenue Proceedings," March 2, 1867, Index No. 6, Proceeding No. 30.

zamindars—and became "little more than a compassionate allowance," which the passing of subsequent legislation on the subject merely confirmed.[50]

Such compensatory measures, even in their more lavish form, could do little to remedy the dislocation which resulted from the disarming of the country and the disbanding of a large part of its former administration. There was no alternative open in most cases to the zamindari families but to turn to the land. "A head is no longer required [by the administration]," Butts wrote of the situation in Lucknow during settlement, "and the coparcenars are all confined to their villages; for, to use an expression of their own, their only trade is zamindari."[51] There was no alternative source of income which could make up the deficits. As J. R. Reid noted in Azamgarh, public works in the district could not replace service "in the Native Army and with Native Princes," from which "extraneous source a good deal of money used to come into this part of the country."[52] The chief sufferers not only from the diminution in income but also from the disappearance of their accustomed trappings of power and prestige were the Kshatri or warrior families : "There is everywhere a tacit refusal of all tribute and homage which cannot be enforced by law. The Raja bitterly complains that the peasant, who pays him rent, no longer bows to him; the lowly salam of the grain-dealers, the shopkeepers, the pilgrims, the dancing-girls, is reserved for the English Magistrate who guards the property and punishes the crimes of all ..."[53] To enforce their dwindling authority, zamindars and talukdars kept up sizeable establishments of retainers, ranging from agents who supervised cultivation and the collection of dues to bodyguards armed with cudgels. Observers commonly mistook the social

[50]For a concise account of malikana from the earliest regulations to Act XVII, 1876 (§35), see *Hardoi Settlement Report*, pp. 342–344. The equivalent compensation granted to talukdars, viz. the official haq talukdari, was fixed at 22.5 percent on each talukdar's revenue assessed under the settlements of Regulation IX, 1833. By Government Order IX of January 17, 1844, it was reduced to 10 percent plus the allowance of "a variable sum over and above the equitable right" (that is, the 10 percent), to be open to revision at the death of the grantee. For a clear illustration of the re-examination of such allowances owing to the financial exigencies of Government, from the late 1860s, see "Petition of the Rajah of Mujhowlee, Zillah Gorakhpur," in NWP, "Revenue Proceedings," February 29, 1868, Index No. 9, February 1, 1868, Proceedings Nos. 27, 28. For the decision of the governor-general in the case, confirming life interest only see *ibid.*, Index No. 10, February 29, 1868, Proceeding No. 20.

[51]*Lucknow Settlement Report*, pp. 89–90.
[52]J. R. Reid, quoted by Colvin, *Memorandum*, p. 126.
[53]McMinn, *Introduction*, pp. 71–72.

necessity of the retainer force—especially in the changed circumstances of the later nineteenth century—for a perverse and wilful Oriental extravagance. "The enormous industrial loss caused by the idle pomp of Indian noblemen and princes has been little lessened," McMinn wrote in 1902. "Though no longer are there to be found a hundred thousand armed men waiting near the Mogul, swaggering around in eager expectation of outrage and plunder, yet still each nobleman keeps numerous gangs of swashbucklers ..."[54]

With the intensification of upper-class interests in the land, the problems of defining the area of each "nobleman's" jurisdiction and liability for revenue payments took on nightmarish proportions. The search for the rent rate was a pastime by comparison. We have seen how tenurial complexities arose from the regular operation of partition and inheritance.[55] Struggles to equate the titular claims which recorded shares represented with a quantifiable area of land now became serious. Where sufficient land was available for adequate partitions to be made, some solution could be attempted, at least as far as the legal record went, and settlement officers were well provided with instructions as to how to conduct the arbitration.[56] But the procedure could mean an exhausting wrangle amongst various "proprietary" parties to a dispute as to how to reconcile their respective claims to shares of almost imperceptible minuteness. Reid collected some standard schematic tables of rights and interests of two parganas in Azamgarh, a single example of which should suffice to illustrate the settlement officer's dilemma.[57] Even where shares in complex mahals could be adequately defined, the extent of each sharer's liability to pay revenue still eluded the settlement officers. G. E. Ward, Officiating Collector of Jaunpur in 1878, described a situation which was only too familiar elsewhere in the

---

[54] C. W. McMinn, *Famine Truths*, p. 119. McMinn suggested, by way of a remedy, the introduction of the Elizabethan Vagabondage acts.

[55] See pp. 52–53 above.

[56] The regulations relating to the partition of estates are as follows : Regulation VI, 1807 (rescinded, 1810); Regulation XIX, 1814; Regulation VII, 1822. Act XIX, 1863, codified the existing law relating to "perfect" (that is, complete) partition, with modifications and elaborate rules of procedure. This enactment remained the basis for subsequent legislative prescriptions on partition under the later Rent and Revenue acts (see Appendix 6). For an examination of the problems raised by "imperfect" (that is, incomplete) partitions at the revision of settlements, see C. H. T. Crosthwaite, "Memorandum on Imperfect or Private Partitions," September 21, 1867, in NWP, "Revenue Proceedings," December 21, 1867, Index No. 12, Proceeding No. 110.

[57] *Azamgarh Settlement Report*, Appendix VII, Examplar I. A share might be an

provinces. His example was a large mahal—a whole taluka—which contained twenty-four mauzas (A,B,C ...) broken up into twelve subordinate mahals (I, II, III ...). To simplify the discussion, Ward supposed each mauza to be exactly 1/12 of the taluka and each mahal to contain 1/12 of each mauza. The composition of the twelve mahals would thus be as follows: Mahal I—1/12 A, 1/12 B, 1/12 C, ... 1/12 X, 1/12 Y, 1/12 Z, and so on for II, III, IV, and the remaining mahals. But in practice, the arrangement was much more complicated owing to the fact that the divisors were not equal. The following pattern was more likely to have arisen: Mahal I—1/60 A, nothing in B, 1/10 C, ... 1/100 X, nothing in Y, 1/2 Z; Mahal II—1/30 A, 1/15 B, 1/10 C, ... nothing in X, 1/50 Y, 1/4 Z. On top of this came partition. As a result, mahals of an aggregate area of twenty acres existed which had to be identified on twenty village maps and which were owned by a "proprietary" body of several families. Here was the crux. The "proprietors," as well as the revenue they paid, were arranged by mahals but, as Ward commented, if Mahal I pays Rs. 1,000, "we do not know how much revenue 1/12 A is charged with, or how much 1/12 B pays. We only know that 1/12 A + 1/12 B + 1/12 C ... + 1/12 Z pays a total revenue of Rs. 1,000 ..." The rental assets provided the final complication, since cultivators under each set of proprietors paid them rental but not according to mahals. A cultivator—Ram Baksh of Mahal I, for example—might hold one acre in the 1/12 of A belonging to Mahal I, nothing in 1/12 B, one and one-half acres in 1/12 C, two acres in 1/12 D, one acre in 1/12 E, and nothing in any other mauza. His total holding aggregating eight and one-half acres rented at Rs. 50, but neither Government nor Ram Baksh knew precisely how much of this he paid for his acre in 1/12 A or for his half-acre in 1/12 C ...[58]

---

entire *mahal* or a specific share in a mahal, or a mauza or a specific share in a mauza, or a fixed area measure (a *bigha*, for example).

Division of Shares in Terms of the Rupee as Unit (representing one proprietary share) and Parts of That Unit (representing the possible sub-divisions of a share amongst the proprietary community)

Rupee		Annas		Pies		Kants		Jans		Tils
1	=	16	=	192	=	3,840	=	34,560	=	1,866,240
		1	=	12	=	240	=	2,160	=	116,640
				1	=	20	=	180	=	9,720
						1	=	9	=	486
								1	=	54

[58]E. C. Buck, "Note on the Preparation of a Record-of-Rights in the Permanently-

Even this presented an ideal and simplified situation owing to the assumption that proprietors could be clearly distinguished from cultivators. This had never been the case in reality. Zamindars stood as cultivators in respect to their sir land and any fields which they might lease—under cultivating pattis—from other zamindars for additional income where their shares had dwindled below an economically viable level or where such lease provided them with an entree into a neighbour's territory, enabling them to threaten his power and prestige. The pressure on the land by upper-class claimants displaced from service could not but increase such sub-division. Take Lucknow district, for example. If the rights of some 37 talukdars to a mere 376 mahals could be clearly established in law, whatever the complexities of physical distribution of liability might be, no such easy solution could be found for the overwhelming majority of superior rights : the remaining 1,122 mahals had to be divided amongst no fewer than 14,756 proprietors. Here, too, the distribution was highly unequal. Whilst rights to some 603 mahals were held by a mere 2,832 zamindars, a further 501 mahals aggregating 329,855 acres had no less than 11,574 recorded sharers.[59] In these circumstances and especially in view of the number of subordinate rights established within each mahal or mauza, co-sharers had to take additional fields on lease, an easier task for cultivating classes than for the Kshatris who, like most of the Brahmans, looked first to service for supplementary income.[60] The pattern of rights of a numerous "proprietary brotherhood"—*bhaiachara* tenure—was to the settlement officers nothing more than a tangled mass of confusions. W. E. Neale's problems in defining bhaiachara rights in Etawah were characteristic : "Not only are hereditary rights hard to discover, but they are made doubly hard by the endless inter-transfers and mortgages which the brotherhood always effect, and which are the necessary prelude to the stronger part of the community gradually eating up and ousting the weaker. The transactions are hardly ever recorded as they occur during the current settlement; but at the commencement of a new one they all crop up, and have to be minutely followed out and noted; many, indeed most of them, concerning the smallest areas, and the same area being often several times involved. . . ."[61] Officers continued

Settled Districts," in NWP and Oudh, "Revenue Proceedings," September 1878, Index No. 40, August 24, 1878, Proceeding No. 51.

[59]*Lucknow Settlement Report*, pp. 59, 88–89.
[60]*Kheri Settlement Report*, pp. 26–27.
[61]*Etawah Settlement Report*, p. 126.

assiduously to compile statistical statements of acreages or percentages of cultivated area held by the various categories of the official model of tenurial structure—proprietors, occupancy tenants, tenants-at-will—whilst other passages of their reports showed how the common phenomenon of multiple status rendered such statistics useless. With the operation of mortgage and lease, legal holdings would show the patterns in Table 3, which is based on H. F. Evans' data from Agra district.

TABLE 3
PATTERNS OF LEGAL HOLDINGS

Class of Cultivator	Percent of Total Cultivated Area Held	As Sir (acres)	Average Cultivated With Occupancy Right (acres)	Area Held As Tenants-at-Will (acres)	Total Average Holding (acres)
Proprietors	23.5	9.7	1.2	0.8	11.7
Occupancy tenants	52.1	0	7.7	0.4	8.1
"Privileged tenants"	2.0	0	2.0	0	2.0
Tenants-at-will	22.4	0	0	6.0	6.0

SOURCE: *Agra Settlement Report*, p. 58, for the parganwar statement of average holdings.

The range of revenue-payers throughout the provinces stretched from the few all-powerful talukdars in Oudh districts, controlling large areas—as in the case of the thirty-seven talukdars of Lucknow referred to above—to the mass of zamindari and bhaiachara coparcenars who composed the majority of the proprietorial group. The number of co-shares concentrated on the family or clan holding placed them in a position that was hopelessly uneconomic, whether subdivision had actually taken place or not. The situation of the small coparcenar was, to say the least, unenviable: "little richer than the ordinary cultivator, ... he has generally the richer zamindar's position and liabilities," as Butts observed.[62] Meanwhile, the final assessments, as drawn up on the basis of soil rates and such vernacular records as were broadly consonant with them, had to be declared before the disparate "proprietary bodies" of each pargana and distributed amongst them. The general rule was that a proposed distribution of the demand other than according to the quality of the soil must be approved unanimously. Agreement could hardly be hoped for—predictably, perhaps—where populous zamindaris held

[62]*Lucknow Settlement Report,* p. 90.

or rather struggled to hold superior rights in mahals, that is, over the greater part of the provinces. The distribution of the demand therefore tended either to be entrusted to "the people," by which the more powerful elements of the revenue-paying body were meant, or to be imposed according to the quality of the soil.[63] Where the spread of canal irrigation had accentuated disparities in productivity, improving some parts of a mahal and at the same time causing gross deteriorations in other, usually more low-lying areas, settlement officers laboured to establish a compromise, to strike a mean between soil and recorded rates or between the rate on cultivated as distinct from total revenue-paying area and the proportion of the old jama to the new.[64] As far as the condition of excessively sub-divided tenures was concerned—a more tortuous problem than canal deteriorations—the settlement officer could only use his discretion, hedged about by the necessary regard for Government interests. When Maconochie had completed his calculations for the settlement in Unao, he found it impossible "in many instances . . . to fix a demand on full assets as given by our rates." He was obliged to show some consideration in view of the lengths to which sub-division had gone in the district (severely affected by annexation); otherwise, "the Settlement would have broken down, by the landowners not paying or, more probably, as the good old Nawabi days are still remembered, and men will live, they would have taken to crime. It would probably have been put down in time by the law, but the moral effect of a Government forcing its subjects into crime would have been most fatal in its results. . . ."[65] The settlement officer had to aim in such circumstances at a level of demand as near to the official requirement of "half-assets" as the proprietors had the power of paying. But what standard could they use to estimate this power? The suspicion of fraudulent understatement dominated their view of local records. Little else remained available to them beyond cautious conjecture.

Once the settlements were completed, after years of tireless devotion by the field staff, little could be done to modify them. When complaints were voiced against obvious imperfections and maladjustments, the conventional response from the uppermost reaches of the adminis-

---

[63] *Muttra Settlement Report,* p. 98.

[64] See, for example, A. Cadell's computations, *Muzaffarnagar Settlement Report, Canal Tract,* pp. 88–90.

[65] *Unao Settlement Report,* p. 56.

tration was to emphasize the sacrosanctity of precedent and to "enjoin the necessity of extreme caution" :

On the one hand, we have to consider a system which has been built up by the labours of some of the most eminent men whom India has seen; we are bound to confine our suggestions to that which is practical, and which will confirm itself to the state of property indigenous in these provinces, and as confirmed and modified by the course of nearly three-quarters of a century's legislation; we are bound, also, to consider the prosperity of the country and its ability to resist misfortune of season; and, above all, to remember that the maintenance of a contented and substantial peasantry and proprietary is a condition that must take precedence of every other. On the other hand, we are bound unprejudicially to consider whether the Imperial revenues are in any respect unnecessarily sacrificed, and if so, to the best of our ability to provide a remedy. . . . [66]

The settlements met with little modification, and the demands fixed by them were for the most part met.

The Realization of the Demand

The Board of Revenue accorded to the seasons a paramount role in revenue affairs. Its annual reports began with an account of climatic conditions and a description of the state of the harvests in each division. "To write of the administration of the land revenue," the board maintained, "without some notice of the character of the seasons by which, more than by any other cause, the land revenue is controlled, would be to analyze results without attempting an explanation of the causes which have chiefly produced them. . . ."[67]

District officers of the Revenue Department did not always agree with the board. Cadell, for example, compared the state of things in Banda district—a poorly endowed area where farmers coped with difficult conditions by a semi-shifting pattern of agriculture—under "native" governments with the present-day situation under British rule. The land (that is, the revenue) administration prior to the British had, he concluded, been superior in certain important respects. It had been generally more moderate; it had been unquestionably more elastic; in short, it had been adapted to existing circumstances.

[66]Government, NWP, to Board of Revenue, NWP, June 28, 1871, in NWP, "Revenue Proceedings," March 1874, Index No. 27, March 7, 1874, Proceeding No. 73.
[67]NWP Revenue Administration Report, 1871–72, p. 3.

Since then, British rule had brought with it a number of advantages to Banda—greatly increased security of living, prosperity, and a better administration. Moreover, the extension of British power had meant markets for Banda's produce in the Doab, and the East India Company's operations had already created a greater demand for certain products (Cadell does not specify which), although the fact that no material improvement had taken place in Bundelkhand communications for nearly fifty years (prior to the 1870s) had tended to make these benefits more apparent than real. Then, too, there were the advantages of the reformed revenue system. These, however, did not include either of the two cardinal virtues of the old administration. The severity of British assessments was notorious, as was the inelasticity of demand : collections of revenue in full were insisted upon, irrespective of the seasons.[68]

Who was right, Cadell or the Board of Revenue? A comparison of the statistics of the revenue demand and collections with the state of the harvests over the period 1864-65 to 1884-85[69] suggests the board was arguing more from principle than practice. In 1865-66, for example, the "landholders" were said to have been enabled "to meet their engagements with ease" owing to the prevalence of high prices for all kinds of agricultural produce over the greater part of the provinces. The following year, the same was said of the Rohilkhand landholders. In 1878-79, an indifferent year, prices said to be "fortunately high" everywhere "materially assisted the people to meet the rent and revenue demand" in Allahabad Division, although the kharif there had been only fair and the rabi considerably below average. In the scarcity year 1883-84, nearly all the revenue was collected "without pressure or any approach to difficulty within the year"—a year in which, over many hundreds of square miles, an estimated three-quarters of the total food supply of the people was said to have been annihilated in a crop failure which extended over the greater part of the provinces.[70] The situation was the same for Oudh. In 1864-65, the inadequacy of the monsoon caused an almost total failure of the (staple) rice crop everywhere. Its effects were felt particularly in Sultanpur and the trans-Gogra districts. The price of agricultural produce increased bringing "some distress amongst

[68]*Banda Settlement Report*, p. 95. Details of the pre-British system follow at pp. 96 ff.
[69]Compare Figure 1 with Figures 7 and 8.
[70]*NWP Revenue Administration Reports*, 1865–66, pp. 1–4; 1866–67, pp. 1–3; 1878–79, pp. 1–4; 1883–84, pp. 1–6.

the poorer classes" but enabling "the landholders ... to pay up the revenue" : "It is a matter of much satisfaction that under these circumstances so clear a balance sheet should be shown. The rent-roll exhibits an increase of 1 lakh [Rs. 100,000] over that of 1862-63; out of a Total Demand of Rs. 10,403,660 only Rs. 87,390 (not %) remained uncollected at the end of the year, and of this sum, only Rs. 1,309 were irrecoverable ..."[71] District officers had the authority to apply to the board, in the event of severe natural disorders, for suspension or even remission of a portion of the revenue demand. Little use was made of this prior to 1873, when the principle was enshrined in the new rent and revenue statutes, Acts XVIII and XIX. The collector of Basti even reported that he had not asked for remissions when a hailstorm damaged crops in the district "on the ground that the relief would not reach the cultivator." The board found this regrettable, and trusted in the new legislation to make such relief more readily available.[72] However, implementation of the statutory provisions was obstructed, as a narrative of relief operations during the scarcity of 1877-78 and 1879 clearly shows : "Not the least important question for decision at a time when the condition of all classes of the community was one of grave anxiety was : what course to follow regarding the realization of land revenue? were there any remissions or suspensions to be granted? if so, under what circumstances and to what extent?" Such was the issue before the local Government. But external pressures had to be considered. "The time when the kharif fell due [the kharif had failed] was one of great financial pressure, in consequence of heavy expenditure incurred in famine relief in Bombay and Madras. The Government of India thought it necessary under the circumstances to remind the local Government that, with reference to the character of the settlement, proposals or promises for remission ought not to be encouraged, and, in view of the experience of past famines and droughts in these provinces, held that it would be a direct encouragement to thoughtless unthrift were the demand even to be suspended on any great scale." With this admonition, the matter was left "to the discretion of the local Government."[73] Over those years of widespread failure in the

[71]*Oudh Revenue Administration Report*, 1864–65, Pt. I, p. 1. The error in accounting—Rs. 87,390 is more than one-half of one percent of the total demand—is in the report. From 1873–74, the order of presentation in the Oudh reports was changed. The section on revenue from then on included one paragraph only on agricultural conditions, accompanying an annual rainfall statement.

[72]*NWP Revenue Administration Report*, 1872–73, p. 9.

[73]D. G. Pitcher, *Report on the Scarcity*, 1877–1879, pp. 12–13.

harvests, neither a general remission nor a general suspension of revenue was sanctioned.[74] This position, however loudly lamented, did not change. The Board of Revenue reported the (minimal) amount of kharif suspensions made during the drought of 1881, and at the same time stated "their fear ... that the discretion allowed to Settlement Officers was too cautiously exercised, and considering the period of trial which the cultivating classes have passed through, principally in Allahabad division and Agra district, it is a matter of surprise that the Government revenue has been so easily got in, and that without recourse to coercive measures. ..."[75] The revised rent law, Act XII of 1881, included the same provisions on remissions and suspensions as its predecessor—and implementation of these ran into the same obstructions from the procedure which protected the Government against rash action. R. S. Aikman, the Collector of Etah, inveighed against the elaborate rules formulated under Section 23 of the act, which necessitated the already hard-worked district establishment to go out and assess, field by field, the damage done in the event of hailstorms, floods, or drought. Their purpose was to calculate the amount of rent and the proportionate amount of revenue to be remitted or suspended and to distribute this between the tenants and under-tenants in the case of rent, and amongst the different pattis and mahals in the case of revenue : "It is little wonder that men blaspheme because of the plague of the hail. The rules are workable where the harvest of a limited number of villages is destroyed. But the procedure is so laborious that it would be impossible to apply it to a calamity of any great extent—say, for instance, the destruction by drought of the crops of a whole tahsil ..."[76] The 1877-78 situation thus remained unchanged. Government continued to lose little of its collections on account of remissions. It was the same story as takavi,[77] attributable to the same causes.

[74]*Ibid.*, p. 282. For 1873 to 1876, the official figures for remissions of rent in NWP came to Rs. 208,000 and of revenue Rs. 111,000. Suspensions over the same period amounted to Rs. 89,000 in rent and Rs. 42,000 in revenue. See E. C. Buck, "Note on the Collection of Land Revenue," in "Report of the Indian Famine Commission, 1879," *P.P.*, 1881, 71, Appendix I, p. 171.

[75]*NWP Revenue Administration Report*, 1880–81, p. 12. The total demand in the affected districts was Rs. 15,614,604. Of this, only Rs. 736,519 (less than 5 percent) remained uncollected on account of scarcity at the close of the revenue year. Returns for the following year showed that a great proportion of those outstandings was "being rapidly got in."

[76]*NWP Revenue Administration Report*, 1882–83, pp. 4–5.

[77]See pp. 110–118 above.

Far from being controlled by the condition of the harvests, the realization of the revenue demand depended on the zamindars' capacity to mobilize their resources and pay it. These resources were, first, the extent of cultivated and cultivable area under the control of a zamindar or zamindari group; second, the charges levied under the authority of a haq zamindari on all who lived or farmed within the limits of a mahal; and third, the amount which could be raised by borrowing. The total yield had to cover the Government's demand, the claims of dependants, and the requirements of conspicuous consumption for the maintenance of prestige; in many cases it had also to satisfy a simple urge for rapacity.

Increases in the revenue demand under the revised settlements necessitated increased exploitation of these resources by the zamindars, but the rate of increase of their wealth could be effectively cancelled out by the satisfaction of prior claims. Assessments which were pitched in accordance with sound if abstract principles of political economy and the equitable claims of Government could represent an increase of from 40 percent to 100 percent over the previous jama within a single tahsil which was regarded as highly productive by the settlement officer—as, for instance, tehsil Jalalabad in Shahjahanpur district. Even the well-to-do proprietors found it difficult to meet the new demand; to others who had suffered even under light assessments in the past it brought absolute ruin. "The larger the number of share-holders, the more mouths dependent on the surplus profits," R. G. Currie wrote. "It is not a mere matter of some luxury being temporarily given up, but perhaps one meal a day given up or a daughter left unmarried for several years for want of means ..." Nonetheless, Currie ordered reductions in the demand only where "considerable" increases had occurred—a course which was duly approved by the Board of Revenue.[78]

Expansion of cultivation offered little by way of a solution to zamindars to the problem of how to increase their means, since it almost automatically entailed an enhancement of the revenue demand and the result could not be other than a vicious spiral. Far more commonly, zamindars looked to their haqs to cope with new pressures and chiefly to the charges on cultivators which secured the greater part of their income. "Almost all, if not all, the extra and abnormal demands made on the zamindar by Government were passed on

[78]Shahjahanpur Settlement Report, pp. 43–44.

by him to the tenants," as A. M. Markham commented apropos of Bijnour district.[79]

Viewed as a landlord-tenant relationship, the dealings of zamindars with cultivators on their mahals invariably left much to be desired. Butts' picture of Lucknow landlords was typical of those found in official reports : "They would seem to spend little in improving their estates, little in promoting the comfort or happiness of the numerous classes of labourers who till their lands. If a kachha well is to be dug, it is the tenant that finds the capital. If seed grain is to be purchased, it is the landlord perhaps who will supply the money, but a rate of interest of 25 or 36 percent, to be afterwards repaid with the capital. This is the chief intercourse of the landlord, and in valuing his lands and collecting his rents lie his only acknowledged functions . . ."[80] Such functions might be acknowledged as the landlords', but they were exercised by agents, which sent McMinn into one of his characteristically vehement denunciations of the upper classes of Oudh : "Their tenantry are so numerous, their farms and interests individually so petty, the nobles themselves are so indolent, their state and customs are so obstructive of rapid locomotion or personal enquiries, that there is no chance of their ever becoming well acquainted with their tenantry. An English landowner knows far more about his tenantry than any native noble, who cannot take a morning walk without a retinue consisting largely of rogues and eavesdroppers. . . ."[81] The revised settlements, in adding to the zamindar's needs and inclinations to exact charges, could hardly bring about an improvement in his relations with cultivators. As far as Butts could see, the Lucknow zamindars tended to by-pass the privileged groups of Thakurs and Brahmans and come down hard on "the remaining classes—the labourers of the soil, without traditional privileges, without resources, and without ambition, who cling to the soil as affording them the only visible means of support . . . It is these classes that largely make up the population, and it depends upon the forbearance of the landlord whether their life is to be one of comfort or of want and poverty."[82]

The vulnerability of this unprivileged majority is undeniable. But the position of upper-class cultivators vis-a-vis the zamindars

[79]*Bijnour Settlement Report*, pp. 89–91.
[80]*Lucknow Settlement Report*, p. 92.
[81]McMinn, *Introduction*, pp. 109–110.
[82]*Lucknow Settlement Report*, pp. 1–2.

was more complicated than Butts' note suggests. The Bengal Recovery of Rents Act, X of 1859 (extended some months later to the NWP), was the pioneer of agrarian legislation. It recognized *inter alia* a landlord's power to enhance the rent of his tenants in accordance with the power assumed by the chief landlord—Government—to enhance its claim to revenue. S. M. Moens, for one, saw in this power of enhancement a cause for bitter antagonism between zamindars and cultivators: to the latter, at least as far as Bareilly district was concerned, it was nothing but a curse.[83] But the zamindar was not unobstructed in the exercise of his new power over the whole cultivating community. It was only the unprivileged "tenants-at-will"— the majority of the population, it is true—to whom no new legal rights were extended. The regulation of the zamindar's relations with this class of cultivators was regarded, in accordance with contemporary theory, as being beyond the duty of Government. Act X of 1859 strengthened potential opposition to the zamindar from privileged groups. It created a prescriptive right of occupancy, to be claimed at law by cultivators on presentation of proof of their continuous occupation or cultivation of a given holding over a period of not less than twelve years.[84] Occupancy status was attractive. It had no direct liability to revenue; it was legally constituted as free from the guarantee of the zamindar; it entitled the holder to resist, in the courts, the zamindar's attempts at enhancement; in short, it enabled cultivators so designated to threaten the zamindar's authority. The struggles between "landlord" and "occupancy tenant" manifested themselves in a variety of forms. Suits by zamindars for ouster generally aimed at preventing the accrual of occupancy rights within their mahals; legal status and the power of access to the courts dominated the issue, whilst physical possession was a secondary concern. In one district alone, Saharanpur, the number of suits brought under Act X of 1859 rose from 711 in 1861 to 1,029 in 1863 and 2,075 in 1864—a fact attributed by the officiating collector to the zamindars' anxiety to secure themselves against occupancy claims.[85] Some zamindars achieved this by the subtle means of refusing to accept rent payments. The tenant would, it was expected, find the temptation to spend the money irresistible, arrears would accumulate—and the zamindar would win a decree in the courts for ouster. The law offered

[83]*Bareilly Settlement Report*, pp. 55–56.
[84]See Appendix 8.
[85]*NWP Revenue Administration Report*, 1864–65, p. 6.

no corrective for such practices.[86] Enhancement suits provided the stiffest legal battles, which in many cases zamindars were forced to fight by reason of the revised settlements themselves:

The Settlement Officers in these Provinces assess the land revenue estimated on the estimated rents obtainable for the various kinds of soil in an estate, and not on the actual rents paid in any estate. Hence it frequently happens that a landholder finds himself compelled to sue suddenly for generally enhanced rents in order to enable him to realize the full amount payable by his tenants, but which from one cause or another may not have been exacted during currency of the last settlement. Under the Court Fees Act he is called upon to pay heavily to do this, though he very often cannot afford the risk of the expense. If however he should succeed, the costs of the suit are frequently thrown on a body of cultivators, who have at the same time to pay a higher rent and are burdened with the expenses of the suit. . . .[87]

The fact that no adequate solution could be found for enhancement disputes made the struggles more bitter and more prolonged.[88] The amount of enhancement was to be fixed legally by reference to a "standard rate for the pargana or vicinage." What could this be? Not the settlement officer's estimates which were themselves impugned. Nor the vernacular records which were manipulated by local interests, that is, by the zamindars. No practical standard existed. Litigation merely served to perpetuate the issue, whilst the relations between zamindars and occupancy tenants worsened. "Rents will rise as civilization progresses and intelligence increases," Butts concluded cheerfully, "but rent enhancement in many cases seems to amount to mere spoliation, or that is how the tenants look at it."[89] The necessity for rents to rise was a pious wish voiced in the Secretariat, where the obstinate refusal of rural phenomena to follow the principles of political

[86]Board of Revenue to Government, NWP, September 26, 1867, in NWP, "Revenue Proceedings," November 23, 1867, Index No. 78, October 12, 1867, Proceeding No. 48. The same practices were used by zamindars against co-sharers. Zamindars found other means of preventing cultivators from acquiring the prescriptive right of occupancy; for example, they compelled them to change their fields, thus breaking the continuation of the tenancy before the twelve-year period expired. See W. Crooke, "Note on the Famine Commission's Note on the Relations of Landlord and Tenant," in NWP and Oudh, "Revenue Proceedings," May 1882, pp. 26–29.

[87]Board of Revenue to Government, NWP, December 5, 1870, in NWP, "Revenue Proceedings," October 1872, Index No. 4, December 31, 1870, Proceeding No. 30.

[88]On the (insoluble) problem of proof of adequate, and equitable, enhancement, see Board of Revenue to Government, NWP, March 13, 1872, in NWP, "Revenue Proceedings," October 1872, Index No. 7, April 13, 1872, Proceeding No. 2.

[89]*Lucknow Settlement Report*, p. 70.

economy brought forth a stream of comments and enquiries. To Auckland Colvin, for one, it was clear that the answer could not be found in the text-books but was to be sought "in the history of the public land revenue assessment, and the agricultural economy of the people." But the financial exigencies of Government cut short any such attention to the realities that ruled the differentiation of local charges. As Colvin himself went on to state, "it is nevertheless to a rise in rents that the Provinces must in future mainly look to [for] an increase of the public revenue from the land."[90] With the move to enhance rents, dictated by the revised settlements, came attempts to consolidate zamindari "cesses" with "rents" and thus bring them within the range of assessment. Under the NWP Revenue Act, XIX of 1873, cesses regarded as "deriving from the occupation of land" were henceforward to be included with the zamindar's rent.[91] Miscellaneous *sayer* revenues were legally abolished—though the settlement officer's only sanction against zamindars continuing such exactions seems to have been to refuse to record them in the official set of village papers. In one instance, however, the new prohibition on the levy of fees on trades provided local competitors with an opportunity to dispute a zamindar's authority: in Moradabad, Banias refused to pay the rent assessed on their shops.[92]

Where such orders were strictly carried out (no evidence exists as to what extent this was done) with the aim of preventing trade from being unduly hampered, they must, as Alexander commented, "have caused rather severe loss to the zamindars."[93] Theoretically, this could be made up by increased legal charges, where a zamindar was strong enough to take them. But where this was impracticable or the yield insufficient, there remained another resource: the widespread practice of borrowing. The supply of funds for revenue payments had been an established business of "agricultural capitalists" prior to British rule, as the bankers of Oudh so clearly illustrate.[94] The British revenue assessments provided these "agricultural capitalists" with increased opportunities for business. This was not merely the result of increases in demand exacted irrespective of the state of the harvests,

[90]Colvin, *Memorandum*, p. 130.

[91]Act XIX, 1873, § 66.

[92]*Moradabad Settlement Report*, pp. 64–65. For examples of the nature and extent of zamindars' bazar charges, see pp. 45–46 above.

[93]*Ibid*. No evidence was given as to the precise extent of loss resulting from such restrictions.

[94]See pp. 57–58 above.

nor was it confined to areas where such increases coincided with a greater concentration of numbers within the limits of zamindaris; the way in which the timing of collections throughout the provinces was arranged necessitated it.

The principle on which the *kists,* or instalments for the payment of revenue, had been fixed under the first settlements in the NWP was as follows. Since Government, "according to India's ancient constitution," held a right to a portion of all produce of the soil, it had in consequence a lien on this portion and could insist on the satisfaction of its claim before the crops were actually harvested. This Government not only could do but did, for the kists were fixed at dates prior to the harvest times. Collectors and the deputy local officials, the tehsildars, were empowered to appoint their own watchmen to prevent the removal of crops before the Government demand was paid or before adequate security at least was furnished against its eventual payment. Thirty years later, official opinion came to deplore the "hardship and impolicy of thus forestalling, as it were, the country's revenues" and dismissed the old arrangement of kists as nothing more than "the rude device of a state of society, where there was little security for life or property, and where property had consequently lost its right value." In 1840-41, Government formally renounced its lien for the current revenue account on the standing crop. The number of kists was reduced from eight, or in some districts from nine, to four, and these were theoretically timed to allow for both the cutting of the crops and their marketing: the two kharif kists were set for November, December, or January, and rabi kists were set for after May 1, with a month's interval between the two kists for each harvest. Further, Government now looked to the estate on which the demand was levied and to other property of the *malguzar* (revenue-payer) for its security and to the standing crop only where estates were in arrears with their payments. The value thus conferred on the property would, it was believed, guard against any loss to Government. Opposition to the new procedural changes was voiced in two quarters: first, by the tehsildars whose power was legally circumscribed by the re-arrangement of the kists in that it removed an instrument for the control of cultivators from their grasp; and second, by "the money-lenders" who were said to be now "less necessary to the agriculturists." The people themselves were said to have "failed generally to understand or appreciate the boon and, like all ignorant people, were suspicious and apprehensive of further design." Government, however, was enthusiastic : the new system was reported in 1846 to be working well, and agricultural prosperity was evident wherever the assessments themselves had been moderate.[95] No further enquiry therefore as to how the revenue was being paid was encouraged. It was expressly stated in the official *Directions* that "so long as the Revenue is punctually paid, it is most important that the Collector, as a fiscal officer, should abstain from all interference with the mahal. The great desire and object of the Government is to teach the people self-government and punctual payment to bar all direct interference by Government fiscal officers."[96]

The question of the arrangement of kists was reopened, inevitably, by the revision of settlements. In 1872, the Board of Revenue presented its summary of district officers' reports on the matter to the local Government. Its conclusions were clearly stated : the revised kists had provided for crops to be cut but not in practice to be marketed before the revenue demand was collected. One month before marketing, cultivators had to pay up those charges to the zamindars which Government labelled "rent." Since the revenue payments had to be made in cash, it was cash which had to be borrowed for this purpose; therefore, "besides the rent and revenue payable, a large sum was annually charged to cultivators and landlords in the shape of interests."[97] Nor was this all, as Crosthwaite observed : "The simultaneous demand for £1,000,000 sterling from the agricultural classes must, and does, cause the value of money to rise very much. And a loan which at another time could be had at the rate of 36% p.a., at the time of the revenue instalments costs 72% ..."[98] Moneylenders—and this included zamindars and rich peasants who also supplied cultivators with loans—rather than becoming less necessary to agriculturists, had retained their position of control in spite of the legal re-adjustment of the kists; if anything, they had strengthened it. The burden of the land revenue, which may in itself have been a moderate estimate, was enormously increased by credit charges with the advantage, as the board concluded, accruing "only to the moneylender. Unless for the administrative purposes of Government the maintenance of such a system is desirable, the Board consider that

[95] *Directions for Collectors of Land Revenue*, paras. 30–32, pp. 13–14.

[96] *Ibid.*, para. 34.

[97] Board of Revenue to Government, NWP, March 16, 1872, in NWP, "Revenue Proceedings," May 1873, Index No. 9, April 6, 1873, Proceeding No. 55. See also *Cawnpore Settlement Report*, pp. 102–103.

[98] *Etwah Settlement Report*, pp. 89–90.

no time should be lost in relieving the agricultural community of the heavy pressure now placed upon them. Nothing but the most urgent public benefit can justify the Government in imposing, in addition to the demand for revenue, an annual payment of interest which falls probably little short of two millions sterling. . . ."[99] It was true that the kists as fixed in the 1840s had been intended to cover the time required for the marketing of produce. That they had failed to do so "was owing to an error of judgment on the part of the officers who formerly fixed the dates of those instalments."[100]

If, however, a greater interval were permitted between the time of the crops' disposal in the markets and the exaction, in cash, of the revenue demand, how could Government guard against the zamindars' misappropriation of funds thus lying idle for a time, funds which belonged legally to Government? Government could not risk the resignation of a part of its income since, as the officiating collector of Farukhabad observed, the cash balances at the Government treasuries had to be maintained at a certain figure which varied not with fluctuations in local conditions but "with the State's financial circumstances."[101] Yet if the interval were not allowed, how could the burden of interest on the agricultural community be lightened? The board called for opinions from the settlement officers as to practical action.

The great majority advocated the reduction in the number of kists from four to two, with one for the kharif and one for the rabi. As to actual dates, the board could only give a general directive : no kist should fall due till fifteen days after the ripening and harvesting of all or part of the crop. As a rule, the kharif kist was to fall not earlier than December 15 or later than February 1, the rabi kist not earlier than April 15 or later than June 15. On this principle, the settlement officers were to fix the dates themselves—no uniform date for the whole province being possible in view of the irregularity of local harvesting times—and to fix the proportions of revenue payable at each date.[102] After five years of discussing "this urgent problem," the Government's conclusion was that the practical result of the new rules "would not delay the incoming revenue substantially." Before

[99]Board to Government, NWP, cited above, n. 97.
[100]*Ibid.*
[101]Officiating Collector, Farukhabad, September 8, 1870, in "Abstract of Replies to Board's Circular AAA, 20 July 1870, on the . . . Payment of the Revenue Instalments," in NWP, "Revenue Proceedings," May 1873, Index No. 12, April 6, 1873, Proceeding No. 58.
[102]Board's general directive in "Abstract of Replies," cited above, n. 101.

the revision of the kists, the revenue had seldom all been collected before January; after it, in 1875, it was reported to be reaching the Treasury at much the same time.[103] The board's conclusion, of the same year, showed no advance on the position it had held at the beginning of the enquiry: the information and knowledge of agricultural facts, upon which the arrangement of revenue instalments should be based, were "too little advanced to enable district officers to frame their proposals in accordance with the instructions enunciated by Government and by the Board. But the collection of facts, and the application of the knowledge gained from them must be a work of time, and it is for this reason that the rules which the local Government have lately issued contemplate a gradual rather than an immediate change."[104]

Any more effective action by settlement officers was prevented by certain a priori restrictions. To accommodate the range of local needs, a flexibility in the arrangement of kists was demanded which could not be met by the administration: "The Board are anxious to fetter district officers' discretion as little as possible but they think that except for very special reasons, the number of instalments payable in the year should not exceed four, and in many cases three (two for the kharif and one for the rabi) would suffice. The people's convenience is undoubtedly the main point to be looked to but the multiplication of instalments means additional work in keeping the accounts and additional trouble and expense in collecting the revenue, to which considerations some weight may be attached ..." In the same communication, the Board of Revenue insisted that "no effort has been spared to fix those dates which are convenient to the people."[105] The general practice of settlement officers was to draw up sets of three or maximum four kists from which the zamindars of mauzas grouped according to similarity in soil conditions were to choose the set they would prefer.[106] Zamindars were understandably reluctant to loose

[103]Board of Revenue to Government, NWP, January 11, 1875, NWP, "Revenue Proceedings," February 1875, Index No. 17, February 6, 1875, Proceeding No. 36. For the procedure of the *kist* enquiry, 1870 to 1875, see pp. 264–266 below.

[104]NWP, "Revenue Proceedings," cited above, n. 103.

[105]Board of Revenue to Government, NWP and Oudh, February 28, 1881. The board attacked an unspecified "London magazine" for criticizing Government on the basis of information of 1870 to 1872. "The whole system," said the board, "has been entirely remodelled in the past ten years." NWP and Oudh, "Revenue Proceedings," April 1881, Index No. 47, March 26, 1881, Proceeding No. 35A.

[106]For the procedure, see, for example, *Etah Settlement Report*, pp. 69 ff. (S. O. B. Ridsdale, pargana Mahrehra); *Shahjahanpur Settlement Report*, pp. 48–49 (R. G. Currie,

such hold on cultivators as the kists had given them and therefore tended to choose such re-adjusted sets as left the former system virtually unmodified. The Board of Revenue was aware that the "agricultural interest"—as the zamindars were termed collectively in a communication of 1872—was "generally averse to a change," but they (the board) agreed with district officers in believing that "native opinion in such a matter must not be too jealously respected. The economic advantages of a change in the system are probably not easily appreciated by the majority ... Native opinion here is probably more guided by a characteristic dislike to change of any kind in any established system, than by well-grounded reasons for fearing the consequences from which it professes to recoil ..."[107] For the most part, zamindars were given such power to manipulate the proposed alterations in the kists that their interests and Government's coincided. Where complaints against innovation did break out was where zamindars feared that change of dates deprived them of their former power of distraint over the cultivators' crops. Such fears were owing to forgetfulness or ignorance, as F. N. Wright noted apropos of the outraged Cawnpore zamindars. They could continue to distrain the crops of tenants-at-will whose rents fell due, as before, at the ripening of the harvest :[108] "as the law stands, the landlord can demand his rent from a tenant-at-will whenever he pleases."[109] The occupancy tenant had some measure of protection, but even his crops could legally be distrained by the zamindar at the harvest subsequent to his default on rent payment.[110] These provisions added to the vulnerability of the tenant-at-will and created a further *casus belli* in the relations between zamindar and occupancy tenant.

Given these conditions, no formal re-adjustment of kists could alter the way in which revenue was realized to any significant degree. As W. A. Forbes commented in 1873, "whether you have two kists for each harvest, or half a dozen, revenue is, as a fact, collected in the same way as rent—that is, when you can get it."[111] Zamindars either

tehsil Jellalabad [Jalalabad]; *Muzaffarnagar Settlement Report, Canal Tract* (Alan Cadell), pp. 90–91.

[107]Board of Revenue to Government, NWP, March 16, 1872, in NWP, "Revenue Proceedings," May 1873, Index No. 9, April 6, 1873, Proceeding No. 55.

[108]*Cawnpore Settlement Report*, p. 103. See also *Muttra Settlement Report*, p. 98.

[109]Since "this class of tenants have no security to offer except the crop"; see NWP and Oudh, "Revenue Proceedings," April 1881, Index No. 48, March 26, 1881, Proceeding No. 36 (comment on *Oudh Revenue Administration Report*, 1874–75, paras. 126–133).

[110]*Cawnpore Settlement Report*, p. 103.

[111]W. A. Forbes, Officiating Junior Member, Board of Revenue, NWP, "Note

accepted the change in timing because it perpetuated their control or they ignored it. The result for the cultivators was predictable. As Neale reported sadly from Etawah, "a better arrangement of the revenue instalments ought at once to give them [the agriculturists] in a great measure the desired opportunity to escape from their thraldom. But though this change has been instituted and is now in operation in this district, it has so far neither benefited nor even en-lightened the great mass it was specially designed to help ..."[112] This thraldom was exacerbated but not caused by the working of the revenue system. The dilemma facing the administration over the adjustment of kists touched on a more complex problem which involved the greater part of the population : indebtedness.

---

on Revenue and Rent Instalments," in NWP, "Revenue Proceedings," May 1873, Index No. 16, April 19, 1873, Proceeding No. 42.

[112]*Etawah Settlement Report*, p. 111.

Chapter IV

THE PROBLEM OF INDEBTEDNESS

Lending cash and grain to meet the needs of local farmers had long been an essential feature of agriculture in the provinces. Creditors came from all but the poorest strata of rural society: well-to-do peasants acquired an interest in their neighbours' produce through the loan of a few maunds or a few rupees; mahajans (dealer-bankers) lent out a portion of their stocks as a regular part of their trade; and maliks used loans to tighten their control over subordinate cultivators and to enhance their local prestige which was measured in numbers of dependants.[1] The working of the British revenue system created further incentives to borrow, but Government supplied no alternative agency of any significance to provide credit. Quite the reverse: the supply of loans from the Treasury to the rural population contracted under British rule because of the marked decline in takavi advances.[2] Private creditors were therefore free to exploit the increased need for credit, and the provision of loans became indisputably the most profitable area for investment of local capital in the later nineteenth century. The reverse side of the coin was the problem of indebtedness.

The Supply of Local Credit

Contemporary estimates of the number of peasants who resorted to borrowing as a regular source of supply were vague. In the absence of detailed local enquiry into the "question of agricultural indebtedness,"[3] such information as was officially recorded on the subject came

[1]See p. 36 above.

[2]See pp. 110–118 above and Figure 6.

[3]Between 1860 and 1900, only one official enquiry into indebtedness was made, prompted by reports of severe distress among cultivators in Oudh in 1868–69 and restricted to that province. The evidence collected in the course of this (cursory) enquiry by the revenue administration was published as "Correspondence Relating to the Indebtedness of Cultivators in Oudh," in *Selections from the Records of Government*

from the observations of district officers incidentally in the course of settlement work. Statistics accompanying these observations were little more than arithmetical translations of a general impression : the most frequent estimate—75 to 80 percent of the cultivating body— meant simply the majority.[4]

"Except in masonry wells," commented R. H. Davies, then Chief Commissioner of Oudh, summing up the results of the 1869 indebtedness enquiry, "little capital is permanently invested in the soil. Cultivators and their families, unlike the *metayers* of Europe, provide their own farming stock, bullocks, ploughs, tools, gear, manure. They are mostly too poor to store seed for the better sorts of produce, or maintain themselves on poorer grains from harvest to harvest ... Therefore they are very generally, though in varying degrees, dependent on extraneous aid ..."[5] Besides the common bijkhad (seed and food) loans, a peasant might borrow cash to pay dues, where his zamindar's share of the produce was taken in cash, to buy cattle, or to spend on festivals, weddings, or funerals in order to fulfill his social obligations.[6] The actual volume of debt varied with the seasons in any given area, since a significant section of the peasantry—the exact extent of which could never be defined with the means of enquiry to hand—borrowed when adverse circumstances compelled it, as E. C. Buck concluded from enquiries in pargana Bilhaur, Cawnpore

(Oudh), 1868–69 (hereafter cited as *Oudh Selections*, 1868–69). According to the terms of the enquiry, the deputy commissioner of each district was requested to submit a brief report (generally six to eight paragraphs), including an area statement of kharif and rabi crops, a description of the ways in which unindebted and indebted cultivators disposed of their produce, a description of their interest charges and modes of account, and practical suggestions as to how cultivators might be "rendered more independent." *Ibid.*, pp. 1–3.

[4]See A. H. Harington, "Economic Reform in Rural India : Agricultural Indebtedness," *Calcutta Review*, LXXVI (1883), 153–181, citing settlement reports and district gazetteers of the NWP and Oudh. In Moradabad (1881) and Agra (1871), for example, the majority of cultivators were said to be indebted—so also in Unao (1867), for seed loans. In Gonda and Pratabgarh (1868), a "large majority" borrowed. In Fatehpur, Sitapur, Kheri, and Fyzabad (1878), 75 percent were said to be indebted ; in Sultanpur, Rae Bareli (1868), and Bara Banki (1878), 80 percent. Only in Bareilly, during settlement, was an attempt made to take a rough sample from specific villages ; a random sample taken from ninety-three villages showed that the majority of cultivators were indebted for some purpose, and that 66.8 percent borrowed their seed grain.

[5]R. H. Davies, "Memorandum on the Correspondence Relating to the Indebtedness of Cultivators in Oudh," November 10, 1869, *Oudh Selections*, 1868–69, pp. 71–72.

[6]See, for example, *Bareilly Settlement Report*, p. 55; *Oudh Selections*, 1868–69, p. 64 (Rae Bareli). In Muttra district, a large proportion of the cultivators was reported to borrow or hire ploughs and plough cattle; see *Muttra Settlement Report*, p. 48.

district, in 1871.[7] A debt once borrowed, especially in circumstances of hardship owing to crop failures, was difficult to clear: A. Young reported from Sultanpur that much of the indebtedness current in 1868 dated back to the bad harvests of 1864-65.[8]

Mahajans, the stereotyped "village creditors" of Government records, made their loans according to recognized—and written—systems of account. The charges reportedly levied by dealers on rabi grain loans in Bareilly, for example, where cultivators' indebtedness was looked on "as the natural state of affairs,"[9] are set out in Table 4, while local modes of account common in Oudh in 1868-69 are set out in Table 5. Charges were also exacted in advance; *daswana* and *bilsah* or *kast* deductions were common in Oudh. According to the first, Rs. 100 was recorded as the loan, Rs. 90 was paid over to the debtor, and Rs. 100 was to be repaid; the deduction amounted thus to a 10 percent interest charge. According to the second, 2.5 to 6 seers per rupee of recorded debt were deducted in advance, with the actual amount of the deduction determined by the relative fineness or coarseness of the grain.[10]

TABLE 4

CHARGES LEVIED ON RABI GRAIN LOANS IN BAREILLY

Indigenous Term	Amount/Value Borrowed in Kartik (October-November	Amount/Value Repaid in Jeth (May-June)
Deora (1.5 times)	5 maunds	7.5 maunds
Bhao up siwaia (1.25 times the current prices at harvest)	5 maunds (worth Rs. 10)	Rs. 12.8.0 worth of grain
No indigenous name given	Rs. 10 worth of grain	Rs. 10 worth of grain calculated at 2.5 seers per rupee lower than market price
Deora nirikh katke[a] (1.5 times the current price, at harvest)	5 maunds (worth Rs. 10)	Rs. 15 worth of grain (50 percent)

SOURCE: *Bareilly Settlement Report*, p. 55.
[a] This type of charge was exacted by only a few extortionate zamindars in pargana Aonlah.

[7]E. C. Buck cited by Harington, "Economic Reform in Rural India," *Calcutta Review*, LXXVI (1883), 155.
[8]*Oudh Selections*, 1868–69, pp. 64–65.
[9]*Bareilly Settlement Report*, p. 55.
[10]Davies, "Memorandum on . . . the Indebtedness of Cultivators in Oudh," *Oudh Selections*, 1868–69, pp. 72–73. The literal meaning of *daswana* is "one-tenth"; that of *bilsah* or *kast* is unknown.

TABLE 5

MODES OF ACCOUNT COMMON IN OUDH IN 1868–69

Indigenuous Term	Borrowed	Amount Entered in Books	Repaid
Ugahi	Rs. 10	Rs. 11	Rs. 11, in instalments, Re. 1 per month
Up	1 maund	1.25 maunds	Value of 1.25 maunds repaid in money at 25 percent interest; in case of default, amount to be increased to 5 seers for each rupee unpaid
Sahogat	1 maund	1 maund	Value of 1 maund at rate of 2 maunds per rupee below current price till debt is satisfied

SOURCE: R. H. Davies, "Memorandum on the Correspondence Relating the Indebtedness of Cultivators in Oudh," November 10, 1869, in Government of Oudh, *Selections from the Records of the Government,* 1868–69, pp. 72–73. The precise meaning of the vernacular terms in unclear.

The range of charges included under the general head of "interest" defied any supposition of the existence of a uniform rate. As in the case of their fruitless search for a rent rate, district officers were baffled as to what might be the principle governing this business of loans. "I know of no rational explanation," E. Thompson reported from Sitapur in 1869,

of the extraordinary difference between the rates of interest prevailing in localities removed perhaps only a few miles from each other and in which, so far as we know, the risks are alike; why in one village the cultivator should pay 50%, and in another 100%, and yet there is nothing unusual in this. The rate of interest on mortgage of landed property in parts of Sitapur was for many years fixed by the same inexorable custom at $37\frac{1}{2}$% p.a. without limitation as to amount, while in others no more interest could in any case be claimed than 50% on the original loan, the security in both cases being the same. These great discrepancies cannot be reconciled by considerations of the disparity of risk, and the variation in the supply of capital for investment. ...[11]

As rational an explanation existed, however, for the apparent irrationalities of interest charges as for the variations in "rent" — namely, a creditor's relationship to his debtor, or rather the extent

[11]E. Thompson, Officiating Commissioner, Sitapur, in *Oudh Selections,* 1868–69, pp. 40–44.

of the debtor's dependence. The principle on which a creditor operated was not to recover his principal with the profit of added charges for its use but to secure a regular source of income from high charges on money or goods loaned.[12] It was his interest to keep his debtor in a state of dependence by means of heavy charges so that he must continue to pay up indefinitely.

The timing of loans and their repayment also worked to the creditor's advantage. Given the small amounts which in the main constituted a borrower's seasonal requirements, short-term loans were the norm. Accounts were balanced every six months: kharif loans in the harvest months of Aghan and Pus (November–December), and rabi loans in Jeth (May–June).[13] A cultivator borrowed his grain for sowing or to feed his household in the thin months of the year, when stocks were lowest and prices were consequently at their highest level. At the harvest, when his creditor demanded repayment, the situation was reversed: most cultivators had to pay off their dues as soon as their grain was threshed and local markets were therefore glutted with produce. Prices naturally fell, with the result that the cultivator might pay back two or three times the amount of grain originally loaned in order to arrive at its cash value at the time of borrowing.

The comprehensiveness of the borrowing clientele, the wide variety of purposes for which they borrowed, and the fact that deficiencies in some part of the harvest were as frequent as abundance was rare kept creditors in business. The custom by which sons were liable for debts incurred by their fathers, without any express stipulation that inherited wealth should be sufficient to cover the debts inherited, ensured the continuation of payments to the creditor in the event of the death of his original debtor.[14] Against these advantages, the creditor had to set his risks: bad debts owing to poor harvests, and impoverished or recalcitrant debtors who might on occasion abscond without payment.

The comprehensiveness of the clientele of borrowers—the majority

[12]Compare A. O. Hume's observation: "They [i.e., moneylenders, prior to British rule] lent money, but only at enormous rates of interest; but this was not unfair as they never hoped even to recover the principal while for such interest they were to get they were dependent on the good will of the debtor, or the rare paternal influence of some superior"; *Agricultural Reform,* pp. 38–39. See also p. 39 above.

[13]This timing seems to have been universal in Oudh. See reports of the deputy commissioners, answers to Question 4, in *Oudh Selections,* 1868–69.

[14]See *Oudh Selections,* 1868–69, p. 41 (Sitapur); *Kheri Settlement Report,* pp. 17–18; *Unao Settlement Report,* p. 18 (this last relating to zamindari families). On ancestral debt in Hindu law, viz. the Pious Obligation, see p. 221 below.

of peasants who were unwilling or unable to accumulate reserves—
was matched by a wide range of creditors—the rural minority who
held sufficient stocks from which to make loans. Davies concluded
from the 1868-69 enquiries that the suppliers of "extraneous aid"
to the majority of Oudh cultivators were most frequently "petty
moneylenders," whose numbers included, however, "not only professional village bankers and *bannias,* but also many speculative and
thriving members of the agricultural classes."[15] Reports from Lucknow
showed the range of creditors from whom cultivators commonly
borrowed. According to H. H. Butts, a talukdar's relationship with his
"tenants" was commonly that of creditor to debtors.[16] J. W. Quinton
noted in 1868 that the agriculturists' "so-called mahajan" was frequently himself a petty zamindar or prosperous cultivator who had
managed to save some money which he immediately tried to increase
by lending it out to fellow villagers.[17] Meanwhile, in the "agricultural"
parganas of Mohanlalganj and Mohan Auras (that is, in parganas
distant from Lucknow city), professional moneylenders were said to
number more than one to every two villages.[18] The same range of
creditors was found elsewhere. Bareilly cultivators, for example, were
"more or less in debt to their mahajans or their zamindars or mokud-
dums."[19]

The provision of agricultural loans was the means *par excellence*
of earning a rapid and sizeable return on capital, as compared with
other pursuits. William Crooke, in his report on conditions in parts
of Etah district for the Dufferin Enquiry of 1888, listed the regular
sources of income of a family of Telis (oilmen). Their traditional
occupation of pressing oilseeds brought in an estimated Rs. 100 a year.
From their 3 acres 2 roods of cultivated land on which, in the year
under report, they grew five crops in the kharif and only one, bejhar,
in the rabi, the value of the total outturn was estimated at Rs. 50.6.0.
From their capital employed in moneylending, some Rs. 3,500, they
were reported to realize an annual income of Rs. 1,200.[20] A mahajan's
family holding 29 acres 6 poles as tenants-at-will sublet (in 1886-87)

[15]Davies, "Memorandum on ... the Indebtedness of Cultivators in Oudh," *Oudh Selections,* 1868–69, p. 71.

[16]*Lucknow Settlement Report,* p. 56, and see p. 151 above.

[17]J. W. Quinton, Deputy Commissioner, Lucknow, *Oudh Selections,* 1868–69, p. 10.

[18]*Lucknow Settlement Report,* p. 56.

[19]*Bareilly Settlement Report,* p. 55.

[20]Dufferin Enquiry (Enclosures, NWP and Oudh), pp. 77–78: tehsil Kasganj, mauza Abhaipur, family of Chhote.

23 acres 1 rood and 15 poles, from which they drew a net income, after paying their rent, of Rs. 56. The remaining 5 acres 2 roods and 31 poles, which they cultivated themselves with three kharif crops and two rabi crops, brought in an income of Rs. 79. Their income from moneylending, however, was estimated at Rs. 350 per year.[21]

In the same district, a Thakur family lived off the combined resources of zamindari, cultivation, and moneylending. The family's sir holding was 81 acres; added to this were another 17 acres which were held under occupancy tenancy in the name of the wife in another village belonging to another zamindar. Theirs was a typical multiple holding. The family's earnings from cultivation over this large area were, in the year under report, some Rs. 1,231—the value of the outturn of seven kharif and seven rabi crops. From moneylending, their annual income came to some Rs. 750 on a capital of Rs. 2,000.[22]

Of all potential creditors, a talukdar or zamindar occupied the strongest and most profitable position. To the income from his charges over his mahal were added the charges on his loans. Most important, his jurisdiction as talukdar or zamindar over subordinate cultivators provided him with greater means of controlling his debtors than were available, for example, to a rich peasant or mahajan. Restrictive principles could govern a mahajan's accounts with his debtors. Rules existed, for example, against excessive compounding, whereby a debt became invalid once it had risen to more than twice the amount of the principal.[23] But few effective restrictions existed to obstruct the exactions of a strong zamindar-creditor, and few checks could be kept on the debtor's "account" which seems seldom to have been itemized separately from charges due by him under the head of zamindari.[24] S. M. Moens noted how in Bareilly the uncommonly

[21]*Ibid.*, tehsil Etah, family of Bijai.

[22]*Ibid.*, pp. 53–54, tehsil Kasganj, mauza Abhaipur, family of Narayan Singh.

[23]For legal rules restricting the compounding of debts, see p. 219 below.

[24]A report from Farukhabad district in 1877, for example, stated how moneylending and "rent" accounts were indistinguishable in the zamindars' records (the *patwaris'* papers); see Board of Revenue, NWP, to Government, NWP and Oudh, October 4, 1877, NWP and Oudh, "Revenue Proceedings," May 1880, Index No. 71, November 3, 1877, Proceeding No. 46. A comment by F. N. Wright in a note on the reh problem in parganas Akrabad and Sikandra Rao, Aligarh district, is instructive : "I have carefully analysed the causes of decrease of rent-roll (where found), and especially the arrears of rent, with the view of ascertaining if they could be directly attributed to the effect of *reh*. In many instances this was most unmistakably the case, but in others I found that cultivators holding all good land and with no *reh* in their fields were in arrears; in others, the area affected by *reh* would be trifling, but arrears heavy; in others, again, the patwari asserted that the heavy arrears were in no way due

high charge of 50 percent *(deora nirikh katke)* was levied by "a few extortionate zamindars" of pargana Aonlah,[25] whilst the local bania creditors could not "screw their debtors too hard for fear of driving them to emigrate to Turai [terai], a safe haven of refuge ..."[26] In Sitapur, as Thompson noted in 1869, peasants were aware of the dangers inherent in borrowing from a zamindar, even where his charges were no higher than a mahajan's. There was

no doubt a general idea that zamindars are bound to help their tenants by liberal advances of takavi, but these advances are not popular among culti- vators. Many zamindars make advances to their cultivators on the same terms as mahajans and exact the same profits. But peasants prefer money- lenders to landlords : landlords have much greater facilities for realizing the debt to the last farthing than mahajans have. The zamindar would take everything due to him before it left the field, but the mahajan can be inde- finitely put off, and if he is quite overbearing the cultivator can leave him for another man. The cultivator borrows from his mahajan hoping to cheat him, but he knows he cannot cheat his landlord.[27]

The regular drain on cultivators' produce in the form of charges which provided the mahajans and maliks—especially the zamindar- creditors—with a sizeable income made it impossible for the culti- vators themselves to store up reserves. The conditions under which the vast majority of farmers in the provinces produced their crops year after year were as J. R. Reid described them apropos of Azamgarh district in 1870 :

If the rice and rabi crops of the preceding year had been good, the agriculturist has generally grain in his house to feed—from April to the middle or end of August—himself and his family; and if he employs anyone to help in watering his sugar-cane, or in ploughing his land, to pay in kind for the hired labour. He may have rice to use as seed, but is not likely to have seed for the rabi

---

to *reh* (though *reh* was injuring the village), but to the fact that the zamindars mixed up their banking and rent accounts, credited receipts to the former, and showed any balance due under the head of arrears of rent—that is to say, the ordinary condition of indebtedness in which the cultivators usually are was utilized as a means of holding arrears over them and keeping them in the landlord's power." Wright, Settlement Officer, Cawnpore, to Commissioner, Meerut, March 22, 1878, para. 9, in NWP and Oudh, "Revenue Proceedings," June 1879, Index No. 125, December 28, 1878, Proceeding No. 63.

[25]*Bareilly Setllemenl Report,* pp. 80–81.

[26]*Ibid.,* p. 55.

[27]*Oudh Selections,* 1868–69, pp. 35–36. For a classic example of efficient use of takavi by the Begam Sumroo, see pp. 48–49 above. In pargana Fatehabad, Agra district, "village bankers" were reported at settlement to be "proprietors" in much larger numbers than

crops, and will probably have to borrow, in addition to the rabi seed, grain for food during September. When the Bhudawi [early kharif] crops are ready, he is in need of grain for his domestic use, and little or none of his crop will be sold. Though poor eating, it will somehow carry him and his family on till the rice is cut and threshed. Meantime he needs cash to pay the first and second instalments of his rents, and this he borrows. When the rice crop is ready, he perhaps repays part of the money and grain he has borrowed. But rice is a favourite food grain, and it generally sells very cheap at harvest time. Besides the crops must supply food for himself and his family for three or four months at least. The agriculturist therefore parts with as little of his rice-crop as possible. Then comes the sugar-cane season. The price that he gets for his *gur* [molasses] is set against his old debts for grain and cash and out of it he pays the first of the rabi instalments, and his banker through it realizes debts that have been caused during the past year by marriages, domestic trouble and the like. Out of his rabi grain the cultivator saves as much as he can, but part of it he will have to sell in order to pay the last instalment of his rent, or square his account with his banker ... ; for grain that he borrows, the agriculturist pays in kind 37%, for cash and grain repaid in cash, he pays interest at 25%. The ordinary run of agriculturists lay by very little. Anything they might from adventitious circumstances—such as exceptionally good harvests, high prices, rent-rates below average—be able to save, they spend in marriages and other petty extravagances. As a rule they live from hand to mouth, and probably always will do so.[28]

In addition, there was always the problem of shortfalls in the harvest. Reid himself estimated elsewhere that seasonal disorders regularly reduced the Azamgarh farmers' yields by some 25 percent,[29] and Quinton had noted earlier in Lucknow how deficiencies in the seasonal outturn erased the hope of any remainder being left to the cultivator once he had met—wholly or only in part—the charges for which he was liable.[30]

---

elsewhere in the district and to have far greater control over cultivators "than would be possible if they were unconnected with the land." The statistical statement of landholdings for the pargana showed that these "banker-proprietors" were not *Banias*, but Brahmans and Thakurs, the dominant landholding castes in the pargana, who held proprietary titles to 21 and 28 percent, respectively, of the zamindaris. See *Agra Settlement Report*, p. 39, and Transfer Statement F, p. 41.

[28]J. R. Reid, Settlement Officer, Azamgarh, August 3, 1870, in "Abstract of Replies to Board's Circular AAA, 20 July 1870, on ... the Payment of the Revenue Instalments [Azamgarh]," in NWP, "Revenue Proceedings," May 1873, Index No. 12, April 6, 1873, Proceeding No. 58.

[29]See p. 25 above.

[30]*Oudh Selections*, 1868–69, pp. 7–9.

Amongst the peasantry throughout the provinces, there were relatively few who combined privileged status—by reason of their kinship or service relationship with the dominant zamindar—with freedom from debt, and who were therefore independent enough to control the distribution of their own produce. Such cultivators were able to sell off only so much of their crops as would clear their liabilities to the zamindar, disposing of the least and most valuable produce at the highest prices and retaining the bulk of their crops—the coarse food grains—for their own consumption or for store, to sell later in the season as need or a shrewd eye for the market might dictate. The vast majority, however, were compelled to pay heavy charges to their zamindars and, at the same time, to sell more of their produce at the harvest time in order to satisfy their creditors : deductions for the repayment of loans reduced the low selling price still further.[31] They were subject to the control of the zamindar with his charges and to that of the creditor with his loans, and could rarely escape from them, least of all when they were one and the same.

Indebtedness and the Expansion of Agriculture

The introduction by Government of measures to ensure the continued development of the agricultural resources of the provinces principally by means of public works resulted *inter alia*, as we have seen, in greatly increased production of the crops recognized as having the highest market value : indigo, sugar cane, cotton, and the finer grains such as rice, wheat, and barley. This was most noticeable in areas opened up to canal irrigation.[32] The changes in local crop patterns towards the predominance of such crops were greeted with enthusiastic approval by Government officers who saw in them clear indications of progress away from the apparent barbarity of indigenous practices and towards agricultural prosperity. It was assumed that the benefits of rising prices—the fruits of sound expansion—for this category of produce would naturally be available to the "agricultural community," or at least to that section of it which deserved such benefits as a reward for enterprise and industry.

[31]The distinction between indebted and unindebted cultivators, crucial in relation to the local distribution of produce, was clearly drawn in the Oudh enquiry of 1868–69. For observations on Lucknow Division, see *Oudh Selections*, 1868–69, p. 4; Lucknow district, *ibid.*, pp. 7–9; Unao district, *ibid.*, pp. 14–15; Bara Banki district, *ibid.*, p. 20; Sitapur Division, *ibid.*, pp. 23–26; Sultanpur district, *ibid.*, pp. 63–64.

[32]See pp. 71–74 above. For the extent of the expansion of "valuable" crops in canal-irrigated areas of the NWP, see Figures 2, 3, and 4.

Such expansion was deceptive. Although it had in many cases caused substantial ecological changes, it brought no revolution in the techniques traditionally used by local farmers, and, even more important, it left untouched the local networks of charges and loans which so largely controlled the production and distribution of their crops. The burden of the small farmer's dependence on his superiors could in no way be relieved by an increase in "valuable" crops. W. S. Robertson warned in a paper published in 1876 that "any actual increase in rice cultivation does not denote a corresponding increase in the welfare of the ryot who, as a rule, has to grow his crops, and the rice one in particular under the pressure of a heavy mortgage."[33] Not only were the "valuable" crops commonly grown by means of loans; they were also subject to the heaviest zamindari charges and were graded according to the scale of values ruling in local markets. Sugar cane generally topped the list, followed by indigo, cotton, and tobacco, then by opium and vegetables.[34] Local creditors who already reaped benefits from the reduction in takavi loans by Government[35] and from the increased pressure on zamindars and cultivators to borrow owing to the system of revenue collection,[36] were presented with increased opportunities for business in those areas where the cultivation of finer grains and commercial staples had expanded.

Indigo cultivation in the NWP provides a clear case in point. In Farukhabad district, for example, indigo was already extensively cultivated under the stimulus of the Ganges Canal by 1860 : in that year the collector estimated that some 50 different indigo concerns operated in the district, totalling some 150 factories with each supplied

[33]W. S. Robertson, "Grain and Seeds," *Indian Agriculturist,* June 1, 1876, at p. 163.

[34]In Bijnour district, the scale of *zabti* charges (fixed dues, paid in cash) was recorded during settlement as follows :

Change (Rs. per acre)

Crop	Minimum	Maximum
Sugar cane	3.1.6	18
Cotton Vegetables Safflower	3.12.0	12
Tobacco	—	15
Opium	—	10

See *Bijnour Settlement Report,* pp. 87–88. For further examples, see *Bulandshahr Settlement Report,* pp. 5–6.

[35]See pp. 110–118 above, and compare Figure 6 with Figures 7, 8, and 9.

[36]See pp. 156–160 above.

by 25 to 30 villages. Both seed and dye were sent from Farukhabad "in large quantities" to the Punjab, Rajputana, Central India, and Calcutta.[37]

Purchasers of plant, seed, or *gaud* (partially manufactured indigo) contracted with cultivators or, more commonly, with their zamindars for maximum security, for each season's supplies. Each transaction was governed by a *satta* (contract) drawn up by the gomashta (the purchaser's agent) before witnesses, who were generally servants attached to the local indigo factory. The terms of the satta established the area to be sown with indigo, the quality of plant, seed, or gaud to be delivered by the contractor, and the rate at which he was to be paid. The sum agreed in the satta as the full value of the indigo was commonly paid over to the contractor in advance, though payment by instalments according to the various stages in cultivation was not unknown. The contractor received all or the most substantial part of his advance payment in January and paid over 1 percent of the amount (*sattawan*, according to the terms of the satta) on receipt as a charge to the go-mashta. The remainder was his, theoretically, to dispose of as he wished; the only condition stipulated in the contract was that he should cultivate or ensure the cultivation of indigo on the specified area of his holding from April to June. Supervision was entrusted by the factories' agents to peons—called *sepahis* in this context. On the average, they numbered some eight to a factory. Since they received no special payment by way of *dasturi* (officially recognized charges), they invariably lived at the cultivator's expense when inspecting his indigo plots.[38]

Four seers of indigo seed per bigha were required for a good average outturn, ranging from fifteen to thirty maunds of plant. This would

[37]C. R. Lindsay, Collector, Farukhabad, to Officiating Commissioner, Agra, August 18, 1860, in NWP, "Revenue Proceedings," April 27, 1861, Index No. 196, September 8, 1860, Proceeding No. 30. Lindsay's note included no statistics corroborating his impressions of the extent of indigo cultivation in 1860. Statistics provided by the settlement survey, however, in the early 1870s gave the total cropped area of the district as 1,242,620 acres, of which 477,578 acres were estimated as under kharif crops with indigo occupying a total area of 31,156 acres. Four parganas had less than 100 acres under indigo; a further four had between 100 and 1,000 acres; a further four had between 1,000 and 2,000; and only one had between 2,000 and 4,000. Three parganas had over 4,000 acres under indigo. See "Statement of Crops Grown During the Year of Measurement [survey year not specified] by Parganas," *Farukhabad Settlement* Report, p. 11. Note the value of indigo, in relation to its proportion to the total cropped area.

[38]C. R. Lindsay, in NWP, "Revenue Proceedings," April 27, 1861, Index No. 196, September 8, 1860, Proceeding No. 30.

give between fifteen and twenty seers of gaud together with one maund of seed.[39] The average net profit (costs deducted) per bigha to a cultivator who contracted to grow indigo was estimated by C. R. Lindsay, the Collector of Farukhabad, at a mere rupee, where he was advanced Rs. 15 for every 100 maunds of plant he was bound to deliver, and no more than a rupee and a half where Rs. 20 was paid for every 100 maunds. So much for the cultivator. The purchaser was in a better position : Lindsay estimated his profits at some Rs. 20 per maund of gaud and Rs. 45 per maund of manufactured indigo.[40]

Given these minute profits of cultivation, it may well be asked why farmers contracted to grow indigo. The answer to this lies in the time at which indigo advances were paid. As P. C. Wheeler candidly explained when commenting on indigo cultivation in Jaunpur district in the 1870s, "Indigo planting is pursued, like so many other industries, by taking advantage of other people's necessities. The planter's object is to procure so much plant. This is effected by advancing money to zamindars and tenants when they need it."[41] With these cash advances paid in January, cultivators could clear the charges due to their zamindars, and the latter, in turn, could meet their revenue obligations—the cultivators' payments falling due before crops could in most cases be marketed. The advance offered by indigo purchasers in January was, consequently, "a temptation not to be resisted," as Lindsay observed in 1860.[42] Predictably, the majority of cultivators in the indigo-growing districts—the lower castes of Kurmis and Kachhis—found the advances irresistible, in spite of the meagre remuneration. The produce of these cultivators was subject to heavy charges, unrelieved by any reductions on account of privileged status. (Lindsay drew attention to the fact that the high-caste Brahman and Thakur farmers in Farukhabad took to indigo cultivation "only occasionally."[43] Even the few rupees' profit from indigo had to be paid over in meeting these charges, and the cultivators accumulated nothing.

[39]G. E. Lance, Collector and Magistrate, Cawnpore, to Officiating Commissioner, Allahabad, July 2, 1860, in NWP, "Revenue Proceedings," April 27, 1861, Index No. 190, August 15, 1860, Proceeding No. 185. Compare J. R. Reid's estimate for Azamgarh, viz. approximately 25 maunds of plant per bigha as a fair yield; *Azamgarh Settlement Report*, p. 118.

[40]C. R. Lindsay, cited above, n. 37. It is not stated whether the expenses of entertaining *sepahi*-inspectors were included in "costs deducted."

[41]*Jaunpur Settlement Report*, pp. 113–114.

[42]C. R. Lindsay, cited above, n. 37.

[43]*Ibid.*

The service provided by indigo contracts in meeting obligations created by the temporary settlements in the NWP goes far to explain the relatively peaceful history of indigo cultivation, particularly in the Doab, when compared with the riotous affairs earlier in permanently settled Bengal, where no such regular dependence compelled acceptance of the institution and where the matter was rather one of zamindars' and planters' attempts to force their will on cultivators.[44] In 1860, the collector of Mainpuri emphasized that in his district indigo cultivation was indeed "highly popular with zamindars and ryots," unattended by breaches of the peace, and explicitly ascribed this "in great measure to the value set, and the use made, of the indigo advances for paying the rabi instalments of the revenue."[45] In his report in the same year from Cawnpore, G. E. Lance also dwelt on the voluntary nature of the indigo "bargains," which were found to cause no trouble to civil, revenue or criminal authorities.[46] Significantly, where zamindars seem to have held effective control over the production of indigo—in parganas Aonlah and Crore of Bareilly district, for example—it was reported to be unpopular. There, the zamindars owned the "small native factories" which had sprung up in the two parganas during the years of the settlement survey and controlled their cultivators by loaning indigo seed at the extortionate charge of 1.25 maunds per maund advanced.[47]

In parts of Aligarh district, other problems arose for indigo growers, stemming from the combination of the control of production by local zamindars and the disastrous effects of canal irrigation. In the late 1870s, extensive indigo cultivation was reported in the district: the official estimate, admitted to be short of the actual figure, was 29,013 acres. Under the stimulus of the Ganges Canal, the country was by this time "studded with indigo factories"—some 171 in all and mostly controlled by local zamindars.[48] As a direct consequence of excessive distribution of canal water, the irrigated areas of parganas Akrabad and Sikandra Rao had already become badly infected by reh.[49] The situation was serious enough to warrant a recommendation

[44]On this aspect of indigo cultivation in Bengal, see B. Chowdhury, *Growth of Commercial Agriculture*, especially pp. 190–192.

[45]Cited by L. A. Ross, Officiating Commissioner, Agra, to Government, NWP, August 27, 1860, in NWP, "Revenue Proceedings," April 27, 1861, Index No. 195, September 8, 1860, Proceeding No. 29.

[46]G. E. Lance, cited above, n. 39.

[47]*Bareilly Settlement Report*, pp. 98–99.

[48]*Aligarh Settlement Report*, p. 37.

[49]On the connection of canals with the increase of reh, see pp. 76–79 above, and Appendix 5.

by the executive engineer to stop the supply of canal water to thirteen selected villages where the spread of reh appeared most damaging. But both cultivators and zamindars of those villages had come to depend on indigo advances as a regular source of income : stoppage of the canal water supply would bring ruin. What was Government to do? Should it close the canal to limit the deterioration of the land, and reduce the zamindars' revenue liability accordingly? Enquiries, however, showed that the zamindars, fed regularly by the cultivators' indigo payments, were in no way willing to reduce their "rents" on a scale corresponding to the proposed reduction in revenue. Government's final recommendation was that the canal should be closed for one year, whilst the collector or his assistant should be invested with a settlement officer's powers to adjust the revenue demand and, titularly, the "rents" in the selected tracts.[50] But since Government had no power to compel zamindars to reduce their charges, it had no means of protecting the cultivators in such a situation. No action could be taken on the district officers' reports.

The focus of Government zeal in promoting the expansion of crops which it believed to be essential for agricultural prosperity was not indigo but sugar cane. The cultivation of sugar cane had long been associated in the provinces with first-class soil conditions exploited by skilled and industrious farmers.[51] The complicated processes of local sugar manufacturing, both of gur (molasses) and khand (refined sugar), and the trade in these products provided considerable opportunities for employment and not merely to the cultivators themselves. The spirit of agricultural industry so manifestly expressed in the sugar trade of the provinces was early encouraged by Government with "liberality and perseverance."[52] The Crown continued the Company's work on a wider scale. While the canal developments in the Doab provided some stimulus to increased cultivation, the construction of a network of road and rail communications—particularly by the Oudh and Rohilkhand Railway Company [53]—provided the

[50]For the correspondence on the problem of Akrabad and Sikandra Rao, see NWP and Oudh, "Revenue Proceedings," May 1880, Index Nos. 100–106, May 22, 1880, Proceedings Nos. 17–23. The executive engineer also recommended takavi advances to be made directly to cultivators to enable them to sink wells for an alternative source of irrigation. Ibid., Index No. 103, Proceeding No. 20. On the procedural problem of takavi loans to cultivators, see pp. 112–118 above.

[51]For sugar cane as a traditional index of top-class cultivation, see p. 32 above. For its method of cultivation, see p. 22 above.

[52]Moradabad Settlement Report, p. 44.

[53]For the dates of construction of lines, by sections, see Appendix 7.

established and flourishing controllers of sugar growing, manufacturing, and trading in Rohilkhand with new incentives in the form of opportunities for large-scale distribution.

The kolhus (sugar mills) and *khandsaris* (small-scale refineries) rapidly multiplied in response. A. M. Markham recorded some 4,821 kolhus in Bijnour during his settlement survey in the early 1870s—on the average, 1 kolhu to every 9.5 acres of cane.[54] In Bareilly district, the number of khandsaris had increased from 174 in 1848 to 561 in 1872—that is, by more than 300 percent. This, in the official view, was clear evidence of the "generally remunerative character of the trade."[55]

But to whom was it remunerative? The long period of cultivation and of manufacture, from the crushing of the cane for the extraction of ras (juice), to the boiling of ras for gur, and in refining khand, required not only machinery but time to work it. The greater proportion of cultivators could neither afford the initial cost of machines nor wait so long (some three months from cane-crushing to the boiling of the gur) for a return on their crop.[56] Most sugar, therefore, was grown on advances. In Bareilly, these were provided by the owners of khandsaris, who were more often than not the local zamindars.[57] In Pilibhit, all "castes and creeds, ... whoever has sufficient capital," were reported to be in the business.[58] In Shahjahanpur, owners of *bels* (small factories for the manufacture of gur) controlled the district's sugar production by a notoriously extortionate system of advances which tied cultivators firmly to their local bel.[59] Here again, cultivators benefited little from increased production. As Reid commented in the official resolution on Moens' *Bareilly Settlement Report,* "it is to be feared that the portion of the value filtering into the tenants' hands is comparatively small. The crop is usually grown on advances by sugar-refiners ... When (as often) the refiner is also the landlord, or is supported in his dealings by the landlord, the tenant, who has opened up an advance account with the refiner is in an unequal struggle. He has no option left but to sell his *ras* at a price considerably below the rate at which, when it is ready, it might be sold by him for cash in the market."[60] What did the cultivator do with his minimal profit

[54] *Bijnour Settlement Report,* p. 75.

[55] *Bareilly Settlement Report,* p. 94.

[56] For details of sugar-making in north-western districts, see *Moradabad Settlement Report,* pp. 47–48; in eastern districts, see *Azamgarh Settlement Report,* pp. 123–124.

[57] *Bareilly Settlement Report,* pp. 94–95.

[58] *Pilibhit Settlement Report,* p. 10.

[59] *Shahjahanpur Settlement Report,* p. xvi.

[60] NWP Revenue Department, "Resolution," January 29, 1883, *Bareilly Settlement Report,* pp. 3–4.

from the controlled sale of his cane crop? Once again, the timing of advances provided a service, albeit a costly one. Bargaining between purchaser and grower began in Jeth (May–June) in Rohilkhand, and was usually concluded in Kuar (September–October), prior to the cutting of the cane. This was convenient to cultivators for the payment of their kharif dues. As with indigo, advances for sugar-growing proved irresistible for the regular remittance of rent charges.[61] Again, the cultivator could keep little or nothing of his earnings since no sooner did he receive the advance than he paid all or most of it over to his zamindar.

If contemporary estimates were sound—and in this respect there seems little reason to doubt them—the local market value of sugar in the districts where it was most extensively cultivated, that is, in Rohilkhand, bordered on the prodigious. In Bareilly, for example, Moens recorded some 50,078 acres under sugar cane in the year of his survey: a mere 5.7 percent of the cultivated area of the district. The approximate value of the crop, however, which was given in the official review of Moens' report nearly ten years after its publication, was quoted at Rs. 31 lakhs (calculated on the basis of Moens' acreage statistics). This was nearly twice the district's assumed rental and four times its annual revenue demand.[62] The proportion of total zamindari charges in the Rohilkhand districts paid by means of the proceeds from the cane crop was consequently very high. Markham estimated that sugar cane covered a mere 7 percent of the cultivated area of Bijnour district—or 14 percent if the area kept fallow for the next season's plantings were allowed for—but accounted for some 36 percent of the gross rental. The entire range of rabi crops, on the other hand, was sown on some 37 percent of the cultivated area but accounted collectively for only 28 percent of the gross rental.[63]

Cultivators rarely shared in the trading of gur and khand, which was chiefly the business of a multitude of commercial agents. Manufacturers—including zamindars who owned bels or khandsaris—commonly sold their products to traders in the larger commercial centres situated at road and rail junctions; they in turn exported it south and west by train or by cart. The small number of cultivators who processed their own gur sold it to *beoparis*, itinerant petty dealers, who in turn sold their stocks at local markets to the agents of more

[61]*Bareilly Settlement Report*, pp. 94–95.
[62]*Ibid.*, p. 94.
[63]*Bijnour Settlement Report*, p. 75.

substantial trading concerns.[64] Each trader at each stage in the passage of the product through the district took his commission fixed at a percentage on the value of the commodity. Prices fluctuated with the seasons but measures existed to lessen trading risks. In Burragaon, Shahjahanpur district, a *"khatunti* system" operated to ensure some profit for the manufacturer and the dealer except where gross climatic disorders caused a near-total failure of the crop. The prices of all agricultural produce for the area were fixed by agreement between local traders, zamindars, and cultivators at an annual assemblage in a central market.[65] Since the majority of cultivators produced their sugar crop by means of advances provided by the traders and zamindars, they had little alternative but to accept the terms agreed on by the controlling minority.

Of the "valuable" crops grown on a large scale in the provinces in the later nineteenth century, cotton was the least stable index of prosperity. The successful cultivation of the plant undoubtedly matched up to contemporary official standards for industrious and progressive agriculture : it demanded good soil—preferably *dumat* or loam—and careful watering and weeding. The frequency of disorders in the kharif seasons, to which cotton was especially vulnerable, meant however that success was more rarely obtained and never over as wide an area as it was in the case of indigo and sugar cane.[66] The problems posed by climatic irregularities were not in themselves insuperable, given the existence of promising soil conditions, skilled farmers, and, most important, a regular incentive to overcome them. In the few districts where cotton was grown extensively—most notably in Muttra even prior to the opening of the Agra Canal in 1874[67]—the incentive was provided once more by advances. "The exportation of cotton is one of the largest sources of income in this district," G. E. Watson, the Collector, reported in 1873. "Agents are sent up from Allahabad and Mirzapore, who make advances on the crop even before it is harvested. This ready sale is, I believe, one of the principal reasons for the greatly extended cultivation of the crop . . . This year,

[64]For details of the Rohilkhand sugar trade, see *Moradabad Settlement Report,* p. 48.
[65]*Shahjahanpur Settlement Report,* pp. xviii, xx-xxi.
[66]For details on the consistently disappointing outturn of the cotton crop for the NWP as a whole, see *NWP Reports on the Actual Outturn of the Cotton Crop,* 1869–70, 1872–73, 1873–74. For the failure of Government-sponsored experiments in improved cotton production, see p. 102 above.
[67]See pp. 71–72 above.

as last, the Government demand due on the autumn harvest was paid principally from the proceeds of this crop."[68] Consistent expansion was prevented by the instability of available markets for the provinces' cotton output. Cotton exports from British India rose from 563,000 bales (of 400 pounds each) in 1860 to 1,848,000 in 1866 but dropped to 1,064,000 by 1870.[69] At the outbreak of the American Civil War, European textile entrepreneurs had turned in desperation to India in the hope of securing an adequate alternative source of supply. Their experiences during the next five years showed clearly the insurmountable obstacles which prevented them from establishing control over the supply of agricultural produce and the utter impossibility of direct investment of European capital in local agriculture. It was the systems of advances and the endless convolutions of commercial agencies through which all marketable produce was distributed which reduced the entrepreneurs' expectations to uncomprehending despair : "In many parts of the cotton districts, there are very unusual and singular difficulties, which arise out of a strange state of society, and which counteract the ordinary effect of the habitual motives of human action," sighed the *Economist,* in reviewing a series of letters exposing the problems of the Indian cotton trade.[70] The discovery of a far more convenient source of supply in Egypt cut short the agonies of the merchants and fed their urgent needs, with the consequence that the powerful stimulus of the export market for the Indian product was and remained substantially diminished.[71] On the home markets, instability resulted from the importation of Manchester-processed yarns and from fluctuations in the purchasing power of the cotton traders' rural clientele, which varied from season to season according to the outturn of their crops. These problems remained unrelieved throughout the period.

The Grain Trade

In contrast to the suddenness of the cotton boom, the export trade in food grains expanded slowly and at a steady pace. The stimulus here

[68]G. E. Watson, Collector, Muttra, to Board of Revenue, NWP, March 29, 1873, paras. 7–9, in *NWP Report on the . . . Outturn of Cotton,* 1872–73, p. 24.

[69]G. Watt, *Dictionary,* IV, 50, cited by D.S. Landes, *Bankers and Pashas,* p. 73.

[70]"On the Best Practical Method of Augmenting the Culture of Cotton in India," *Economist,* October 4, 1862, at p. 1094.

[71]For details of the cotton boom and the history of Indian cotton exports in the nineteenth century, see p. 102 above. The British colony of Fiji experienced at the

was not provided by any overriding urgency on the part of European entrepreneurs in search of immediate supplies but by the gradual development of public works. While the canals stimulated the production of finer food grains on an unprecedented scale, railways and roads provided wider opportunities for distribution both within the districts of the provinces and outside their borders. Exports of grain from the provinces to Europe were not made on a large scale before the mid-1870s. The entrepreneurs from abroad were in no way interested in repeating the experiences of the cotton merchants, and they made no significant attempt to establish a footing in the territory ruled by local agricultural and commercial interests; rather, they tapped the sources of supply which the indigenous trading networks offered them : "The majority of cultivators are not brought into contact with European purchasers."[72] It was left to the local Banias to acquire the cultivators' grain in the first instance, and any communication between the regional agents of the European grain-trading concerns and the growers—concerning, say, specific requirements of the buyers as regards types of staples—was entrusted to the "kanungo and patwari staff,"[73] which for the most part consisted of servants of the zamindars and talukdars.[74]

Agents of the European grain-exporting companies were based in the great marts and banking centres of the provinces. In 1860-61, Colonel Baird Smith ranked Mirzapur and Farukhabad first amongst the provinces' markets, with Lucknow, Allahabad, Cawnpore, and Agra in second place. Both Benares and Muttra were also considered important as seats of large indigenous banking firms.[75] Beyond these, and beyond the great road, rail, and river junctions which supplied them, trading networks intersected the districts, connecting up local marts and bazars. While Moradabad district, for example, grew into an important thoroughfare of trade between Rohilkhand and the Doab, Punjab, and Rajasthan districts to the south-west under the stimulus of the Oudh and Rohilkhand Railway, its local grain-trading patterns

same time a similar boom, followed by slump, owing to similar causes. See Evelyn Stokes, "The Fiji Cotton Boom in the Eighteen-Sixties," *New Zealand Journal of History*, II, 2 (October 1968), 165–177.

[72]E. C. Buck, Director, Agriculture and Commerce, NWP, to Government, NWP, "Note on the Wheat Trade," 1877, para. 12, in Government of India, *Selections from the Records of Government*, No. CLX, p. 198.

[73]*Ibid.*

[74]For further details on the problem of patwaris as subordinate Government officials, see pp. 246–252 below.   x

[75]R. Baird Smith, "Report", p. 3.

with its immediate neighbours seem to have persisted. This trade followed the seasons. Since in districts to the south of Moradabad crops ripened a full month earlier, there was "an ebb and flow" in the movement of the staple coarse food grains of the cultivating population, that is, in the movement of "articles of almost universal production and consumption; . . . barley will thus be brought up in large quantities [to Moradabad] early in March, to be repaid in April . . ."[76] Grain was merely one item—usually the largest—of the aggregate imports and exports of a district. Azamgarh's list of principal imports included, according to Reid, English cloth and yarn, cotton, silk, dried tobacco, salt, metals and hardware, and leather, in addition to staple and export grains (rice, for example)—all purchased chiefly with the proceeds from local sugar products, indigo, opium, and country cloth.[77] A sizeable "commercial community" dealt in these commodities. According to the 1872 census for Azamgarh, the number of adult males (of 15 years and over) engaged in commerce was 9,840 or 2.17 percent of the adult male population of the district, excluding a further 5,768 (1.27 percent) employed in transport of commodities.[78] These figures were admittedly only a rough guide, since many besides members of hereditary merchant castes took some part in trade—all those who had carts, pack animals, or sufficient reserves and time to do so—whilst all persons registered as belonging to trading castes did not necessarily follow this occupation. In trade, as in agriculture, many participants were working on borrowed capital or as brokers; the number of wealthy traders who owned all their capital was said to be small. Estimation of the volume of local trade was hazardous : no figures were available to Reid of the quantity let alone the value of imported commodities; no statement could be drawn up of the earnings of agents.[79]

Local distribution focused on small commercial towns which usually had a resident population of bankers (who made loans to agriculturists), a few cloth dealers, money-changers, small grain dealers, artisans, and cultivators with holdings and interests in the neighbourhood. The size of the town and the complexity of its dealings both locally and with larger centres determined the number of markets held per week. Bahadurganj, for example, in Ghazipur district lay on

[76] *Moradabad Settlement Report*, p. 18.

[77] *Azamgarh Settlement Report*, pp. 159–161.

[78] 1872 census returns, cited by J. R. Reid, *ibid*. The total number of persons registered as members of banking and trading castes in the districts was 36,243.

[79] Reid, *ibid*.

the Chhoti Sarju River, a principal trade route from Azamgarh to Patna, and was linked by road also with Ghazipur and Mahomadabad. Special bazars were held there twice weekly (in addition to the usual daily markets) and were attended by large numbers of the rural population from six to eight miles around and by itinerant traders. Peasants procured their supplies at these markets, but seldom brought cash to pay for them. The common practice seems to have been for them to bring in their produce—grain, oilseeds, and vegetables—and to sell it to certain dealers and buy from others what they required with the proceeds. Or they would exchange their grain, valued at the current market rate (less deductions, if they owed charges to the dealers) for oil, salt, cloth, and tobacco.[80]

The development of new and distant markets for food grains distorted the old seasonal rhythms of the grain trade. In Bundelkhand, changes in the early 1860s amounted to a complete reversal of direction. In 1864, J. P. Stratton, the Political Assistant stationed at Nowgong, observed that whereas formerly grain had come up through the district from Saugor, Jubbulpore, and Narbada and had passed on to the British districts to the north, the traffic now came down from Banda, Hamirpur, and Cawnpore, through Bundelkhand to the south. What had caused this? Stratton explained that better markets for the grain of Saugor and Narbada were now to be found in the south rather than the north; response to these new attractions had led to Bundelkhand's having to draw some of its grain supplies of late from the Doab. He suggested a number of reasons for the rise of better markets to the south : recent deficiencies in the harvests of "various southern districts"; extensive cultivation of cotton in the Deccan taking up former grain land; a similar situation in Malwa owing to the increase in opium cultivation; and extensive public works in the Deccan. "All these events combining either to diminish production or enhance price or both, they have raised prices in Malwa and the Daccan and thus attracted Narbada grain to those marts."[81]

[80]*Ghazipur Settlement Report*, pp. 106–107. In pargana Zahurabad alone, markets included Bahadurganj, with a population of 5,007 (according to the 1881 census), two other small towns with a few resident Banias and indigo and sugar factories, and eleven minor markets. Three of these last functioned four times a week, three twice a week, and four once a week. For a survey of market facilities in all parganas, see *ibid*., pp. 94–112. Numerous centres for small-scale local trading seem to have been the rule in other districts. See, for example, *Lucknow Settlement Report*, p. 39; *Fatehpur Settlement Report*, pp. 7–8; *Bareilly Settlement Report*, pp. 58–59.

[81]J. P. Stratton to Agent to Governor-General for Central India, June 11, 1864, in NWP, "Revenue Proceedings," September 24, 1864, Index No. 53, Proceeding No. 18.

The enormous extension of communications further north, in the provinces proper, meant greater access to the higher-priced export markets. Inevitably, with this extension, price levels at the larger trading depots rose. By 1882, the Board of Revenue thought it "hardly necessary to notice that the equalization of prices in the provinces was becoming more and more apparent." Equalization, that is, at high rates, for "it is only in a few outlying tracts that low prices still prevail for some time immediately following the date of the harvest."[82] Whilst districts still far from the major lines of communication preserved considerable stocks, local storage of grain elsewhere was said by the same year to have "greatly fallen into disuse."[83] Bulk stores at railway stations, road junctions, and *ghats* (landing places) on the navigable rivers were now becoming the centres of regional accumulation.[84]

"It is probable that any sudden extra demand for export is met chiefly by drawing on the surplus store of the province in hand from previous years," the secretary to the financial commissioner of Punjab noted in 1879; "but it may also be met to some extent by a decreased local consumption, consequent on the rise in price which a demand for export causes."[85] Officials in the NWP and Oudh were similarly cautious in accounting for the source of supply of the increasing exports. Government's role was to observe the passage of trade and collect its dues. It was slow to set about the basic task of calculating the volume of the regional traffic in food grains. "Except on such channels as the East Indian Railway and the Ganges Canal, and at such points as the customs' hedge and the bridges over the great rivers, and the octroi barriers of the principal towns, there is no

[82]*NWP Revenue Administration Report*, 1881–82, p. 6. Compare the observation seven years later: "With the extension of railway communications in Rohilkhand, the prevalence of low prices may be said to have come to an end." *Ibid.*, 1888–89, p. 6. A. B. Patterson, Settlement Officer, Fatehpur, was similarly convinced of the efficacy of railway development—"the great export trade to Europe provides a security against any possible return to low prices"; *Fatehpur Settlement Report*, p. 47.

[83]*NWP Revenue Administration Report*, 1881–82, p. 6. Compare *Shahjahanpur Settlement Report*, p. xiii: due to the railway "grain is exported south to a much greater extent than before."

[84]Chandausi junction, for example, in Moradabad district, on the Oudh and Rohilkhand Railway. According to E. B. Alexander, who noticed a large quantity of wheat being carted at the end of October to the railway station for export to Rajputana, grain was often kept in store at centres like Chandausi for "a long time." *Moradabad Settlement Report*, p. 57.

[85]J. A. E. Miller to Government, Punjab, December 8, 1879, in Government of India, *Selections from the Records of Government*, No. CLX, p. 207.

machinery existing for the registration of trade," Frederick Henvey
noted in his report on the scarcity of 1868-69 and 1870; ". . . accordingly, for a general view of the exports and imports, as well as the
internal traffic, dependence must be placed in great measure upon
the conjectural estimates of tehsildars."[86] The situation did not
change rapidly. Although great stress was laid by Sir John Strachey
on the prime duty of the new Department of Agriculture for the provinces, established in 1874, to collect statistics of production and
distribution,[87] no system of trade registration was in force till 1877.
The system then implemented was admitted at the outset to be imperfect, and remained defective throughout the period.[88]

If overall patterns of trade movements could be gauged only in
the most approximate fashion, local statistics were even more inadequate. A. F. Millett in discussing the exports and imports of Fyzabad
district—said to act as an emporium for eastern Oudh—gave the
aggregate value of exports for one year (unspecified) in the late 1870s
as Rs. 4,864,074 and of imports as Rs. 1,979,768. But, he promptly
added, "It appears that the official returns do not accurately represent
either the one or the other; they only indicate the course of river
trade at marts within the district boundary, and the internal trade
by road or river with other parts of Oudh is not given . . ." Millett
despaired: "The actual exports of the district cannot be determined;
its large population probably consumes most of the produce."[89]

The calculation of prices was also beset with uncertainties. It was
officially recognized that the passage of the product from the cultivator
to the local dealer and on to the commercial centres entailed a number
of transactions, each governed by its price "rate." Village prices
were held to differ according to the relative distance between the

---

[86]F. Henvey, *Narrative*, p. 6.

[87]See p. 101 above.

[88]An adequate statistical series for trade in staple food grains cannot be compiled
from the official NWP and Oudh trade reports. Trade registration posts multiplied
from year to year; frontier divisions within which statistics were officially collected
were altered from time to time; figures for one year's road but six months' rail traffic
were combined in the same entry; figures of quantity sometimes alternate with those
for (estimated) value. The trade figures given in *Oudh Revenue Administration Report*,
1872–73, Statement XXV, are identical with those in *Oudh Revenue Administration
Report*, 1871–72, Statement XXIV. The *Report* for 1873–74 contained no statistical
statement, while the *Report* for 1874–75 included neither a statistical statement nor a
descriptive account in the text.

[89]*Fyzabad Settlement Report*, p. 28. G. B. Maconochie made similar observations in
Unao in the 1860s. No data as regards exports and imports were available from which
reliable figures could be obtained; *Unao Settlement Report*, p. 20.

village and the nearest market town : Moens maintained that Bareilly village prices were, on the average, about two to three seers per rupee below the market "rate."[90] These local prices were in turn divided officially into two categories : harvest or threshing-floor "rates" and bazar or local dealers' "rates." As with rents, the estimation of any viable rate which governed local prices proved to be a problem. Harvest "rates" covered a multitude of individual transactions, governed by the precise relation of purchaser to seller and the extent of the latter's obligations to the former. W. C. Benett's remark, apropos of Gonda prices, that it was always extremely laborious and in some places impossible to ascertain correctly what price the "corn factor" (corn dealer) pays the cultivator on the threshing floor[91] is therefore by no means surprising. This is true also of Markham's finding that the recorded threshing-floor "rates" were fictitious—that they were "to a great extent *pro forma* rates, fixed on to facilitate settlements among sharers, etc., and with an eye to the entries of rent to be made in the village papers."[92] Here again, it had become impossible for officers to detect genuinely fraudulent practices. For Benett, the arduousness of disentangling actual prices was restricted to the harvest category in Gonda. "Retail prices in the bazar," he declared, "may be discovered at once."[93] Others, however, encountered difficulty here too. F. N. Wright, for one, was thwarted in his wish "to show the prices at which the grain-dealers sold back the grain to the cultivators at seed time, when it would be at its highest price," since he could not gather sufficient information to tabulate them.[94] The problems of enquiry into grain transactions were complicated still further by the imposition of the Licence Tax. E. B. Alexander commented that because of this tax traders in Moradabad had become suspicious of all enquiries as to their business and that "the information they give us is so utterly misleading that it is extremely hard to give any accurate account of trade dealings."[95] These difficulties precluded

[90]*Bareilly Settlement Report*, p. 81. For an early twentieth-century all-India survey of local grain prices in relation to distance from major market centres, see Th. Engelbrecht, *Die Feldfrüchte Indiens*, price maps, Figures 1–16; price tables, pp. 60–111, Tables 1–12.

[91]*Gonda Settlement Report*, pp. 77–78.

[92]A. M. Markham, Settlement Officer, Bijnour, to Commissioner, Rohilkhand, January 23, 1871, in NWP, "Revenue Proceedings," September 2, 1871, Index No. 12, July 29, 1871, Proceeding No. 38.

[93]*Gonda Settlement Report*, p. 78.

[94]*Cownpore Settlement Report*, p. 58.

[95]*Moradabad Settlement Report*, pp. 56–57.

any sound estimate of dealers' profits. Benett's conjectures on this score are perhaps instructive. From a comparison of bazar prices (culled from Banias' books) with field prices (conjectured), he hazarded the conclusion that, in Utraula and Gonda, the profits of a corn factor were little more than 27 percent—but, he added, there was also a differential in types of grains and areas: in Gonda investments in oilseeds paid 40 percent while in Utraula they paid 20 percent.[96] What, therefore, is the reader to assume the corn factor's profits to have been? The difficulties in compiling the most basic information of this kind also made any valid comparison of local price conditions impossible, since each officer collected what information he could, when, where, and how he could, making full use of his discretionary powers. No uniform method could be imposed at the local level, and the divergence could be extreme. For Cawnpore district, two totally different sets of statistics were offered for the same periods— 1814-1836, 1840-1856, and 1859-1877. These periods were selected so as to avoid distortion owing to severe irregularities occurring in the intervening years. The explanation for the discrepancy was that W. S. Halsey's list, compiled earlier in the revision of settlement, had neglected to rule out the special influence of Cawnpore city over the prices of produce in the neighbourhood, whereas Wright's list had taken this anomaly into account.[97] S. O. B. Ridsdale offered detailed statements of prices for each pargana of Etah district; these, however, were averages struck from Banias' books in three principal marts of parganas Sahawar, Karsana,[98] and Azamnagar,[99] and from zamindars' as well as Banias' books in four principal marts of pargana Sirpura.[100] Bazar "rates" were listed for Mainpuri district for the period 1815-1871, but the rates quoted were not derived from Mainpuri records since no district bazar rates for the whole period were in fact available and such fragments as were procurable could not be relied on. What was given therefore were the averages of rates current in Agra bazar for the periods 1815-1840 and 1857-1871. Since no details from Agra were available for the period 1840-1857, the settlement officers "were obliged to substitute Muttra rates for that interval." This was asserted to matter little inasmuch as rates in Agra and Muttra "are

[96]*Gonda Settlement Report*, p. 78.
[97]For F. N. Wright's comments on W. S. Halsey's errors, see *Cawnpore Settlement Report*, p. 59.
[98]*Etah Settlement Report*, p. 100.
[99]*Ibid.*, p. 86.
[100]*Ibid.*, p. 120.

and have been always almost identical."[101] Further confusions were added by variations in local weights and measures. Alexander commented that although the figures he had taken for prices for Moradabad district from the pargana rent-rate reports were the most accurate obtainable, "the perpetual confusion which occurs in all these early returns between the different seers and the kucha and pucka maunds renders it impossible to rely much on them."[102]

Given the impossibility of making accurate calculations, Government officers could offer only the most general estimates in reporting the rise in local prices during the past settlements (approximately 1840-1870). Their conclusions in the main ranged between 25 and 50 percent by way of a permanent rise in the prices of staple produce.[103] Prices had always risen inevitably whenever harvests were deficient, but the tendency had formerly been—so far as is known—for them to fall on the subsequent occurrence of better seasons. While deficient harvests continued to push prices up,[104] increasing exports of agricultural produce kept them from falling back to old levels when outturns improved.[105] Prices fell noticeably only when exports diminished, as happened for example during the course of 1889-90[106]

[101] *Mainpuri Settlement Report*, p. 70.

[102] *Moradabad Settlement Report*, p. 61.

[103] The increase in prices of agricultural produce between 1840 and 1870 for Etawah, for example, was estimated at 40 percent (*Etawah Settlement Report*, pp. 55–56); for Fatehpur, 25 percent (*Fatehpur Settlement Report*, pp. 46–47); for Mainpuri, 47 percent (*Mainpuri Settlement Report*, pp. 72–73); for Muttra, 50 percent (*Muttra Settlement Report, Canal Tract*, p. 76); for Etah, an average of pargana estimates, 60 percent (*Etah Settlement Report*, cited above in notes 98, 99, 100); for Moradabad, 60 percent in *gur*, 70 percent in edible grains (*Moradabad Settlement Report*, p. 61); for Farukhabad, 300 (sic) percent ("Resolution," *Farukhabad Settlement Report*, pp. 2–3). For Oudh by 1872 C. W. McMinn quoted an average rise of 20 percent since 1858; *Introduction*, pp. 189–190.

[104] According to the Commissioner of Agra Division and "native" opinion, for example in 1886–87 the "late sudden rise" in grain prices was owing to deficient harvests of the preceding three years; see *NWP Revenue Administration Report*, 1886–87, p. 4. Prices in Jhansi Division in 1888–89 were reported to be high—the "natural consequence" of bad harvests; see *ibid.*, 1888–89, pp. 5–6. For the frequency of poor harvests in the period 1864–65 to 1884–85, see Figure 1.

[105] Prices in 1887–88 were reported to be considerably higher than in 1886–87 (in which they had also exceeded markedly those of the preceding year). The continuing rise was generally attributed to deficient harvests of previous years, an indifferent kharif outturn, and larger exportations. See *NWP Revenue Administration Report*, 1887–88, pp. 5–6. S. M. Moens was informed, "frequently," by leading grain merchants of Bareilly that "provided internal peace is maintained, they never expect the average wheat price on a series of years to fall again below 25 Bareilly seers the Rupee" (formerly a sign of impending scarcity); *Bareilly Settlement Report*, pp. 60–61.

[106] As reported in "up-country" districts, diminished exports tended to keep the

and again in 1892-93.[107] The marked fall in the value of silver, which was widely commented on by the early 1870s, also contributed to maintain this upward trend in prices. "Bullion [in payment for raw materials exported] has been poured into the Indian empire at the rate of £1,500,000 p.a. for the last ten years, 1862-71," C. W. McMinn reported. "Whether ... an advantage or not, the fact remains that prices must rise ..."[108]

Who could benefit? "The rise in prices might reasonably be expected to have affected the condition of the people very materially," Alexander commented as regards Moradabad, "but," he added, "it is better to defer consideration of this point."[109] Since, as we have seen, only a minority of cultivators disposed of their produce free of obligations to local Banias or beoparis, the upward climb in prices could benefit but a few producers directly by bringing them a better return on their crops. In the bargain between purchaser and cultivator which the harvest prices represented, "the grip of the purchaser [Bania- or zamindar-creditor] on the seller ... is a very tight one," the settlement officers commented with regard to the situation in Mainpuri, which was typical of the districts as a whole. "In fixing the harvest prices, the grain-dealer, who is the purchaser, has generally the best of it. Therefore, on a general rise in market rates, harvest prices, although they will not remain stationary, will not increase in the same proportion."[110] A. H. Harington noted how the common phenomenon of the combination, in one person, of moneylender and grain dealer—"the simple system [sic] of rural economy is entirely based on the dealings of this man"—prevented the borrowing ryot, a similarly common phenomenon, from getting a fair price for his produce.[111] In Muttra the combination was seen at its most

price of wheat down despite generally poor harvests. *NWP and Oudh Revenue Administration Report*, 1889-90, pp. 7-8.

[107] Prices of food grains were reported to be easing, in 1892-93, as compared with several years past. Coarser grains became, temporarily, comparatively cheap in most parts of the NWP owing *inter alia* to "a falling-off in the foreign export trade" and the fact that heavy rainfall during threshing made the grain unfit for storage. See *NWP and Oudh Revenue Administration Report*, 1892-93, p. 5.

[108] McMinn, *Introduction*, p. 189, For a contemporary summary of the question of depreciation in the 1870s, see Harington, "Corn in Egypt," *Pioneer* (June 1876), as cited by Harington, "Economic Reform in Rural India," *Calcutta Review*, LXXX (1885), 445. According to Harington, basic data essential for calculating the average extent of depreciation had never been collected.

[109] *Moradabad Settlement Report*, p. 61.

[110] *Mainpuri Settlement Report*, pp. 73-74.

[111] "Economic Reform in Rural India," *Calcutta Review*, LXXX (1885), 436.

formidable : these men constituted a grain-dealing "guild or fraternity, to which not only no outsider not of the caste can get admittance, but which monopolizes the moneylending or banking trade." A rise in market prices could not filter through to producers subject to their control, for the members of this guild, "be they Baniyas or zamindars, can compel the producer, who lives solely by the advances they give him, to bring his produce to their shops and prevent him getting the full open market value for his goods. The cultivator is therefore not only crippled by the heavy interest he has to pay, but also by the low prices he is compelled to take for his produce."[112] Moreover, with the rise in prices, indebtedness could be seen not merely to persist but to grow. Alan Cadell observed in the Muzaffarnagar canal tract how, "greatly as the agricultural community has prospered in recent years" (mid-1870s), indebtedness had in fact increased, since old habits of borrowing were further encouraged by improved credit and lower interest rates, which were the direct consequences of an overall rise in the prices of agricultural produce.[113] Throughout the provinces, the granaries of talukdars, zamindars, privileged peasants, and mahajans were stocked by the produce paid over by the peasants in remitting their seasonal charges.[114] The most the majority of cultivators could hope for by way of benefits from price increases was some easing of the pressures of local control.

"Unimproved" tracts in which no large-scale public works had been constructed shared along with "improved" districts in the general rise in prices, but the result here was that existing inequalities in the distribution of wealth from trade were aggravated. Take the case of Bijnour. The price of wheat in markets lying on or near major lines of communication—the rivers—might well have doubled or quadrupled within the space of a few years by the late 1870s, enriching local mahajans and zamindars, especially those who continued to claim bazar dues. But internal communications in Bijnour remained poor. The existence of only a few roads meant that the majority of minor rivers in the district were never bridged. Cultivators living "on the other side of an impassable stream" or impeded by the lack of a direct road from reaching the flourishing markets could not take advantage of their benefits.[115] While the costs of imported commodities

[112] *Muttra Settlement Report*, pp. 89–90.

[113] *Muzaffarnagar Settlement Report, Canal Tract*, pp. 18–19.

[114] See, for example, the description given by "Xenophon, Duab" in "The Last Rubee and Khureef," *Indian Agriculturist*, October 1, 1876, p. 284.

[115] Observations by Officiating Senior Member, Board of Revenue, NWP, in NWP Revenue Department, "Resolution," 1880, *Bijnour Settlement Report*, p. 3.

they needed for daily use—such as salt, spices, and household utensils—
had risen, cultivators in the district's hinterland had no corresponding
increase in the proceeds from the sale of their produce with which
to meet them.

By 1892, the cultivators' predicament as a result of the increasing
stimuli applied to local markets was obvious. W. E. Neale, then
Commissioner of Agra Division, observed that prices which were
"slowly rising, first of all in the luxuries [sic] of life, such as ghi, wheat,
oil, firewood, horses and cattle," would be "ultimately followed
by an appreciable dearness in the millets and other staple food of
the vast agricultural and labouring population."[116] Elsewhere Neale's
gloomy predictions had already become reality. In Hardoi district,
settlement returns on grain prices from Madhoganj, the principal
mart, showed that in the late 1870s kharif staples—jowar and bajra—
were "often sold to the poor by the grain-dealers at prices actually
exceeding the rates at which the wealthy purchase wheat." Although
the admitted unreliability of such returns ruled out precise and
detailed calculations, the conclusion seemed indisputable to the
officials: "the broad fact remains ... that the food of the poor is
increasing in price with greater rapidity than the food of the rich."[117]
The expansion in "valuable" crops directly contributed to the problem.
Bareilly was one of the few districts where wheat, prior to the great
developments in the export trade, was commonly grown by cultivators
for food. The price of this staple was said to have risen between 1859
and the revision of the settlement because, *inter alia*, of the "increased
area as compared with former years devoted to the cultivation of
sugar-cane and cotton, and the consequent comparative diminution
of the area devoted to food-grains."[118] In the canal-irrigated districts,
enormous increases were reported by the mid-1870s in the export
rabi staples: in 1873-74 alone, the area under wheat was increased by
39,225 acres and that under barley by 25,555 acres. The area under
pulses, the prime source of vegetable protein for the rural population,

[116] *NWP and Oudh Revenue Administration Report*, 1891–92, p. 6. Compare the situation
reported in Basti district in 1888–89. "The rise in prices makes it impossible for the
cultivator to get sufficient food whereas prior to the increase in exporting facilities,
he kept his grain and had it in store for an unfavourable season." The Board of Revenue,
however, was "not prepared to endorse the view that the cultivator has been a loser
by the extension of railway communication and the consequent rise in prices. His
former thrift is perhaps somewhat overstated." *NWP and Oudh Revenue Administration
Report*, 1888–89, pp. 5–6.

[117] *Hardoi Settlement Report*, pp. 20–21.

[118] *Bareilly Settlement Report*, p. 60.

registered a decrease in that year of some 9,000 acres.[119]

It was not only the cultivator's diet which was affected to his detriment by the attractions the grain trade offered his purchaser-creditors. His supplies of seed grain could be similarly jeopardized. W. S. Robertson, in a note published in the *Indian Agriculturist* in 1876, explained how "extortionate moneylenders," to whom most ryots were in debt, "compel their unfortunate victims not only to sell under compulsion at their own prices, but to purchase some inferior grain for seed. Thus inferior qualities of grain are gradually being diffused over the land, to the serious detriment of rice in particular, from the fact of this being the more expensive grain, and most in demand for exportation."[120]

Government and the Problem of Indebtedness

Local society, as Moens noted in Bareilly, tended to accept persistent borrowing as the natural state of things—cultivators even considered it prestigious to keep a running account with the Bania for a sizeable sum.[121] Official opinion, on the other hand, deplored the peasants' indebtedness and saw in it—not without reason—the fount of all local evils. A. O. Hume's view, characteristically dramatic, was representative of current opinion on the problem: "Wherever we turn, we find agriculturists burdened with debts running on at enormous rates of interest. In some districts, even provinces, the evil is all-absorbing—a whole population of paupers, hopelessly meshed in the webs of usurers."[122]

The problem was not viewed solely as an index of peasant pauperization. There was also the far from unimportant question of the moneylender's interception of legitimate profits of Government. Robert Knight accused Government of resigning its just claims to the *sahukar* (moneylender) and thereby strengthening the latter's position

[119]*NWP Revenue Administration Report*, 1873–74, para. 14. The increases in Etawah district alone that year were recorded as 19,507 acres for wheat (over 50 percent above the 1872–73 figure) and 12,257 for barley (nearly 50 percent above the 1872–73 figure).

[120]"Grain and Seeds," *Indian Agriculturist*, June 1, 1876, at p. 163.

[121]*Bareilly Settlement Report*, p. 55.

[122]Hume, *Agricultural Reform*, p. 36. Hume attributed this condition pre-eminently to the "ruinous system of civil litigation" introduced by the British. On landlord and tenant litigation, see pp. 152–153 above. On litigation generally, see Chapter V below.

to the detriment of his agriculturist clients. In an article published in 1871, Knight expostulated that "by lowering the assessment [from 66⅔ to 50 percent, the new revised proportion of 'rental assets' to be taken by Government][123] we simply enrich the sowkar [sahukar]; for what we abandon as *rent* he takes as interest." Knight therefore recommended loftily that the creditor-middleman be removed, and he preached to Government the advantages offered by a serious study of the Book of Genesis : "for we believe that the Scriptures, though not teaching political science dogmatically, do nevertheless contain very striking examples of political wisdom."[124] Instructions for ending the iniquities of the interception of profits, and the consequent evils for the agricultural population, were to be found in the story of Joseph who, by advancing grain to cultivators in time of severe scarcity on the condition of regular payment of one-fifth of their produce to the state, gained total control over agricultural production, which ruled out any danger of interference by "private creditors." Knight urged that since "the revolution made 3,500 years ago in Egypt by the young and inspired Hebrew minister was suggested to him by Divine wisdom, Government should pay attention to this historic expedient."[125]

The Government of India and the local administrations of the NWP and Oudh were in no position to be confident of a viable analogy between themselves and Pharaoh. Their problem was one not merely of responsibility but also of cost. Hume estimated that "the native mofussil capital employed in usury [for British India as a whole] is believed to be more than three-fold that employed in trade. By no means could the amount of the latter be more than doubled for many years, so that for a long time two-thirds at least of the capital now employed in moneylending in the mofussil *must* continue to be so employed."[126]

[123]See pp. 123–124 above.

[124]"Corn in Egypt," *Indian Economist*, April 15, 1871, at p. 234. The article discussed a question raised (by A. H. Harington) in the columns of the *Pioneer* under the head "Corn in Egypt," viz. : "Is it creditable to a landlord that his rent is paid regularly by a debt-ridden tenantry with money borrowed at 37½%?"—a question provoked by the current debate over the adjustment of revenue kists, on which see pp. 155–160 above.

[125]Knight, *ibid.*, p. 235. He believed the state might well appropriate three-fifths of the rental with nothing but advantage to all classes. Less would benefit only the malguzar and *sahukar*, at the expense of the state and the ryot.

[126]Hume, *Agricultural Reform*, p. 46. "Native" capital was never solicited for contribution to the massive investment in the provinces' public works (see pp. 64–66

Official statistical estimates of the volume of debt throughout the provinces were as vague as those of the numbers of debtors. Even under heads of account which seemed most significant to observing revenue officers—chiefly the rent payments—no specific information could be assembled. Harington commented in 1883 on the "extraordinary lack of data for estimating the probable proportion between rent and advances."[127] In 1869, C. A. Elliott had conjectured that throughout the NWP some £10,000,000 total value were borrowed annually by "agriculturists for seed, food grains, rent, revenue, clothing and other expenses."[128] Enquiries made by J. S. Mackintosh, Secretary to the NWP Board of Revenue, to "many European and native officers" led him to conclude that "not less than the rent paid or payable for the land [that is, an estimated sum of twice the land revenue demand] was borrowed yearly for the cultivation of it." Mackintosh's own view as expressed in a personal communication to Harington was that the amount borrowed in an ordinary year was nearer £15,000,000 than £10,000,000, and that in a year of severe distress this rose to between £20,000,000 and £30,000,000 and was probably nearer the latter.[129] Harington's own calculations of the "probable magnitude of the financial part of the business"—the capital required annually for loans—provided an estimate that some £19,000,000 would be regularly involved per year.[130] The Government land revenue then stood at some £20,000,000 for British India. Harington asked whether the state could furnish the amount needed for loans, and, if it were so able, should it "buy up the creditors" or leave "the enterprise to private capitalists"?[131]

Government could not afford to contemplate such a radical overthrow of existing conditions as would be necessitated by the replacement of the machinery which existed—even that portion of it run by mahajans—for the supply of credit to agriculturists. The chief

above), nor was any other area for large-scale, productive, and systematic investment opened up for it.

[127]"Economic Reform in Rural India," Calcutta Review, LXXVI (1883), 164.

[128]Revenue Reporter, IV 11 (1869), 84, cited by Harington, ibid.

[129]Ibid. Harington gives no exact date for Mackintosh's enquiry.

[130]Ibid., p. 163. Harington's calculations were as follows. One-half the gross produce he assumed to be equivalent to the maximum amount borrowed, which would be equal to one-and-one-half times the cultivator's rent. Two-fifths of the cultivators of the seven temporarily settled provinces would pay, he assumed, two-fifths of the gross rental of those districts and consequently one-fifth of the land revenue, assuming the rental stood at twice the land revenue.

[131]Ibid., p. 166.

commissioner of Oudh had asked for recommendations by district officers in the course of the 1869 enquiry into indebtedness as to how the cultivator's state of dependence on extraneous aid might be improved.[132] In their replies the district officers were almost unanimously of the opinion that "no direct interference can advantageously be exercised by the administration," an opinion in which the chief commissioner concurred.[133] If Government not only refused to interfere with a landlord's activities but even gave him specific legal protection in recognizing his power of enhancement of rent and distraint of tenants' goods on default of rent payments, how then could Government legitimately obstruct the moneylender in the pursuit of the profits of his trade?[134]

Practically speaking, since both the realization of land revenue and the zamindars' collection of their charges were heavily dependent on the timely assistance of "the mahajan," it was inconceivable that Government should interfere with what was in fact its vital source of supply.[135] Nor could it disturb "the mahajan" in his role as universal provider, *faute de mieux*, to the cultivating population. However deplorable the profiteering of creditors might seem, official opinion was resigned to admitting that "with all his faults, the village banker has been and probably will continue to be a useful member of the agricultural community. He finds much of the capital with which the cultivating system of the country is worked and advances it on little better security than the agricultural labourer's verbal promise, the fulfilment of which depends on the seasons."[136] Patrick Carnegy's official statement in 1868 for the Oudh enquiry made the position, and the dilemma, of Government abundantly clear : ". . . anything

[132]*Oudh Selections*, 1868–69, p. 3.

[133]Davies, "Memorandum on the ... Indebtedness of Cultivators in Oudh," *Oudh Selections*, 1868–69, p. 74.

[134]For a statement of the problem of the *mahajan's* dealings and Government control, see the observations of E. Thompson, Officiating Commissioner, Sitapur, in *Oudh Selections*, 1868–69, pp. 39–40. The policy of non-interference early found its clearest expression in the repeal of the Usury Laws by Act XXVIII, 1855. For a discussion of this legislation and its problems, see pp. 217–220.

[135]W. P. Harrison, Assistant Commissioner, Pratabgarh, in *Oudh Selections*, 1868–69, pp. 68–69. See also A. B. Patterson in *Fatehpur Settlement Report*, p. 12.

[136]NWP Revenue Department, "Resolution," 1883, *Allahabad Settlement Report*, p. 8 (and see text of *Report*, p. 48). See also *Bareilly Settlement Report*, p. 81, and Sir John Strachey's eloquent observation, "Moneylenders are obviously as necessary to the Indian agriculturist as the seed which he sows, or as the rain which falls from heaven to water his fields," quoted by Harington, "Economic Reform in Rural India," *Calcutta Review*, LXXVI (1883), 153 (headnote).

like official interference in the interests of the cultivator would only lead to ill-will between him and the mahajan, who often stands between him and starvation. However much, therefore, the Officiating Commissioner [Carnegy] might like to see the position of the cultivator improved, he is of the opinion that, in the interests of the latter ... the less we interfere the better."[137] The welfare of the cultivator was, after all, the landlord's responsibility.

Scarcity years, in pushing prices beyond the high levels which had become the norm beginning in the early 1870s and beyond even those recorded for famine years in the past,[138] brought a scramble for the profits of local trade in food grains. "Besides the regular traders, men of all sorts embarked in it who had or could raise any capital, jewellers and cloth dealers pledging their stocks, even their wives' jewels, to engage in the business and import grain."[139] But failure in the kharif could bring no profit to local cultivators. As June and July wore on and little or no rain fell, the threat of imminent scarcity drove up prices of all available stocks of grain. Farmers could not benefit as they had nothing now to sell, having long before disposed of the greater part of their outturn from the previous rabi to meet their obligations. At most, they kept back sufficient for a few months' food. By September, local stocks were drained, and cultivators could only buy or borrow their seed and food at prices which rocketed to famine levels.[140]

The breakdown in the local supply of grain which became apparent on the occurrence of severe scarcity was no isolated happening but the consequence of years of rising prices combined with uneven yields. The danger as far as Government's awareness of the deteriorating condition of the rural population was concerned lay, as McMinn remarked, "in the slowness of Indian starvation and the absence of outward indications of the approach of famine."[141] The threat of poor outturns had subtle and damaging consequences for the majority of cultivators in that it led creditors to refuse further advances. As

[137]Oudh Selections, 1868–69, p. 48.

[138]McMinn, for example, noted how "at present [early 1870s] when a good harvest is reported all over India, the price of wheat is higher in Lucknow than it was in the NWP during the 1837–38 famine." Introduction, p. 189.

[139]Meerut district, NWP Revenue Administration Report, 1876–77, pp. 6–7.

[140]Ibid. For the agriculturist's problems in his role as consumer, see NWP and Oudh Revenue Administration Report, 1889–90, p. 4.

[141]Introduction, p. 187.

C. J. Daniell commented on the situation in Jhansi in August 1877, "Whenever little or no crop is sown, or when the sown crop is endangered by drought, banias close their money bags and refuse food or its equivalent. The people are then thrown on their own resources (nil, in so many cases)."[142] This problem was in no way confined to Jhansi. Elsewhere in the provinces during the scarcity of 1877 large stocks accumulated from previous good seasons were in the hands of the zamindars and dealers; throughout the summer, as the gross deterioration in the kharif conditions became more and more apparent, a brisk exportation persisted nevertheless. But the kharif failure induced creditors to turn away their cultivator clients from fear that their diminishing stocks might not be replenished in that season. It was in their interest to withhold loans and thus to drive prices still higher.[143]

Throughout, Government's policy was to interfere as little and as briefly as possible with the channels of private trade. The modicum of official control believed indispensable in easing straitened circumstances in neighbouring Bihar in 1873, when imports from the NWP on which the area relied were held back owing to the attraction of the famine prices ruling in the provinces, was designed as a temporary measure : such needs should disappear, it was expected, "as means of communication are extended and the wealth of the country increases."[144] The needs, however, persisted, but the control diminished even further, and the principle of non-interference triumphed—as the Famine Commission of 1879 in fact recommended. The seal was set on this policy by the publication of the Famine Code in 1896.[145] Grain continued to flow throughout the provinces (earning Government a handsome profit from freight charges and customs dues),[146] not in response to the distress of cultivators who could neither pay for it nor, in the face of imminent scarcity, borrow it, but as the high

[142]C. J. Daniell, "Demi-Official Report on the Condition and Prospects of Agriculture in Jhansi," August 16, 1877, in Government of India, "Famine Proceedings," September 1877, Proceeding No. 72.

[143]*NWP Revenue Administration Report*, 1876–77, pp. 6–7. Henvey, *Narrative*, p. 9.

[144]This "control" amounted to a minor reduction in the rates for the carriage of grain by railway. See Agriculture, Revenue and Commerce Department, India, to Government, NWP, February 25, 1875, in NWP, "Revenue Proceedings," March 1875, Index No. 2, March 20, 1875, Proceeding No. 2.

[145]*Resolution on the Administration of Famine Relief*, IV, 118.

[146]From October 1896 to June 1897, rail-borne imports of grain into the NWP and Oudh totalled 645,628 tons, exports 306,377 tons. "This vast and beneficient trade movement was effected not only without difficulty or apparent effort, but with great pecuniary advantage to the State." *Ibid.*, p. 119.

prices of local famine conditions and the expanding export trade dictated.

When his zamindar or creditor refused to oblige him, what did a cultivator do for grain? He could rob a store, or he could riot; the latter was a frequent occurrence in the "distressed districts" of the Doab during the grain crisis of 1877, for example, and was met by vigorous police measures.[147] He could also emigrate; this was a common cource of relief for farmers in the Lower Doab and Bundelkhand, who made their way to Malwa when scarcity threatened and returned one or two seasons later.[148] He could, on occasion, earn a temporary subsistence wage—for the duration of the most obviously critical period only—on Government relief works. This remedy became more worthless as the century wore on. To cut costs Government entrusted the actual expenditure on schemes of village relief works to the zamindars, with the result that they employed only the able-bodied at starvation wages.[149]

The peasantry was subject to the ravages of scarcity years without adequate relief; occasional abundant harvests provided no significant alleviation. The predicament of the impoverished cultivator faced with a fair season's outturn was well known and was aptly summarized by the lieutenant-governor of the NWP himself as early as 1872: "The seed and food borrowed at a high rate have to be repaid by a far larger weight of grain when prices have fallen, and the forced sales to which he is compelled in order to pay rent or revenue lower

[147]Government, NWP and Oudh, to Government of India, October 4, 1877, in Government of India, "Famine Proceedings," October 1877, Proceeding No. 14. For details of grain robberies and the consequences meted out to robbers, see D. G. Pitcher, *Report on the Scarcity,* 1877–1879, pp. 3–5. For details of the steep rise in the rate of incidence of "ordinary crime" in scarcity years, see Henvey, *Narrative,* pp. 126–127 (1868–69, 1870); see also *Resolution on the Administration of Famine Relief,* IV, 126 ff.

[148]Baird Smith described emigration as the only important relief "adopted by the sufferers" in the famine of 1860–61. Migrants from western districts were estimated to number 120,000, from central districts (i.e., Central and Lower Doab), 255,000, and from eastern districts 500,000; "Report," pp. 36–39. In comparison, emigration in the famine of 1877–78 was reported much reduced, and only from Jhansi Division from the end of July, and Agra Division during August. No figures were given; see *NWP Revenue Administration Report,* 1876–77, pp. 1–3. The official report in the scarcity of 1896–97 made no reference to emigration. But by this time regular migration of labourers to Assam, Bengal, Bihar, and Bombay had begun in earnest. See p. 275 below.

[149]Relief works in Bundelkhand on roads, tanks, wells, and embankments were reported accomplished under the administration of local zamindars at the cost of Rs. 4.8.0 per 1,000 feet of excavation. See *Resolution on the Administration of Famine Relief,* IV, 14.

the market price below the level at which the abundant crop would of itself place it ... To the well-to-do farmer, who has grain to sell, high prices bring fortune; to the indebted man, who has to borrow, they are loss and ruin ..."[150] In 1874-75, Benares Division saw good harvests reaped throughout. Gorakhpur especially "enjoyed a plenty enough to compensate for the scarcity of the year before." But abundance worked, as of old, against cultivators in clearing their accounts of loans borrowed to tide them over the previous year's drought. "If they took 1 maund of grain in October 1874, when selling at 20 seers the Rupee," the Collector, J. J. F. Lumsden, suggested by way of a typical example, "they would have to repay in April or May 1875, the value in grain of Rs. 2, with interest at 25 percent, and as grain was then selling at 30 seers, they would have to give back 1 maund and 35 seers for every maund they borrowed. Considerations such as these must temper to a certain extent the cultivator's joy at a bumper harvest."[151] A. B. Patterson, the Settlement Officer of Fatehpur, reported that the abnormally low prices in pargana Khaga owing to exceptionally good harvests gave cause for anxiety: "many moderate settlements would press severely if low prices recurred on a par with those of 1850–1857, or April–November, 1876." For low prices brought great distress: cultivators "had more grain than they knew what to do with, but money to pay their rents was hardly to be got."[152]

In the Secretariat meanwhile, it was an acknowledged fact that the actual division of "rental assets" between Government and zamindar differed markedly from the nominal egalitarian proportions of 50 percent on which the revised assessments had been calculated. "It will hardly be denied," H. S. Reid, Junior Member of the Board of Revenue, admitted in a minute of 1873, "that a rental, equivalent to double the Government demand, is collected only in good years. Assuming the pay of the patwari to be 5 percent on the jama, the zamindar, what with the payment of cesses, expenses of collections, balances of rent and patwaris' allowances, nets little more (if any

---

[150]Government, NWP, to Board of Revenue, NWP, June 25, 1872, para. 3, *NWP Revenue Administration Report*, 1870–71. For detailed observations by divisions, see *Report*, pp. 2–3.

[151]*NWP Revenue Administration Report*, 1874–75, pp. 2–3. The same situation was reported from Ghazipur district, viz. excellent harvest, abundant grain, sufficient food but money scarce—and "rents" therefore were paid with difficulty.

[152]*Fatehpur Settlement Report*, p. 45.

more) than 30 percent of the rental, a clear 50 percent of which goes to Government. The Government will probably gain an increase of 30 to 40 lakhs p.a. [Rs. 3,000,000 to 4,000,000] by the revision of settlement at 50 percent on present, in lieu of 66 percent on old assets."[153]

The zamindars' share was not merely depleted by the regular payment of cesses; it was subject at the same time to the risk of further reductions owing to a wide range of irregular circumstances. Among these were the increased pressure, not to mention the conflict, stemming from excessive numbers dependent on proprietorial claims within the zamindari group; the inability of zamindars, especially the idle aristocrats displaced from service, to turn themselves into industrious landlords; the fact that poor harvests on the one hand leading to unrealizable balances of charges from cultivators, and good harvests on the other resulted in a glut of local markets and the plummeting of grain prices. Government however continued to collect its revenue on the basis of the theoretical distribution of assets; its demand could not be adjusted to allow for the inroad of regular, let alone irregular, charges on zamindars' incomes.[154]

The combination of scientific revenue assessments and untoward circumstances rapidly singled out the prosperous zamindars from the economically incapacitated even within the space of a single pargana. S. N. Martin reported from Muzaffarnagar in 1862 how the assessment (of pargana Muzaffarnagar) had been "unfortunately preceded by several bad years, including those of the mutiny and famine ..." with the result that "the wealthy capitalists have alone been able to hold out but the Bhyachara villages have been greatly depressed ... The zamindars of unirrigated lands have suffered immensely while those proprietors whose estates border on the canal were making, during the last year of distress when grain was selling at 8 seers the Rupee, large but temporary profits ..."[155] All through the district, the old zamindari families of Syuds faced ruin: "though their numbers

[153]"Minute on the Patwari's Status and Remuneration," August 8, 1873, in NWP, "Revenue Proceedings," March 1874, Index No. 13, November 8, 1873, Proceeding No. 85. For an enumeration of regular cesses payable to Government, estimated on every Rs. 100 of "rental" theoreticall due to the zamindars, see the example, from Jhansi, at p. 136 above (Table 2). For comparable payments collected from Oudh zamindars, see H. C. Irwin, *Garden of India,* pp. 32–33. Compare the Stracheys' assertion that modernization was achieved without extra charge on the revenue; see p. 2 above.

[154]Compare Figure 1 with Figures 7 and 8.

[155]*Muzaffarnagar Settlement Report,* p. 60.

have greatly increased, out of all proportion to the minute quantity of land from which they now draw subsistence, they cannot be induced to curtail expenditure," Martin observed, "and are deeply involved to the moneylenders."[156] The predicament of the upper classes, confronted with the consequences their abrupt displacement from service and unable or unwilling to forsake the obligations of their social position and the lure of prestige in order to save the means to meet Government's demands, was widespread. "What are we to do to live?" a "well-to-do" Thakur asked in the course of a conversation with Wright, the Settlement Officer in Cawnpore district. "Our profession of soldiering is closed to us; some few of us indeed get employment in the forces of the native chiefs, but Ahirs and sweepers fill the ranks of the [British] native army. Chamars are writers in the courts; our caste forbids us to handle the plough." Wright could find no answer "but that he must either swallow his pride or go to the wall."[157] The zamindars of Hardoi district to the north-west faced the same alternatives. In the early 1870s, assessments were increased under Government sanction while the settlement officers (who provided the calculations) drew attention to the fact that zamindars were struggling in vain to pay them, their assets having been ravaged by three years of deficient outturns (by 1871) owing to floods and hailstorms. The next year, 1872-73, drought struck the rabi; the following kharif produced a miserable outturn over most of the district; and this was succeeded by another moistureless rabi together with severe frost. Complaints of over-assessment reached the Viceroy's ear. Lord Northbrook's subsequent instructions, "to strike off irrecoverable balances, suspend demands too suddenly imposed, and to relieve generally the universal distress in the country," did not reckon with the scrupulous attentiveness of the local Secretariat to the interests of Government. As a result, suspensions in demand were granted "only to persons in actual distress," whilst "well-to-do landowners considering themselves aggrieved in the matter of assessment, were left to proceed by petition."[158] To the south of Cawnpore, the old zamindari families of Fatehpur district faced ruin in 1871 when Government imposed a 10 percent cess for the expenses of local

[156]S. N. Martin to G. E. Williams, Commissioner, Meerut, May 22, 1865, *Muzaffarnagar Settlement Report*, p. 33. It is probable that the increase Martin noted was not absolute, but a relative increase in numbers dependent on zamindari claims.

[157]*Cawnpore Settlement Report*, p. 47.

[158]*Hardoi Settlement Report*, pp. 314-315. On the procedural problems of remission and suspension of revenue, see pp. 148-149 above.

administration with no account taken of the existing debts of the zamindars nor of the ravaged state of the district following the great drought of 1868-69.[159]

Such instances were representative of the risks confronted by the majority of zamindars in both the NWP and Oudh as an inevitable consequence of their obligatory as well as voluntary commitments being perpetually out of step with their means. Abundant harvests, when they occurred, could bring about no adjustment in this position. Like the cultivators, zamindars had necessarily to borrow.

The problem of zamindars' indebtedness was not confined to the persistence of pressures which encouraged or enforced borrowing. It had in the later nineteenth century an additional dimension in the complicated procedure of the legal transfer of proprietary rights as a consequence of the contracting of debts and the working of the principle of limitation. The title awarded to zamindars under the earliest settlement in the NWP conformed in its incidents with contemporary principles of proprietorship: it was established as both heritable and transferable. Further, insofar as the quantifiable proprietary assets in land to which the title referred were held liable for the payment of the revenue demand, Government declared its right in the case of default to compel the sale of the zamindar's title to realize its debt, that is, arrears of revenue. Meanwhile, the transferable nature of the title enabled the zamindar to take out legally recognized mortgages on its security. In the course of the nineteenth century, the principle of compulsory sale was extended. It came to cover the acquisition of land, on payment of compensation, for public purposes—the construction of public works.[160] More important, Government's rights as creditor against its debtor for the satisfaction of its debt were extended in accordance with the principles of equity to private creditors; the civil law in this respect was brought in line with the revenue law by the Code of Civil Procedure.[161] The zamindar's title had been liable to pass to Government and thence to the auction purchaser at revenue sales; now it could pass in addition to his creditor, who might in turn be the auction purchaser.

[159] *Fatehpur Settlement Report,* p. 40. In "ordinary times," A. B. Patterson believed, the 10 percent cess "would perhaps have been managed without much difficulty." For further, similar observations, see *ibid.,* pp. 10–11.

[160] Act VI, 1857 (acquisition of land for public purposes), amended by Act II, 1861, repealed by Act X, 1870, § 2. On the procedure, especially of valuation, see S. C. Dutt, *Compulsory Sales,* Lectures II and III.

[161] Act VIII, 1859, § 205. For the procedure of compulsory sales in execution of a decree, see Dutt, *ibid.,* Lectures IV to VI.

The combination of increased pressures on zamindars and the liberalization of the machinery of compulsory sales for debt resulted in a spate of litigation and alarming statistics of completed transfers. The average annual number of registered sales of immoveable property in the NWP climbed steadily: there were 32,188 between 1878 and 1883, 32,361 between 1883 and 1888, 35,928 between 1888 and 1893.[162]

Theoretically, the transfer procedure inherited from the Company's revenue administration fitted neatly into the framework of Government's intentions to modernize agrarian conditions. It was a cardinal principle of classical political economy that insolvent proprietors must not be permitted to waste away their estates for unproductive purposes; their property must be cleared of its debts (legally termed "encumbrances") and sold off to a relatively few efficient capitalists who were able to transform a number of broken-down estates into a large-scale, viable economic unit which by judicious investment would become prosperous.[163] G. B. Maconochie for one viewed the extensive transfers in Unao district during the revision of settlement with this type of economic optimism. The existing situation of the zamindars appeared hopeless to him. There were on average some ten divided pattis to a single village, with four sharers to each patti. These sharers were all directly affected by their displacement from service following annexation and did not work in the fields. The expenses of hired labour for cultivation had to be found, in addition to their other charges. Their mounting debts seemed to leave no alternative "but that their land must pass into the hands of those with capital, and therefore into the hands of the few." This seemingly harsh remedy would, Maconochie commented, prove ultimately beneficial to both country and people.[164] The transfer procedure would provide the means for the introduction of wealthy landowners "who can and will for their own sakes, spend money in improving their estates, displacing a pauper proprietary who, without the means of purchasing labour are, in too many instances too proud, or too lazy, to work with their own hands."[165] The sufferings of impoverished

[162]"Note on Land Transfer and Agricultural Indebtedness in India," in Government of India, *Selections from Papers on Indebtedness*, p. 35. Oudh figures for the same periods were 6,257, 6,672, and 7,075, respectively; *ibid.*

[163]For the analogous application of principles of classical political economy to encumbered estates in Ireland, see R. D. C. Black, *Economic Thought*, especially pp. 35-40, 121, 125-126.

[164]*Unao Settlement Report*, pp. 67-68.

[165]*Ibid.*, p. 18.

zamindari families were seen as the price of modernization. District officers could accept them—yet not without compassion—as the necessary outcome of Government's adherence to its just cause. "Is the healthy circulation of landed property an unmixed evil? Is not the same process, the supplanting of old families by the nouveaux riches, going on elsewhere, wherever civilization is at a high pitch?," Wright demanded in the course of a description of the lamentable state of the Cawnpore zamindars, with whom the British Government had, obligatorily, broken faith in sacrificing their interests in the pursuit of progress.[166] "The principle on which the whole machinery of the British Government works is of giving every one his exact due, at the same time exacting rigorously its own rights to the uttermost farthing. Such a principle is directly opposed to that on which old families maintained their status under other Governments. When precise definition of rights did not exist, the strongest was master, and failing other resources, the favour of the ruling authority could raise the beggar of yesterday into the talukdar of today ..."[167]

Government was not however in a position to be so rigidly consistent as such proclamations implied. Unhappily, the progressive aspirations of economic theory and equitable principles were not backed by suitable means for enforcement, nor, ironically, was it in the interests of Government, in view of its fundamental requirements of political expediency, that it should seek to enforce them. The logical extension of the working of the modernized legal machinery in co-ordination with economic pressures should ideally have resulted in the disintegration of the structure of superior rights over land accompanied by the dispersal of the proprietors from their seats of local power. This preparing of the way for a "capitalist succession" implied in fact an upheaval of revolutionary dimensions, and the collapse of that stratum of society upon which Government depended for its maintenance. Hence, in practice, Government was obliged to correct its forward-looking principles after the conservative fashion of its predecessors. It implemented grace and favour schemes for the relief of insolvent proprietors of influence: *kham tehsil* management, whereby the management of an estate was taken over temporarily by tehsili staff; the Court-of-Wards caretakership; the Jhansi Encumbered Estates legislation, designed to shore up the zamindars of the most backward district in the provinces; and, lastly, the move in the 1890s towards

[166]*Cawnpore Settlement Report*, p. 47.
[167]*Ibid.*, p. 46.

restriction of the transfer procedure itself. Meanwhile, the unacknow-ledged ally of Government was none other than the litigious zamindar. In fighting off the competitors for his position—still, in spite of the cost of mounting pressures, the only means of access to the widest range of local resources—he acted in the political interests of Govern-ment. In obstructing the processes of the judicial machinery by seemingly wanton litigation and in frustrating their successful outcome by fraud and physical coercion, he kept his place de facto in society and ensured that the essence of the old order was perpetuated, albeit at a price: the gross distortion of the modernized legal machinery and, often enough, the economic ruin of litigants. This unnatural but inevitable coalition between Government and the litigious zamindars can best be examined by an enquiry into the working of the law, focusing on the central problem of debt and alienations.

Chapter V

THE FRUSTRATION
OF LEGAL REMEDY

In 1879, a report from the assistant collector and magistrate of Budaon reached the Secretariat in Allahabad. It drew attention to the way in which the land revenue had been realized from "proprietary" communities of Thakurs in tehsil Dataganj following the ravages of the previous year's scarcity: "The whole demand of nearly Rs. $6\frac{1}{2}$ lakhs [Rs. 650,000], except for the paltry sum of Rs. 69,000, was screwed out of the people between November 15 and March 31, in the face of a total loss of the kharif from which according to theory the assets were obtained ... Where did the six lakhs come from? They were roughly speaking raised on mortgage bonds at abnormally heavy rates of interest ... The balance of Rs. 68,903 was outstanding because the money could not be screwed out of the people before the rabi was cut." The revenue law took its normal course: there were 176 arrests against 22.26 mahals where distraint occurred, compared with a mere 56 arrests the previous year; 39 mahals, shares, or pattis were attached, compared with the preceding year's total of 4.[1]

Surveying the scene some fifteen years later, in 1896, when all but a few shreds of the Thakurs' proprietary titles had been swept away through transfer litigation, J. S. Meston, then Settlement Officer, arrived at the gloomy conclusion that "nothing save special and

---

[1] A. Wyer, "Memorandum on Resolution No. 3268 A of 1878," in NWP and Oudh, "Revenue Proceedings," June 1879, Index No. 75, June 14, 1879, Proceeding No. 35. Figures for registered deeds were as follows:

	October–February 1876–77	October–February 1877–78
Documents	346	992
Value (Rs.)	104,619.6.0	213,502.0.0

Wyer's diary of February 19, para. 48, gave as examples of local interest rates 7 percent per month (84 percent per year) and in some cases 16 percent per month (192 percent per year); see *ibid.*, Index No. 71, June 14, 1879, Proceeding No. 31. For the regular procedure of "coercive process" under revenue law, see *Directions for Collectors of Land Revenue,* §§ 90–100, pp. 41–47.

drastic legislation" would keep the last of their ancestral property (that is, the legal titles to it) in their hands. The disastrous role played by the earlier revenue assessments in forcing mortgages which were subsequently foreclosed had either lapsed into official limbo or merely escaped Meston's notice. Instead, he turned the full blast of his accusations against two targets : excessive ceremonial expenditure, and the whole machinery of the civil law which, in provoking incessant litigation at untold expense, worked against the integrity Meston claimed for the summary dealings of the revenue administration.

Such special and drastic legislation, I confess, I should like to see directed at the roots rather than at the spreading boughs of the Upas-tree of indebtedness. Its roots are only two : ruinous extravagance in marriages and ruinous indulgence in litigation. To devise a direct remedy for the former evil is a Utopian hope : to mitigate the latter is surely no more impracticable than many of the schemes which the Government of India now meditates with academic approval. The facilities for litigation regarding the land, its titles and its burdens, especially lend themselves to restriction. Nothing saddens a settlement officer more than to see fine properties frittered away in cumbrous, lengthy and expensive law suits regarding them, when a summary decision of the revenue courts, if invested with finality, would have given substantial justice and nipped the quarrel in the bud. I know scores of villages in Budaun where a petty dispute about a mortgage or a succession has been carried to the High Court and has ruined the weaker party, whether successful or not. The kurmis, a sturdy, frugal and industrious caste of cultivators are egregious sinners in this respect; and their vicissitudes at the law are their frequent boast. Imagine a small green-grocer in an English village priding himself on having fought a suit about the title-deeds of his shop up to the House of Lords ! The parallel is by no means exaggerated.

The fever of land litigation is augmented ... , I cannot help thinking, ... by the growing popular appreciation of the helplessness of the revenue law in questions of title, and also by the timidity of the revenue and settlement courts in dealing with trespassers. The more that the people understand how bound down a Settlement Officer is to record possession and not property in land, the more will litigation in the civil courts run riot after a revision of settlement, and the more animosity and waste will such a revision bring in its train. As the law at present stands, an elaborate settlement record is pure waste of money : hardly an entry of importance can be made in it that is not liable to be immediately nullified at the nearest munsifi. It is only the extremely poor and ignorant who "still regard the settlement as a sort of Jubilee, and the Settlement Officer as the redresser of wrong." But I confess I am conservative enough to desire the rehabilitation of that ideal. The people are rapidly coming to look on us as getting all we can for the Government and giving nothing in return; as raking in the revenue with utter disregard for the concerns of those who pay it.[2]

The Modernization of the Legal Machinery

Litigiousness itself was not the product of the sophistications of the Civil Procedure Code, but it had long been a topic for discussion—and the anonymous author of a tract published in 1830 had noted shrewdly how the Company's revenue demands inevitably contributed to it.[3] The modernization of the law, in extending to private citizens property rights and causes of action previously confined to Government, meant an increase in judicial facilities with which to pursue local contentions of long standing. Meanwhile, the revision of assessments under Crown Government in no way lessened the provocations to litigiousness provided by the revenue demand.

The upmoding of the legal precedents inherited from the Company's administration, which placed the relatively swift and summary procedures of revenue law further and further in the background, was inevitable in view of the role assigned to a modern judicial system by contemporary European opinion in administrative and entrepreneurial circles. The legal codification of sound principles guaranteeing the security of property was a *sine qua non* for a progressive state of society.[4]

Experiences of Company justice in the mofussil courts recounted by prominent entrepreneurs to the Select Committee on Indian Colonization and Settlement on the eve of the transfer of Government revealed the disparities between entrepreneurs' requirements, the provisions of existing law, and the consequences of its operation. "The population is so depraved," William Theobald, the mouthpiece of indigo-planter zeal, informed the committee, "and the lower classes are so deficient in good faith, corruption seems to be so much increasing under the influence I believe of our institutions, that we want something

[2]J. S. Meston, January 6, 1896, paras. 11–13, in "Replies of Officers Consulted by the Board of Revenue," in NWP and Oudh, *Opinions . . . on the Subject of Land Transfer*, p. 19. Compare Hume's denunciation of the "ruinous system of civil litigation" as the root cause of indebtedness; see p. 191, n. 122 above.

[3]"The endless litigation to which the natives of India are, as it were, condemned, is one of the many evils, and certainly not one of the least of them for which the burthensome amount of the public imposts is, as I conceive, in a great degree responsible." *An Inquiry into the Alleged Proneness to Litigation*, p. 2.

[4]For the incidents of the concept of security in classical political economy, see R. D. C. Black, *Economic Thought*, pp. 136, 147, 157–158, 242.

like a strong pressure and police upon them for the protection of our interest and capital ... In our view, the laws are very defective."[5] The problem was, with what should they mend them? The radical solution would have been the wholesale introduction—and enforcement—of English law into the courts of justice throughout India, suppressing the existing hybrid growth of "native" laws administered in the light of European juristic principles in favour of a uniformly modern system.[6] John Freeman, an indigo planter with an intimate knowledge of the back-breaking litigation involved in attempting to establish a viable property title in up-country Bengal, opted for this remedy. After all, he insisted, "English law is administered to 600,000 people without distinction of creed, caste or colour in Calcutta, and has been administered for 80 years, and afforded satisfaction to all."[7] Others recommended merely that English law should be introduced, in the interests of modernity, alongside the recognized "native" institutions—which would require none of the unfortunate consequences involved in the adaptation of the one to fit the other. Theobald himself was of this view : "I do wish permanently to see one law for the natives and another law for the Europeans. The natives here have always had one law and we cannot have their law. There is the Hindoo law for the Hindoos, and the Mahommedan law for the Mahommedans; I do not see why we should not have the Christian law for the Christians."[8]

The Crown Government could provide no such cut-and-dried solutions to satisfy the entrepreneurs' demand for protection. Its policy and practice were, as in the case of public works, revenue assessments, and the structure of local administration, not to demolish existing institutions but to remodel them. The new Government's inheritance of judicial machinery bequeathed by the Company included the means by which it was to be overhauled and modernized : the recommendations of the Indian Law Commissions. The Second Commission, set up under a direction of the Charter Act of 1853,

[5]Evidence of April 22, 1858, "Reports of the Select Committee on Colonization and Settlement in India"—First Report : *P.P.*, 1857–58, 7, 1 (261), p. 68.

[6]For the early history of the British administration of law in India, see C. Fawcett, *First Century of British Justice*. On the origins and application of the fundamental guiding principle of equity, imported from Europe, see J. D. M. Derrett, "Justice, Equity and Good Conscience," in J. N. D. Anderson, ed., *Changing Law*, pp. 114–153.

[7]"Reports of the Select Committee on Colonization and Settlement in India"— First Report, pp. 130–131. For Freeman's account of his experience of mofussil litigation, see *ibid.*, pp. 108–109.

[8]*Ibid.*, pp. 88–91.

issued its report the following year, and it appeared "markedly conservative in comparison with the ambitious plans of its predecessor.[9] The abstract principles of scientific law derived from European juristic traditions but believed to be universally applicable, with which T. B. Macaulay had striven, largely in vain, to "reform and preserve,"[10] had given way to sober assessment of narrower range of practical issues. In the commission's view, a code of substantive civil law was required to consolidate the mass of regulations and enactments; this, they recommended, should be formed on the basis of "simplified English law, modified in some instances to suit Indian conditions"[11]—which was logical enough, since no other source of law could be found to fulfill such a need. The task of drafting a modern law for British India was carried on subsequently by the Third Law Commission but, after the enactment of its first draft as the Indian Succession Act of 1865, the legislature in India refused to comply further. The impasse which resulted when the commission refused the objections of the legislature which in turn refused to enact the draft laws ended in the commission's resignation. The Fourth Commission appointed in 1875, headed by the Law Member of the Governor-General's Council, Whitley Stokes and including for the first time three Indian judges (that is, European judges serving in India), introduced no essentially new element—other than that the commission itself represented the Government of India in Calcutta and was thus a stage removed, procedurally, from the India Office. In its drafts, however, it followed on from where the Third Commission had left off.[12]

Between 1859 and 1882, the fundamental measures of reform in codifying and amending the civil law reached the statute book. The great Code of Civil Procedure of 1859 was followed in the same year by the Limitation Act (regulating *inter alia* the institution of suits).

[9]E. Stokes, *English Utilitarians,* p. 258. On the First Commission, preceded by James Mill's despatch of 1834, see *ibid.,* pp. 193–196.

[10]*Ibid.,* p. 196. For a summary of T. B. Macaulay's work with the commission, a pale reflection of stated aims, see *ibid.,* pp. 213–214.

[11]*Ibid.,* p. 258.

[12]On the general question of English legal influence, see M. Anantanarayanan and G. C. V. Subba Rao, "The Influence of English Common Law and Equity upon Law in India," *Revista del Instituto del Derecho Comparado,* Nos. 8–9 (Nov.-Dec. 1957), pp. 118–127. For a brief account of the drafts of the Third and Fourth Commissions, see A. Gledhill, *Republic of India,* pp. 155–156. More detailed analyses are to be found in G. C. Rankin, *The Background to English Law,* and M. P. Jain, *Outlines of Indian Legal History.*

In 1870, the Court Fees Act established a uniform system of charges for the presentation of suits. Rules for the submission of evidence were codified in the Evidence Act of 1872. Parallel reforms meanwhile took place in the structure of the courts themselves. In 1861, the Sadr Diwani Adawlat and Supreme Courts in the presidency towns were amalgamated under the High Courts Act, which was extended to the NWP in 1866. By 1868, the reorganization of mofussil courts was completed : the principal *sadr amin* became subordinate judge; the office of sadr amin was abolished; the jurisdiction of the lowest court in the hierarchy—the *munsifi*—was extended to include the hearing of suits of up to Rs. 1,000 in value, in place of the former limit of Rs. 500; and Small Cause Courts were established in which subordinate judges, empowered by the local Government under an order of 1871, might hear suits of up to Rs. 500.[13] The jurisdiction of the Small Cause Courts was summary : no right of appeal was granted. The main progression of litigation, therefore, was from the *munsif's* courts through to the High Court at Allahabad;[14] the wealthiest and most determined litigants might take their case on to the Judicial Committee of the Privy Council in London, the supreme legal authority. In both the higher and lower strata of the Indian courts, business was conducted in English.

Developments in the formulation of a substantive civil law determined the form according to which business might be conducted. The series of major statutory provisions designed to govern property transactions which were enacted between 1859 and 1882 were the embodiment of equitable principles but showed little evidence of modification to fit a specifically Indian scene. The Civil Procedure Code of 1859 codified and amended the creditor's rights of attachment and sale of his debtor's property, together with the first provisions regarding insolvency outside of the presidency towns—the former being an extension of Government's right of compulsory sale for revenue arrears, the latter a development in step with contemporary English practice.[15] In 1864 the first comprehensive measure codifying and amending the existing law relating to the registration of deeds was enacted; however, the effectiveness of legal registration, admit-

[13]Stokes, *English Utilitarians,* p. 265.

[14]Appeals to the Privy Council were instituted by the Charter Act of 1726, on which see Jain, *Outlines of Indian Legal History,* p. 441.

[15]On compulsory sales, see p. 201 above. For the chronological developments in insolvency law, see D. F. Mulla, *Law of Insolvency,* "Introduction," and the brief summary in Gledhill, *Republic of India,* p. 198.

tedly an essential feature of a modern administration, was, and continued through successive enactments to be, hampered by the preservation of optional categories.[16] Six years later, the first Contract Act became law—a distillation of entrepreneurs' desiderata and English legal principles.[17] The last great pioneering property statutes followed in 1882 : Negotiable Instruments, Trusts, Easements, and, most important of all, the codifying Transfer of Property Act. Developments meanwhile in the law of mortgage, largely through judicial decision, established the incidents of foreclosure and the equity of redemption, major innovations in the Indian legal scene.[18] The modernization of revenue regulations relating to landlord and tenant in a series of enactments beginning with the Bengal Recovery of Rents Act of 1859 rounded off the development of property law.[19]

By the time the first Indian judge was appointed to a High Court in 1885, a formidable body of statutes laid down the law, together with twenty years' accumulation of precedent in the form of High Court decisions. The personal laws of Hindus and Mohammedans had escap-

[16]For a summary analysis of registration enactments, see M. Krishnamachariar, *Law Of Registration,* pp. i–ii. Certain deeds recording transfer of property, in which no consideration (sum of money involved in the transaction) was stipulated, were not compulsorily registrable (see Indian Registration Act, XVI of 1864, § 17).

[17]For characteristic objections by entrepreneurs to the imperfect state of contract laws prior to 1872, see A. N. Shaw, "On the Best Means of Promoting the Growth and improving the Quality of Cotton in India," *Journal of the Society of Arts,* XI (1863), 235–242. See especially the note to pp. 242–243. See also J. MacNair's evidence of May 6, 1858, before the Select Committee on Colonization and Settlement. The imperfect law of contract, he argued, prevented any control of advances made to cultivators (chiefly of indigo), and enhanced production costs; see Second Report : *P.P.,* 1857–58, 7, 1, 165 (326), pp. 26–27. On the British Indian contract law, see C. Rajaraman, "The Law of Contracts in India," *Revista del Instituto del Derecho Comparado,* Nos. 8–9 (Nov.-Dec. 1957), pp. 180–185.

[18]By the principle of the equity of redemption, property, when mortgaged, was held legally to pass to the mortgagee, the mortgagor losing his right of ownership per se but retaining an equity of redemption, a guarantee that his original right of ownership should be restored on his redemption of his security by repayment of his debt within the period specified. The debate as to whether such a provision was or was not contrary to indigenous legal practice became irrelevant once the equity of redemption was recognized as legally established in British India by the Transfer of Property Act. See R. Ghose, *Law of Mortgage,* pp. 210, 218. For a summary statement of the principles of transfer law, see K. Krishna Menon, "English Law in India : The Law of Transfer of Property," *Revista del Instituto del Derecho Comparado,* Nos. 8–9 (Nov.-Dec. 1957), pp. 90–101.

[19]See p. 152 above. For categories of tenant right as defined in successive statutes, see Appendix 8. For a select list of principal statutes relating to property, and agrarian conditions generally, in NWP and Oudh, see Appendix 6.

ed codification as such,[20] but in being administered in the modernized courts in conjunction with modern juristic principles, they were subject to interpretation in the light of European concepts. Not that this was a new departure in their history: the selection of texts on which the administration of these laws in the British Indian courts was based had initiated the process of infiltration by European juristic ideas, which grew apace under the regular interpretations of officially recognized texts in the light of equity.[21]

In some respects, the reforms brought cohesion to the highly disparate body of law officially recognized under the Company administration. The old distinction between laws operative in the presidency towns and those operative in the mofussil was removed; a degree of uniformity, though far from John Stuart Mill's and Macaulay's ideal, was achieved in the new statutes; and the Mohammedan and more especially the Hindu personal laws were drawn closer to the British Indian law. But reform was piecemeal. A large section of Government's machinery for social control lay outside it: the revenue administration kept its magisterial system, of summary decisions by the collector and/or magistrate in his district court, with a right of appeal lying to the commissioner of the division.[22] The jurisdiction of revenue and civil law, however, overlapped—

[20]On the proposed codification of personal laws, see Stokes, *English Utilitarians*, pp. 225, 228, 329 (note U).

[21]Hindu law was essentially—in the form administered then in British Indian courts—the law of the joint Hindu family. This property-controlling institution of great complexity had no comparable counterpart in Mohammedan law. Hindu law was by far the most vulnerable of the personal laws to modern re-interpretation. On the history of Hindu law from the eighteenth to the twentieth century, see J. D. M. Derrett, "The Administration of Hindu Law by the British," *Comparative Studies in Society and History*, IV, 1 (1961), 10–52. For a short summary of points where Hindu law was most radically re-interpreted in the light of English law, see A. Gledhill, "The Influence of Common Law and Equity on Hindu Law since 1800," *International and Comparative Law Quarterly*, III (1954), 576–603, and S. Venkataraman, "The Influence of Common Law and Equity on the Personal Law of the Hindus," *Revista del Instituto del Derecho Comparado*, Nos. 8–9 (Nov.-Dec. 1957), pp. 156–179.

[22]Further distinctions operated within the jurisdiction of the revenue administration. Settlement courts, for example, presided over by settlement officers, were separately constituted from regular revenue courts, for the hearing of claims preferred during settlement operations. For the complicated history of the precise constitution of settlement courts, first defined as "Courts of Civil Judicature," then under Act XVI, 1865, as "Courts of Revenue," and subsequently under Act XXXII, 1871, as civil courts once more (the judicial power of the officers changing according to each definition), see *Fyzabad Settlement Report*, pp. 489–490. For one example of many conflicting decisions by revenue and settlement courts on a question of definition of tenancy categories, see *Jaunpur Settlement Report*, p. 174.

especially in the sphere of tenancy law—and the lack of co-ordination between the two could not but produce conflict. Disparities also arose within the civil law itself on account of the inevitable divergence of decisions by different courts and different benches as to the precise application of statutory provisions. Further, the statutes themselves could conflict with incidents of the personal laws, which they had no authority to override. Lastly, the administration of law—a Government preoccupation—could come into conflict with dominant local interests : a powerful malik or a prosperous occupancy tenant might use the new institutions of civil law or modernized personal law to his advantage, or he might obstruct their working; there was little the judicial administration could do to enforce its interpretation of equal rights in such cases.

With the opportunities extended by the modernized civil law, on the one hand coinciding with the pressures of revenue law under the revision of assessments on the other, the "natives' proneness to litigation" blossomed forth with renewed vigour. Settlement operations throughout the provinces compelled the preferment of claims regarding the definition of rights, titles, and interests in landed property—and within a limited period, since settlement courts were closed on the cessation of operations in a district. Returns from Fyzabad district signalled an all-time record : some 71,728 suits were disposed of during the course of settlement, more than three times the district average for Oudh, which was a mere 19,151.[23] Elsewhere, disputes between the overcrowded bhaiachara sharers, which were further complicated by confused *khewats* (proprietary records), were added to those of minute sub-division; together, these two types of disputes constituted the greater proportion of the 40,719 cases heard in Agra district's settlement courts.[24] At the same time, the collector exercised his routine magisterial powers in adjudicating in routine suits brought under the revenue law. Here also annual returns showed a steadily upward trend, with increases in litigation registered by 1899-1900 which, in comparison with the figures for 1864-65, cannot but be described

---

[23]Returns for the several districts of Oudh were as follows : for Sultanpur, 26,043; Partabgarh, 20,736; Rae Bareli, 22,693; Lucknow, 27,139; Sitapur, 17,290; Bahraich, 7,496; Unao, 12,658. See *Fyzabad Settlement Report*, p. 490. For details of settlement litigation, see *ibid.*, pp. 491–511. Compare *Mainpuri Settlement Report*, pp. 99–100, for examples of litigation created by the compilation of the *wajib-ul-arz*. For the range of this document, considered to be the basic "village record," see pp. 254–257 below.

[24]*Agra Settlement Report*, p. 4.

as astonishing.[25] Meanwhile, business in the local civil courts throve in response to the provision of improved legal facilities, which were hardly designed to discourage litigation. The munsifs of three districts in Agra Division alone dealt with 6,299 cases, instituted in accordance with the elaborate technical prescriptions of the reformed law, within one year, 1872. Of these, 5,043 were registered as of not more than Rs. 100 in value. The following year, the total number of cases had risen to 6,568, of which only 1,435 involved sums of more than Rs. 100. [26]

The duplication of legal apparatus was the inevitable consequence of Government's introduction of the contemporary juristic concept of "private property" and the codification of its incidents. While Government's needs dictated the perpetuation of a system of revenue courts, dealing almost entirely—predictably enough—with matters connected with the land, the recognition of "property" and "proprietary title" entailed the maintenance of a parallel system of courts of civil judicature, where in accordance with accepted English practice all questions regarding "property"—largely equated in the mofussil, inevitably, with interests in land—were cognizable. Colonel William Sleeman, for one, saw what this had led to. "The Government committed a great political and social error when it declared all the land to be the property of the lessees and all questions regarding it to be cognizable by the Judicial [that is, civil] Courts," he declared, and dwelt upon its cost. "Why force men to run the gauntlet through both series? It tends to make the Government to be considered as a rapacious tax-gatherer, instead of a liberal landlord, which it really is; and to foster the growth of a host of native pettifogging attorneys, to devour, like white ants, the substance of the landholders of all classes and grades."[27] Sleeman's question was necessarily to remain a rhetorical one, since the problem was insoluble. The expenses which followed as its corollary grew as the passage of time graced the legal system with procedural refinements. The Bengal Recovery of Rents Act (X of 1859), for example, abolished in the interests of up-to-date justice the principle whereby a plaintiff had previously been allowed to sue several defendants collectively. In the eyes of the collector of

[25]For the volume of legal business transacted by collectors, according to divisions, from 1864–65 to 1899–1900, see Figure 10.

[26]The districts of Mainpuri, Etawah, Etah; see *Etawah Settlement Report*, p. 110. Figures for suits of low value are dubious, since the fact that court fees were fixed ad valorem (see n. 29 below) encouraged fictitious declarations of trifling sums.

[27]W. Sleeman, *Journey*, II, 70 n.

Meerut, this new provision, or rather the extra expense entailed in bringing a separate suit in each case, constituted the principal objection against the act itself. Sixty-four suits had been brought by the landlords of a single mauza, he maintained, at a total cost of Rs. 194, whereas under the old system three suits would have sufficed and the costs would not have amounted to more than Rs. 7.11.0. To this the Board of Revenue very properly replied that

the more exact and regular procedure required by the present law would seem to preclude the latitude of suing several defendants collectively, as was formerly allowed. Although there might occasionally be cases where causes of action were precisely the same, and which might be tried as one suit without inconvenience, each individual claim must be decided on its own merits and the option of suing collectively could be allowed only subject to the Court's approval. The discretion of admitting such collective suits could not with safety be trusted indiscriminately to all officers presiding in Revenue Courts . . . [28]

To the cost of hiring vakils, whose business it was to be skilled in the increasingly intricate ways of the law (which made them increasingly necessary), were added stamp charges on all documents—such as plaints and written submissions of evidence—and court fees which were fixed under the codifying Court Fees Act, VII of 1870, at an ad valorem rate.[29] To these expenses were added those of time and, frequently, the costs of travelling from the hinterland of a district to the court at the sadr station. The theoretical provision of equal law for all was in practice effectively restricted by these cumulative access charges.[30]

A certain atmosphere of bargaining which hung about the local courts diminished to some degree Government's claim (as voiced by Sir John Strachey, for example)[31] concerning the efficacy of its legal machinery in protecting the interests of its subjects with a general disinterestedness. Litigation could be an attractive (as well as an obligatory) pursuit—and not merely to the "educated classes" who

[28]Board of Revenue, NWP, to Government, NWP, January 25, 1861, in NWP, "Revenue Proceedings," November 16, Index No. 86, August 17, 1861, Proceeding No. 30.

[29]Act VII, 1870, Schedule I (table of ad valorem fees). 35 of the act empowered the governor-general of India to reduce or remit fees, with such changes to be published in the *Gazette of India.*

[30]The provisions for suits to be instituted *in forma pauperis* covered exemption from court fees only.

[31]See, for example, p. 2 above.

had some knowledge of the law. "From the proximity of the law courts," F. W. Porter wrote from Allahabad in the mid-1870s, "the people, especially of [pargana] Chail (containing the city of Allahabad and, consequently, one-third of the district's educated population), have gained a smattering of the law and an insatiable thirst for the excitement of the legal lottery. A Chail tenant is used as a synonymous term for a village lawyer." His neighbours on the other side of the Ganges, however, though not so well educated and "utterly ignorant of the law," rivalled him in litigiousness, making up "for ignorance by tenacity."[32] Along with litigiousness went fraud, which was encouraged by the technical complications of the imported law and by the relative impersonality of the modern courts. G. B. Maconochie's observations on this point as regards Unao district are instructive. "When I joined the Settlement Department [in the late 1850s], an old zamindar would seldom tell a direct lie but before I left the district [less than ten years later] this had greatly altered for the worse. Men who but a few years before would have scorned to lie before their 'Punch' or a 'Hakim' came into Court, with a lie in their mouths, as readily as the veriest bazar witness." Maconochie, with an eye to circumspection, gave no reason : "I merely state the fact. But I believe in a few years, the people of Unao will far surpass in fraud their brethren across the Ganges in the old British provinces."[33] If the courts could offer a temptation to duplicity which seems at times to have been irresistible, new legislative enactments unwittingly provided the provocation to defraud. While increasing pressures from multiple claims to the zamindari together with a rising revenue demand tended to encourage zamindars to bear down upon the cultivators with greater vigour and regularity, their efforts to raise cultivators' charges could be substantially hampered by the working of the rent law. The creation of a legally privileged class of occupancy tenants by Act X of 1859 brought with it restrictions on the zamindars' legal power of exaction.[34] To raise the "rents" of his occupancy tenants in accordance with the law, a zamindar had to take them to court and prove that a higher "rate" than he at present exacted from them was "the prevailing rate payable by the same class of ryots for land of a similar description and with similar advantages in the places adjacent."[35] The dictates of procedure demanded that

[32] *Allahabad Settlement Report*, pp. 48–49.
[33] *Unao Settlement Report*, p. 25.
[34] See pp. 152–153 above.
[35] Act X, 1859, § 17. The other statutory grounds for enhancement were as follows :

the zamindar bring a separate suit in each case of enhancement. He was met, however, by collective obstruction on the part of the occupancy tenants. Since no occupancy tenant wished to pay more to his zamindar, all had a vested interest in declaring their "rents" at a low figure—which, under the provisions of the act and in line with interpretations placed by the High Court on the key phrase in Section 17, "of the same class," became the standard. Instead, therefore, of the general "rate" of rent for a given area being raised—in accordance with the revenue—to a generally equitable level, which was what the statute was intended to achieve, rents paid by the occupancy tenants as recorded at law might persist at a privileged low rate. No legal remedy existed to ease a zamindar's frustrations in such cases. He must resort to extortion—or, as S. M. Moens observed to be the case in Bareilly district, to fraud. This took the form of payments to the kanungo, who undertook commissions from the local Government to ascertain and record the rents of a pargana for the official accounts.[36] No amendment of this situation could be sought in the later tenancy enactments, which faithfully preserved the incidents of occupancy right and therefore perpetuated the conflict.

The Modernization of the Law
Relating to Debt and Alienations

It was not merely the zamindars' struggles with cultivators which were complicated by the modernized machinery of the law. Recognition of a creditor's rights in accordance with established tenets of judicial practice in England added a further dimension to the longstanding antagonism between zamindar and moneylender. The removal of statutory restrictions on interest rates by the Repeal of the Usury Laws in 1855, combined with the codification of principles of limitation and the codification of the liability of a debtor's property to attachment and sale in 1859, provided creditors with a formidable array of new weapons for battle in the courts. The zamindars of

(1) when the value of the produce or the productive powers of the land have been decreased otherwise than by the agency or at the expense of the ryot (which provided the zamindar with an incentive to discourage attempts by occupancy ryots to improve their holdings); (2) where the quantity of land held by the ryot has been proved by measurement to be greater than the quantity for which rent has previously been paid by him (providing the zamindar with an incentive to enter fictitious measurements in records).

[36] *Bareilly Settlement Report,* pp. 116–117. For the whole summary of the local consequences of the act, see *ibid.,* pp. 114–117.

Allahabad who petitioned Government in 1872, drawing attention to these legal innovations which were in their eyes tantamount to discriminatory measures, spoke for many of their ills elsewhere in the provinces : "Petitioners complain of the evils attendant on the usury laws now in force, under which Native usurers and money-lenders charge exorbitant rates of interest and compound interest, and by unfair and cruel practices so increase the amounts of the loans due to them that they at last force the sale of hereditary estates of their debtors, and either themselves purchase them at adequate prices, or get others to do so, thus causing the ruin of thousands of landholders and keeping petitioners in perpetual fear of the loss of their estates . . ."[37]

Sympathy for the zamindars was not wanting—even from the bench of the High Court which tried innumerable cases of foreclosed mortgages which led to compulsory sales in execution of the decree awarded to the creditor. "The real protection the borrowing landholders want," ran the comment of an Allahabad judge in a letter of 1871, "is return to a reasonable legal rate of interest; but as this is rank heresy in these later days I dare not dwell further on the point."[38] The proposition that artificial controls should be placed on the natural movement of interest was anathema to the dominant group of contemporary theorists in England. "Next to the system of protection," J. S. Mill had argued, "among the mischievous interferences with the spontaneous course of industrial transactions may be noticed certain interferences with contracts. One instance is that of the usury laws."[39] In 1855, legislation was passed to abrogate all restrictions on interest rates hitherto recognized in the regulations and thus to clear the way for the uninhibited operations of the market : the Act for the Repeal of the Usury Laws, XXVIII of 1855, was, as Mr. Justice Raymond West put it, "a mere adoption of an English doctrine supposed to have been proved correct by impregnable reasoning."[40] West himself, aware from his experience at the law of

[37]Sheikh Mohamed Raza-coddeen and others, zamindars, Zillah Allahabad, "Petition to H.E. the Viceroy and Governor-General of India," February 19, 1872, in Government of India, *Selections from the Records of Government*, No. CLV, at p. 287.

[38]Letter No. 76, February 7, 1871, Government of India, *Report of the Deccan Riots Commission*, 1875, Appendix B, p. 60.

[39]J. S. Mill, *Principles of Political Economy*, Book V, Ch. X, as quoted in *Report of the Deccan Riots Commission* 1875, Appendix B, p. 60. For a selection of similar contemporary opinions held applicable to Indian conditions, see *ibid.*, pp. 60–64.

[40]West, "The Land and the Law in India," in *Report of the Deccan Riots Commission*, 1875, Appendix B, p. 56.

the realities of the Indian scene as far as borrowing practices were concerned, opposed the wholesale abandonment of controls—and sided with his colleague in Allahabad as to the desirability of some restriction to protect borrowers' interests. The law should coax the people into sounder commercial habits, not coerce them. "... for India, perhaps the maintenance of the limitation, or a still closer approximation to the native practice by giving to the courts an extended discretion to deal with interest, would have been a more politic course to follow until its people had acquired the capacities of a self-asserting and intelligent mercantile community." Even West, however, conceded the necessity of large-scale transactions being "left to the operation of supply and demand" : his liberal proposals were recommended for application only to "small debts."[41] Such academic criticism of Government's modernizing measures had little effect. Impediments to the implementation of the new act arose not out of the comments of practitioners, but from judicial decisions as to the applicability of its provisions. Fragments of Hindu law, for example, had been included in the provisions of early revenue regulations on the subject of usury : the rule of *damdupat,* which prevented a creditor from recovering as interest at any one time a sum more than equal to the principal, had thus enjoyed recognition in the officially recognized personal law of the Hindu community and in secular British Indian regulations. What then was the scope of the 1855 act? The courts differed, with the result that reform of the legal restrictions on interest rates throughout British India was a decidedly piecemeal affair. Damdupat remained in force in the town of Calcutta, but not in the mofussil of Bengal where the repeal by the 1855 act of Regulation XV of 1793, which had given the rule legal recognition, was upheld. Damdupat also disappeared in the NWP under the High Court's interpretation of the act.[42] In Madras, Act II of 1889 finally deprived the rule of legal force. In Bombay, however,· the rule was held consistent with equity—and a series of decisions preserved it.[43]

[41]*Ibid.*

[42]*Kuar Lachman Singh* v. *Pirbhu Lal,* 6 *NWP High Court Reports—Full Bench Rulings* 358.

[43]For successive Bombay decisions, to 1875, see *Report of the Deccan Riots Commission,* 1875, Appendix B, p. 360. For the history of *damdupat* in Hindu and British Indian law, see J. R. Gharpure, "The Law of Damdupat," *Bombay Law Reporter* (Journal), VI (July 1904), 129–143; F. R. Vicajee, "The Rule of Damdupat," *Journal of Comparative Legislation,* New Series, II (1900), 464–472; R. K. Ranade, "Damdupat in Hindu Law," *Bombay Law Reporter* (Journal), LIV (July 15, 1952), 49–57.

The provisions of a law designed on an English model, the principle of which was "perhaps"—as the Allahabad petitioners rightly observed—"to place no limit to the amount of benefit an owner may derive from the employment of his capital, whether money or goods,"[44] could not but deprive debtors of the modicum of legal protection available to them under previous restrictions imposed by the courts on interest exactions. Their difficulties were increased by further innovations—similarly demanded in accordance with progressive opinion ruling in the upper reaches of Government. Attachment and sale in execution of decrees for debt might, like the repeal of usury laws, be recognized by contemporaries for what they were : "entirely the creatures of British legislation";[45] but the principle was theoretically sound and, in addition, formed the basis of Government's security for its revenue. The just principle, as Sir George Edmonstone, then Lieutenant-Governor of NWP, insisted in a note of 1860 on the provisions of Section 205 of the Civil Procedure Code *inter alia*, was that "the whole of a man's property is liable for the liquidation of his bona fide debts. It is important that this principle should be maintained. On this principle, land is held to be hypothecated for the Government revenue assessed on it. Whatever intermediate processes are now preferentially adopted for the realization of revenue, it is the proprietary right in the land itself which is looked to as the real security, and its sale as the ultimate means of coercion." Government could not, "with any prudence or safety, give up the security," while abstract principles compelled it to extend its rights as public creditor to the private sphere.[46] As a result, debtors were not merely less protected under the new laws, but open to new attack.

The extension of compulsory sales also raised problems of uniformity in the law : it ran directly counter to recognized incidents of the joint

[44]"Petition" cited above, n. 37, para. 8, pp. 290–291.

[45]R. West and G. Bühler, *Digest*, IV, 642. Compare Government, NWP, to Board of Revenue, NWP, March 27, 1873, apropos of Jhansi Division : The lieutenant-governor agreed with the board that the compulsory sale of ancestral property under the provisions of the Civil Procedure Code was an innovation, "and moreover the debts for which this process is put into action, were incurred under a system in which the lenders had no just ground of expectation that the Regulation system would be enforced for their recovery." NWP, "Revenue Proceedings," September 1873, Index No. 32, March 29, 1873, Proceeding No. 87.

[46]Sir George Edmonstone, May 26, 1860, in Government of India, *Selections from the Records of Government*, No. CLV, pp. 12–13. For details of procedure, see S. C. Dutt, *Compulsory Sales*, Lectures II–VI. For an historical summary, see R. K. Ranade, "Legal Proceedings in Respect of Debts," *Bombay Law Reporter* (Journal), LXI (August 15, 1954), 81–90.

Hindu family. "It has been held by our highest courts of justice," ran a despatch of 1858 from no less an authority than the Court of Directors, "that under the Hindoo law, as it prevails wherever the Mitakshara is respected, the alienation by a father of immoveable ancestral property without the consent of the sons, except on proof of necessity, is illegal; and it is not easy to understand how property, which cannot legally be sold by the individual himself may be legally sold by a court of justice in satisfaction of his personal debts."[47] Modern statutory prescriptions were, in this instance, an irresistible force. Conflict between them and the Hindu law persisted throughout nearly twenty years of divergent judicial decisions to be resolved authoritatively by the Privy Council decision of 1877 that a coparcenar's interest was to be held liable to attachment and sale in satisfaction of his debt.[48] The next move, inevitably, was towards liberalization of joint-family restrictions on alienations by the admission (tantamount to creation) of an undivided coparcenar's right to alienate, voluntarily, his interest in the joint-family property for value. This was sealed by a Privy Council decision of 1879; the procedural difficulties involved in the division of undivided assets were dealt with by extending the principle of partition—hitherto resorted to by members of the family in order to set up separate units—by means of the unfailing device of equitable construction. The undivided coparcenar's right to alienate his share was, their lordships decided, "founded on the equity, which a purchaser for value has, to stand in his vendor's shoes and work out his rights by partition."[49]

Provisions for the realization of debts under the law of the Mitakshara joint family also came in for stringent re-assessment in line with the principles of property. The institution known as the Pious Obligation, whereby a son was bound to pay his father's debts provided they had not been contracted for immoral or illegal purposes, stood as a guarantee for the father's absolution after death—and, more practically, for the creditor's security of repayment. The obligation was an unlimited liability and was in no way conditional on the receipt of assets from the father. Modern interpretations changed that, tying

[47]"Despatch," August 4, 1858, para. 4, in Government of India, *Selections from the Records of Government*, No. CLV, p. 62.
[48]*Deen Dayal* v. *Jugdup Narain Singh* (1877), *The Law Reports*, 4 *Indian Appeals* 247.
[49]*Suraj Bunsi Koer* v. *Sheo Persad* (1879), *The Law Reports*, 6 *Indian Appeals* 88. For a brief summary of the essential conflict and its resolution, see A. Gledhill, "English Law in India," in W. B. Hamilton, ed., *Transfer of Institutions,* at pp. 185–186.

the obligation by equity to the quantum of assets—joint-family property—inherited.[50]

The powers of manager of a joint-family—the father or other seniormost member—to alienate family property as laid down in the Mitakshara text were similarly refurbished by equitable interpretations. Traditionally, such alienations could be made only on the grounds of distress, necessity, or benefit to the family. The legal validity of a manager's alienations could depend, in the context of the modernized Hindu law, on the construction placed by the courts on these provisions. Meanwhile, an equitable extension gave the alienee protection against the dangers of voidable transactions. The pioneering decision in Hanuman Persaud's case established the point that, provided the alienee satisfied the court that he had made such honest inquiries as befitted a reasonable man to ascertain the technical soundness of the alienation within the limits of the law, the alienation must be upheld.[51]

Against these innovations, the joint family retained some power to hit back at the creditor or alienee, through subsequent litigation, and thus save the property at stake. Sons might seek to prove—at times with their father's collusion—that the paternal debts were "tainted" (the technical term), that is, contracted immorally or illegally; a successful plea would absolve them from parting with the family assets to satisfy the debts. The joint family as a whole, acting through its representatives, might obstruct the passage of their interests to an alienee by proving prior knowledge on his part of the unsoundness of the deal. Both situations admitted abundant opportunities for fraud to ward off intruders.

Obstructions to the smooth processes of the transfer law by joint Hindu families belonged to the wider area of conflict between the proprietor and his creditor-alienee competitor. Complications which beset the procedure of transfer of property through foreclosure of mortgages and forced legal sales and which frustrated the intentions of the legislature to clear away encumbrances on landed property

[50]In Bombay, the liability of Hindu heirs was limited by statute (Bombay Hindu Heirs Relief Act, VII of 1866). Elsewhere, such limitation was established by judicial decision. On the re-interpretation of the Pious Obligation by British Indian lawyers, see Gledhill, "The Influence of Common Law and Equity on Hindu Law since 1800," *International and Comparative Law Quarterly*, III (1954), 583–584. For a catalogue of summarized decisions on the Pious Obligation, see V. S. Pantulu, *Hindu Law Relating to the Liability for Debt.*

[51]*Hanuman Persaud* v. *Mst. Babooee* (1856), 6 *Moore's Indian Appeals* 393.

were not necessarily detectable however from a reading of the statistical returns of alienations officially registered. Indeed, the returns themselves could prove deceptive on close inspection. Compulsory sales involved not one but a series of procedures : proposal, actual sale, and confirmation. Statistics collected at one stage might be taken, as Philip Robinson had cogently suggested in commenting on Wilton Oldham's memorandum on revenue sales in Benares district, as recording completed transactions with the result that the extent of actual sales was exaggerated.[52]

Risks of such errors were not diminished by provision, made in the later part of the century, for improved recording and registration of legal transfer. By 1894, a seemingly comprehensive system existed : copies of assurances were to be preserved in public offices, registered under the Registration Act (as amended in 1877); changes in actual or presumed rights of parties to land were to be recorded in the revenue administration's official documents prescribed for the purpose, the statistics being compiled from district officers' reports.[53] Registration itself however was neither comprehensive nor, in relation to such alienations as it covered, wholly compulsory.[54] At the same time, the revenue officers ran into difficulties in attempts to collect district statistics of any value. A. M. Markham, for example, "in obedience" to a directive of the board in 1873, submitted a report regarding the extent of transfer of landed property from the "old proprietors to the non-agricultural classes" in Bijnour since 1840, but he expressed misgivings about its validity. The statistics were incomplete, and even where complete they were not satisfactorily correct : an approximation to facts was the net result for some three-fifths of the district. The board's scrupulous distinction between agricultural and non-agricultural classes on the theoretically defined grounds of sources of income could not be applied in practice "without special inquiry, far outside the sphere of settlement operations." Nothing in Markham's records informed him "whether a certain Bunniah, Brahmin, Khuttra, Bishnoi and others, recorded as a landowner, obtains his income chiefly from land or chiefly from trading; or who is and who is not a Government servant. There are many other castes besides Bunniahs, some of whose members are traders, and who obtain landed property by

[52]Philip Robinson, Untitled Notes on W. Oldham's Memorandum (no pagination).
[53]"Note on Land Transfer and Agricultural Indebtedness in India," in Government of India, *Selections from Papers on Indebtedness*, pp. 25–26.
[54]See p. 211, n. 16 above.

making advances on it; and there are some Bunniahs ... whose ownership of land is centuries old. Many Government servants were hereditary landowners for generations before they became Government servants. A hard-and-fast line of distinction is impossible ..." Markham submitted tables of transfer statistics, nonetheless, drawn up in accordance with a slightly modified version of the board's instructions—an "imperfect and inexhaustive classification, but the best possible."[55] Other officers reported the same unsatisfactory state of affairs. Of the total number of transfers, 1,447, recorded in pargana Azamnagar, Etah district, details of only 754 were entered, and S. O. B. Ridsdale regarded the statement, "even if it were complete, of very little intrinsic value."[56] The collation of returns from the separate parganas of tehsil Tilhur alone in Shahjahanpur district involved improbable amounts of labour : the statements were not all given in the same form; in several cases, information that was clearly incorrect had been obtained from the tehsil office; details on each decade of the past settlement were lacking; prices were either not entered or were not to be believed; and areas shown were deceptive as many properties recurred several times, some villages having been involved in three or four transactions since the previous settlement. In view of this, the settlement officer decided to omit statements of transfer altogether.[57] The simple classifications of "landowner" and "moneylender" were retained—and official recognition of their impracticality was reiterated.[58] By 1894 the Government of India confessed itself defeated in the attempt to secure an adequate statistical account of the working of its transfer machinery : "In view of the unsatisfactory nature of the figures quoted it is difficult to form any general conclusions regarding the sale of land for debt. What we chiefly wish to know is the area of agricultural land sold yearly in each province (a) for secured and unsecured debt respectively and (b) to agriculturists and non-agriculturists respectively; this information we have not got, and pending the improvement to be made

---

[55] *Bijnour Settlement Report*, p. 93.

[56] *Etah Settlement Report*, p. 82.

[57] *Shahjahanpur Settlement Report*, p. 79. For further examples of incomplete returns, see *Fyzabad Settlement Report*, p. 37 (registered sales only), and *Kheri Settlement Report*, p. 22 (assorted statistics, from sub-registrars' and judicial records together with the district register of mutations; no complete returns were obtainable from any one source).

[58] "Note on Land Transfer" (cited above, n. 53), p. 72, referring to *NWP Revenue Administration Reports*, 1882–83, p. 57, and 1889–90, p. 68.

in our Agricultural Statistics Return E there is really only little information of any kind on which we can rely."[59]

Clearly, the defective statistical returns could not be relied on to test the truth of zamindars' complaints as to the extent to which creditors were usurping their rights—insofar as these were encompassed by the recognized proprietary title. Comments of settlement officers which accompanied the figures assiduously compiled to satisfy the Secretariat's requirements were more informative as to the working of the new laws on old rivalries. A broad distinction could in fact be drawn as regards the extent and nature of transfer of title between the greater part of Meerut district on the one hand and Benares on the other. "Changes in Meerut since Sir Henry Elliot's time [1836]," wrote E. C. Buck, in summing up the settlement officers' accounts of transfer in the several parganas, "have not altered to any great extent the distribution of proprietary castes, except in the neighbourhood of the cities of Delhi and Meerut, where the mahajuns and tradespeople have invested their capital in land. As a rule, the transfers throughout the district have been confined to the four prominent classes . . ."[60] Meerut had emerged from the revision of settlements with much of its previous reputation for prosperity undiminished; in fact, it was even enhanced owing to the ability of its most powerful Jat and Taga zamindar-maliks to utilize the opportunities of canal irrigation greatly to their advantage by controlling the production of "valuable" crops which it stimulated.[61] Such resources had provided the means to repel threats of competition. The same was true of other districts where zamindars controlled the benefits of expanding production: in Shahjahanpur, for example, where Thakur zamindars held large interests in the sugar industry, extensive transfers were reported "amongst the brotherhood."[62] In Ballia, it was the loan business generally which provided the means for the more astute

[59]"Note on Land Transfer," p. 77. On problems of collecting statistics relating to agrarian conditions in general, see pp. 258–270 below.

[60]E. C. Buck to C. A. Elliott, *Meerut Settlement Report*, p. 4. The four principal castes seem to have been Jats, Tagas, Rajputs, and, near the major towns, Banias. For details of transfers compiled by W. A. Forbes, by parganas, see *ibid.*, pp. 21–22 (Kotanah), pp. 24–25 (Gurmukhtesur), p. 30 (Hapur), p. 39 (Jalalabad).

[61]On the traditionally renowned expertise of the Jat farmer, see p. 61 above. For the benefits of canal irrigation to the most fertile areas of Meerut, see pp. 69–70 above. On the general prosperity of the district, see A. Colvin, *Memorandum*, pp. 108–109.

[62]*Shahjahanpur Settlement Report*, pp. xxxvii–xxxix (generally as regards tehsil Tilhur, and especially pargana Jalalabad of that tehsil).

members of upper-caste families to consolidate their interests through the transfer laws. "There is no indication," D. T. Roberts reported during the course of settlement,

that proprietary right in the district is passing into the hands of the mercantile classes by the dispossession of the hereditary Rajput zamindars. The old zamindars, as a class, hold their own; if some are sold out for debt, their places are taken by others of the same class and the redistribution does not bring in new men, aliens to the soil. The Rajput zamindars contain a full and fair proportion of shrewd and saving men who are continually extending their estates by purchase. If one family ruins itself by extravagance, its property is bought up by another family of the same or some adjacent mahal. Moneylending is far from being a monopoly of the trading castes, but is largely engaged in by well-to-do Rajputs and Brahmans.[63]

Brahman zamindars in Aligarh, whose holdings were commonly found in amongst collections of Jat villages, exploited both the money-lending trade and the transfer machinery with similar success. "To the power derived from the possession of money they add the influence of caste," T. E. Smith noted, "and some of them have been among the largest accumulators of property in the district."[64]

Zamindari interests elsewhere could be more vulnerable to attack owing to the lack of comparably secure resources. Catastrophes such as famine years tended to break an already weakening resistance, as in the case of those zamindars of parganas Meerut and Burnawa of Meerut district[65] for whom the profits of canal irrigation during the drought of 1860-61 lay, or were kept by their neighbours, beyond reach. The districts in the east of the provinces and south in Bundelkhand offered more frequent examples of failing zamindars, deeply indebted and entangled in consequence in the toils of transfer litigation. Relatively poor natural conditions in comparison with the near-proverbial fertility of the best Doab districts, a depressing series of low outturns at the harvests[66] and, as far as certain districts of Benares Division were concerned, intense pressure of population on the land[67]

[63]*Ballia Settlement Report*, p. 53.

[64]*Aligarh Settlement Report*, pp. 33–34. See also p. 168 n. 27 above.

[65]*Meerut Settlement Report*, p. 47 (Burnawa), pp. 53–54 (Meerut).

[66]See Figure 1, Allahabad, Jhansi, and especially Benares divisions.

[67]According to statistics recorded during the revision of settlements, in the 1870s, the population of Azamgarh district then stood at an estimated 613 persons per square mile, of Ghazipur 688 persons per square mile. The figures are significantly higher than those for western districts (for a selection of which see p. 68 above). The 1872 census set the average density of population for NWP at 381.24 persons per square mile. The 1869 Oudh census gave the average density figure of 474 persons per square mile.

(the picture commonly presented by many of these areas) hardly made for agricultural prosperity. Added to these circumstances were the minute sub-division of zamindari claims following service displacement[68] and the rigorous exaction of Government's revenue demand, which worked against the consolidation of interests. It is hardly surprising, therefore, to find evidence there of a more rapid disintegration of mahals into partitioned shares than one finds in the west.[69] In Benares Division, the number of recorded mahals had increased from 18,218 in 1864-65 to 28,634 by 1884-85, and by 1899-1900 it was given as 42,763.[70] Transfers of zamindari title seem also to have been considerable—by way of a general impression, in view of the notorious unreliability of statistics. William Irvine estimated that an area equal roughly to one-quarter of the district of Ghazipur had changed hands in sales between 1840 and the end of the revised settlement forty years later. Here again, however, the "moneylending classes" had not ousted the hard-core zamindars, who retained a little more than one-half of the district's "property."[71]

What in fact was the result of legal alienations, by sale and mortgage? Few settlement officers reported signs of physical dispossession as a result of the incessant activity of the courts.[72] W. C. Benett summed it up in a single illuminating phrase : "the result of all these transactions is the creation of a number of concurrent interests in the same soil."[73] Cases were reported, from Unao for instance, where the parties to the alienation settled in to a compromise : "the purchaser after the sale having allowed the ex-zamindar and his family some land at favourable rates and being content to have the land secured to its recipients with the sole proviso that it was not transferable, the ex-zamindar is content to accept the substantial advantages rather

[68]For examples, see pp. 141–142 above.

[69]Benares Settlement Report, pp. 23–24.

[70]The figure for Benares Division for 1899–1900 includes the newly created Gorakhpur Division. Compare the figures for the western divisions :

	Meerut	Rohilkhand	Agra
1864–65	9,314	17,547	8,603
1884–85	12,029	23,289	12,281
1899–1900	23,461	31,419	20,692

Source : NWP Revenue Administration Reports (years as given above), Appendix X, "Statistical Précis of the Revenue Administration of the NWP."

[71]Ghazipur Settlement Report, p. 157.

[72]One example at least is reported from pargana Kandla, Muzaffarnagar district; Muzaffarnagar Settlement Report, p. 107. Observations in "Note on Land Transfer," at p. 42, suggest that this may well be an isolated case.

[73]Gonda Settlement Report, p. 67.

than push matters to extremity and gain or lose everything."[74]
Gentle acquiescence in the processes of the law was also encouraged
(after 1873) by the rent acts. Ex-proprietary tenants were granted,
by a provision intended to prevent the decline of the hitherto "landed
gentry" into landless degradation, an equitable right of occupancy
in land designated as their sir previous to its alienation.[75] Being
classed as a tenant, the ex-proprietor was rid of his revenue liability;
armed with his occupancy right, he could at least obstruct attempts
by the new zamindar to raise his charges.

Not all were content to compromise. The difficulties which even
a bona fide purchaser of proprietary title might encounter subsequent
to the alienation itself were many and complex. There were the
problems of establishing physical possession, or realization, of a claim
where the legal title acquired referred to a share reduced by sub-
division to proportions beyond the reach of practicality. There were
problems where rights acquired by law constituted a share, physically
undefined, in joint-family property—which, until actual partition
"by metes and bounds" was made (for which a purchaser would
have to litigate), was liable to fluctuate in accordance with an increase
or decrease in the number of coparcenars owing to births or deaths
in the family.[76] Moreover, there were other dilemmas : if the purchaser
enforced partition, as the law entitled him to do (by reason of "the
equity [which] a bona fide purchaser for value has, [enabling him]
to step into his alienor's shoes and work out his rights by partition"),
he gave up the protection from the full force of the revenue liability
which the joint responsibility of the coparcenary provided; if he did
not enforce partition, he risked persistent impediment by "the village"
to the realization of his interests.[77]

[74]*Unao Settlement Report*, p. 75. G. B. Maconochie described such compromises as
"the acknowledged custom in one small taluka in Lucknow ... In all recent sales
the ex-zamindars were secured in possession of some land under the same terms.
The rents of the land were usually fixed and at favourable rates" (the price of the
tenants' prospective allegiance). Compromises elsewhere, however, had harsher
consequences. Concessions made by Bania purchasers to Thakur zamindars in pargana
Thakurdwara, Moradabad district for example, were merely the first stages of a
process working towards legal ouster. See E. B. Alexander's comments on a report
of 1859 by Sir John Strachey, in *Moradabad Settlement Report*, pp. 76–77.

[75]See Appendix 8, under Act XVIII, 1873. For a discussion of the award of such
a right to a judgment debtor in Oudh, see Oudh Revenue Department, Circular
Letter, December 9, 1884, in NWP and Oudh, "Revenue Proceedings," 1884, File
No. 620, Serial No. 1, Proceeding No. 1.

[76]See *Report of the Deccan Riots Commission*, p. 36.

[77]*Aligarh Settlement Report*, pp. 128–130. The Settlement Officer, T. E. Smith,

The coparcenars could also contrive, by a variety of means, to upset the alienation. Courses of action to this end which were open to a joint Hindu family have already been outlined.[78] The ingenious manipulations of the law by Mst. Umrao Begum, a seasoned litigant, in the case of Tika Ram provide one illustration of the devices open to zamindari coparcenars to repulse the auction purchaser—with untoward consequences in this case for Government itself. Tika Ram had bought at an auction in 1863, for the sum of Rs. 5,000, the title deeds to Mohanpur village in Bareilly district which had been confiscated for its owners' part in the "Mutiny"; in due course he was awarded legal possession. Umrao Begum had been the principal sharer, amongst the eight recorded coparcenars. Prior to the "Mutiny," balances had accrued on her share, which had then been farmed out on lease under the operation of revenue law until such time as the arrears might be realized. The farmer-lessee himself was a mere hireling of the Begum who, by meeting the formal requirements of the law (as an "external" party), preserved her interest in the village. On the expiration of the lease, towards the late-1860s, Umrao Begum instituted a suit for the release of her share and obtained a decree accordingly from the court of the Principal Sadr Amin. Tika Ram, understandably alarmed, appealed to the judge but to no avail. Government—that is, the local revenue administration—meanwhile was unaware of the proceedings taken in this way against Tika Ram in the civil court by Umrao Begum. Tika Ram promptly brought an action against Government for Rs. 4,236.4.6, this being the value of Umrao Begum's share which he had lost, estimated on the basis of the purchase price paid over for the village. The Board of Revenue, after some discussion, called on the collector to compromise the case : Tika Ram was to be awarded Rs. 5,000, for which he was required to surrender that part of Mohanpur in his (legal) possession—nearly one-quarter of the entire estate. On May 27, 1868, the collector made it known that Tika Ram refused to abide by the terms of the compromise. The commissioner of Rohilkhand forwarded the collector's letter to the board on July 20. On July 10, however, Tika Ram's case had been heard in the civil court and had been decided ex parte against Government, which was compelled to pay Rs. 4,236 and costs.[79]

believed that the greatest mistake a cultivating proprietor could make was to oppose an incoming Bania's "petition for partition."

[78]See p. 222 above.

[79]Extract from Board of Revenue, NWP, to Government, NWP, August 31, 1869, on the case of *Tika Ram* v. *Government*, NWP, in "Report of the Legal Remembrancer,

The resistance of powerful zamindars could break the force of the transfer law. The Thakurs of pargana Aonlah, Bareilly district, successfully repulsed any threat to their zamindari, and to their thriving credit operations.[80] Moens had no illusions about their flagrant subversions of the judicial machinery, or about the consequent deterrent to capitalist enterprise which the law was titularly to encourage : "No capitalist would risk money in a share in a village with the knowledge that he would have a half dozen suits to fight through the Civil Courts to get even nominal possession of his purchase, and the subsequent certainty of an annual suit for even the small share of profits assigned to him in the village papers." As a measure of "these difficulties," Moens cited the predicament of a "well-known Hakeem, Saadut Ali Khan, ... [an] unusually strong, wealthy and intelligent landholder, who had bought numerous shares in this pargana, of which neither he nor his successors were ever able to obtain possession."[81]

When legal obstructions failed, became wearisome, or were merely adjudged impractical, determined zamindars mustered their resources of manpower to fight off the auction purchaser. "The old tradition [of local means of coercion] still protects former *quasi*-proprietary bodies," Auckland Colvin wrote from the Secretariat in Allahabad in 1871,

or, if tradition fails them, they are not slow to assist themselves. Within sixteen miles of my writing-table there are villages where it is as much as the auction-purchaser's life is worth to shew his face unattended by a rabble of cudgellers. He may sue his tenants and obtain decrees for enhanced rents; but payment of those rents he will not get. A long series of struggles, commencing in our Courts, marked in their progress certainly by affrays, and very probably ending in murder, may possibly lead him at length to the position of an English proprietor. But in defence of their old rates the Brahmin, or Rajpoot, or Syud community, as the case may be, ignorant of political economy, and mindful only of the traditions which record the origin and terms of their holding, will risk property and life itself.[82]

NWP, 1868–69," in NWP, "Revenue Proceedings," January 22, 1870, Index No. 52, October 23, 1869, Proceeding No. 82. For the complete correspondence on the case, see *ibid.*, Index Nos. 45–56.

[80]See pp. 163, 174 above.

[81]*Bareilly Settlement Report,* p. 283.

[82]Colvin, *Memorandum,* p. 114. Colvin's syntax suggests that the attainment of proprietorship on the English model in the NWP was tantamount to martyrdom (an appropriate sentiment for the times). For further examples of the vigorous repulse

The range of obstructionist tactics employed by zamindars in frustrating the dispensation of justice according to the law and in violating the peace tended to make something of a mockery of the principle of security for which Government ostensibly strove, but at the same time these tactics served Government's political ends. Nothing could have been less desirable, politically, than that the transfer laws should have worked through to their logical—revolutionary—end. "The indebtedness of proprietors becomes a serious political question," a spokesman for the Government of India recorded in a note of 1894, "when it is found that their insolvency means dispossession and that the soil is passing into the hands of classes who have the ability neither to cultivate nor to rule." As far as the NWP and Oudh were concerned, there was little cause for alarm. "The transfer of land is still sufficiently common," the note continued, "but the landowning and cultivating classes compete with the moneylender for the possession of it. There is little indication in the recent economic history of the provinces of any reason for apprehending wholesale dispossession of any class it is desirable to retain on the soil."[83]

This was no new realization on the part of Government. Even if the combined pressures of the British administration and local society drained away their means, the position of the old proprietors had nonetheless to be zealously guarded. The revenue administration, accordingly, exercised powers which contradicted not merely the civil but also the revenue sale laws. In Banda district alone, 117 confiscated villages were restored in 1867 to the "old zamindars, who had been ousted either by the Civil Courts, or from inability to pay the revenue in former years, on the sole condition of the proprietors evincing a capacity to manage the estates during a short specified term of years." "I am to add," the secretary to the board continued, "that, speaking broadly, the sale of estates for arrears of revenue has ceased to be a process in use, and that the sympathy of the Board, as well as of Government, is ever on the side of the ousted or embarrassed zamindar."[84] Provision was made not merely for restoration after the

of auction purchasers, see *Farukhabad Settlement Report,* p. 158 (trans-Gangetic parganas); *Shahjahanpur Settlement Report,* p. xxxviii (tehsils Jalalabad and Shahjahanpur).

[83]"Note on Land Transfer," pp. 41–42.

[84]Board of Revenue, NWP, to Government, NWP, October 23, 1867, apropos of the alleged collusion of a tehsildar with a Marwari creditor in transfer litigation with certain zamindars of Hamirpur district, in NWP, "Revenue Proceedings," November 2, 1867, Index No. 5, Proceeding No. 13.

completion of sale—a further potential obstacle for the auction purchaser to take into account; Section 244 of the Civil Procedure Code of 1859 itself empowered the collector to intervene in the course of a compulsory sale and seek to compromise the transaction between the parties by temporary alienations in order to rescue the estate from the direr consequences of insolvency[85] and thus preserve some security for continued revenue payments.

As the distress of impoverished zamindars and the threat to the revenue and to Government's political stability which this necessarily implied grew increasingly obvious during the revision of settlements, rescue operations to shore up the crumbling structure of proprietorship in the provinces became more comprehensive. In both the NWP and Oudh, Courts of Wards functioned busily to extricate the more promising of encumbered estates from the vicious circle of debt and transfer litigation, appointing Government managers to bring them back to solvency, with a little experimentation with agricultural improvements on the side, as befitted a benevolent proprietor.[86] In 1870, the jurisdiction of the Oudh Court of Wards was extended to cope with cases provided for under the Oudh Talukdars' Relief Act, XXIV of 1870. In the NWP, the appalling condition of the indebted majority of zamindars in Jhansi Division demanded special legislation, passed after some nine years of notes, memoranda, and draft enactments :[87] in its final form this was the Jhansi Encumbered Estates Act, XVI of 1882. By the 1890s, this essentially paradoxical progression in the amendment of transfer law had reached its next

[85]The collectors' attempts met with varying success. Statistics for 1864–65, for example, showed sale had been "warded off" in fifty cases in Meerut district, but only in one in Bulandshahr (out of forty-nine in which preventive steps had been taken); in Aligarh, in three (100 percent success); in Budaon, in thirty-one; in Bareilly, in seventy-five; in Bijnour, in three; in Moradabad, in three (no rates of success are given for these last four districts). *NWP Revenue Administration Report*, 1864–65, pp. 9–10.

[86]See pp. 104–107 above.

[87]For details, see B. W. Colvin, Officiating Commissioner, Jhansi, to Board of Revenue, NWP, November 13, 1873, "Indebtedness of the Agricultural Classes in Jhansie Division," in NWP, "Revenue Proceedings," March 1874, Index No. 34, January 17, 1874, Proceeding No. 65. Board of Revenue to Government, NWP, September 17, 1875, "Condition of the Zamindars of the Jhansie District," in NWP, "Revenue Proceedings," January 1876, Index No. 15, January 8, 1876, Proceeding No. 55. Government, NWP and Oudh, to Government of India (Department of Revenue, Agriculture and Commerce), August 9, 1878, apropos of distress in Jhansi, in NWP and Oudh, "Revenue Proceedings," August 1878, Index No. 4, August 10, 1878, Proceeding No. 1. "Bill to Provide for the Relief of Encumbered Estate in the Jhansi Division," in NWP and Oudh, "Revenue Proceedings," November 1878, Index Nos. 30–44.

stage : the compilation of a wide-ranging set of papers (bearing on all the provinces of British India) to introduce formal restrictions into the transfer laws themselves.[88]

If the debt and transfer laws had proved unequal in practice to the task theoretically expected of them, the history of their working provided a striking vindication of at least one dictum of John Stuart Mill—". . . that government is always in the hands, or passing into the hands, of whatever is the strongest power in society, and that what this power is does not depend on institutions, but institutions on it."[89]

[88]The pioneer enactment restricting the right of alienation was the Punjab Alienation of Land Act, I of 1901. For a detailed account of the passing of this legislation, see N. G. Barrier, "The Punjab Alienation of Land Bill of 1900," *Duke University Program in Comparative Studies on Southern Asia*, Monograph No. 2 (1966).

[89]J. S. Mill, *Autobiography*, p. 137.

Chapter VI

THE DILEMMAS OF
ADMINISTRATION

Government was at pains to stress publicly the overriding benevolence
of its aims in promoting the moral and material progress of British
India and a corresponding awareness of the responsibility it considered
inherent in its supreme power. Official apologists were anxious that
too narrow an interpretation should not be placed on its historic role :
"The Indian Government," as Sir W. W. Hunter defined it in the
Imperial Gazetteer, "is not a mere tax-collecting agency, charged
with the single duty of protecting person and property. Its system
of administration is based upon the view that the British power is a
paternal despotism, which owns, in a certain sense, the entire soil
of the country, and whose duty it is to perform the various functions
of a wealthy and enlightened proprietor ..."[1]

Government's concern for the state of its "property," in line with
contemporary principles, was inseparable from its need to ensure
the regular collection of its "rent." It was logical that responsibility
for the welfare of the land should fall principally on the revenue
administration. It proved increasingly difficult for that administration,
however, to discharge the duties which such proprietorial responsibility entailed. Measures introduced to repair apparent deficiencies in
the condition of the "estate" had brought a multitude of unforeseen
problems in their train which deterred by their range and intensity
subsequent attempts at remedial action. Nowhere was this more
obvious than in the NWP and Oudh. Public works aggravated imbalances in productivity. Small-scale agricultural improvements
failed persistently to achieve practical objectives of any significance.
The refinements of administrative procedure robbed the old principle
of takavi loans of most of its utility. Government's concern to secure
its revenue in accordance with equity and an ill-defined image of
dawning prosperity compelled its officers to labour at endless com-

[1]Quoted by A. H. Harington, "Economic Reform in Rural India," *Calcutta Review,*
LXXX (1885), 435 (headnote).

promises in matching impractical principles with incomprehensible practices. New incentives for production and distribution resulted in bloating the power of local creditors at the expense of the bulk of the rural population. The decorous application of law and order by means of the modernized judicial system proved time and again an illusion when confronted with the realities of the rural scene.

The persistence of problems of such dimensions, in overburdening the revenue administration, aggravated fundamental weaknesses in its capacity which made consistent action by Government in the sweeping style of a capitalist proprietor utterly impracticable. Geared first and foremost to meeting Government's requirements, the design of the revenue administration was not of that comprehensive quality which Government's much-publicized responsibility demanded. Here, too, modernization brought problems which were insuperable by the means to hand : innovations in bureaucratic procedure introduced in line with contemporary notions of order and security hampered the exercise even of essential powers—the collecting of taxes and the dispensing of justice. Each aspect of the revenue administration— the co-ordination between senior and subordinate officers; the state of official records; the machinery for enquiry into agrarian conditions; and procedural impediments and restrictions on expenditure—came to reflect in some degree the predicament of the British Government in its adopted environment.

The Structure of Administration

In accordance with instructions from the governor-general in Calcutta and the India Office in London, the lieutenant-governor of the provinces took all decisions as regards fiscal affairs in consultation with the Board of Revenue. The board, with its two members—senior and junior—and its secretary drawn from amongst the highest-ranking revenue officers in the field, was the co-ordinating link between the Secretariat in Allahabad and the administration's offices in the mofussil. It prepared the revenue agenda for the lieutenant-governor's adjudication from the correspondence it conducted in the first instance with the commissioners of the revenue divisions—six in the NWP and four more in Oudh. Each commissioner's office was in turn a central reference point for the officers who staffed the district collectorates within each division.[2] The district collectorate was the hub of the

[2]For the geographical areas of the revenue divisions and the districts included in

administration—it represented the "paternal despotism" of British power in miniature. The collector and magistrate was responsible for the collection of the "rents" of his "estate"—his district—and for its welfare. He had to supervise the revenue accounts and administer criminal, and to some extent civil, justice. He was responsible, logically, for the local police. He had to see to the efficiency of local Government institutions, such as schools and dispensaries, and to the construction and maintenance of all roads and bridges other than those which were part of the main communications systems of the provinces (and therefore the responsibility of the Public Works Department), and of virtually all Government buildings.[3]

From his office in the sadr station of the district, the collector presided over an administrative establishment which reflected in microcosm the ranking of the Revenue Department as a whole. His assistants were of various grades, the degree of subordination of each official being relative to his distance from the collectorate. The assistant collector and magistrate was the most senior of the subordinate office staff; he was a trainee collector, based like his superiors at the sadr station. Beyond, in the district itself, deputy collectors or tehsildars carried out the functions of the collector in their sub-divisions, tehsils, under his absolute authority. Beneath the tehsildars came the subordinate establishment proper : this consisted of the village officers who were recognized and partly paid by Government and who included amongst their numbers the mokuddams (headmen), the lambardars (tax collectors), and, most important, the patwaris (accountants) on whom Government relied for the maintenance of local records, its basic source of information on agrarian conditions. Lastly, the subordinate establishment also included the clerks and messengers who populated the collectorate and *tehsili* (the tehsildar's office), recording and communicating every transaction as official procedure demanded.[4]

"It will be seen," C. H. T. Crosthwaite concluded on summarizing

them, see endpaper map. Prior to its amalgamation with the NWP in 1877, the Oudh administration was separately constituted (along lines parallel to those of the neighbouring province), headed by a chief commissioner who was assisted by a Board of Revenue. Commissioners and deputy commissioners, respectively, staffed the Oudh divisions and districts. In 1877, the offices of lieutenant-governor and chief commissioner, and the two Boards of Revenue, were amalgamated. The structure of divisional and district administration remained as before.

[3] C. H. T. Crosthwaite, *Notes on the North-Western Provinces*, pp. 3–4.

[4] For the numbers employed in the administration, and establishment costs, see pp. 272–273 below.

the structure of the revenue administration, ". . . that the organization at the disposal of the Government of these provinces is such as to enable them to reach the very lowest strata of which society is composed."[5] Effective use of this organization was another matter : it depended on the co-ordination of the various ranks and efficient communication from the top to the bottom of the hierarchy.[6] The distance, however, between the collector and his assistant at the sadr station and the patwaris in the villages was vast and was measured not merely in physical terms. A formidable barrier stood between the superior and subordinate ranks of the district administration, between the European collector and his handful of European assistants—and the "natives" beyond. Prior to 1900, it was rarely crossed by subordinates who earned promotion in view of their recognized experience. "We are as oil to water out here," Frederick Layard, an officer in the Indian army, wrote to his brother A. H. Layard, in 1858 shortly after the suppression of the "Mutiny" disorders; "luckily we are the oil and stay at the top."[7] Administrative power was distributed accordingly. In local affairs, the collector was supreme; he was "to the natives," in Crosthwaite's words, ". . . the personification of Government."[8]

In the exercise of his power, however, the collector was accountable to his superiors. Every official action and its justification had to be documented, with the result that the collectorate stood as a clearing-house for the local administration, and the collector, at his desk or holding court day in and day out, became increasingly alienated from the remote rural world beyond his office which his duties prescribed him to care for but which the procedure for executing them prevented him from investigating at first hand. "There is in fact no real revenue administration," C. J. Connell expostulated in a critique of Government compiled from his experience as an officer of the Bengal Civil Service.

... the Collector, especially in Oudh ... , is a tax-gatherer and nothing more; he is a compulsory jack-of-all-trades whose days are spent in inditing countless reports on all miscellaneous matters of great or small importance, upon which the local Government of the day sets, or is forced to set great

[5]Crosthwaite, *Notes on the North-Western Provinces*, p. 5.

[6]"Whether the machine works so as to attain this end depends very much upon the *personnel* of the District Officers," *ibid.*, p. 6.

[7]Quoted by G. Waterfield, *Layard of Nineveh*, p. 291. Frederick Layard denounced the provocatively segregated administration. He expressed his surprise that the Indian had not in fact retaliated by massacring all Europeans during the "Mutiny."

[8]Crosthwaite, *Notes on the North-Western Provinces*, p. 4.

store; he has to draw up portentous memos on conservancy, municipalities, drains, and self-government all the morning; his afternoons are occupied with his appellate work, and an odd half hour or so, as leisure permits, is with difficulty snatched for the real work of a Collector, namely, the disposal of the revenue reports; those papers, which have to do with the future prosperity or ruin of villages, must be perfunctorily rushed through, while a proposal for a new latrine has taken up hours of valuable time.[9]

Restrictions on the collector's mobility grew with the passage of time. While the Secretariat in Allahabad expanded into numerous departments, the district collectorates remained the single source of local information and the principal executive agency. While correspondence became more and more voluminous, superior orders from Allahabad and Calcutta insisted on greater formalization in procedure: witnesses were demanded for an increasing number of transactions; signatures had to appear on more documents; written submissions usurped the place of verbal orders even in the most ephemeral matters. Reporting all these developments at the end of the revenue year 1880-81, the collector of Jaunpur bewailed the consequences which he—in the position of greatest administrative power in the district—was obliged to suffer: "It is almost impossible at the present to get through the mere manual and mental labour required to keep the business going. There is actually no leisure for thought or examination of what is going on."[10] The board found itself reluctantly in agreement with "the general tendency" of the collector's remarks, but could make little by way of positive recommendations: "There must be a limit to the constant increase of establishments [in Allahabad]. There is certainly a limit to what can be done by existing ones ..."[11] The succeeding twenty years proved the board wrong. The business but not the staff of the collectorates swelled to majestic proportions, as the figures for correspondence and judicial work show.[12]

More problems for the harassed collector arose with the revision of settlements which dominated the revenue administration, and consequently the agrarian scene so far as Government was concerned, from the late 1850s. Principles of Government dictated that

[9]C. J. Connell, *Land Revenue Policy*, pp. 72–73.

[10]*NWP Revenue Administration Report*, 1881–82, para. 137, p. 79.

[11]*Ibid.*, p. 79 n.

[12]For the increase in the collector's business, measured in terms of letters issued and received and cases instituted and disposed of, by division, from 1864–65 to 1899–1900, see Figure 10.

the new assessments were to surpass their predecessors in careful attention to minute detail, district by district.[13] To execute these plans, given top priority by Government, staff had to be found to assist the European settlement officers—and where else but in the collectorates could subordinate officers be found in sufficient numbers and with the required local experience?

The means of meeting this demand for assistance were not unlimited. Government's requirement that the new scientific principles of assessment be applied with accuracy and impartiality meant that few district officers were eligible for such service. The Settlement Department could not, as Sir William Muir, then Lieutenant-Governor, noted in 1868, "especially in all matters connected with assessment, be confided with safety to Native officials."[14] The problem this created for the routine administration was also abundantly clear to Muir. Since district officers—the collectors—were necessarily involved in settlement work, and since some twenty-one of the most promising (European) assistants throughout the NWP were posted to the Settlement Department, the day-to-day business of the collectorates devolved increasingly on junior ("native") staff.[15] In answer to Muir's protest concerning the "great strain which the Land Revenue Settlement ... was bringing to bear on the Civil Service in the conduct of the Administration's ordinary business," Government could only attempt to relieve what was an insoluble problem of two irreconcilable claims by an informal compromise. A circular order published in July 1868 instructed commissioners, district officers, and settlement officers that the junior assistants attached to the Settlement Department should aid in general district administration in the rains and summer months, for example, when they were sometimes "insufficiently supplied with ... Settlement work."[16] The order remained more of an exhortation than a command : so long as the settlements were the dominant concern of Government, there was little incentive for aspiring officers to turn from opportunities for recognition and promotion which assessment work offered and bury themselves amongst the papers in the collector's office.

In the Doab districts, canals could bring similar problems to the

[13]See pp. 123–127 above.

[14]"Minute," in NWP, "Revenue Proceedings," June 27, 1868, Index No. 29, Proceeding No. 14.

[15]Ibid.

[16]Circular Order 74, July 10, 1868, in NWP, "Revenue Proceedings," July 11, 1868, Index No. 1, Proceeding No. 40.

collector, but here it was the "native" subordinates who were torn between the conflicting claims of Government on local field staff. For the assessment of direct and indirect revenue from the canals, so important an item of Government's budget,[17] the irrigated area of each district had to be measured each season, and the charges which were calculated initially on an acreage basis had to be distributed according to the intricacies of local cultivating and proprietorial interests. In a district such as Etawah in the mid-1860s, where a mere 40,000 acres were irrigated on the average each year by the Ganges Canal, the business of recording the irrigation statistics was entrusted to the collector's tehsil staff which seemed to cope with this additional burden without undue strain. However, the system of measurement devised for Etawah was carried over with unfortunate results to Meerut, where already in 1866 an estimated 200,000 acres were annually watered by canals. W. A. Forbes, the Collector, was moved to protest vehemently against this "most hideous system of canal-irrigation measurement . . . which, without the slightest exaggeration is likely to cause disaster to our land revenue system." In tehsil Meerut alone, seven separate measuring parties were employed—simultaneously—during six months of the year (three months for each harvest); to each party, one of the fixed tehsil establishments of amins (field clerks) had to be attached according to the Etawah system. The collector was left to carry on his business insofar as possible "by the aid of casual and inexperienced subordinates." "I trust," Forbes wrote beseechingly, "the system may be crushed at once, for the anxiety it causes not to mention the labor, can hardly be described."[18] Forbes's plea roused the board. Faced with the unwelcome choice as to which of Government's needs was to be served by the less reliable agency, the board decided it should not be the collectorate and the land revenue itself which suffered. They recommended therefore that, if necessary, canal-irrigation measurement be "superintended by a casual employé in preference to the deputation of members of the fixed establishment for this duty whenever the Collector may find the number of measurement parties and the duration of their operations interferes prejudicially with the regular work of his district."[19]

[17]For the direct and indirect revenue from the canals in NWP, from 1876–77 to 1899–1900, see Figure 5.

[18]W. A. Forbes, Collector, Meerut, to Board of Revenue, NWP, February 7, 1866, in NWP, "Revenue Proceedings," May 26, 1866, Index No. 48, Proceeding No. 24.

[19]Ibid., Index No. 47, Proceeding No. 23.

While the collector continued officially to dominate the local administration, the increasing demands made upon him by the range of his duties together with the dictates of procedure diminished both his means and his opportunity to discharge them with the vigour which his authority theoretically required. As a result, he was compelled to entrust more and more of the business of local government to his "native" officers. Their responsibility grew correspondingly out of all proportion to their status and consequently their power as recognized by Government. From the point of view of official ranking, they remained throughout entirely subordinate to the collector but, as far as effective action was concerned, the collector was in the paradoxical position of being entirely subordinate to them.

The collector's dependence on his "native" establishment was reinforced by the mobility accorded him by the conditions of service in the modernized Crown administration. It was an easier matter for European officers in the later nineteenth century to leave a district for another or for a sanctioned spell abroad than it was for them to move about within one during the performance of their duties. The upper ranks of the administration were becoming increasingly remote from their environment, as Hunter himself showed in pointing to the contrast between Company service and the improved conditions of modern times :

The Company's servants accepted India as their home, and generally remained a long time in one District. But under the beneficent policy of the Queen's Proclamation, the natives of India every year engross a larger share of the actual government. The English administrators are accepting their ultimate position as a small and highly mobilised superintending staff. They are shifted more rapidly from District to District; and the new system of furlough, with a view to keeping them at their utmost efficiency, encourages them to take their holidays at short intervals of four years, instead of granting long periods of idleness once or twice in a quarter of a century's service. They have not the same opportunities for slowly accumulating personal knowledge of one locality; on the other hand, their energies are not allowed to be eaten away by rust ...[20]

The "native" officers, ineligible for promotion beyond the rank of assistant and consequently immobilized in the.r sub-districts, were expected to acquire that "minute and extended knowledge of the people and the country"[21] beyond the reach of their European superiors.

[20]W. W. Hunter, ed., *Imperial Gazetteer of India,* p. xxxi.
[21]Crosthwaite, *Notes on the North-Western Provinces,* p. 5.

It was early established as a central tenet of Government revenue policy that the administration should interfere as little as possible—in any direct sense—with the affairs of local proprietors.[22] The tehsildar's office was the last outpost of the administration, the co-ordinating link between the collectorate and the mahals. Zamindars were required to make their submissions and their revenue payments to their local tehsildar, who kept the accounts for the sub-district. Dealing with estates the proprietary title of which had been given to a numerous body of co-sharers were more complicated, and here Government had long seen fit to provide some means of assisting the tehsildar. At the earliest regular settlements, the honorary local office of lambardar had been created. Lambardars were to be the elected representatives of proprietary brotherhoods, whose principal duty was to collect the group's revenue payments and hand them over to the tehsildar. They were officially nominated by the brotherhood at an assembly presided over by the settlement officer, according to the recognized procedure stipulated in the *wajib-ul-arz,* or record of rights drawn up at settlement.[23] At this point, Government's participation in relations between the brotherhood and its lambardar-representative ended. The office was partly hereditary, subject to the qualification that a lambardar's eldest son should prove fit to manage affairs. The brotherhood itself held the power to depose a lambardar who failed to satisfy their requirements and to elect a new one.[24]

With the revision of settlements, the office of lambardar came in for some intensive questioning. Was it an efficient agency for the collection of the revenue? Did it assist the tehsildar? C. A. Elliott, Officiating Collector in Farukhabad in 1868, was convinced that the lambardari "system" had proved totally impractical. "We have tried for nearly thirty years to introduce this system, thinking it congenial to the spirit of the country, and have failed; it is no use trying any more or refusing to acknowledge our failure."[25] In Farukhabad, where each shareholder by-passed the lambardar and paid his share of the land tax direct to the tehsildar's office (thus complicating

[22]See p. 105 above.

[23]For the details of official procedure regarding the appointment of *lambardars,* see *Unao Settlement Report,* pp. 76–77.

[24]*Ibid.,* p. 49.

[25]C. A. Elliott to Commissioner, Agra Division, April 30, 1870, "Note on the Selection of Lambardars," in NWP, "Revenue Proceedings," April 29, 1871, Index No. 2, December 31, 1871, Proceeding No. 26.

his accounts), the lambardar's office had grown into a much-coveted sinecure. The degree of effective representation which lambardars could exert depended on their power within their community. Where a lambardar was already strong, he could stand as the "village representative" before local officers and use his influence to arbitrate private quarrels. However, like all other prestige posts which were heritable, this one had become the preserve of families of maliks who were determined to control it. According to Elliott, the incumbent was in many cases a woman, an infant, or a non-resident,[26] all of whom were singularly unqualified to represent the community but were at the same time legally capable of passing the titie to their heirs. Elsewhere, cabals of lambardars had grown up within the brotherhoods owing to manipulations in the election procedure.[27] The offices multiplied with no reference to the needs of the community as far as representation, let alone tax-collecting, was concerned. In Farukhabad, many villages had three or four lambardars; it was not uncommon to find six or even eight to a village, and rare cases of twelve and more were known to Elliott.[28]

With such confusions obliterating the neat outlines of administrative agencies, what was Government to do? Elliott suggested that any notion of legal status attached to the lambardar should be abolished, and that the idea of his collecting revenue from others or of others paying it through him should be abandoned. But where ownership was in the hands of a large community, a recognized representative was clearly required for those times when Government wished to consult the proprietors or act through them. "We cannot summon up 50 or 100 Rajputs every time we have to appoint a chaukidar or patwari, or to put pressure to obtain the apprehension of a thief: for these purposes we must select lambardars"; moreover, Government had to hold to the principle that the lambardar should be "the representative of public opinion in the village." To see that this principle was honoured, however, Elliott recommended that the lambardari system be reformed—by the direct action of Government. Hereditary status should be abolished and the office made elective forthwith, with the appointments to be made from candidates selected by the proprietors and the collector on the principle of *quamdiu se bene gesserint*—"or words to that effect in Hindustani."[29]

[26] *Ibid.*
[27] *Unao Settlement Report*, p. 50.
[28] Elliott, "Note on the Selection of Lambardars," cited above, n. 25.
[29] *Ibid.*

W. A. Forbes, Commissioner of Benares in 1870, recalled a similar state of affairs from his days as Collector in Meerut. To the detriment of Government's links with society, local maliks who could not be brought under supervision controlled the lambardar's office and through it the "village community." The system had "become hateful" to those elements of rural society it had been designed to assist; the proprietary brotherhoods, "for the simple reason, that the care imposed upon us [revenue officers] by the Government in *Directions to Settlement Officers,* para. 157, has not been observed, and fractions of the brotherhood who have then for very good reasons separated themselves from time to time from the main body have found their interest still left against their will in the hands of the persons from whose tyranny and affliction and oppression they had attempted to free themselves, and that, moreover, they have to pay them as their unaccepted agents."[30] If these observations provided a strong case for some measure of reform in the lambardari system, how was it to be achieved? Both Elliott and Forbes had left their respective districts for higher posts; they could no longer carry on their protestations at the district level, and a new accumulation of official duties prevented them from paying much attention to old causes of concern.

More formidable obstructions to corrective action came from the senior echelon of the field staff, the divisional commissioners. R. M. Lind, Commissioner of Agra Division, made no attempt to muffle Elliott's disclosures in his covering note to the board but, at the same time, in prophesying the unwelcome consequences in terms of a dissolution of the status quo which must necessarily follow an attempt to act upon them, he showed the inexpediency of adopting any of Elliott's recommendations: "admission of the principle [of Elliott's proposals] would go far to break up the remaining bonds of union in village communities ... Depriving a lambardar of his most important function, the collection of revenue from his co-sharers, would be apt to disorganize the social status of communities in which the custom was permitted to prevail."[31] Others, like F. O. Mayne,

[30]W. A. Forbes to Board of Revenue, NWP, June 29, 1870, in NWP, "Revenue Proceedings," April 29, 1871, Index No. 5, December 31, 1870, Proceeding No. 29.

[31]R. Lind to Board of Revenue, NWP, May 11, 1870, in NWP, "Revenue Proceedings," April 29, 1871, Index No. 2, December 31, 1870, Proceeding No. 26. Lind considered the "primitive state of village communities ... particularly favourable to the lambardari system." That "evils" were creeping in was owing no doubt to imperfections in the system—or rather, specifically, to an abuse in the mode of nominations to the post of lambardar. It will be remembered that the lambardari was a creation of the early British administration.

Commissioner of Allahabad in 1870, saw it as a practical issue : "If Elliott does away with the lambardar's legal status ... with whom will engagements be made to pay the Government Revenue? It is impossible to take enagagements from a whole bhyachara community ..."[32] True, shareholders often preferred to pay their revenue quota directly to Government, and it was right that they should have this power. Moreover, no tehsildar who understood his work would decline to take their payment (how else would Government get its revenue?). It was also true that there were faults in the selection of lambardars : no woman or child should be elected. But these were minor objections. Elliott, in questioning the lambardars' utility, had challenged the whole principle of Government's non-interference. Mayne sided with Lind : "We interfere a great deal too much ... From my experience, lambardars, although not always made use of for collecting the revenue, are nevertheless mostly men of great influence and power in a village and are very useful and necessary institutions, and I think we should do wrong to destroy their legal status."[33] The board agreed with the commissioners, and Government did nothing to remedy the defects in the lambardari system. It was "an easier matter," in H. S. Reid's words, "for the Collector to deal with large agricultural communities through the more intelligent and powerful members of the body."[34]

The status quo was thus preserved, and the lambardars were retained. At the same time, however, the board recognized the collector's authority to allow co-sharers, separate in respect of the legal possession of an estate but with a joint liability to meet the revenue assessed on it (a common situation), "to pay their quota of demand direct into the tehsili without the lambardar's intervention."[35] Yet it was "obviously undesirable," the board admitted, that "the work of collection from a large number of individual sharers should be thrown on the tehsil officials when a recognized agency for such collection already exists."[36] In addition to the burden of paperwork on the tehsildars, there was also the greater risk of errors being made

[32]F. O. Mayne to Board of Revenue, NWP, June 11, 1870, in NWP, "Revenue Proceedings," April 29, 1871, Index No. 4, December 31, 1870, Proceeding No. 28.
[33]Ibid.
[34]H. S. Reid, Junior Member, Board of Revenue, NWP, July 16, 1870, in NWP, "Revenue Proceedings," April 29, 1871, Index No. 8, December 31, 1870, Proceeding No. 32.
[35]Board of Revenue, NWP, Circular No. 1, March 22, 1871, in NWP, "Revenue Proceedings," April 29, 1871, Index No. 13, Proceeding No. 34.
[36]Ibid.

in the increasingly intricate accounts—a danger about which the board had expressed its anxiety some four years earlier, in 1866.[37] The collector was therefore urged to use his authority with the co-sharers "sparingly and with discretion."[38]

Such orders were of little practical assistance to the overworked tehsildars. Government's reliance on them to supervise its relations with proprietors demanded, theoretically, that they should be allowed a certain mobility to keep their tehsils under inspection. Modernized procedure, and the acceptance of the breakdown in the lambardari system, created problems for the tehsildar which reflected those of the collector above him. "What modern Tehsildar has leisure, even if he has the aptitude, for ... constant visits to a distance from his headquarters?" asked G. H. M. Ricketts, Collector of Allahabad in 1865. "Owing to the elaboration of our Revenue system, its intimate combination with judicial functions, and the accuracy required from all Tehsildars in all their numerous statements, they are chained to their desks; the means of communication with their zamindars, or the source whence they obtain the knowledge of their villages, is through the Putwarees, who are never impartial or to be relied on ..."[39]

The patwari held hereditary office under a zamindar as the keeper of his accounts and transactions with the cultivators of his mahal. Government, in taking up these "village records" as the basis of its revenue assessments in the settlements under Regulation IX of 1833[40] recognized the "village accountant," the patwari, as "a Government as well as a village servant."[41] The application of new scientific

[37]Board of Revenue to Government, NWP, July 13, 1866, in NWP, "Revenue Proceedings," July 28, 1866, Index No. 1, Proceeding No. 12.

[38]Board's Circular No. 1, 1871, cited above, n. 35.

[39]G. H. M. Ricketts to Officiating Commissioner, Allahabad, January 9, 1865, in NWP, "Revenue Proceedings," May 6, 1865, Index No. 8, February 18, 1865, Proceeding No. 23. Further problems arose where tehsildars were "appointees of influential men." The tehsildar was also induced to stay in his office by blandishments provided by legal duties : "The tehsildars [in Oudh], who are the officers primarily responsible for the collection of the revenue, prefer judicial work, partly because it is more attractive and vested with more dignity in the ordinary native mind, and partly because it affords a better opportunity of attracting attention and thereby attaining promotion. Under such circumstances, it is not surprising that these officers do not find time to move about in their circles and acquire that knowledge of the character and condition of the people which alone can give them the means of forming an opinion how best to collect their revenue." *Oudh Revenue Administration Report*, 1874–75, p. 76.

[40]See p. 123 above.

[41]"Correspondence Regarding the Lieutenant-Governor's Proposed Alterations in

standards to the business of assessment which came with the revision of settlements[42] did not diminish the patwari's importance vis-à-vis the administration. The reluctance of Government to dispense with any of its recognized agencies was increased in this case by the overriding necessity to cut costs. As R. C. Oldfield, Collector of Farukhabad, noted in the course of a discussion in 1863 on the establishment required for the revision of his district's settlement, "The employment of the Putwarees will be no new feature, as they have always been the instruments through which all the operations of the Settlement have been primarily conducted, and as I presume it is not contemplated to dispense with anyone of the systematic series of operations or the preparation of the various records which comprise a regular Settlement, I conclude the object of the Government is rather to reduce the amount of labour and expense of supervision, hitherto falling on the Government, by taking the fullest advantage of the existing records, and of the aid of Putwarees and Zamindars by enlisting their willing co-operation."[43] The patwaris were indispensable to the revenue administration not merely for the collecting of taxes but also for the conduct of its judicial business. According to a note by the lieutenant-governor in 1862, nine of ten summary suits (heard in the revenue courts) had to be decided "almost entirely on the Patwari's evidence."[44]

The principles of modern administration demanded more of the patwari than had been required under Company rule. He should understand his work thoroughly; he should know the circumstances of the people within his jurisdiction; most important, he should be "quite independent."[45] At the same time, Government was anxious that measures to improve the patwari's services should leave his rightful position in the "village community" undisturbed—he must remain the "village" servant as well as Government's. The problem of how the patwari's independence might be secured under these conditions could not but persist.

Government's requirements for increased efficiency at the village

the Existing System of Farming Settlements in NWP," in NWP, "Revenue Proceedings," April 14, 1864, Index No. 35, Proceeding No. 29.

[42]See pp. 123–127 above.

[43]R. C. Oldfield to Officiating Commissioner, Agra, October 7, 1863, in NWP, "Revenue Proceedings," March 26, 1864, Index No. 52, Proceeding No. 5. On the problems of co-ordinating local records with new scientific standards of assessment, see pp. 127–129 above.

[44]Government, NWP, to Board of Revenue, NWP, August 9, 1862, in NWP, "Revenue Proceedings," August 9, 1862, Index No. 25, Proceeding No. 20.

[45]Ibid.

level were clear; it was—and remained—a matter of how to achieve them. The first attempt was the introduction of the patwaris' *halkabandi* system early in the 1850s. Under this system contiguous villages were grouped together in *halkas* (circles), each of which was to be served by one of the local patwaris appointed by the district officer in consultation with the zamindars. An official enquiry into the working of the system some seven years later[46] revealed the problems which modernization entailed. The greatest concern was shown for the zamindars' opinion. In Agra and Meerut divisions, the halkabandis had met with general approval;[47] minor adjustments a few years later showed that Government was prepared to continue to follow the zamindars' wishes. The commissioner of Meerut reported in 1863 that the patwaris' halkas in Saharunpur had been completed with as little change as possible—and where such had occurred, it was "generally with the idea of bringing the various villages of one landlord into the jurisdiction of one patwari; a fact to which the zamindars themselves attach great importance."[48] Government in this respect was even prepared on occasion to forego the interests of efficiency. Some twelve years after the enquiry, M. A. McConaghey found that villages in Mainpuri situated at opposite extremes of a pargana were grouped together in a halka because they happened to belong to the same body of proprietors.[49] Elsewhere, the Government measures were not so well tailored to zamindars' requirements. With the exception of Cawnpore, where the halkas were drawn up with the zamindars' consent[50] as they had been in the Upper Doab districts, the new system met with vociferous disapproval in Allahabad Division, for there it threatened to remove some patwaris and their offices from zamindari control.[51]

[46]Instituted under NWP Revenue Department General Order 1567 A, November 15, 1860; see Board of Revenue, NWP, Circular Order S, December 15, 1860, in NWP, "Revenue Proceedings," December 15, 1860.

[47]Commissioner, Agra, March 25, 1861, Index No. 134, Progress No. 3618, in NWP, "Revenue Proceedings," January 11, 1862, Index No. 40, Proceeding No. 16 (in Aligarh only, some zamindars opposed the policy). See also Commissioner, Meerut, April 30, 1861, Index No. 276, Progress No. 5359, in *ibid.*

[48]G. E. Williams to Board or Revenue, NWP, September 30, 1863, in NWP, "Revenue Proceedings," April 2, 1863, Index No. 24, January 30, 1864, Proceeding No. 24.

[49]M. A. McConaghey, late Settlement Officer, Mainpuri, to Officiating Commissioner, Agra, March 24, 1873, in NWP, "Revenue Proceedings," March 1874, Index No. 11, November 8, 1873, Proceeding No. 83.

[50]Collector, Cawnpore, March 20, 1861, in NWP, "Revenue Proceedings," January 11, 1862, Index No. 40, Proceeding No. 16.

[51]Commissioner, Allahabad, April 1, 1861, Progress No. 3817, in *ibid.*

Reports from Jhansi and Benares told a similar story of discontent amongst the dominant zamindar-maliks.[52]

The fate of the halkabandi system in the overwhelming majority of cases was clear, as was the choice of action open to strong zamindars : they either controlled it or obstructed it. Little opportunity remained for the patwari to become the independent agent of Government as modern administrative principles so urgently required. The commissioner of Rohilkhand was alone in his cautious conclusion that his district officers "generally approved" of the new system "as furnishing a more qualified class [of patwaris], more trustworthy because not so immediately dependent on the zamindars."[53] This was the most optimistic assessment of the measure in the whole enquiry. The lieutenant-governor was satisfied nonetheless on the receipt of these reports that the advantages of the system were patent and that such discontent as was expressed was "partial." The board was asked to keep the system in view and to notice it in their administration reports as a supervisory check.[54] Later in the same year—1862—the lieutenant-governor recommended that the halkabandi system be extended to districts lying outside it up to that point, in order to correct frauds and abuses by introducing an enlightened professionalism into patwaris' activities.[55]

Independent status for patwaris might well conform to the theoretical needs of Government, but its situation in practice militated against it. For one, there was the general principle of non-interference in the affairs of rural society for fear that disturbance of the zamindars might result in an upheaval of "Mutiny" proportions. More immediately, there were chronic problems of shortage of trained staff and of the means to pay them.

As far as the patwaris were concerned, Government had made its position clear soon after its decision to retain the halkabandi system. The expenses of the patwaris were to be shared, but Government was to be a junior partner in the enterprise : "For the proper remuneration

[52]Deputy Commissioner, Jaloun, January 25, 1861, Index No. 1, and Collector, Azamgarh, December 31, 1860, Index No. 509, Progress No. 358; Collector, Ghazipur, January 3, 1861, Index No. 4, Progress No. 364; Collector, Mirzapur March 7, 1861, Index No. 78, Progress No. 2842—all in *ibid.*

[53]Commissioner, Rohilkhand, July 16, 1861, Index No. 229, Progress No. 8483, in *ibid.*

[54]Government, NWP, to Board of Revenue, NWP, January 6, 1862, in NWP, "Revenue Proceedings," January 11, 1862, Index No. 41, Proceeding No. 17.

[55]Government, NWP, Board of Revenue, NWP, August 9, 1862, in NWP, "Revenue Proceedings," August 9, 1862, Index No. 25, Proceeding No. 20.

of the Patwaris, the zamindars are entirely and solely responsible."[56] Government's essentially supplementary payment for the patwaris' official services was also paid by the zamindars—indirectly, such payment being fixed at a proportion of the revenue. Prior to the publication of the Saharunpur Rules in 1855-56, this stood at some 2 percent on the jama of each district. Thereafter, patwaris' salaries were fixed by order at Rs. 80 per year, and the zamindars' contribution increased to 5 percent on the revenue. This system of payment became legally standard throughout the NWP in 1860.[57] Incentives to improvement and good conduct were officially provided by the classification of patwaris into three groups: the first drawing Rs. 120 per year, the second Rs. 100, and the third Rs. 80. Appointments were made to each class according to experience and merit.[58] Subsequent rulings on the status and remuneration of patwaris provided for their supplementary allowance from Government as before: a circular order of 1874 fixed the rate of payment at Rs. 5 to Rs. 12 per month, varying according to the size of a patwari's halka and the amount of revenue drawn from it.[59] These rates remained in force.

Not surprisingly, patwaris tended to maintain a certain diversity of interests, as circumstances suggested or compelled it. Things were no different in this respect between the temporary settled districts of the provinces and the permanently settled parts of Benares Division, where the halkabandi system had been introduced as elsewhere with the pious hope of cutting down local administrative establishments to a size more manageable with the finances in hand. The board soberly reported observations by the collector of Benares showing that neither

[56]Government, NWP, to Board of Revenue, NWP, January 30, 1864, in NWP, "Revenue Proceedings," April 2, 1864, Index No. 26, January 30, 1864, Proceeding No. 20.

[57]Board of Revenue, NWP, Circular No. 4, August 4, 1860. Under the board's Circular No. 8, September 23, 1862, the 5 percent patwari cess was to be paid into the tehsili and the patwaris were to draw their wages through the tehsildar.

[58]G. E. Williams, Commissioner, Meerut, to Board of Revenue, NWP, September 30, 1863, in NWP, "Revenue Proceedings," April 2, 1863, Index No. 24, January 30, 1864, Proceeding No. 24.

[59]Board of Revenue, NWP, Circular No. 3, February 25, 1874, in NWP, "Revenue Proceedings," March 1874, Index No. 16, February 28, 1874, Proceeding No. 30. Compare the salary scales for appointments in the higher reaches of the revenue administration; see pp. 272-273 below. The law relating to patwaris and to their superiors in charge of pargana units, the kanungos, was codified by the NWP Land Revenue Act, XIX of 1873, amended by Act XV, 1886; the Oudh Land Revenue Act, XVII of 1876; the NWP and Oudh Kanungos and Patwaris Act, XIII of 1882, amended by Act IX, 1889.

the new system nor the fixing of salary scales had cut the village patwari free from his reliance on local resources : ". . . still in some cases the Patwari retains his Jagheer [jagir], and makes a private settlement with the zamindar about his pay, and in some cases still collects his pay from the assamees, instead of receiving it from the hands of the zamindar . . . The Patwari then becomes a cultivator as regards his Jagheer, and a collector of his own pay in petty items from the whole community, whose accounts he is expected to keep honestly, and regarding whose affairs he is expected to speak truthfully. The duties of his office, if properly discharged, leave little time for agricultural employments . . ."[60]

This "proper discharge of official duties" was frustrated a priori in the majority of cases by the patwari's necessarily multiple status vis-à-vis Government and his own local society. It was a common assumption of the revenue administration that, as W. C. Plowden put it in reviewing collectors' reports in 1868 on the state of the patwaris' papers, "if things are properly and systematically looked after, village accountants are the Revenue Officer's most useful coadjutors."[61] Officers' experiences in putting the requirements of administration into practice continually proved Government's expectations to be as far out of proportion to the agency provided as the official remuneration was to the prescribed range of duties. Patwaris might prove themselves ignorant and unskilful (in the use of measuring instruments and in surveying the fields of the mahal), given to delegating tasks to relatives[62] and, most irritating of all, absent when required by the district officer for some specific duty.[63] The impatience of superiors is understandable—the more so in view of the impossibility of many of their tasks— but it blinded them to some not unimportant distinctions. As a conse-

[60]Board of Revenue, NWP, to Government, NWP, April 29, 1867, in NWP, "Revenue Proceedings," May 25, 1867, Index No. 35, Proceeding No. 5. For illustrations of the animosity roused by the halkabandi system between (a) zamindars and Government and (b) zamindars and patwaris, and aggravated further by the imposition of the percentage cess on the revenue for the patwaris' payment, see the correspondence preceding the board's report, in *ibid.*

[61]NWP, "Revenue Proceedings," August 15, 1868, p. 6.

[62]See, for example, the complaints of the settlement officer, Allahabad district, in *NWP Revenue Administration Report*, 1867–68, pp. 23–24.

[63]Extract from Captain D. G. Pitcher's diary, kept while on special duty in connection with the investigation of excessive mortality in Rohilkhand, in NWP and Oudh, "Revenue Proceedings," July 1880, Index No. 39, May 3, 1879, Proceeding No. 85. Compare E. B. Alexander's comments on the "very large" number of non-resident patwaris from old-established families, most of whom were living in the large towns; *Moradabad Settlement Report*, p. 113.

quence, the inefficient, slothful, or fraudulent patwari became confused
with the dutiful official, co-operating with Government and zamindar
but saddled with an unending variety of conflicting claims to his
services.[64]

The State of the Records

The confusions surrounding the patwari's status hampered the revenue
officers in their Sisyphean task of compiling and maintaining a valid
set of administrative records. Modern principles of government
demanded the accumulation of accurate and comprehensive data
on the condition of the provinces such as would be provided—it was
claimed with all confidence—by the amalgamation of scientific
techniques of measurement with the miscellany of village papers
corrected in the light of thirty years of settlement experience and
the equitable principles of property.

Here [in the NWP] there has been a professional survey of the country:
the boundaries and areas of all estates have been ascertained and carefully
recorded. Field maps, showing every field, every uncultivated patch, every
orchard and garden, every pond or water-course, the village-site,—in fact
every portion of the estate in full detail, plotted to scale and admirably
executed, have been prepared. In these Index maps, every field or plot is
numbered. A list of fields, with corresponding numbers, forms part of the
record; in this list the number of the field, the details of measurement, the
name of the field, the name of the proprietor and cultivator, the area, the
rent, are all recorded. Records of right, showing the tenure, share or position
of every proprietor, sub-proprietor and cultivator, have been carefully

---

[64]See, for example, the draft circular of instructions for a projected system of village
(that is, famine) relief, 1880. A debate followed as to which executive agency should
implement the proposal, and how it should be supervised. The lieutenant-governor
opposed the entrusting of the scheme to wealthy landlords, as was done in Bengal.
Their inexperience would, he considered, result in inaccuracies and they "would
resent any interference in the shape of supervision unless it was conducted by high
officers." But the "cost of these would be so great that the game, in ordinary parlance,
would not be worth the candle." Therefore, the lieutenant-governor preferred "to
work with the agency we find ready to our hand in the village patwari and in the
supervising kanungos." Government, NWP and Oudh, to Government of India,
September 13, 1880, in Government of India, "Famine Proceedings," October 1880,
Proceeding No. 1. In reply, the Government of India regretted this rejection of
landowners' assistance, which deviated from the Famine Commission's recommendations, and trusted that the agency of patwaris and kanungos would be supplemented
by that of "landowners of good character, high position and local influence who
possess and enjoy the respect of district officers." *Ibid.*, Proceeding No. 2.

prepared. Village administration papers, or bye-laws, noting the customs and rules for village management, present and future, providing for all contingencies connected with transfer of right by sale and purchase; mortgage; the rules regarding right of pre-emption, partition, succession, election of managers—are entered. In short, whereas in Bengal nothing was known, or hardly anything was known beyond the amount of the demand which was made permanent, here in the North-West every atom of information which can be required is immediately forthcoming.[65]

This in theory was how things should have been. However, the tidy world of G. E. Williams's vision (from his vantage point as Commissioner of Meerut in 1866) lay far from reality, as reports from settlement officers showed it to be. For a start, the myriad of cultivated patches, criss-crossed by strips of waste, which made up a pargana frustrated attempts at accurate measurement even on the relatively small scale adopted by the professional survey. The approximations registered by the surveyors were also ephemeral: field boundaries fluctuated from season to season according to the fallowing practices of different localities and of individual cultivators within them.[66] Surveyors' amins (field clerks), saddled with this impractical business of detailed measurement, chose understandably on occasion to cut the Gordian knot. A map drawn up of part of an estate in Mirzapur in 1865-66 turned out on inspection to be an exact copy of an original compiled in 1840, "except that lines defining the fields were all drawn straight and at right angles to one another ... In the North-east corner ten additional fields were inserted" to represent the increase in cultivation.[67]

The employment of amins brought other problems in that the expense of maintaining them fell heavily on local society. "What can be done is done to stop this, or rather to stop anything like exaction," Crosthwaite reported from Moradabad in 1873, "but the people think that the ameens can save or injure them, and are only too ready to bribe them, while the better class of zamindars would think it mean not to entertain them while they are in the village."[68]

[65] *Muzaffarnagar Settlement Report*, p. 11.

[66] G. B. Maconochie's observations, in *Unao Settlement Report*, p. 45. On the typically diversified cropping patterns in the provinces, see pp. 25–27 above. On the substitution of "estimated" for "actual" in official records, under explicit sanction, see p. 125.

[67] A. R. S. Pollock, Collector, Mirzapur, to Commissioner, Benares, February 15, 1868, "Report on ... *Khari* Holdings [under Government Management] ... Lately Separated from the Possession of the Rajah of Singrowli," in NWP, "Revenue Proceedings," May 2, 1868, Index No. 13, Proceeding No. 19.

[68] *NWP Report on the Progress of Settlement Operations*, 1872–73, "Abstract of Reports,"

Zamindars who spurned the services of the amins, on the other hand, and who turned their backs on the survey were liable to fines levied by the settlement officer; these were required by regulation to ensure the attendance of zamindars on the surveying parties as a safeguard for their interests.[69] One way or another, the survey was an expensive business.

After the lengthy processes of surveying came the lengthy processes of the settlement. As far as zamindars and cultivators were concerned, this meant a second set of minor officials and their demands following on the footsteps of the first.[70] The administration however was saddled with new problems resulting from a marked lack of co-ordination between the two field operations. While the surveyors turned out maps of some 700 square miles per year, the settlement department was hard put to reach a total of between 350 and 400 square miles per year, inspected and assessed. This disparity was aggravated by the fact that the survey department did not always supply its maps to the settlement department as soon as required.[71] There seemed to be a choice of two remedies available to Government: decrease the survey staff or increase the settlement establishments. The board recommended the latter, finding the other course of action impossible. As E. C. Buck, then Officiating Secretary to the board pointed out, it was "almost too late to do anything in this direction, even if it were advisable to do so. The Board doubt whether survey parties could be materially reduced without interfering with the departmental arrangement, and increasing the average cost of measurement."[72] The expenses of local communities on the other hand in entertaining settlement amins in greater numbers could not but increase.

The settlement officer's difficulties in co-operating with the survey department were little more than an irritant in comparison with the problems he confronted in the course of registering rights over land. Government's needs dictated the arduous procedure of compiling

----

§ 5, Rohilkhand Division, Moradabad district, p. 16; § 8, Agra Division, Agra district, p. 24. For similar happenings in connection with the subordinate administrative establishment of the canals, see pp. 88–89 above.

[69]C. H. T. Crosthwaite's observations, *NWP Report on the Progress of Settlement Operations*, 1872–73, p. 15. Crosthwaite stated his reluctance to coerce the zamindars into attending the survey parties (costly in time as well as money) and to use fines for the purpose, "except where neglect is contumacious and very marked."

[70]*Ibid.*, p. 16. On the duration of settlements, see pp. 130–131 above.

[71]Board of Revenue, NWP, to Government, NWP, January 27, 1875, in *NWP Report on the Progress of Settlement Operations*, 1873–74, p. 2.

[72]*Ibid.*

the wajib-ul-arz (record of rights), the basic "village" document. "It is of course absolutely necessary that the proprietary rights should be clearly defined in order to distribute the revenue," E. B. Alexander commented, "and it is also necessary to have some fairly corrected record of occupancy and tenant right."[73] Alexander made no bones about the labour involved in supervising the preparation of such documents (one for each village) : "by far the heaviest work in the settlement." The headings of a typical wajib-ul-arz suggest that this was no understatement :

1. The history of the village, including all changes in proprietary possession.
2. A detailed record of present proprietary holdings, with the distribution of Government demand in villages held in severalty.
3. Mode of collecting rents, rendering of accounts, and payment of Government demand.
4. Right of transfer and manner of succession.
5. Appointment and removal of lambardars.
6. Lists of rights in groves.
7. Rent-free holdings.
8. Rights to irrigation from wells, tanks, and so forth.
9. Rights in homesteads, *surais* (encampments), bazars, and so forth.
10. Rights to grazing and manure.
11. Appointment and removal of village servants.
12. List and rights of under-proprietors in talukadari villages.
13. List and rights of *chakdars* (subordinate official, in charge of a chak) and subordinate proprietors in independent villages.
14. "Cultivators, their customs and rights, what they give, and what they are entitled according to the custom of the country to receive."[74]

The wajib-ul-arz was an elaborate local codification of the principles of Pax Britannica, and as such it warranted an attitude of solemn responsibility on the part of the officers charged with compiling it. "It contains a summary and acknowledgement of every man's right and interest in the village," G. B. Maconochie declared; "therefore much of the future peace of the community depends on it, and unless

[73] *Moradabad Settlement Report*, p. 88.
[74] *Unao Settlement Report*, pp. 49–51. For further details on the same scheme of classification (general throughout the provinces), see *Muttra Settlement Report*, pp. 106–120.

every custom, and procedure, is provided for, and laid down, disputes of all kinds will be constantly cropping up."[75]

Such hopes could rarely be satisfied. As in the case of the survey, local phenomena proved too elusive for the settlement officer with his cumbersome recording apparatus. The formality of the wajib-ul-arz added interminable frustrations to his task of redacting material to fit the various headings, tying each piece to an artificial base in 'the village.' "So great is the vitality of a real custom, neither party wishes ... [it] to be entered ... ," S. M. Moens complained from his experience in attempting to meet Government's requirements in Bareilly. "The cultivator is afraid of the payment becoming stereotyped, and that henceforward he will be deprived of all powers to refuse compliance with the demand. The zamindar is afraid; (1) of the endless disputes which a demand for entry of the custom would excite; and (2), lest a refusal of entry should be followed by a general refusal of the asamis to give the dues and services."[76] Where the impasse was resolved, it was usually in favour of the zamindar. Astute officers such as T. R. Redfern in Kheri district warned that too great a reliance should not be placed on the record of rights (thus contradicting Government's own directives) because of the undue weight given to the proprietor's case. "The fact is," Redfern explained candidly, "that the persons who are interested in traversing any custom alleged by the proprietor are not always known to the verifying officer, and are not specially called or consulted; while they on their part do not voluntarily attend, unless a dispute between themselves and the proprietor is already aglow."[77] If some administrative papers were merely one-sided, others had the more serious defect of being decidedly unreal. Crosthwaite asserted that these were in fact in the majority— that most were records "not of existing usages but of usages the Settlement Officer wished to establish or of conditions the then proprietors (or some of them) were anxious to introduce."[78] Some officers, faced with manifestations of local custom which they found frankly deplorable, employed the tactics of an ostrich and refused to recognize their

[75] *Unao Settlement Report*, p. 49.

[76] *Bareilly Settlement Report*, p. 110.

[77] *Kheri Settlement Report*, pp. 29–30.

[78] "Note on the Wajib-ul-arz," in NWP, "Revenue Proceedings," December 21, 1867, Index No. 16, Proceeding No. 15. Crosthwaite cited, by way of an example of such errors, the settlement officer in Mainpuri (at the previous settlement) who inserted clauses regarding tenants' right to compensation for improvements amongst other things which "may or may not have been beneficial but were not records of an existing custom or usage."

validity by recording them—which was R. G. Currie's method of
resolving the problem of the Raja of Powayn's extortionate zamindari
charges.[79] Meanwhile, legislation and judicial decisions on tenancy
had resulted in several of the record's categories becoming obsolete,
thus adding to the settlement officer's selectivity as regards the recording of existing usages.[80] In spite of all these known compromises,
the wajib-ul-arz continued to be held in great regard from the point
of view of the judiciary. "The Civil Courts," stated the Honourable
Mr. Justice Turner, "in compliance with the intention of the Legislature, have accepted the administration proper as entitled to the
highest weight as evidence of the matters it purports to record ... ,"
and he enjoined settlement officers to aim at accuracy, "that as far
as possible it may be worthy of the authority with which it is regarded
by the Civil Courts," and at simplicity, "that it may be easily understood by those whose rights may be affected by it."[81] The courts
tended to be more plain-spoken in their recognition of the nature of
the wajib-ul-arz. The highest judicial authority, the Privy Council,
had on one memorable occasion defined it simply as "the proprietor's
document."[82]

The compilation of the wajib-ul-arz and the jamabandi, or "rent
roll," was the focal point for the recording of local information for
the purposes of Government under the revision of settlements. It
was considered essential that proprietary title should be locally
registered and that the incidents of the landlord and tenant relationship be classified in detail at the village level according to a compre-

[79]*Shahjahanpur Settlement Report*, p. 99. See p. 46 above.
[80]*Mainpuri Settlement Report*, p. 99. According to R. S. Whiteway's information
at settlement, in villages in Muttra owned by a single proprietor "the law has now
to a great extent settled the relations of the landlords and their tenants"; *Muttra
Settlement Report*, p. 106.
[81]"Note on the Wajib-ul-arz," in NWP, "Revenue Proceedings," December 21,
1867, Index No. 16, Proceeding No. 15. Mr. Justice Turner endorsed Crosthwaite's
views; see *ibid.* For a summary history of the legal recognition of the wajib-ul-arz
in the provinces, see R. N. Cust, Junior Member, Board of Revenue, "Minute on
the Wajib-ul-arz," August 16, 1867, in *ibid.*, Index No. 13, Proceeding No. 12.
[82]Extract from the judgment of the Judicial Committee of the Privy Council in
the case of *Uman Parshad* v. *Gandharp Singh*, July 6, 1887, as reported in NWP and
Oudh, "Revenue Proceedings," February 1888, File No. 261 A, Serial No. 1, Proceeding No. 10. For further statements of the legal value of the wajib-ul-arz, see
Muhammad Hasan v. *Munna Lal*, 8 *Indian Law Reports—Allahabad Series* 434, and *Ishri
Singh* v. *Ganga*, 2 *Indian Law Reports—Allahabad Series* 876 (both cases on the right of
pre-emption).

hensible, if imported, set of criteria. It was equally important that regular accounts should be kept of the payment of rent—the economic basis of the contract between a landlord and his tenants. These two documents were to assist Government in its role as tax-collector and magistrate. Its proprietorial interests were to be served in addition by statistical information on the condition of the estate, again collected at the village level—figures of population distribution, of the outturn of principal crops per harvest, of facilities for irrigation and for local marketing of produce, and so on.

The task of assembling and maintaining such detailed local records demanded a high degree of co-operation between the most senior members of the district administration—the European district and settlement officers—and the local, part-time officials with their ambiguous status as servants of Government and the village, the patwaris. Data accumulated in the first instance by the patwaris was to be processed under European supervision in accordance with modern principles.

Problems which soon manifested themselves in the course of the settlements destroyed much of the symmetry of such a plan. The supervising officer's position in the administrative hierarchy placed him forever at a distance from the sources of his information, a predicament which the growing burden of paperwork and his mobility in terms of furlough and promotion could only aggravate. Moreover, the standards of scientific precision proved in practice difficult if not impossible to meet with the means to hand : the settlement officer could not establish the rent rate except by his own estimates;[83] and the surveyors could not plot the agricultural pattern of a pargana. The standards however remained unaltered, and Government, forever assuming the existence of a phenomenon which it was unable to create, namely the patwari as a disinterested public servant, required not merely local records but also local officials to conform to them. Correspondence between the records patwaris kept for village purposes, in accordance with their zamindars' requirements, and the criteria set up by the administration to serve its needs was inevitably coincidental and relatively rare.

The European officers' position was unenviable. While they admitted to the central importance of the patwaris' records, their field experience led them to question the extent to which such data could and should be relied on for administrative purposes. Auckland Colvin's report

[83]See pp. 123–130 above.

in 1864 on the lax state of morals as regards public accounting in a pargana of Muzaffarnagar district reflected a widespread concern over the state of the patwaris' records, which on inspection continually turned out to be highly dubious. Amounts of produce were "invariably entered at haphazard" in the official accounts; foreclosure of mortgages went unnoticed; details as regards possession remained unspecified; deaths of proprietors escaped registration. All of which led Colvin to conclude, legitimately, that "the present system of village registration is very imperfect and carries in it seeds of serious mischief." Meanwhile, these records were accepted as "the basis of hundreds of decisions affecting landed property."[84]

Colvin was aware that the circumstances of the patwari, in spite of the halkabandi system, made this inevitable. He pleaded for practical encouragement (in the form of a rise in salaries), for increased facilities for supervision, and for the removal of the "most dangerous duties" from the patwari's charge in order to overcome fraudulence in error and safeguard the integrity of the official records.[85] Government did not see itself in a position to implement any of Colvin's recommendations, and official misgivings about the state of local records could not but persist. "It is a crying shame," exclaimed R. N. Cust, Junior Member of the Board of Revenue in 1867, "that, with such a machinery, costing so much to the State in the salaries of the two higher grades, and to the landholders in the salaries of the lower grades, there should be such indifferent results. It comes to this, that if during the next five years something better cannot be attained, the time will have come to ... dismiss the whole establishment ... The Patwari must not be allowed to be the bailiff, or private servant of the landowner, or the money-lender and shopkeeper of the village ..."[86] Five years passed, and an enquiry into the status and remuneration of the patwaris of the NWP in 1873 revealed the same lamentable state of affairs; the compilation of papers was corrupt; the maintenance of correct records was impossible.[87] Settle-

[84] *Muzaffarnagar Settlement Report*, pp. 111–112, and generally, C. A. Elliott, "Note on Registers of Landed Property," in NWP, "Revenue Proceedings," December 21, 1867, Index No. 24, Proceeding No. 23.

[85] *Muzaffarnagar Settlement Report*, pp. 111–112. In Muzaffarnagar district, it was reported as usual for bhaiachara villages to auction the patwari's appointment. The highest bidder took it.

[86] R. N. Cust, "Note on Registers of Landed Property," in NWP, "Revenue Proceedings," December 21, 1867, Index No. 23, Proceeding No. 22.

[87] C. W. Carpenter, Settlement Officer and member of the Nauri Tal Revenue Code Committee, to Board of Revenue, NWP, April 17, 1873, in NWP, "Revenue

ment and district officers had in these circumstances little alternative but to decide their revenue cases on the basis of a fraudulent anachronism. The patwari still tended to be the bailiff or private servant of the landowner.[88] The importance of the documents had not diminished; neither had the need for better supervision to ensure correctness, nor the awareness of the Board of Revenue of such need, nor Government's intransigence in meeting this need. "The Government agency [as regards payment of the patwaris] is not sufficiently effective," H. S. Reid declared flatly, "and is not likely to be strengthened ... The benefit of correct papers is chiefly felt by landlords and cultivators, and charges necessary to ensure their accuracy may be properly debited to them from existing funds if the Treasury cannot meet them."[89] This pronouncement carried a note of finality, as was borne out in later years. No adequate standard of correctness could be attained and careful supervision could not be ensured while the patwari's rate of pay remained below subsistence level, while the zamindars' control persisted undisturbed, and while the senior field officers remained remote and overworked.[90]

The impasse persisted, with faulty records adding to the burdens of routine administration, which in turn prevented the senior officers from applying such correctives as their supervisory powers allowed. Meanwhile, the reliance of all branches of Government on the (unreformed) patwari showed no signs of abating in deference to the acknowledged shortcomings in the rich miscellany of documents which stood as "village records." "Without the co-operation of the village accountant," J. A. Baines, Census Commissioner in 1891, wrote with enthusiasm, "I must admit our statistical information about India would be grievously circumscribed. Births, deaths and the census are all within his province in addition to his more special functions in connection with the record of cultivation, assessments and transfers of land.

Proceedings," March 1874, Index No. 7, November 8, 1873, Proceeding No. 79. See also J. F. D. Inglis, Senior Member, Board of Revenue, "Minute Regarding the Remuneration and Status of Patwaris," August 15, 1873, in *ibid.*, Index No. 12, November 8, 1873, Proceeding No. 84.

[88]H. S. Reid, Junior Member, Board of Revenue, NWP, "Minute on the Patwaris' Status and Remuneration," August 8, 1873, in *ibid.*, Index No. 13, Proceeding No. 83.
[89]*Ibid.*

[90]On the impracticability of E. C. Buck's proposals, owing to the settlement officers' lack of power to control the payment of patwaris, see E. B. Alexander's comments in *Moradabad Settlement Report*, pp. 113–114. The same state of affairs persisted in Oudh, where the patwaris were generally under the thumb of talukdars, with whom district officers could not interfere. See I. F. Macandrew, *Some Revenue Matters*, pp. 82–84.

A demand for information on any one of these and even more various topics, rolls down from the seat of Government over the three steps of the district officer, his assistant, and the sub-divisional officer, till it falls on the village accountant, who duly provides the data required, which are hoisted back by the same route, losing at each stage, I fear, some of their picturesqueness and originality."[91]

If something of the special flavour of local records seemed lost in this process of refining, much undoubtedly remained—including a certain obstinate refusal to conform to the official requirements of accuracy. District officers, for example, were instructed to submit four statistical statements annually, as follows: I. Classification of lands and crops; II. Distribution of principal crops in (1) irrigated and (2) unirrigated lands; III. Average outturn of principal crops per acre; IV. Distribution of produce : whether exported or retained for consumption. By 1872, experience had led to sharp questioning of this procedure. The board agreed that reports from officers on the subject showed the uselessness of continuing with the statements and qualified its conclusions with the following suggestion for remedial action : "If irrigation otherwise than by canals were struck out of Statement I, that and Statement II might in time be fairly reliable. But except at large cost, there seems ... little hope of getting information on the other heads, which is worth the paper it is printed on. In short, it is absolutely impossible for the District Officers to give the returns required in Statement IV, or those in Statement II and III, without a special establishment for the purpose, and though No. I can be given, it is hardly necessary to do so."[92] The lieutenant-governor duly recommended to the Government of India that the statements be discontinued.[93]

In 1874, the Department of Agriculture was founded in the NWP with the avowed aim, *inter alia,* of collecting adequate statistics on agrarian and commercial conditions, but it did not possess the means to set up the special establishment required to transform aims into action.[94] Its parent body in Calcutta suffered from the same funda-

[91]J. A. Baines, "The Distribution and Movement of the Population in India," *Journal of the Royal Statistical Society* (March 1893), pp. 15–16.

[92]Board of Revenue, NWP, to Government, NWP, December 6, 1872, in NWP, "Revenue Proceedings," January 1873, Index No. 3, January 4, 1873, Proceeding No. 25.

[93]Government, NWP, to Government of India, December 30, 1872, in *ibid.,* Index No. 4, Proceeding No. 26.

[94]On the India and NWP agricultural departments and their necessary reliance on the revenue administration, see pp. 100–102, 108 above.

mental deficiency. Two years later, Knight launched the first number of his *Indian Agriculturist* with a tirade against the administration which appeared on the first page. "Remembering that the Indian Government is the great landlord of the soil," he taunted, "it is a heavy reproach to its Department of Agriculture and Revenue that it knows nothing with certainty to this hour of the cost of cultivation, or the yield of any single product whatever, but—the poppy! although we possess exceptional means of information at our command."[95] Annual reports of the provinces' Agriculture Department, filled with accounts of the Court-of-Wards' estates and with lavish details concerning experiments in progress on the model farms,[96] maintained a discreet silence on the question of general crop statistics, which lay far beyond its means to ascertain. Descriptive information of any comprehensive order on the state of agriculture from year to year was confined to a few paragraphs in the administration reports of the Board of Revenue; after 1884-85, even this source dwindled to token estimates, in annas, of the total outturn per division. More precise data on detailed questions were theoretically forthcoming from the patwaris and were subject in consequence to a variety of hazards. In Jhansi Division, where the condition of the cattle frequently gave serious cause for concern, no mortality figures for livestock were registered for 1889-90. The year appeared to have been "comparatively healthy" for this respect, "but as the patwaris were on deputation to Settlement work, the Deputy Commissioner has not found it feasible to obtain the usual statistics."[97]

Trade figures for both the NWP and Oudh were notoriously inadequate.[98] Twenty years after the first official system of traffic registration was established for the NWP in 1877, deficiencies in information as to the movement of staple articles of trade remained substantially unremedied. J. S. Meston, Director of Land Records and Agriculture in the provinces in 1898 drew the Government of India's attention to the limitations of available data on the balance of export and import: "The statistics for this factor . . . are by no means absolutely complete and probably never will be so." Returns consisted of accounts of rail-borne traffic and road traffic between the provinces and Tibet and Nepal. No registration had ever been instituted for the

[95]*Indian Agriculturist*, January 1, 1876, p. 1.
[96]See pp. 103–106 above.
[97]*NWP Revenue Administration Report*, 1889–1890, p. 7.
[98]See p. 184 above, notes 88 and 89.

"large avenue of trade" by road between the NWP and the adjoining provinces and native states except at isolated points "and incidentally in connection with other objects of investigation"; for the other "large avenue," along the Ganges and Gogra to Bengal, "only fitfully collected figures" were available for 1886-87, 1888-89, and 1893-94. Meston believed the total traffic statistics to "involve a margin of error [omission] up to 10%."[99]

The collection of comprehensive trade statistics was hampered both by the complexities of communication lines linking the provinces and their neighbouring districts and by the paucity of registration points. In addition problems arose in this connection from the "subordinate establishment." The Oudh Board of Revenue cautiously suggested in their report for 1870-71 that the trade returns for the year represented an advance on their predecessors in terms of correctness, "but," it added,

so long as the funds at the disposal of the Administration compel it to keep the salaries of the registering clerks at a limit of Rs. 4 per mensem, it is hopeless to expect accuracy and steady work at the registration posts. The clerks are of too poor a class to command respect; they are armed with no real authority. There hence arises a difficulty, which as yet is less real than conceivable. "If a carrier represents his cotton as Berlin wool or his brick-dust as diamonds, the clerk may doubt the information but may not satisfy himself by practical demonstration." At the same time the clerks are absolutely in the hands of the carriers, as regards the weight and value of the goods exported and imported and it is hard to say in what degree the returns approximate to the truth.[100]

The registration of vital statistics was, understandably, entrusted to local agency: to village officers and chaukidars, or police (paid by the zamindars).[101] Government had taken a stand against systematizing population counts as far as agricultural communities were concerned, probably in view of the momentous task of maintaining

---

[99]"Memorandum on Existing Food Stocks in the NWP and Oudh," in Government of India, "Famine Proceedings," March–June 1898, File No. 127, Serial No. 16. Ten percent is undoubtedly an underestimate.

[100]*Oudh Revenue Administration Report*, 1870–71, p. 47. The numbers of clerks increased, but not their salaries.

[101]*Unao Settlement Report*, pp. 30–31. See also Sir William Muir, "Minute on the Agreement and Payment of Rural Police (Chowkidars)," May 28, 1868, in NWP, "Revenue Proceedings," June 27, 1868, Index No. 30, Proceeding No. 35. A cess of a fixed percentage on the revenue was to be instituted for police maintenance, according to districts.

regular records, not to mention the expense. As late as 1893, in answer to a query as to why the Famine Commission's recommendations in this respect had not been implemented, Government made its position plain. "Generally speaking, the existing law makes registration of vital statistics compulsory in towns and municipalities, but . . . it has not been found practicable or desirable, having regard to the conditions of native society, to extend this system generally to rural areas."[102] Trouble could arise when Government needed statistical information as regards rural communities, as for example in the famine years of 1877 and 1879, in order to measure the extent of the phenomenon. D. G. Pitcher reported how Government, in its zeal to secure accurate mortality figures in Shahjahanpur, warned the chaukidars by a circular order that failure to register deaths would result in six months' suspension. "It is not surprising then," Pitcher continued, "seeing that house-to-house verification had never been carried out, if some chaukidars thought that a higher rate of mortality might get them a better name, or that when deaths began to occur very frequently a panic seized them, and they elected to report every disappearance in a death."[103]

Whether dictated by the incoherence and inadequacies of local records for the purposes of administration, or merely reinforced by them, Government's zeal for special enquiries as an obligatory condition precedent to official action was marked. Even matters which were the direct concern of the revenue administration and which would seem at first sight subjects for a brisk report and a correspondingly succinct decision were exposed to the procedure of a full-scale enquiry, in deference to the serious concern of the administration.

The "urgent problem" of the re-adjustment of revenue kists[104] was one such matter. The question of the policy involved in the timing of the kists was first raised—inconsequentially—in 1839. C. A. Elliott revived it thirty years later,[105] and it was taken up by

[102]Government of India (Home Department, Sanitary Branch), August 15, 1893, "Summary of Measures Adopted on the Recommendation of the Famine Commission," in Government of India, "Famine Proceedings," January 1894, Serial No. 7, Proceeding No. 19. For the recommendation, see "Report of the Indian Famine Commission," *P.P.*, 1881, 71, Pt. II, Ch. II, § 1, and Ch. VI, § 1.

[103]D. G. Pitcher, "Report on the Excessive Mortality Recorded for Rohilkhand, 1877–78," para. 21, in NWP and Oudh, "Revenue Proceedings," June 1879, Index No. 17, Proceeding No. 118.

[104]See pp. 155–160 above.

[105]C. A. Elliott to Commissioner, Agra, in *Revenue Reporter* (1869), cited in NWP, "Revenue Proceedings," May 1873, Index No. 12, April 6, 1873, Proceeding No. 58.

the Secretariat. The board's Circular Order AAA of July 28, 1870 invited the opinions of revenue officers. An abstract of these was forwarded, with the board's views, for Government's orders on March 16, 1872. In reply, the Government's General Order of April 2 requested J. F. D. Inglis's opinion as Senior Member of the board. Inglis's opinion was subsequently recorded in a note sent to Government on December 13. According to General Order of April 18, 1873, Government then "fully discussed" the question, laid down its principles, and requested the board to frame instructions on them for the revenue officers' guidance. A draft circular was submitted by the board to Government, dated May 22, 1873. However, it was subsequently found necessary to amend this draft, and a revised version was sent in substitution, dated September 23. Meanwhile, the board had "received for compliance" (through the local Government's General Order of August 20, 1873) a requisition from the Government of India (which had seen the correspondence in the "Proceedings") for a statement showing the proposed changes in instalments and their financial results. The board stated nothing could be done towards meeting this requisition till orders were passed on the circular they had submitted. The circular was approved by a General Order of October 23, 1873 and issued on November 25. The first replies however showed that the information submitted was likely to be insufficient to enable the board to form any opinion on the propriety of such proposals as were made. The board therefore issued a second circular, dated March 6, 1874, requiring fuller details on answers supplied to the original circular. Replies which were sent in to the board subsequent to the second circular, "though still wanting for many districts," were reviewed by the board in August. It then appeared that Paragraph 7 of the original circular had not been properly followed, in that the instructions to state the date and amount of each instalment had not been sufficiently observed. Therefore, a tabular form was issued with the board's next circular, of October 7, 1874. By January 11, 1875, replies to this were being received and were stated to be nearly complete.[106] The submissions of the overburdened district officers had not however proved satisfactory. In view of the gravity of the matter at issue, the board concluded cautiously, after five years' deliberation, that "The information and knowledge of agricultural facts, upon which the arrangement of revenue instalments should be based, is [sic] too

[106]Governor, NWP, to Government of India, February 2, 1875, in NWP, "Revenue Proceedings," February 1875, Index No. 23, February 6, 1875, Proceeding No. 42.

little advanced to enable district officers to frame their proposals in accordance with the instructions enunciated by Government and by the Board."[107]

The Secretariat's craving for more detailed information could never be satisfied. Reports compiled by district and settlement officers in the course of their duties provided data and often acute observations on a wide range of specific matters, such as the mode of cultivation of indigo or the spread of reh in certain zamindars' estates in canal districts; or they gave comprehensive descriptions of conditions ruling generally in a district within the period when its revenue settlement was revised. As far as administrative purposes were concerned, however, the official records suffered from two serious defects : lack of co-ordination and of continuity. In the absence of adequate means to maintain and improve them regularly, the records could not be amended satisfactorily by such special enquiries as Government launched from time to time. These were prompted by disasters engulfing agricultural communities so severely as to attract public notice : the appointment of a commission of experts to examine the agrarian conditions of India in relation to the great famine of 1877-78 and 1879 is a case in point. Inevitably, it fell to the overworked revenue establishments to supply the local information for the experts' judgment. Inevitably, the data collected failed to meet the requirements.

In 1887, irked by public assertions in England to the effect that "the greater proportion of the population of India suffers from a daily insufficiency of food," Government in the person of the Viceroy, Lord Dufferin, ordered a large-scale enquiry into the condition of the lower classes of agriculturists.[108] The seriousness of the procedure was marked. A circular order—confidential—was sent to the provincial administrations, defining the limits of the enquiry and placing great emphasis on precision : Government demanded not general comments, but facts and statistics relating to selected households in each district.[109] Subsequent reminders followed the initial circular order, enjoining

[107]Board of Revenue, NWP, to Government, NWP, January 11, 1875, in *ibid.,* Index No. 17, February 6, 1875, Proceeding No. 36.

[108]For brief summaries of the immediate background to the Dufferin Enquiry, see W. Digby, *"Prosperous British India,"* p. 306, and also pp. 157–158, 316–317, 448, 565; see also B. M. Bhatia, "An Enquiry into the Condition of the Agricultural Classes in India, 1888," *Contributions to Indian Economic History,* I (Calcutta, 1960), 80–81. Both Digby and Bhatia place undue reliance on the statistical data collected by the enquiry.

[109]Government of India, Circular Order No. 44 S-I (Confidential), August 17, 1887.

urgency in view of Lord Dufferin's departure from India earlier than anticipated and the necessity of completing the enquiry accordingly.[110]

The local Governments set to work organizing the collection of information as instructed, a time-consuming task. In the NWP and Oudh, the circular order (again confidential) which instructed the commissioners of divisions as to how to proceed with local investigations was published by the Secretariat on January 12, 1888,[111] nearly five months after the first order from Calcutta. By June 8 following, such reports as had reached the Government offices at Allahabad were collected together and, with a covering letter by the director of land records and agriculture summarizing their content, were despatched to Calcutta on July 25; the submissions covered fourteen of the forty-two districts.[112]

The obstacles encountered in the course of the enquiry had been formidable. Throughout Agra Division, and especially in the districts of Muttra and Etah and in parts of Etawah, the kharif of 1887 had been a near-total failure. Since, as the commissioner observed, "the cultivator lives on the autumn harvest's produce, and pays his rent chiefly from the spring harvest ... , a year where the cultivator has no autumn crop is a bad one to inquire into the sufficiency of the cultivator's food. During the past winter months, the cultivator had certainly not a sufficiency of food. The particulars collected in Muttra at any rate," he added, "are interesting only as showing how this class pull on in times of scarcity."[113] Otherwise, the reports of his district officers could offer nothing beyond general facts as to the common condition of local food supplies. Elsewhere, frustrations arose from the failure of the Secretariat to time its requests in conjunction with district officers' routine. "Such an inquiry as is contemplated in the orders of Government can only be made during the tour season," J. J. F. Lumsden commented from Benares, "and it is to be regretted that the orders on the subject were not received before half the tour season had passed."[114] By this time, the officers were well occupied with their inspection of tehsili accounts, the hearing of

[110]Government of India, Circular Order No. 35 (Confidential), March 21, 1888.

[111]Government of India, Circular Order No. 53 I-6 (Conficential), January 12, 1888.

[112]For the districts covered by the enquiry, and by the Famine Commission report, 1879–1880, see endpaper map.

[113]W. Kaye, Commissioner, Agra, to Director, Land Records and Agriculture, May 29, 1888, in Dufferin Enquiry (Enclosures, NWP and Oudh), p. 3.

[114]J. J. F. Lumsden, Commissioner, Benares, to Director, Land Records and Agriculture, April 14, 1888, in ibid., p. 129.

revenue disputes, and a myriad of items of routine business. Their reports did little more than corroborate the general impressions which already filled bulging files in Government offices—a conclusion which the commissioners of Allahabad and Rae Bareli admitted without surprise, given the circumstances.[115]

The greatest impediments of all were raised by the nature and terms of the enquiry itself. It asked the impossible, even of officers whose duties in the field placed them in an unrivalled vantage point vis-a-vis agrarian conditions. Thomas Stoker, Settlement Officer in Bulandshahr district in 1887, in submitting "the following considerations," showed one reason why:

My daily work for five months in the year brings me into contact with the people in their fields and villages; I am surrounded by them for hours every day; for weeks together I speak to nobody else; I see them under every condition, and hear all their complaints. It is part of my business to visit every one of their homesteads, and to note generally their style of living, their appearance, the character of their houses, their surroundings, their stock and equipment. It is impossible that any person of ordinary intelligence and observation can mix on these terms with the people and remain in ignorance of such broad facts as to whether they are sufficiently fed and clothed and properly equipped for the business of agriculture. If no more than this were required, I could at once and with some confidence give an answer to the inquiry which is now made. ... But ... generalizations are not required, ... an inquiry is to be instituted into specific cases. This I feel bound to represent that I do not think I can carry to a useful or safe conclusion. It is the object of every person who lives by the land to place the condition of himself and his industry before the Settlement Officer in the most disparaging light. It will be useless for me to say that the inquiry has no connexion with settlement; I will not be believed. I cannot divest myself of my official character. Every man whom I question will believe I am seeking a basis on which to assess his rent or revenue, and he will answer accordingly. He will declare that his fields do not return even the seed and labour, and that he and his family are starving. The evidence of my own sight will show him to be lying; but unless I make an inquisition and hunt up evidence, the record will

[115]A. J. Lawrence, Commissioner, Allahabad, to Director, Land Records and Agriculture, April 10, 1888, in *ibid.*, p. 120; F. Currie, Officiating Commissioner, Rae Bareli, to Director, Land Records and Agriculture, April 2, 1888, in *ibid.*, p. 173. See also the comment by T. W. Holderness, Collector, Pilibhit, in forwarding "notes of such enquiry as I have been able to make at intervals during the last three months ... The enquiry is very imperfect, but as the sole European officer here, I have found my time occupied by other matters." Holderness to Commissioner, Rohilkhand, April 13, 1888, in *ibid.*, p. 106.

misrepresent the facts. And, indeed, the evidence being that of his fellows, will most likely support than contradict him. These are not mere speculations. I find . . . that since I have been engaged in settlement work my relations with the people are much changed. I am regarded as an enemy, to be opposed by their only weapon, that is to say, deception. I tried at first when going among the fields and villages to help the people by explaining to them such matters as the great improvements which have recently been made in the methods of well-sinking, or the better methods of cultivation I had seen followed, or better staples grown in other parts of the country. I desisted only when I found myself credited with the Machiavellian policy of seeking in this manner fresh grounds and reasons for raising the revenue. My object in making a house-to-house inquiry will certainly be misunderstood, and the facts will certainly be misrepresented. I can answer for the accuracy of my own observations; but I do not think the information supplied by cultivators or proprietors will be equally trustworthy.[116]

Where European officers were replaced by "native" subordinates, for example in Etawah during the furlough of Alexander (the Collector), and where tehsildars were consequently entrusted with the compilation of data for the enquiry, impossibilities persisted. Alexander subsequently reported how the tehsildars' calculations of cultivators' annual budgets had been reckoned theoretically on the basis of so many people per family and so many seers' expenditure on food at such and such average price, with little or no regard to the actual amount involved. In any case, it was a hopeless task, Alexander himself admitted, "dealing with a long period like a year and after an interval of several months."[117] Others amongst his colleagues were more sweeping in their condemnation of the terms of the enquiry. "I have the honor to state," J. S. Porter wrote from Shahjahanpur, "that, after much consideration and consultation with persons well acquainted with the subject, I have found it impossible to make an exact valuation of the normal income and expenditure of the poorer

[116]T. Stoker, Settlement Officer, Bulandshahr, to Commissioner, Meerut, February 3, 1888, in *ibid.*, pp. 1–2. The effect of local suspicion on the validity of agricultural enquiries was early acknowledged. See, for example, a note of 1864–65 apropos of returns on the value of agricultural produce to be submitted by collectors. "As their value will depend upon their accuracy, and as the habitual distrust of the natives of the motive by which the Government is actuated in directing such information to be furnished will for a long time tend to the concealment of the real outturn of the crops by the cultivators, much reliance cannot be placed upon the results which will be reported for some years to come." *NWP Revenue Administration Report*, 1864–65, p. 2.

[117]E. B. Alexander, Collector, Etawah, to Commissioner, Agra, May 15, 1888, in Dufferin Enquiry (Enclosures, NWP and Oudh), p. 101.

classes in this part of the country . . ."[118] The problem was fundamental. The food supply of the majority of cultivators, the object of
the enquiry, could not be assessed by the statistical means of monetary
calculations which official instructions insisted should be employed.
As C. W. McMinn had noted nearly twenty years earlier with regard
to conditions in Oudh, "the poorer classes habitually use as food things
which never appear in the market quotations : dried blossoms of the
mahwa tree, stones of the mango and other fruits, leaves and tops
of gram, a very wholesome and palatable vegetable, and millet
stalks—all are common articles of diet."[119] Like the Famine Commission's report, the Dufferin Enquiry resulted in an accumulation
of a wealth of accurate, informative, but unwanted observations which
the administration could not utilize and a mass of budgetary statistics
conforming nominally to requirements but useless in content.

[118]J. S. Porter, Collector, Shahjahanpur, to Commissioner, Rohilkhand, May 15,
1888, in *ibid.,* p. 106. See also W. Lane, Commissioner, Meerut, to Government,
NWP, and Oudh, April 3, 1888, in *ibid.,* p. 1.

[119]C. W. McMinn, *Introduction,* p. 181. For attempts at an adequate estimation
of the amount of food grains required for local consumption which, on deduction
from the estimate of total outturn, was assumed to leave the amount available for
export, see A. B. Patterson's notes from Fatehpur district. Allowing for a consumption
rate at 1.5 lbs. per capita per day, he calculated that 4,542,972 maunds would be
required annually for the district, the total produce of which he estimated at 5,905,136
maunds; see *Fatehpur Settlement Report,* pp. 22–23. C. A. Elliott estimated consumption
throughout the province in a famine year at 1/6 ton per capita; see "Memorandum
on Existing Food Stocks in the NWP and Oudh," January 15, 1898, para. 4, in
Government of India, "Famine Proceedings," March–June 1898, File No. 127,
Serial No. 16. Meanwhile, general observations—of McMinn, the Famine Commission,
and the Dufferin Enquiry, for example—persistently showed the impracticality of
such abstract calculations in the actual circumstances.

EPILOGUE
THE COST OF INNOVATION

The physical presence of British power in India had created an impressive spectacle : canals, roads, railways, telegraph lines; Secretariats and Residences; law courts and jails; the civil lines of bungalows at a discreet distance from every district town, which housed the local administrative and commercial establishments in strict hierarchical demarcation, and beyond, the offices and barracks of the military cantonments. Contrasts between the serene formality of government settlements and neighbouring society were for the most part extreme. To look for coherence in the choked-up habitation of local bazars, in the mud and thatch of the rural hinterland, and in the decaying magnificence of the houses of great estates which stood as sporadic monuments to an old authority was an unrewarding task. The sheer system of British rule dominated its environment by its concrete manifestation of law and order, the prerequisite of modernization. It was this spectacle, emphasized by such contrasts, which bolstered the confidence of European onlookers, especially officers committed to careers in the Indian administration, in the ability of the vigorous West to remedy the ills of the chaotic and dissolute East. "A great deal might be made by a strong European Government out of the united provinces of Lebanon and Damascus," Robert Cust reflected in recording for a British Indian audience his impressions of the Levant visited in the early 1880s. "There are ample natural resources, an industrious people, and a sufficient seaport. Progress has been made since the European powers asserted their authority in 1860, and, if the hateful and baneful Turkish rule were swept away, and replaced by a firm and sympathetic Government, powerful to punish, and yet wise enough to leave the people alone,—which is the secret of our success in India,—these Provinces would be developed, and some day a more secure route for commerce would be found eastward of Damascus to the Euphrates and beyond."[1]

[1] R. Cust, "Tour of a Cook-Party in Egypt and Palestine," *Calcutta Review*, LXXXI

Experience in the NWP and Oudh had early confirmed the existence of formidable obstacles in the official machinery itself. The policy of non-interference, the chronic lack of qualified staff to execute even routine duties, the persistent refusal to take action on fundamental issues on the grounds of dangerous insufficiency of knowledge, which in the circumstances could never be remedied—all contributed to circumscribe Government's activities as the benevolent proprietor of its Indian estate. Public finances, moreover, were subjected increasingly to rigorous scrutiny which could result only in the curtailment of once-ambitious programs for expenditure. While the rents of Government's "property" rose and their collection was ensured in spite of annual fluctuations in the condition of the harvests, a minute proportion of the revenue was returned to the provinces in the form of productive expenditure on agricultural improvement. Procedural obstructions in the major official agency which existed for such purposes, takavi, accounted in part for this. But the major part of the revenue was earmarked for expenditure elsewhere according to a list of official priorities at home and abroad. In India itself, the maintenance of the administrative machinery dominated budget allocations.

The charges for modern government were high. The public expenditure for Oudh, for example, had reached a figure of Rs. 10,039,986 as early as 1870, itemized as follows : civil administration, 6,135,100; military establishment, 2,650,546; imperial public works, 1,233,848; agriculture, 492. The chief source of income was the land revenue.[2] The revenue administrations themselves ran up annual charges of millions of rupees in regular establishment costs. For the NWP alone, the bill for 1871-72 came to Rs. 2,457,398, more than 4.5 percent of the revenue collections.[3] This did not include the prodigious expenses

(1885), 315. For principles and policy of British Indian administration actually implemented elsewhere in the Orient, in British Egypt, see R. Owen, "The Influence of Lord Cromer's Indian Experience on British Policy in Egypt, 1883–1907," *St. Antony's Papers, No.* 17 : *Middle Eastern Affairs,* No. 4 (Oxford, 1965), pp. 109–139.

[2] C. W. McMinn, *Introduction,* p. 6.

[3] "Report of the Select Committee on East India Finance," *P.P.,* 1872, 8 (327), Appendix 19, p. 643. The 138 European members of the higher establishment accounted for Rs. 729,000 total per annum, in salaries ranging from collector and magistrate at Rs. 2,250 per month to assistant magistrate, 2nd class, at Rs. 400 per month. The 6,837 members of the permanent subordinate establishment, which included only 39 Europeans, accounted for Rs. 2,488,225 in salaries, ranging from deputy collector at Rs. 250–800 per month to a conglomerate of quasi-nominal payments of less than Rs. 100 per annum. Contingencies came to a further Rs. 2,908,142. Oudh establishment charges, similarly apportioned, came to Rs. 2,157,398. *Ibid.,* p. 649. The judicial establishment for both the NWP and Oudh, that is, the civil and sessions judges

of survey and settlement operations. From a modest beginning, in 1854-55, of a mere Rs. 5,260.9.7, they had reached Rs. 250,150.1.0 by 1860-61. Five years later, the settlement costs were set at Rs. 417,454.2.6. By 1871-72, they had spiralled to Rs. 1,035,003 annually, with the total cost to date no less than Rs. 7,266,037.12.2.[4]

Government's overriding concern for the land revenue, which provided its staple finance, was manifest not merely in the lavishness of the administration appointed largely for its charge. It was reflected in every decision involving public expenditure of any significance. By 1872, for example, several projects had been prepared by the NWP public works engineers for improving drainage in those districts which suffered from persistent scourges of malarious fever, a condition frequently exacerbated by the construction of canals. Plans for remedial action, however, were for the most part to remain in the files of Government. "The primary object not being the improvement of the land revenue," the Secretary to Government was called upon to state, "the Lieutenant-Governor has not felt himself at liberty to ask for grants from Imperial Funds for the execution of such schemes." The only alternative lay in the allotment of meagre sums from the provincial treasury, with the prospect of partial reimbursement from any increase in rental provided by reclamations.[5] With the growing problem of the depreciation of silver from the mid-1870s and the increase in consequence in the cost of remittances to England, Government looked more closely at the public accounts, but it nonetheless maintained and even increased its administrative establishments on the same scale as before.

The local population paid for the progress bestowed upon them in a variety of ways. Their revenue payments supported the incorruptible upper strata of European administrators, while additional charges were levied for the meagre salaries of "native" subordinates. This much was official. At the same time, an endlessly expanding system of service payments arose from the superimposition of European administrative requirements on local society. Zamindars and cultivators paid their water rates for the use of a canal as well as the increment on revenue levied in view of an actual or prospective increase

plus the staff costs of the High Court at Allahabad, ran into some Rs. 392,872 per annum. *Ibid.*, Appendix 22, pp. 663, 665, Appendix 23, p. 666.

[4] *NWP Revenue Administration Report*, 1871–72, p. 113A.

[5] Government, NWP, to Government of India (Department of Agriculture, Revenue and Commerce), June 19, 1872, in NWP, "Revenue Proceedings," June 1872, Index No. 6, June 22, 1872, Proceeding No. 3.

in production; moreover, minor officials of the canal establishment regularly collected fees for their services. During survey and settlement operations, swarms of amins claimed their maintenance from the rural population and collected their fees for entries in the records. Registration clerks, employed by Government to keep a tally of the approximate movements of trade, took fees for services to traders at the customs and registration posts. At the law courts, *chaprassis* (messengers) exploited the opportunities for commissions which the technicalities of procedure and the increasing demand for documentation extended—as did their confreres in the collector's office. "We ourselves could conduct corruption decently," Sir George Aberigh-Mackay lamented in the course of his observations of the goings-on at the local courts, "but to be responsible for corruption over which we exercise no control is to lose the credit of a good name and the profits of a bad one."[6] Such practices however were ineradicable; they had become the very stuff of local administration.

The cost of innovation had also to be met in terms of the cumulative effects of new stimuli and new pressures on techniques of production and the structure of society itself which had not undergone any radical change. The relationships of cultivator to malik, of the borrower to his creditor, and of the locally dominant zamindars and talukdars to Government were involved inextricably in the activities with which the alien administration sought to modernize its charge. "It is not the heat of the sun which scorches," runs the Bengali proverb, "but the sand which is heated by the sun." The expansion of agriculture, the flourishing trade in agricultural products, the scientific principles of the revenue assessments and the inflexibility of their operation in practice, modernization of the judicial machinery and the structure of Government in line with equitable abstractions—every innovation made demands on existing institutions far out of proportion to their capacity. The inevitable dislocation which followed, at each stage, in the physical and social environment could not be remedied in consonance with the immediate interests of Government, which depended heavily on the maintenance of the status quo, however distorted it may have become. No sources of wealth for Government or society other than the land existed or were created to any appreciable extent; no avenues for employment other than the zamindari were available for the bulk of zamindars, who subsisted in a vicious circle of conflicts with occupancy tenants, debts, litigation, and Government relief which perpetuated

[6]G. Aberigh-Mackay, *Twenty-One Days in India*, p. 106.

their poverty. Neither they nor the majority of cultivators could accumulate resources and improve the land; mahajans, on the other hand, who had the resources, could seldom penetrate the defenses of local society to apply their wealth to the soil. The zamindar- creditor, meanwhile, with his concentration of local power, was provided with irresistible incentives to live for immediate returns, which were all the more desirable in view of the constant need to spend lavishly on ceremonial and the law courts in order to win prestige and deter competitors.

Employment in the lower ranks of government services, in the subordinate revenue administration, the post and telegraph, the railways, the police, the army, fed numerous members of the middle and fewer of the upper ranks of local society at the meagre rate of subordinates' pay. Meanwhile, migration from amongst agricultural labourers was beginning. In the last years of the century, the origins can be detected of a small-scale but definable system which grew from a traditional, ad hoc famine relief into a regular practice. Conditions in eastern districts above all, where the increase in the pressure from conflicting and minutely apportioned claims over the land coincided with deterioration in the productivity of large, rapidly deforested tracts, were such as to suggest a supply of surplus agricultural popu-lation for the recruiting agents from the tea gardens of Assam, the expanding coal fields in Bengal and Bihar, and the nascent cotton industry of the Bombay Presidency.

The sudden and uneven stimulus administered to local agriculture to increase production as rapidly as possible on the largest conceivable scale left its mark. Oases of good soils, well watered and attended by the benefits of the optimum in natural resources allied with the maximum in profitable new lines of cultivation, showed it. The saline deserts and bald patches of alkalinity, the swamps and waterlogged tracts, the erosion of riverine areas most notably in the east also showed it. Meanwhile, a rise in the price of agricultural staples and most especially of food grains led to the confusion of the stimulus of the public works developments and the export trade with the frequent occurrence of deficient harvests, under the assumption of a generalized increase in rural prosperity. The uncertainty of output, the cumber-some machinery of grain-dealing in India, and the refusal of Govern-ment to guarantee their interests in the modernization of production and distribution in a more positive fashion than mere supervision would permit turned the entrepreneurs of the wheat trade inevitably to larger and less encumbered sources. They had no hesitation in shaking off their old and inefficient suppliers who were left, along with their Government, to exploit their distorted ecological and economic environment in the ways to which the stimulus to increase had led them. The great wheat trade, which had re-orientated much of the agriculture of the NWP and Oudh, was in fact doomed to come to a relatively early end. "All wheat must ultimately come from the provinces of the West," a contributor to the columns of the *Indian Agriculturist* commented as early as 1876, "for the reason that the steam ploughs and steam agriculture of the future will only there have adequate range. Cultivated in a scientific manner and on broad Christian principles, Western America could produce more than double enough grain for the whole population of the globe. And of course what can be, will be. And what will the husbandmen [of India] do then, poor things?"[7]

[7]*Indian Agriculturist*, September 1, 1876, p. 241.

REFERENCE MATERIAL

APPENDIX I

THE FASLI YEAR

Fasli Month	Corresponding Month of Luni-Solar Calendar	Corresponding English Calendar Month	Distribution of Significant Climatic Disorder
Asarh	3rd month	June–July	Delay in rains : kharif sowings delayed. Failure of rains : kharif lost.
Savan	4th month	July–August	
Bhadon	5th month	August–September	Heavy rain : ripening kharif damaged.
Kuar (or Asoj)	6th month	September–October	
Kartik	7th month	October–November	Failure of rains : no rabi sowings, except on irrigated land.
Aghan (or Mangsir)	8th month	November–December	
Pus	9th month	December–January	Failure of rains : rabi lost, except on irrigated land.
Magh	10th month	January–February	
Phagun	11th month	February–March	Rain or heat storms : ripening rabi damaged.
Chait	12th month	March–April	
Baisakh	1st month	April–May	
Jeth	2nd month	May–June	

APPENDIX 2

NWP AND OUDH : STAPLE CROPS

Indigenous Name	Crop Botanical Name	Sown in (fasli months) [a]	Sown Alone/Mixed : Required Amount of Seed per Acre (estimate)	Harvested in (fasli months) [a]	Outturn per Acre (estimate in maunds of fair yields) [b]
A. KHARIF					
Sawan	*panicum frumentaceum*	Jeth–Asarh	Alone c. 4 seers. With other crops : Less.	Bhadon	8–10
Kakun	*panicum italicum*	Jeth–Asarh	Generally mixed.	Bhadon	Less than 8
Makra	*cynosurus coracanus*	Asarh	Generally alone : 4–5 seers.	Bhadon–Kuar	14–15
Kodon	*paspalum scrobiculatum*	Asarh	Generally with arahar : 6–7 seers.	Kuar	10–11
Junhari/Makei	maize : *zea mays*	Asarh	Alone : 3–4 seers. Generally with other crops : Less.	Kuar	c 12
Jowar	*holcus sorghum*	Asarh	Alone : c. 4 seers. Generally with other crops : Less.	Kartik	c. 12–14
Bajra	*holcus spicatum*	Asarh	Alone : c. 4 seers. Generally with other crops : Less.	Kartik	c. 12–14

Appendix 2 (Continued)

| Crop | | Sown in (fasli months) [a] | Sown Alone/Mixed : Required Amount of Seed per Acre (estimate) | Harvested in (fasli months) [a] | Outturn per Acre (estimate in maunds of fair yields) [b] |
Indigenous Name	Botanical Name				
Pulses :					
Urd/Mash	dolichos pilosus	Asarh	Alone : c. 4 seers.	Variety 1 : Bhadon Variety 2 : Kartik	Variety 1 : 1.5 Variety 2 : c. 8
Moth	phaseolus acoritifolius	Asarh	Generally with other crops : Less. Alone : c. 4 seers.	Kartik	c. 8
Oilseeds					
Til	sesamum Indicum	Asarh	Generally with other crops : c. 1.25 seers.	Kartik–Aghan	"Very limited quantity"
Fibres					
San	crotolaria juncea	Asarh	Alone : c. 4 seers.	Bhadon–Kuar	22 maunds prepared fibre
Patsan	hibiscus cannabinus	Asarh	Grown around sugar-cane plots.	Kuar–Kartik	Not given
B. RABI					
Gojai (mixed barley and wheat)	barley : hordeum vulgare wheat : triticum sativum	Kartik	Mixed seed : 1.5–2 maunds.	End of Phagun–Chait	Barley grain : c. 25; chaff : c. 25 Wheat grain : c. 20
	peas (several varieties)	Kuar–Kartik	Large peas : 1.5–2 maunds. Small peas : 1.3–1.5 maunds.	Phagun	Peas : 32–33 Chaff : 30
Jaukerai	barley and peas	Kartik	No standard proportion of constituent seeds.	Chait	
Madaraha/Mahobia	gram	Kartik	Generally sown alone, sometimes with linseed—1.25 maunds.	Phagun–Chait	Grain : 18–19 Chaff : c. 22

Appendix 2 (Concld.)

Crop		Sown in (fasli months)[a]	Sown Alone/Mixed: Required Amount of Seed per Acre (estimate)	Harvested in (fasli months)[a]	Outturn per Acre (estimate in maunds of fair yields)[b]
Indigenous Name	Botanical Name				
Rai, Sarson	rapeseed: *brassica* sp.	Kuar	Rai mostly sown with peas. Sarson mostly sown with barley. 1.5 seers.	Phagun	rai and sarson: 3–4
Tisi Varieties	linseed: *linun usitatissimum*	Kuar–Kartik	10–12 seers.	Magh– Phagun– Chait	10
C. KHARIF AND RABI Arhar	*cytisus cajan*	Asarh	Generally sown with early khan: 4–5 seers.	Variety 1: Magh Variety 2: Chait	Grain: 20–25 Chaff: 25
	sugar cane (several varieties	Planted in Chait	c. 5, 000. canes.	After a complete fasli year, cut the following Kartik	c. 90,000 canes

SOURCE : This table is based on data provided by J. R. Reid for Azamgarh district and applies to the general range of soil conditions of provinces and estimates of outturns for "unimproved" tracts; see *Azamgarh Settlement Report*, pp. 114–118.

a The precise time of sowing and harvesting within the fasli months differs regionally. As a general rule, these activities in the eastern and south-western districts precede those in the western and north-western districts by two to three weeks.

b For approximate actual yields, these estimates should be reduced by about 25 percent because of "regular" seasonal disorders.

APPENDIX 3

District[a]	"Average Year"		1860–61	
	Autumn	Spring	Autumn	Spring
	(inches)		(inches)	
Agra	17.33	11.70	9.55	0.40
Aligarh	20.93	—[b]	14.20	1.20
Allahabad	36.40	6.23	32.30	0.90
Azamgarh	35.31	4.98	20.38	2.50
Banda	33.57	4.97	12.37	0.40
Bareilly	32.73	5.21	18.70	0.90
Benares	37.25	3.03	24.18	9.60
Bijnour	32.74	3.42	4.01 (?)	1.70
Budaon	25.99	4.13	—[b]	0.60
Bulandshahr	16.33	4.08	3.13	0.72
Cawnpore	21.72	2.41	48.43 (?)	1.60
Etawah	25.99	2.67	27.22	0.00
Fategarh	21.14	3.63	13.91	0.80
Ghazipur	33.63	3.65	23.22	1.17
Gorakhpur	41.02	5.43	20.88	0.70
Hamirpur	28.00	2.82	20.00	2.30
Mainpuri	21.60	3.06	11.08	0.90
Meerut	17.30	4.67	6.60	1.40
Mirzapur	32.32	3.66	19.87	1.10
Moradabad	23.79	6.31	22.81	0.90
Muttra	16.45	1.83	11.00	1.50
Muzaffarnagar	24.82	9.56	8.99	1.00
Saharunpur	33.00	14.21	11.55	2.21
Shahjahanpur	24.96	5.90	27.21	3.00

SOURCE : R. Baird Smith, "Report on the Famine of 1860–61 in the North-Western Provinces of India," *P.P.*, 1862, 40, Chart III.

a No figures were given for Etah, Fatehpur, Jaunpur, Jhansi, and Jaloun districts.

b No figures given.

APPENDIX 4

INDIGENOUS AND OFFICIAL STANDARD MEASURES OF AREA, WEIGHT, AND CAPACITY, AS CURRENT IN THE NWP AND OUDH, 1860–1900

AREA	
Indigenous Measure	*Official Standard Measure*
Pakka bigha	3,025 square yards, or 5/8 of an acre (standard bigha of NWP revenue surveys)
Kachha bigha (= 1/3 to 1/4 pakka bigha) Biswa (= 1/20 bigha) Biswansi (= 1/20 biswa)	

WEIGHT AND CAPACITY	
Indigenous Measure	*Official Standard Measure*
Maund (= 40 seers)	87 2/7 lb. avoirdupois (standard fixed by Government of Bengal, 1833)
Seer (= 1/40 maund or 80 tolas)	2 lb. avoirdupois (standard fixed by Government of Bengal, 1833)
Chattak (= 1/16 seer)	

SOURCE: H. H. Wilson, *A Glossary of Revenue and Judicial Terms,* 2nd ed., revised with added case notes by Ganguly and Basu (Calcutta, 1950).

APPENDIX 5

NOTE ON NINETEENTH-CENTURY INVESTIGATIONS INTO SALINE-ALKALI SOILS IN NORTH-WEST INDIA

Alarm at the progressive deterioration of land in the command of the West Jumna Canal promoted the Government of Punjab in the late 1850s to draw the attention of the governor-general to the seriousness of the problem of reh and usar tracts. "For some time past," the chief commissioner of Punjab reported, "it has been known that many villages on the banks of this canal, in the Paneeput, Delhi and Rohtuk Districts, have been suffering from a destructive saline efflorescence. The accounts of poverty in some of these villages have been quite distressing ... [The] revenue remitted during the current year amounts to Rs. 19,510. At present, about 60 villages, or one-tenth of the total number of canal villages, are affected. But it seemed clear that the mischief is increasing yearly; that it would soon attain to very considerable proportions, and would entail fiscal loss to Government and suffering to the people."[1] On consultation, Colonel Baird Smith, Superintendent-General of Irrigation in the NWP, stated his view of the cause of the appearance of the efflorescence : he attributed it to the percolation under pressure of the canal water through the soil in various directions, the controlling factor being the volume of the canal and the difference between the surface level of the water within the channel and the surface of the surrounding country. A safety limit for such pressure could not be estimated exactly, varying as it did according to local soil conditions, but Baird Smith knew of no evidence pointing to destructive percolation on either the rajbahas (distributary channels) of the East Jumna Canal or the small branches of the West Jumna Canal.[2] Four years later, while correspondence on the spread and intensity of reh continued to yield corroborating observations from revenue and canal officers, H. B. Medlicott, then Professor of Geology at Thomason College, Roorkee, recorded further scientific investigations in a note prepared for the

[1]Chief Commissioner, Punjab to Government of India (Public Works Department), to Governor-General, August 4, 1858, in *Selections from the Records of Government*, No. XLII, p. 1.
[2]Lieutenant-Colonel R. Baird Smith to Sudder Board of Revenue, April 13, 1857, in *ibid.,* at pp. 21–24.

Journal of the Royal Asiatic Society. Medlicott described the cause as a progressive concentration of soluble and partially soluble salts, originally distributed more widely throughout the profile, in the upper strata of the soil to a degree toxic to plant growth. This was brought about by changes in the rate of movement of sub-soil water through percolation, capillarity, and evaporation, and by the quality of the irrigation water itself. Samples from the Ravi and Ganges rivers (which fed the West and East Jumna canals) were found on analysis to be high in sodium sulphate and sodium chloride, the predominant salts characterizing reh and usar lands. At this point, Medlicott inclined to the view that the canal water was an exacerbating agent but not a prime cause, that the "natural" salt lands were made increasingly so by inefficient drainage—where, owing to low elevation and poor outlets for runoff, evaporation was the only means for the removal of surface water—and that insufficient application of water also played a significant part. Soils in which salts accumulated through high rates of evaporation and of capillarity were parched, never thoroughly soaked; there was no natural sub-soil drainage and no "free connection" therefore could be made with the groundwater stratum. He suggested that canal irrigation could well be used to provide the requisite soaking for the soil, to wash down the salts and establish a groundwater connection.[3] (This proposal for intensive water use clearly conflicted with the official canal policy of distributing canal water over an increasingly wide command area for revenue purposes). A further set of independent chemical analyses of usar samples was made by T. E. B. Brown, Chemical Examiner for the Punjab, in 1863. Brown concluded that the *local* usar, known as *kullur* in Punjab, was of three kinds, and that one, *chikna kullur,* consisting of nitric acid and soluble lime—which enabled it to be used as a neutralizing agent against the injurious compositions of sodium chloride, sulphate, and carbonate—characterized reh-affected soil.[4] Meanwhile, samples of reh had been sent for analysis to Dr. Thomas Anderson, Professor of Chemistry at Glasgow, who corroborated in general the reports of his predecessors : "*Reh* may ... be described as a mixture of common salt [sodium chloride] with much sulphates of soda, potash, lime and a small quantity of alumina." The cause of the condition was, in his view, due in essence to the presence in the soil of "some minerals rich in alkaline, the decomposition of which is promoted by the irrigation water and ... a large

[3] H. B. Medlicott, "Note on the Reh Efflorescence of North-West India, and on the waters of the Rivers and Canals," in *ibid.*, pp. 34–49.

[4] T. E. B. Brown to Deputy Commissioner, Lahore, April 11, 1863, in *ibid.*, pp. 68–69. Brown followed this with a note of July 16, 1863, suggesting a method by which nitrate of lime might be artificially produced as a fertilizer for reh, a modification of the method used for saltpetre production in Prussia (*ibid.*, pp. 69–70). This recommendation was in fact contrary to Government policy. Nitrates and other inorganic components of fertilizers were to remain "under the lock and key of the excise"; see p. 107 above.

quantity of these substances are converted into a soluble form, and gradually accumulate until they become so abundant as to become noxious to plants." For this condition, there was no doubt that drainage was the cure.[5]

Additional reports were received by the Government of India from Oudh. Usar was well known in Fyzabad, Bahraich, Lucknow, Sitapur, and Hardoi. It was in general a combination of reh, a mixture of highly soluble salts, and kankar, a residual insoluble precipitation, or hardpan; the relative proportions of reh and kankar were highly variable and were found in a variety of conditions differing widely in the affected districts. It was generally concluded that capillary action was the prime cause of the condition, in which, in Oudh, carbonates rather than sulphates and chlorides predominated. (It should be noted that modern canal irrigation was not introduced into Oudh until the construction of the Sardah system in the 1920s and 1930s, and that local usar was the product of natural decomposition together with induced ecological imbalance in the form of deforestation, erosion, and increased evaporation.) In their recommendations as to remedies, Oudh officers echoed their counterparts elsewhere: "surface irrigation or continuous flooding for a few seasons, and the application of manures, which, however, in the country the people would rather employ to raise the more valuable crops such as sugar-cane, poppy, tobacco, than to reclaim Oosur land."[6]

This correspondence on reh deterioration published in 1864 represents the first collected documentation on the problem and its scientific analysis. Copies were sent to the secretary of state, followed by the despatch in January 1865, "by the Screw Steamer, *Lady Jocelyn*, of three boxes containing specimens of soil from Reh land on the Western Jumna Canal, and samples of canal and spring-water" for analysis by an agricultural chemist. This was followed by a report on reh lands by the officiating superintending engineer, Punjab, and the executive engineer, Delhi Division, West Jumna Canal, together with notes on the sites from which the specimens were taken.[7] By order of Sir Charles Wood, the specimens were forwarded for examination to the Royal School of Mines and examined by W. J. Ward in the metallurgical laboratory. Ward's analysis of the canal waters differed vastly from Medlicott's earlier analyses of the natural waters of the source rivers in that the canal waters were found to be notably low both in chloride and sulphuric acid (a finding which was to be corroborated by later analyses of Ganges Canal

[5] Dr. Thomas Anderson, note of May 29, 1863, in *ibid.*, pp. 71–73.

[6] Lieutenant W. J. Carroll, R. E., Officiating Assistant Secretary, Public Works Department, to Chief Commissioner, Oudh, "Memorandum on Reports by Commissioners on 'Reh'," in *ibid.*, pp. 74–77. The farmers' preference was in line with Government policy. Carroll also noted the potential of canal irrigation as an inundating agent for reclamation.

[7] "Analysis of Specimens of Soil from 'Reh' Lands on the Western Jumna Canal," March 24, 1869, in NWP, "Irrigation Proceedings," July 1869, Proceeding No. 134, pp. 1–8.

waters by J. W. Leather early in the twentieth century). In other respects, Ward added little to existing knowledge. He concluded that reh was a mixture of highly soluble salts, that water was the vehicle by which it was brought into prominence in the soil, and that the cure was the combination of sufficient irrigation, to wash down the salts, with adequate drainage.[8] The technical reports and accompanying papers were then forwarded for information to provincial administrations. The lieutenant-governor, NWP, recommended by way of immediate action that experiments in leaching (that is, the application of sufficient water to wash through the soil) and drainage should be begun, for which the central portion of the East Jumna Canal provided an opportunity. The governor-general's sanction was forthcoming, but for a moderate outlay, His Excellency being "of opinion that all that is really wanted is that the Canal Officers should select one or two badly-drained plots of ground where *reh* is prevalent; that they should drain them in such a manner as to ensure the relief of the soil from over-saturation to a suitable depth—probably 2 feet should suffice; and then encourage their cultivation with irrigation. . . . The whole operation must necessarily be of an exceedingly simple character."[9]

The progress of these modest experiments in reclamation was reported on annually, and annually they were shown to be of little practical value in that a return on investment was not immediately forthcoming. It was found, for example, that canal silt enabled crops to be grown on usar, but the operation was not directly remunerative. By 1875, the fairest promise seemed to lie in the direction of (non-agricultural) plantations.[10] Meanwhile, co-ordination between the analysis and experiments on reh and, in particular, its connection with canal irrigation, and the implementation of plans to extend the canal systems was non-existent. The construction of the Lower Ganges Canal proceeded, from 1873 to 1878, much of it to cover areas actually or potentially threatened by usar and reh, with no provision for preventive measures, although the existence of "the correspondence on the subject of Reh, its causes and effects, [which] would form a blue book in itself," was noted in a report on the canal plans of 1871.[11] The year of the completion of the Lower Ganges Canal, 1878, also saw the presentation of papers by the Reh Committee, the first specific committee of enquiry

[8]W. J. Ward, "Report upon the Soils and Waters from the Reh Lands on the Western Jumna Canal," in *ibid.*, pp. 8–13.

[9]NWP, "Irrigation Proceedings," July 1869, Proceedings Nos. 135–137.

[10]For typical reports on experiments, see, for example, "Experiments on Cultivation of 'Oosur' Land," in NWP, "Irrigation Proceedings," September 1873, Proceedings Nos. 69–73; "Results of Experiments in Reclaiming Usar Soil in the Aligarh Division, Ganges Canal," in NWP, "Irrigation Proceedings," October 1875, Proceedings Nos. 76–77.

[11]L. G. Jeffreys, "Report on the Lower Ganges Canal Project," in NWP, "Irrigation Proceedings," July 1871, Proceeding No. 21, Sec. 14.

to collate information on the problem. Amongst this collection of papers, the contributions by H. B. Medlicott, then Superintendent of the Geological Survey, deserve special mention for their exceptional clarity. In summarizing his scientific experience of the problem, Medlicott concluded that the combination of deforestation and evaporation and the presence and movement of excessive quantities of moisture in the soil accounted satisfactorily for the pronounced chemical "disturbance" known as reh, a distortion of the natural process of decomposition from parent materials in what would now be described as a semi-arid, alluvial tract. Revenue officers' observations and comments enlarged the empirical scene, but added nothing either to analysis or recommendations as to remedy. A note by Denzil Ibbetson, however, drew attention to Government's dilemma : commenting on Medlicott's papers, which he found academic and impractical, Ibbetson asked rhetorically as to how it was assumed the forest cover might be restored—and, in other parts of his discussion, attributed to the cultivators the harmful practice of flush irrigation, while making it clear that there was to be no alteration in the official canal policy (which had in fact given rise to it). The conclusion to the Reh Committee's deliberations was to adhere to precedent : a modest series of reclamation experiments.[12]

The outcome was as before. Whilst it was stated, for example, in 1888 that the Government of India attached great importance to the experiments, Colonel J. G. Forbes, R. E., Irrigation Secretary to Government, NWP and Oudh, admitted that, so far, all attempts at reclamation had proved unsuccessful.[13] With the implementation of Dr. J. A. Voelcker's recommendation that the permanent post of an agricultural chemist should be created for the Provinces, and the subsequent appointment of Dr. J. W. Leather, local analysis of reh and usar was begun on a more systematic, analytical basis. But the constraints of agency and means persisted. Practical experiments from the late 1880s were confined to the attempted reclamation of usar patches by plantation for fuel and fodder reserves and were rarely successful.[14] The problem and the tradition of experimentation (and its conventional budget) were, along with an invaluable technical literature which is only beginning to be explored, bequeathed to the twentieth century.

[12]For a summary of the Reh Committee, see pp. 77–79 above. Medlicott's classic paper is to be found in NWP and Oudh, "Revenue Proceedings," June 1879, Index No. 115, Proceeding No. 53. For Ibbetson's comments, see *ibid.*, Index No. 116, Proceeding No. 54. For a second note by Medlicott, in answer, see *ibid.*, Index No. 120, Proceeding No. 58.

[13]"Reclamation of Reh Lands in the NWP," in NWP and Oudh, "Irrigation Proceedings," September 1888, Proceedings Nos. 1–13. For Forbes's summary report, see *ibid.*, Proceeding No. 8.

[14]See pp. 83–84 above and, for example, "Reh and Usar Experiments in the NWP, 1891," in NWP and Oudh, "Irrigation Proceedings," February 1892, Proceedings Nos. 1–8; for 1894, see *ibid.*, January 1895, Proceedings Nos. 10–12; for 1895, see *ibid.*, December 1895, Proceedings Nos. 1–3.

APPENDIX 6

CHRONOLOGICAL TABLE OF PRINCIPAL STATUTES RELATING TO THE NWP AND OUDH, 1855–1901

Year Enacted	Number	Short Title
	I.	Acts of the Governor-General in Council
1855	XXVIII	Repeal of the Usury Laws
1859	VIII	Civil Procedure Code
1859	X	Bengal Recovery of Rents Act
1859	XIV	Limitation Act
1863	XIV	NWP Rent Act
1864	XVI	Indian Registration Act
1866	XXVI	Oudh Sub-Settlement Act
1868	XV	High Court Fees Act
1868	XIX	Oudh Rent Act
1869	I	Oudh Estates Act
1869	XXV	Salt Act
1870	VII	Court-Fees Act
1870	XXIV	Oudh Taluqdars' Relief Act
1871	XVII	Oudh Local Rates Act
1871	XVIII	NWP Local Rates Act
1871	XXVI	Land Improvement Act
1872	I	Evidence Act
1872	IX	Contract Act
1873	VIII	N. India Canal and Drainage Act
1873	XVIII	NWP Rent Act
1873	XIX	NWP Land Revenue Act
1876	XVII	Oudh Land Revenue Act
1876	XXI	Land Improvement Act, 1871 : Amendment
1878	II	N. India Licence Act
1878	III	NWP Local Rates Act
1878	IV	Oudh Local Rates Act
1878	XIV	NWP and Oudh Administration Act (amalgamation of local governments)
1879	I	Indian Stamp Act
1879	X	N. India Takkavi Act
1881	XII	NWP Rent Act
1882	II	Trusts Act
1882	IV	Transfer of Property Act
1882	V	Easements Act

Appendix 6 (Concld.)

Year Enacted	Number	Short Title
1882	XII	Salt Act
1882	XIII	NWP and Oudh Kanungos and Patwaris Act
1882	XVI	Jhansi Encumbered Estates Act
1883	XIX	Land Improvement Loans Act, 1883
1884	XII	Agriculturists' Loans Act
1886	XIV	NWP Rent Act
1886	XV	NWP Land Revenue Act
1886	XXII	Oudh Rent Act
1889	IX	NWP and Oudh Kanungos and Patwaris Act

II. Acts of the Lieutenant Governor of the NWP and Oudh in Council

1894	V	Oudh Local Rates Act
1897	I	NWP and Oudh Famine Loans Recovery Act
1899	III	NWP and Oudh Court of Wards Act
1901	II	Agra Tenancy Act
1901	III	NWP and Oudh Land Revenue Act
1901	IV	Oudh Rent Act (1886) Amendment Act

APPENDIX 7

Sections of Line	Date Opened (day-month-year)	Distance (miles)
1. East Indian Railway		
Main Lines :		
Moghal Sarai–Mirzapur	1–1–64	19.28
Mirzapur–South Bank Jumna	4–4–64	52.95
Jumna Bridge–Allahabad	15–8–65	2.75
Allahabad–Cawnpore	3–3–59	119.47
Cawnpore–Etawah	1–7–61	86.46
Etawah–Shikohabad	13–11–61	34.39
Shikohabad–Tundla Junction	1–4–62	22.92
Tundla Junction–Aligarh	1–3–63	48.56
Aligarh–Chola	1–4–64	35.54
Chola–Ghaziabad	1–8–64	29.14
Agra Branch :		
Tundla Junction–Jumna Bridge	1–4–62	12.52
(Jumna Bridge–Agra City	1–1–08	0.96)
Hathras Branch :		
Hathras Junction–Hathras Kilah	1–11–98	5.92
2. Oudh and Rohilkhand Railway		
Main Lines :		
Benares Cantonment–Rae Bareli	4–4–98	138.78
Rae Bareli–Lucknow	15–10–93	48.68
Lucknow–Sandila	1–2–72	30.24
Sandila–Hardoi	15–7–72	33.00
Hardoi-Shahjahanpur	1–3–73	39.00
Shahjahanpur–Pitambarpur	8–9–73	32.00
Pitambarpur–Bareilly	1–11–74	13.00
Bareilly–Moradabad	8–6–94	56.07
Moradabad–Nagina	8–10–84	47.25
Nagina–Najibabad	1–4–85	13.74
Najibabad–Hindan Cabin	1–1–86	55.80
Benares–Lucknow Loop :		
Benares Cantonment–Shahganj	5–1–74	56.03
Shahganj–Bilwai	1–5–74	7.00
Bilwai–Malipur	18–4–74	9.00

Appendix 7 (Contd.)

Sections of Line	Date Opened (day-month-year)	Distance (miles)
Malipur–Akbarpur	2–3–74	12.00
Akbarpur–Fyzabad	10–6–73	38.24
Fyzabad–Bara Banki	25–11–72	61.97
Bara Banki–Lucknow	1–4–72	14.43
Bareilly–Moradabad Loop :		
Bareilly–Mile 5	22–12–73	5.00
Mile 5–Aonlah	1–11–73	11.00
Aonlah–Chandausi	10–6–73	27.00
Chandausi–Moradabad	28–10–72	27.22
Branches on Main Line :		
Cawnpore Branch :		
Lucknow–Left Bank of Ganges (Cawnpore)	23–4–67	40.78
Left Bank of Ganges–Junction with old East Indian Railway at Cawnpore	15–7–75	3.22
Branches on Bareilly–Moradabad Loop :		
Aligarh Branch :		
Chandausi–Rajghat Narora	28–10–72	30.48
Rajghat Narora–Aligarh	1–2–72	30.12
3. Lucknow–Bareilly Railway		
Main Lines :		
Lucknow–Sitapur	15–11–86	55.00
Sitapur–Lakhimpur	15–4–87	28.50
Lakhimpur–Gola Gokaram Nath	15–12–87	21.50
Gola Gokaram Nath–Pilibhit	1–4–91	57.55
Pilibhit–Bhojipura	15–11–84	24.00
Bhojipura–Bareilly	12–10–84	12.00
Branch Extension :		
Bareilly Grain Siding	1–4–94	1.75
Kaurialaghat Extension :		
Mailani–Sarda	1–1–93	
Sarda–Sohela	10–3–93	30.78
Sohela–Sonaripur	18–3–94	
4. Bengal and North Western Railway		
Main Lines :		
Sonepur–Mankapur (via Gorakhpur)	15–1–85	228.00
Mankapur–Gonda	2–4–84	17.36
Gonda–Colonelganj	20–10–91	17.89
Colonelganj–Jarwal Road	1–2–92	10.74
Jarwal Road–Gogra Ghat	18–12–96	2.78
Gogra Ghat–Chowka Ghat	24–12–98	3.67
Chowka Ghat–Burhwal	24–11–96	2.88
Burhwal–Bara Banki	24–11–96	16.38
Gorakhpur–Gonda Loop :		
Gorakhpur–Uska Bazar	15–12–86	39.66

Appendix 7 (Concld.)

Sections of Line	Date Opened (day-month-year)	Distance (miles)
Tulsipur–Balrampur	1–6–98	18.15
Balrampur–Gonda	15–12–96	23.08
Ajodhya Branch :		
Mankapur–Nawabganj (Gonda)	2–4–84	13.48
Nawabganj (Gonda)–Lakarmandi Bridge	1–12–84	6.00
Naipalganj Road Branch :		
Gonda–Bahraich	2–4–84	37.47
Bahraich–Naipalganj Road	15–12–86	33.15

SOURCE : *History of Indian Railways, Constructed and in Progress, Corrected to* 1945 (Delhi, 1947), pp. 78–84, 198, 209.

APPENDIX 8

TENANCY CATEGORIES AS RECOGNIZED BY STATUTE, FROM 1859

ACT X, 1859: Bengal Recovery of Rents Act.
  (1) Ryots holding at fixed rates of rent, unchanged since permanent settlement (Benares, 1795). (Sec. 3)
  (2) Ryots holding with right of occupancy acquired through continuous cultivation or holding of land for minimum of 12 years, provided ryots pay rent payable; occupancy right *not* applicable to : (i) sir (also known locally as *khomar, nijjote*) land of proprietor of estate or tenure and leased by him for a term or year by year; (ii) lands sub-let for a term or year by year by a ryot with occupancy right. (Secs. 5, 6)
  (3) Ryots without occupancy rights, entitled to pattas (cultivating leases) only at such rates as may be agreed on between them and persons to whom the rent is payable. (Sec. 8)

ACT XIV, 1863: NWP Rent Act.
Amending Act X, 1859. No further definition of tenancy categories.

ACT XIX, 1868: Oudh Rent Act.
  (1) Occupancy category as for NWP.
  (2) Non-occupancy (tenants-at-will) category as for NWP.
  (3) Tenants who have lost all proprietary right, superior or subordinate, in lands they hold or cultivate awarded a qualified occupancy right— *heritable but not transferable*—provided they pay rent payable and have been within 30 years from February 13, 1856 in possession by themselves or together with another from whom they have inherited proprietor in a village or estate and provided they have no occupancy right in any village or estate possessed by them or by a co-sharer under any proprietary right. (Sec. 5)

ACT I, 1869: Oudh Estates Act.
  Definition of proprietary title of talukdars.
  Talukdars (i) with whom summary settlement was made, 1st April 1858–10th October 1859; or (ii) to whom a talukdari sanad was granted between 1st April 1858 and passing of Act I, 1869. (Sec. 3)

ACT XVIII, 1873 : NWP Rent Act.

(1) Tenants in permanently settled districts or parts of districts holding land at fixed rates unchanged since permanent settlement awarded occupancy right at those rates : tenants at fixed rates.   (Sec. 5)

(2) Persons hereafter losing or parting with proprietary rights in any mahal awarded occupancy right in land held by them as sir in such mahal at date of such loss or parting, at rent fixed at 4 as in the Rupee below the prevailing rate payable by tenants-at-will for land of similar quality [that is, where a tenant-at-will might pay Rs. 2 in rent per acre, an exproprietary tenant of similar class of land in the same area would pay only Rs. 1.8], with similar advantages : ex-proprietary tenants, with all rights of occupancy tenants.

(3) Every tenant who has actually occupied or cultivated land continuously for 12 years recognized as holding occupancy right in that land : occupancy tenants.

   no tenant may acquire under this section occupancy right in (i) land he holds from an occupancy tenant, an ex-proprietary tenant or from a tenant at fixed rates; (ii) sir land; (iii) land held by him in lieu of wages.   (Sec. 8)

N.B. Occupancy right of ex-proprietary and occupancy tenants transferable *only* between persons who have become by inheritance co-sharers in such right.   (Sec. 9)

(4) Tenants without occupancy right : tenants-at-will.

On application of any tenant to have his class of tenure determined, the Collector or Assistant Commissioner to determine the class to which he belongs, of the 4 legal categories.   (Sec. 10)

All subsequent statutes enacted to consolidate and amend the rent law in the NWP and Oudh confirm these categories.

GLOSSARY

OF VERNACULAR TERMS USED
FREQUENTLY IN THE TEXT

Ahir Caste name; low-caste cultivator.

alsi Linseed.

amin Assistant official, clerk.

arahar Species of oilseed (see Appendix 2).

bahi Account book.

bajra Species of millet (see Appendix 2).

Bania Caste name; dealer, moneylender.

batai Crop-sharing, "rent" calculated and fixed on the threshing floor.

behri Shallow dish, basket for lifting water manually from irrigation ditches.

bejhar Mixed barley and peas.

bel Small-scale *gur* (molasses) factory.

beopari Small-scale itinerant trader.

bhaiachara Coparcenary estate, held in severalty.

bhala manas Respectable man, gentleman of substance.

bhur Sandy soil.

bigha Area measure, varying from region to region; an *ilahi* or official standard *bigha* under Moghul government was equivalent to five-eighths of an acre. See Appendix 4.

bijkhad Loan in kind, for seed and food.

bilmokta Lump sum.

biswa Area measure, one-twentieth of a *bigha*; see Appendix 4.

bund Man-made embankment, for soil and water conservation.

busati Local pedlars (eastern districts vernacular).

chak Block of units of similar productivity, grouped together as "circles" for purposes of administration.

chakdar Subordinate official in charge of each *chak*.

chakladar Revenue official in charge of a fixed region *(chakla)* under the Nawab of Oudh's administration.

chapparbandi Changes on house-building materials (collectively).

chaprassi Office or law-court attendant, messenger.

chari Fodder.

charrus Leather well bucket.

chaukidar Watchman.

chungi haq Service charge, exacted by artisans in kind at each harvest.

dak Mail, also (generally) stationery.

damdupat Rule of Hindu law, whereby a creditor was prohibited from realizing interest which exceeded the principal loaned at any one time.

dasturi Official charges (collectively).

daswans One-tenth (in loan calculations, rate of deduction).

dekhli Lever, with counterweight, for raising water for irrigation from a shallow source.

deora One-and-a-half times.

dhak A species of tree : *butea frondosa*.

dhan Paddy (see Appendix 2).

dholna Wooden club, for breaking up clods of soil.

dofasli Double-cropped land, from which crops are taken in both *kharif* and *rabi*.

dumat Loam, clay loam soils.

faslana Charges (collectively) realized at each harvest.

fasli Of the *fasl*, or harvest; *fasli* year denotes the agricultural year, from the sowing of *kharif* through to the harvesting of *rabi*, approximately June to April–May.

gainti Pickax.

gaon kharch Village charges (collectively).

gaud Partially manufactured indigo.

ghair maurusi Resident tenant, from 1859 defined as occupancy tenant.

ghat Landing place.

ghi Clarified butter.

gojai Mixed wheat and barley (see Appendix 2).

gomashta Steward, agent.

gul Watercourse, irrigation channel leading into a field.

gur Molasses, boiled down from the juice of sugar cane.

hal Indigenous plough of wood, occasionally found tipped with metal.

haldi Spice, turmeric.

halka Circle of villages, grouped together for administrative purposes.

halkabandi System by which such circles are grouped together.

haq Right, fee, perquisite.

haq chaharam Right to one-quarter of the proceeds from transfer of property.

haq-i-raiya Cultivating right.

haq kashtkari Cultivating right.

haq shufa Right of pre-emption.

har Tract of land.

harjins Tract sown with grain.

ilaqa Estate (Moghul revenue term).

jagir Officially granted right to a given tract of land (Moghul revenue term; alternatively, *jagheer*).

jama Revenue.

jamabandi Rent roll, system of revenue accounts.

jarhan Transplanted paddy.

Jat Caste name; cultivator.

jhil Shallow depression in ground surface, filled with rain water during the monsoon which is used for irrigation purposes.

jinswar According to crops (in connection with statistical statements listed thus).

jowar Species of millet (see Appendix 2).

kachha Incomplete, of rough material, temporary.

Kachhi Caste name; low-caste gardener-cultivator.

kachhiyana Garden crops, especially vegetables, traditionally grown predominantly by Kachhis.

kakun Species of millet (see Appendix 2).

kankar Calcareous rubble, found abundantly in alkaline tracts; used in road- and railway-building.

kankut Estimate of rent made from the standing crop.

kans Species of deep-rooted grass, especially common in Bundelkhand.

kanungo Subordinate official in Moghul and British revenue administrations, the immediate superior of the *patwari*.

karinda Agent, manager.

khadir Flood plain, adjacent to a river bank, cultivated in *rabi*.

khalsa Liable to revenue, tax-paying land.

kham Under Government management.

khand Refined sugar.

khandsari Small-scale sugar refinery.

kharif Autumn harvest, crops (collectively) sown with the rains and harvested from September to November (see Appendix 2).

khasra Official field book, index compiled at the time of village survey.

khateoni Classified list of cultivated holdings prepared at time of village survey.

khatunti Local system of account, by which prices for a given commodity were fixed according to a collective interest.

khewat Record of shares, interests, and liabilities of landowners in a village.

khudkasht A proprietary cultivator, cultivating his own holding; the holding so cultivated.

kist Instalment, portion of the annual (revenue) assessment to be paid at specified times in the year.

kodon Species of millet (see Appendix 2).

kolhu Bullock-driven cane crusher.

kubz Revenue contract, under the Nawab of Oudh's administration (alternatively, *qubz*).

kudali Hoe.

Kurmi Caste name; low-caste cultivator.

kurpa Trowel.

kusum Safflower.

lakh One hundred thousand.

lambardar Officially appointed representative of a "village community."

Lodha Caste name; low-caste cultivator.

mahajan Dealer, trader, frequently also moneylender.

mahal Territorially defined right of a zamindar, estate.

mahwah Species of tree, valued for its timber, fruit, and flowers.

malbah Account consisting of summary of cash payments.

malguzar Proprietor of revenue-paying land.

malguzari Revenue-paying land.

Mali Caste name; low-caste gardener-cultivator.

malik Master, powerful man, also landowner, proprietor (literally, one possessing a *milk* [alternatively, *milkiat*], "mastership," "proprietary right").

malikana Dues payable to a *malik*.

masur Species of pulse, grown in *rabi*.

maund Measure of weight and capacity (see Appendix 4).

maurusi Non-resident cultivator, from 1859 included in general category of tenants-at-will.

mauza village.

Mitakshara Title of treatise on Hindu law of inheritance and of school of Hindu law for which that treatise was authoritative.

mofussil Rural hinterland, countryside.

mohurrir Clerk.

mokuddam Headman, of proprietors and/or cultivators resident in a village.

muafi Revenue-free.

munsifi Court of the *munsif* subordinate civil judge (the first or lowest rank in the civil judicature).

nankar Part of a zamindari exempted from revenue or set apart for the maintenance of an aged zamindar.

nijkari Rents taken in kind from common cereal crops.

nikasi Record of rental collected within a zamindar's *mahal*.

pahikasht Holding cultivated by a non-resident cultivator, fields at some distance from a cultivator's village.

pakka Complete, of good material, permanent.

pargana Administrative sub-division of a *tehsil*, consisting of a number of villages.

patti Lease, share in coparcenary estate.

pattidar Proprietary leaseholder.

patwari Village, or zamindari, record keeper, accountant; the lowest rank in the British revenue administration (alternatively, *putwaree*).

peri Tax, known in Pratabgarh district, on *mahwah* timber.

phiri Small service perquisite, claimed by artisans of parts of Bareilly district in addition to their main charges.

pur *Charrus*, leather well bucket.

qasbah Small town, local administrative centre.

rabi Spring harvest, crops (collectively) sown after the *kharif* harvest, in October–November–December, and harvested in March and April (see Appendix 2).

raiyat Cultivator, peasant (alternatively, ryot).

rajbaha Distributary channel of canal systems.

Rajput Caste name; warrior, landholder (sub-caste of Kshatriyas).

ras Juice of sugar cane.

rath Wheeled vehicle, a superior form of cart.

reh Saline efflorescence, crystalized in the dry season on the surface and in the upper strata of salt-affected soils.

rokra Account book, listing cash payments.

sadr Chief, principal (used in connection with administrative institutions).

sadr amin Subordinate magistrate under Company rule:

sahukar Small-scale dealer, trader, frequently also moneylender.

sarson Species of oilseed, fine mustard, commonly sown mixed with wheat and barley.

satta Contract, commonly used in indigo business; *sattawan*, according to the *satta*.

sawai Local zamindari charges realized at harvest.

sawan Species of millet (see Appendix 2).

sayer Miscellaneous dues (other than "rents") paid to zamindars.

seer Measure of weight and capacity (see Appendix 4).

sepahi Attendant, retainer.

shroff Banker-trader.

sir Land held by a zamindar under title of personal cultivation.

siwaia One-and-a-quarter times.

surai Encampment, resting place (properly, *sarai*).

surasuri Form of lease known in Muzaffarnagar district specifying "rent" per *bigha*, irrespective of type of crop sown but classified according to presence or absence of irrigation.

surraon Harrow.

Syud Name of community; member of Mohammedan proprietary community.

Taga Caste name; warrior, landholder (sub-caste of Kshatriyas).

takavi Official advances to cultivators from public funds for agricultural purposes.

taluka Regional sub-division, comprising several *mahals*.

talukdar Dominant member of regional society, appointed as revenue official under Nawabi of Oudh, defined as proprietor under British revenue settlement of Oudh, holding title to a *taluka*.

talukdari The rights of a *talukdar* (collectively).

tashki Form of lease known in Muzaffarnagar district specifying "rent" per *bigha*, irrespective of type of crop sown but classified according to presence or absence of irrigation.

tehsil Administrative sub-division of a district.

tehsildar Subordinate official of the revenue administration, in charge of a *tehsil*.

tehsili Office of *tehsildar*.

Teli Caste name; oilman, one who works an oil press.

terai Marshy wasteland skirting the Himalayan foothills at the northern border of both Oudh and Rohilkhand.

Thakur Caste name; warrior, landholder (sub-caste of Kshatriyas).

thok Local sub-division by lease of proprietary rights in a village.

til Species of oilseed (see Appendix 2).

ubari Right peculiar to part of Bundelkhand, whereby a subordinate chieftain was required to pay as revenue the difference (as *ubari*) between an amount arbitrarily fixed by his Raja and the collections of the estate assigned to him by his Raja, in the case of the latter exceeding the former.

ubaridar Holder of *ubari* right.

usar Barren land (Sanskrit, *ushtra*), commonly of moderate to severe alkalinity.

wajib-ul-arz Record of rights, compiled for each village at settlement.

zabti Cash rents, fixed according to types of crops.

zamindar Dominant member of local society, appointed as local revenue official under Moghul administration, defined as proprietor under British rule.

zamindari The rights of a zamindar (collectively).

zar-i-peshgi Local lease, approximately equivalent to mortgage with possession in British Indian law.

zar-i-peshgidar Holder of such lease, quasi-"mortgagee."

ziladar Subordinate official, heading local branch of canal administration.

zillah District (Mughal revenue term).

BIBLIOGRAPHY

I. Unpublished Sources. India Office Records.

Government of India. "Famine Proceedings" (Proceedings in the Departments of Public Works; Revenue, Agriculture and Commerce; Revenue and Agriculture; Agriculture and Horticulture), 1873–1900.

Government of the North-Western Provinces. "Irrigation Proceedings" (Proceedings in the Department of Public Works, Irrigation Branch), 1864–1876.

———. "Revenue Proceedings," 1860–1877.

Government of the North-Western Provinces and Oudh. "Irrigation Proceedings" (Proceedings in the Department of Public Works, Irrigation Branch), 1877–1900.

———. "Revenue Proceedings," 1877–1900.

II. Published Sources.

A. United Kingdom. Official Reports *(Parliamentary Papers)*.

Baird Smith, R. "Report on the Famine of 1860–61 in the North-Western Provinces of India," P.P., 1862, 40.

"Report of the Indian Famine Commission, 1879," P.P., 1881, 71.

"Reports of the Select Committee on Colonization and Settlement in India" —First Report: *P.P.*, 1857–58, 7, 1 (261); Second Report: *Ibid.*, 7, 1, 165 (326); Third Report: *Ibid.*, 7, 1, 373 (415); Fourth Report: *Ibid.*, 7, 2, 1 (461); Fifth Report: *Ibid.*, 1859, 4, 1 (198); Sixth Report: *Ibid.*, 5, 261 (171).

"Report of the Select Committee on East India Finance," *P.P.*, 1872, 8 (327).

"Resolution Relative to the Canals of the North-Western Provinces of India," *P.P.*, 1865, 39 (343).

B. India. Official Reports.

1. Government of India.

Administration of the Guaranteed Railways. *Reports of the Consulting Engineer to the Government of India on the Oudh and Rohilkhand Railway for the Financial Years 1872–73, 1873–74, 1874–75.*

Finance Department. *Report of the Finance Committee,* 1886. Calcutta, 1887.

———. *Report of the Finance Commissioner,* 1887. Calcutta, 1888.

Report of the Deccan Riots Commission, 1875. Simla, 1876.

Revenue and Agriculture Department. *List of Agricultural Implements and Machines Which Have Been Experimented with and Found Useful in India.* Annually, from 1882–83 to 1891–92.

———. *Memorandum on the Restriction of the Power to Alienate Interests in Land.* Calcutta, 1895.

———. *Papers Relating to the Alienation of Land in India from the Agricultural to the Non-Agricultural Classes, 1891–1899.* Calcutta, 1899.

———. *Papers Relating to the Working and Amendment of Act X of 1859.* 2 vols. Calcutta, 1883.

———. *Selections from Papers on Indebtedness and Land Transfer.* Calcutta, 1894.

Selections from the Records of Government. Home, Revenue and Agriculture Department. No. CLV: "Correspondence Regarding the Law of Land-Sale, 1855–1879." Simla, 1879; No. CLX: "The Wheat Production and Trade of India." Simla, 1879.

Selections from the Records of Government. Public Works Department. No. XLII: "Correspondence Relating to the Deterioration of Lands from the Presence in the Soil of Reh." Calcutta, 1864.

2. Government of the North-Western Provinces.

Colvin, A. *Memorandum on the Revision of Land Revenue Settlements in the North-Western Provinces, 1860–1872.* Allahabad, 1872.

Directions for Collectors of Land Revenue. Agra, 1846.

Directions for Settlement Officers. Agra, 1855.

Henvey, F. *A Narrative of the Drought and Famine Which Prevailed in the NWP During the Years 1868, 1869 and the Beginning of 1870.* Allahabad, 1871.

NWP Court of Wards Reports, 1876–77 to 1899–1900.

NWP Internal Road Traffic Registration Report, 1882–83.

NWP Irrigation Revenue Reports, 1873–74, 1876–77 to 1899–1900.

NWP Reports on the Actual Outturn of the Cotton Crop, 1869–70, 1872–73, 1873–74.

NWP Reports on the Progress of Settlement Operations, 1860–61 to 1876–77.

NWP Revenue Administration Reports, 1860–61 to 1890–91.

NWP Settlement Reports:

Report on the Settlement of Agra District. H. F. Evans. 1880.

Final Report on the Revision of Settlement in the Aligarh District. T. E. Smith. 1882.

Report on the Final Settlement of Allahabad District. F. W. Porter. 1878.

Report on the Settlement Operations in the Azamgarh District. J. R. Reid. 1881.

Report on the Revision of Records in Ballia District. D. T. Roberts. 1886.

Report on the Settlement of Banda District. A. Cadell. 1881.

Report of the Regular Settlement, Bara Banki District. F. E. Chamier. 1879.

Report on the Settlement of the Bareilly District. S. M. Moens. 1874.

Report on the Survey and Revision of Records, Benares District. F. W. Porter. 1887.

Report on the Tenth Revision of Settlement of the Bijnour District. A. M. Markham. 1874.

Report of the Settlement of the Bulandshahr District, 1865. R. G. Currie. 1877.

Final Report on the Settlement of Cawnpore District. F. M. Wright. 1878.

Report on the Settlement of Eta [Etah] District. S. O. B. Ridsdale. 1874.

Report on the Settlement of Etawah District, for the Years 1868 to 1874. C. H. T. Crosthwaite, W. Neale. 1875.

Final Report of the Settlement of Farukhabad District. H. F. Evans. 1875.

Report on the Final Settlement of Fatehpur District. A. B. Patterson. 1878.

Report on the Revision of Records and Settlement, Ghazipur District. W. Irvine. 1886.

Report on the Settlement of Jaloun (Excluding Pargana Koonch). P. White. 1871.

Report on the Revision of Records and Settlement of Jaunpur. P. C. Wheeler. 1886.

Report on the Settlement of Jhansie [Jhansi]. E. G. Jenkinson. 1871.

Report on the Settlement of Mainpuri District. D. Smeaton, M. A. McConaghey. 1875.

Report on the Settlement of Meerut District, 1865–1870. W. A. Forbes, J. S. Porter. 1874.

Final Report on the Completion of the Revision of Records of That Portion of the Mirzapur District Commonly Described as the Gangetic Valley. G. Dale. 1887.

Final Report on the Settlement of Moradabad District. E. B. Alexander. 1881.

Report on the Settlement of Muttra District. R. S. Whiteway. 1879.

Report on the Settlement of Muzaffarnagar District, 1873, and Canal Tract, 1878. A. Cadell, 1878.

Report on the Settlement of Pilibhit. E. Colvin. 1873.

Report on the Settlement of Saharunpur. 1871.

Report on the Settlement of Shajahanpur [Shahjahanpur]. R. G. Currie. 1874.

NWP Trade Reports, 1877–78 to 1899–1900.

3. Government of the North-Western Provinces and Oudh.

NWP and Oudh Agriculture and Commerce Reports, 1877–78 to 1899–1900.

NWP and Oudh Foreign Trade Reports, 1877–78 to 1899–1900.

NWP and Oudh. *Opinions of Local Officers and the Local Government on the Subject of Land Transfer in India from the Agricultural to the Non-agricultural Classes.* Allahabad, 1896.

——. *Resolution on the Administration of Famine Relief in the NWP and Oudh, 1896–97.* 4 vols. Allahabad, 1897.

NWP and Oudh Revenue Administration Reports, 1891–92 to 1899–1900.

Pitcher, D. G. *Report on the Scarcity and Relief Operations in Oudh, 1877–1879.* Allahabad, 1880.

4. Government of Oudh.

Oudh Court of Wards Reports, 1881–82 to 1899–1900.

Oudh Revenue Administration Reports, 1867–68 to 1890–91.

Oudh Settlement Reports :

 Report on the Revision of Settlement of Bahraich District, 1865–1872. E. G. Clark,
  H. Scott Boys. 1873.

 Report on the Settlement of the Land Revenue of Fyzabad District. A. F. Millett.
  1880.

 Final Settlement Report of Gonda District. W. C. Benett. 1878.

 Report of the Regular Settlement of Hardoi District. E. O. Bradford, A. H.
  Harrington, W. Blennerhassett. 1880.

 Report of the Regular Settlement of Kheri District. T. R. Redfern. 1879.

 Report of the Land Revenue Settlement, Lucknow District. H. H. Butts. 1873.

 Report on the Revenue Settlement of Partabgarh District. W. A. Forbes. 1877.

 Report on the Settlement Operations of Rae Bareli District. J. M. Macandrew. 1872.

 Report on the Regular Settlement and Revised Assessment of Sitapur. M. L. Farrar.
  1875.

 Report on the Settlement of the Land Revenue, Sultanpur District. A. F. Millett. 1873.

 Report on the Revised Settlement of Oonao [Unao] District. W. Maconochie. 1867.

Selections from the Records of Government, 1868–69 : "Correspondence Relating
 to the Indebtedness of Cultivators in Oudh."

5. Law Reports.

Bombay High Court Reports, 1863, 1866.

Indian Law Reports—Allahabad Series, 1875–1900.

The Law Reports, Indian Appeals, 1877–1900.

Moore's Indian Appeals, 1856.

NWP High Court Report—Full Bench Rulings, 1867–1869.

C. Printed Books.

Aberigh-Mackay, G. *Twenty-One Days in India, Being the Tour of Sir Ali Baba,
 K.C.B.* London, 1880.

Baynes, A. *The Cotton Trade : Two Lectures*. London, 1857.

Benett, W. C., ed. *Gazetteer of the Province of Oudh*. Lucknow, 1877.

Black, R. D. C. *Economic Thought and the Irish Question*, 1817–1870. Cambridge,
 1860.

Buckley, R. B. *The Irrigation Works of India and Their Financial Results*. London,
 1880.

Carnegy, P. *A Note on the Land Tenures and Revenue Assessments of Upper India*.
 London, 1874.

Chaplin, W. *A Report Exhibiting a View of the Fiscal and Judicial System Introduced
 into the Conquered Territory above the Ghauts under the Authority of the Commissioner in the Dekhan*. Bombay, 1824.

Chowdhury, B. *The Growth of Commercial Agriculture in Bengal*, 1757–1900.
 Vol. I. Calcutta, 1964.

Chunder, Bh. *The Travels of a Hindoo to Bengal*. 2 vols. London, 1869.

Connell, C. J. *Our Land Revenue Policy in Northern India*. Calcutta, 1876.

Cooke, C. N. *The Rise, Progress and Present Condition of Banking in India*. London, 1863.

Corbett, A. F. *The Climate and Resources of Upper India*. London, 1874.

Crooke, W. *The North-Western Provinces of India. Their History, Ethnology and Administration*. London, 1897.

———. *A Rural and Agricultural Glossary for the North-Western Provinces and Oudh*. Calcutta, 1888.

Crosthwaite, C. H. T. *Notes on the North-Western Provinces of India, by a District Officer*. 2nd ed. London, 1870.

Digby, W. *"Prosperous British India."* London, 1901.

Dinker Rao, Raja. *Memorandum of Observations on the Administration of India*. Calcutta, 1862.

Dutt, S. C. *Compulsory Sales in British India*. Calcutta, 1915.

Eliot, J. *Climatological Atlas of India*. Edinburgh, 1906.

Engelbrecht, Th. *Die Feldfrüchte Indiens in ihrer geographischen Verbreitung*. Abhandlungen des Hamburgischen Kolonialinstitutes, Bd. XIX, Reihe E., Angewandte Naturwissenschaften, Landwirtschaft und Technologie, Bd. 3. Hamburg, 1914.

Fawcett, C. *The First Century of British Justice in India*. London, 1934.

Ghose, R. *The Law of Mortgage in India*. 5th ed. Revised by B. Ghose. Calcutta, 1922.

Gledhill, A. *The Republic of India. The Development of Its Laws and Constitution*. London, 1951.

Gupta, S. C. *Agrarian Relations and Early British Rule in India*. London, 1963.

Habib, I. *The Agrarian System of Mughal India*. London, 1963.

Helps, A. *Life and Labours of Mr Brassey*. 1872. Reprinted with an Introduction by Jack Simons. London, 1969.

History of Indian Railways, Constructed and in Progress, Corrected to 1945. Delhi, 1947.

Hume, A. O. *Agricultural Reform in India*. 1879. Reprinted with an Introduction by J. Murdoch. Madras, 1899.

Hunter, W. W. *A Life of the Earl of Mayo, Viceroy of India*. 2 vols. 2nd ed. London, 1876.

———, ed. *Imperial Gazetteer of India*. London, 1881.

An Inquiry into the Alleged Proneness to Litigation of the Natives of India; with Suggestions for Amending Some Part of the Judicial System of British India, by the Author of *An Inquiry into the Causes of the Long-Continued Stationary Condition of India, etc*. London, 1830.

Irwin, H. C. *The Garden of India; or Chapters on Oudh History and Affairs*. London, 1880.

Jain, M. P. *Outlines of Indian Legal History*. 2nd ed. Delhi, 1966.

Jenks, L. H. *The Migration of British Capital to 1875*. 1926. Reprinted, London, 1963.

Krishnamachariar, M. *The Law of Registration in British India*. Calcutta, 1931.

Lal, C. B. *The Taluqadari Law of Oudh*. Allahabad, 1910.

Landes, D. S. *Bankers and Pashas : International Finance and Economic Imperialism in Egypt*. London, 1958.

Lees, W. N. *Land and Labour in India*. London, 1867.

Macandrew, I. F. *On Some Revenue Matters Chiefly in the Province of Oudh*. Calcutta, 1876.

Mann, H. H. *Rainfall and Famine : A Study of Rainfall in the Bombay Deccan, 1865–1938*. Bombay, 1955.

McCord, N. *The Anti-Corn Law League*. London, 1958.

Mill, J. S. *Autobiography*. 1873. Reprinted, Oxford, 1954.

McMinn, C. W. *Famine Truths, Half-Truths and Untruths*. London, 1902.

————. *Introduction to the Oudh Gazetteer*. (A proof copy—one of seven printed —in the India Office Library, n.d., includes information dated to 1872.)

Moreland, W. H. *The Revenue Administration of the United Provinces*. Allahabad, 1911.

Mulla, D. F. *The Law of Insolvency in British India*. Calcutta, 1930.

Oldham, W. *Tenant-Right and Auction Sales in Ghazeepoor and the Provinces of Benares*. Dublin, 1873.

Pantulu, V. S. *The Hindu Law Relating to the Liability for Debt and Alienation for the Same, as Laid Down in the Smritis and Interpreted by the Earliest English Writers, and Decisions of the Courts from 1807 up to Present Day*. Bellary, 1899.

Partridge, M. *Early Agricultural Machinery*. London, 1969.

Rankin, G. C. *The Background to English Law in India*. Cambridge, 1946.

Robinson, P. Untitled Notes on W. Oldham's Memorandum, bound with Oldham, *cit. sup.*, British Museum Cat. No. 8022 g 22 1–9 (No. 2).

Silver, A. W. *Manchester Men and Indian Cotton, 1847–1872*. Manchester, 1966.

Sleeman, W. A. *A Journey Through the Kingdom of Oude in 1849–1850 : by Direction of the Rt. Hon. the Earl of Dalhousie, Governor-General, with Private Correspondence Relative to the Annexation of Oude to British India*. 2 vols. London, 1858.

————. *Rambles and Recollections of an Indian Official*, ed. V. A. Smith, 2 vols. 2nd ed. London, 1893.

Somerville, A. *Free Trade and the League*. 2 vols. Manchester, 1852–1853.

Stokes, E. *The English Utilitarians and India*. Oxford, 1959.

Strachey, J. and R. *The Finances and Public Works of India*. London, 1882.

Thorner, D. *Investment in Empire : British Railway and Steamshipping Enterprise in India, 1825–1849*. Philadelphia, 1950.

Thornton, W. T. *Indian Public Works, and Cognate Indian Topics*. London, 1875.

Voelcker, J. A. *Report on the Improvement of Indian Agriculture*. London, 1893.

Waterfield, G. *Layard of Nineveh*. London, 1963.

Watt, G. *A Dictionary of the Economic Products of India*. London, 1890.

Wedderburn, W. *Allan Octavian Hume, 1829–1912*. London, 1913.

West, R., and G. Bühler. *A Digest of the Hindu Law.* 3rd ed. Bombay, 1881.

Wilson, H. H. *A Glossary of Revenue and Judicial Terms.* 2nd ed. Revised with added case notes by Ganguly and Basu. Calcutta, 1950.

D. Articles in Nineteenth-Century Periodicals and Newspapers.

Baines, J. A. "The Distribution and Movement of the Population in India," *Journal of the Royal Statistical Society* (March 1893), pp. 15-16.

Campbell, G. "The Privileges over Land, Wrongly Called Property" (a paper read before the British Association, Belfast), *Indian Economist,* December 31, 1874, pp. 119-120.

"The Climate and Resources of Upper India," *Indian Agriculturist,* July 1, 1876, pp. 193-194.

Cust, R. "Tour of a Cook-Party in Egypt and Palestine," *Calcutta Review,* LXXXI (1885), 311-329.

Harington, A. H. "Economic Reform in Rural India," *Calcutta Review,* LXXIV (1882), 138-174, 382-418; LXXVI (1883), 153-181; LXXX (1885), 435-459; LXXXI (1885), 346-375.

"India," *Bankers' Magazine,* CLXXIX (June 1858), 430-431.

"India's Financial Position," *Bankers' Magazine,* CLXXX (March 1859), 145-148.

Knight, R. "Corn in Egypt," *Indian Economist,* April 15, 1871, pp. 234-235.

"On the Best Practical Method of Augmenting the Culture of Cotton in India," *Economist,* October 4, 1862, pp. 1093-1096.

"Oudh and Optimism," *Indian Economist,* October 31, 1874, pp. 61-64.

"R." "Indian Corn" (Letter to the Editor), *Indian Agriculturist,* September 1, 1876, p. 241.

Robertson, W. S. "Grain and Seeds," *Indian Agriculturist,* June 1, 1876, pp. 163-164.

Shaw, A. N. "On the Best Means of Promoting the Growth and Improving the Quality of Cotton in India," *Journal of the Society of Arts,* XI (1863), 235-242.

"Sir Charles Wood's Despatch Recommending the Perpetual Settlement of the Land Revenue," *Economist,* September 13, 1862, pp. 1009-1011.

"Tillage," *Indian Agriculturist,* April 1, 1876, pp. 100–101.

"Wheat and Its Culture," *Indian Agriculturist,* March 1, 1876, pp. 61–63.

"Why Is Not British Capital More Largely Invested in India?," *Economist,* October, 9, 1858, pp. 1121–1122.

"Xenophon, Duab." "The Last Rubbee and Khureef," *Indian Agriculturist,* October 1, 1876, p. 284.

E. Articles in Twentieth-Century Periodicals and Books.

Anantanarayanan, M., and G. C. V. Subba Rao. "The Influence of English Common Law and Equity upon Law in India," *Revista del Instituto del Derecho Comparado*, Nos. 8–9 (Barcelona, Nov.-Dec. 1957), pp. 118–127.

Barrier, N. G. "The Punjab Alienation of Land Bill of 1900," *Duke University Program in Comparative Studies on Southern Asia*, Monograph No. 2 (1966), p. 125.

Bhatia, B. M. "An Enquiry into the Condition of the Agricultural Classes in India, 1888," *Contributions to Indian Economic History*, I (Calcutta, 1960), 80–94.

Black, R. D. C. "Economic Policy in Ireland and India in the Time of J. S. Mill," *Economic History Review*, 2nd Series, XXI, 2 (August 1968), pp. 321–336.

Derrett, J. D. M. "The Administration of Hindu Law by the British," *Comparative Studies in Society and History*, IV, 1 (1961), 10–52.

———. "Justice, Equity and Good Conscience," in J. N. D. Anderson, ed., *Changing Law in Developing Countries* (London, 1963), pp. 114–153.

Gharpure, J. R. "The Law of Damdupat," *Bombay Law Reporter*, VI (July 1904), pp. 129–143.

Gledhill, A. "English Law in India," in W. B. Hamilton, ed., *The Transfer of Institutions* (Chapel Hill, N.C., 1964), pp. 165–191.

———. "The Influence of Common Law and Equity on Hindu Law since 1800," *International and Comparative Law Quarterly*, III (1954), 576–603.

Habib, I. "An Examination of Wittfogel's Theory of 'Oriental Despotism,'" *Enquiry*, Old series, No. 6 (Delhi, n.d. [1962]), pp. 54–73.

———. "Usury in Medieval India," *Comparative Studies in Society and History*, VI (1963), 393–419.

Krishna Menon, K. "English Law in India : The Law of Transfer of Property," *Revista del Instituto del Derecho Comparado*, Nos. 8–9 (Barcelona, Nov.-Dec. 1957), pp. 90–101.

Landes, D. S. "Vieille banque et banque nouvelle," *Revue d'histoire moderne et contemporaine*, New Series, III (1956), 204–222.

Leacock, S., and D. G. Mandelbaum. "A Nineteenth Century Development Project in India : The Cotton Improvement Program," *Economic Development and Cultural Change*, III (July 4, 1955), 334–351.

McKinley, E. "The Problem of 'Underdevelopment' in the English Classical School," *Quarterly Journal of Economics*, LXIX (1955), 235–252.

Owen, R. "The Influence of Lord Cromer's Indian Experience on British Policy in Egypt, 1883–1907," *St Antony's Papers, No. 17 : Middle Eastern Affairs*, No. 4 (Oxford, 1965), pp. 109–139.

Rajaraman, C. "The Law of Contracts in India," *Revista del Instituto del Derecho Comparado*, Nos. 8–9 (Barcelona, Nov.-Dec. 1957), pp. 180–185.

Ranade, R. K. "Damduppat in Hindu Law," *Bombay Law Reporler*, LIV (July 15, 1952), 49–57.

———. "Legal Proceedings in Respect of Debts," *Bombay Law Reporter*, LXI (August 15, 1954), 81–90.

Stokes, Evelyn. "The Fiji Cotton Boom in the Eighteen-Sixties," *New Zealand Journal of History*, II, 2 (October 1968), 165–177.

Venkataraman, S. "The Influence of Common Law and Equity on the Personal Law of the Hindus," *Revista del Instituto del Derecho Comparado*, Nos. 8–9 (Barcelona, Nov.-Dec. 1957), pp. 156–179.

Vicajee, F. R. "The Rule of Damdupat," *Journal of Comparative Legislation*, New Series, II (1900), 464–472.

INDEX

works as general stimulus to, 15, 175–176; expansion and advances for cultivation and revenue demands, 176–177, 190; sugar trade, 177–178

Sultanpur district: drought of 1864–65 in, 147–148; indebtedness in, 163

Sumroo, Begam, 6, 32, 48–49, 70

Supreme Court. *See* Courts, civil

Survey, area. *See* Records

Swamps: and canal percolation, 81

Syuds, 199–200, 230

Tagas, 225

takavi, 12–13, 110 ff.; pre-Mughal and Mughal prescription for, 111; Begam Sumroo's practice of, 48–49; under Company, 111, and Crown, 112–118; for works of permanent utility, 112; for seed, 113; in scarcity, 113; distribution of, to maliks, 113; official review of, 113–114; amendment of law relating to, 114–115; revised procedure, 1873, 115–116; subsequent modifications, 116–117; N. India Takavi Act, X, 1879, 117; advances compared with land revenue receipts, 117–118; recommended for well-digging, as alternative to canal, 175 n. 50

talukdari, 7, 13, 41–42; talukdari policy in Oudh, 124 n. 6

talukdars, 1, 17, 41, 54, 59; and revenue contracts, 50–51; as absentees, 57; and Sardah Canal scheme, 66; consequences of annexation of Oudh for, 121–122; economic condition of, and revised settlements, 137 ff.; service of, in Company militia, 138; retainers of, 140–141; distribution of revenue liability among, 143; as moneylenders, 166, 167–168

Tappal, tehsil (Aligarh district), 5

tehsildars: trade estimates of, 184; in administrative structure, 236–237; and revenue collection, 242, 245–246; and Dufferin Enquiry, 269

Tenants; definition of, 13, 14, 122–123; and compensation for damage, 90; occupancy tenants: multiple status of, 144; legal power against zamindars, 152–153, 159, 216–217; and administration of law, 213; see also *haq*; ex-proprietary tenants: 227, 228; tenants-at-will: 127; multiple status of, 144, 152; relations with zamindars,

151–152, 159; and sugar cane advances, 176. *See also* Landlord; Law, civil: Tenancy; Rent

Terai, 58, 65, 97, 168

Thakurdwara, pargana (Moradabad district), 228 n. 74

Thakurs: as cultivators, 44, 151; as zamindars and moneylenders, 167, 168 n. 27; economic condition of, and revised settlements, 200, 205–206; and property transfer, 225, 228 n. 74; and sugar interests, 225; and indigo, 163, 174, 230; and auction purchasers, 230

Thana Bhawan, pargana (Muzaffarnagar district), 75–76

Theobald, W., 207–208

Thompson, E., 164

Thornton, W.T., 85

Tika Ram, 229

Tilhar, tehsil (Shahjahanpur district), 224, 225 n. 62

Tobacco, 32

Trade: internal, prior to public works development, 15, 58–59; local distribution, 181–182; export trade and famine of 1860–61, 70, 75; public works and expansion, 179–180; and indigenous trading networks, 180–181; and local distribution, 181–184; export trade with Europe, 180; export trade and prices, 183; calculation of volume of trade, 183–184; registration of traffic, 183–184, 262–263; private trade and Government control, 196–197; Government profit from grain trade, 196; grain entrepreneurs and American prospects, 275–276

Transfer of Property Act. *See* Law, civil: Property: Transfer

Tremenheere, Lt.-General C.W., xxvi, 91, 94

Trusts Act. *See* Law, civil: Property: statutes

Turner, J., 257

ubari: and *ubaridars*, 51

Umrao Begum, 229

Unao district: irrigation in, 30, 31 n. 32; floods in, 93; rent in, 129; fragmentation and revenue liability in, 145; fragmentation and property transfer in, 202; compromise of transfer in, 227–228; litigiousness and fraud in, 216

FIGURES

Figure 1. NWP and Oudh. The State of the Harvests—Kharif and Rabi—by Divisions, 1864-65 to 1884-85. Source: *NWP and Oudh Revenue Administration Reports*. The key to the divisions is as follows:

NWP	Oudh
1 Meerut	1 Sitapur
2 Rohilkhand	2 Lucknow
3 Agra	3 Rae Bareli
4 Allahabad	4 Fyzabad
5 Jhansi	
6 Benares	

For estimates of 16-anna yields of staple crops in maunds and acres, see Appendix 2.

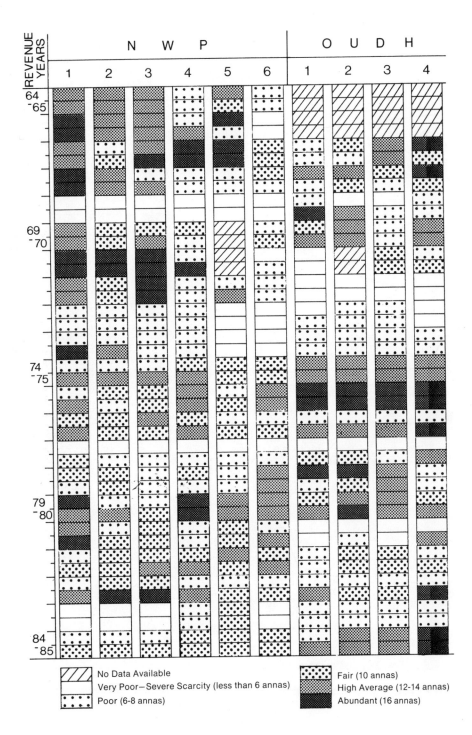

REVENUE YEARS

N W P

O U D H

1 2 3 4 5 6 | 1 2 3 4

64 -65
69 -70
74 -75
79 -80
84 -85

No Data Available

Very Poor—Severe Scarcity (less than 6 annas)

Poor (6-8 annas)

Fair (10 annas)

High Average (12-14 annas)

Abundant (16 annas)

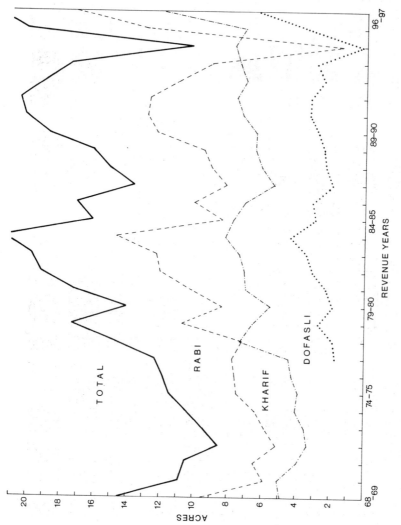

FIGURE 2. NWP. Canal-Irrigated Area, 1868-69 to 1896-97 (in hundreds of thousands of acres). Source: *NWP Irrigation Revenue Reports*. The figures for dofasli land are not available before 1876-77. The dramatic fall recorded for 1894-95 is explained by the excessive rainfall that year and the consequent contraction in the demand for canal irrigation.

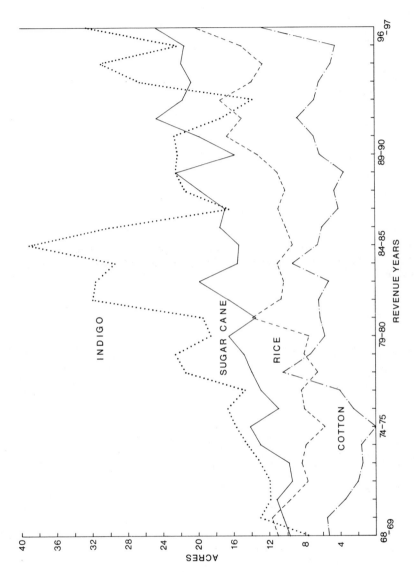

FIGURE 3. NWP. Canal-Irrigated Area: Kharif—Principal Crops, 1868-69 to 1896-97 (in tens of thousands of acres). Source: *NWP Irrigation Revenue Reports*.

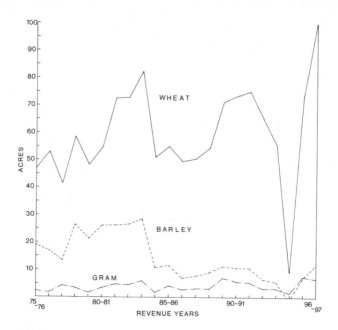

FIGURE 4. NWP. Canal-Irrigated Area: Rabi—Principal Crops, 1875-76 to 1896-97
(in tens of thousands of acres). Source: *NWP Irrigation Revenue Reports*. Figures before
1875-76 are not available.

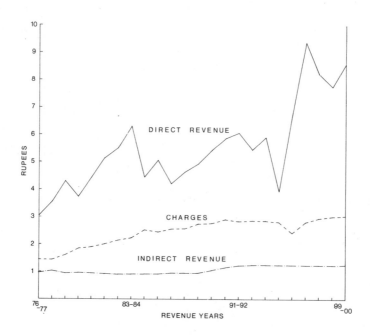

FIGURE 5. NWP. Canals: Revenue and Charges, 1876-77 to 1899-1900 (in millions
of rupees). Source: *NWP Irrigation Revenue Reports*. Direct revenue covers all classes
of water rates. Indirect revenue is the increment to land revenue. Charges are those
for maintenance, improvements, and the canal establishment itself (including leave
and pension allowances).

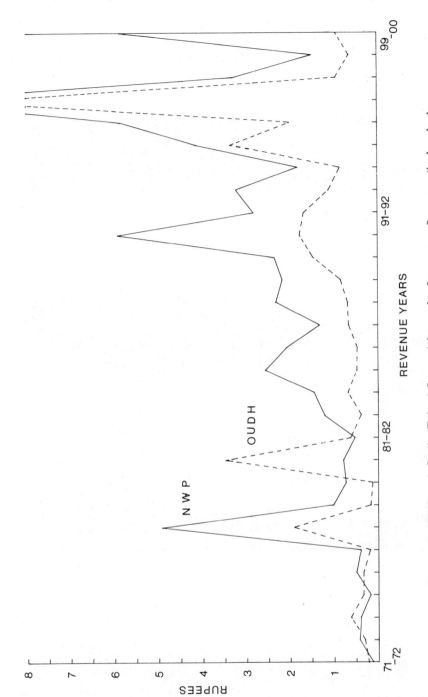

FIGURE 6. NWP and Oudh. Takavi Loans Advanced, 1871-72 to 1899-1900 (in hundreds of thousands of rupees). Source: *NWP and Oudh Revenue Administration Reports.*

REVENUE YEARS

64-65   74-75   84-85

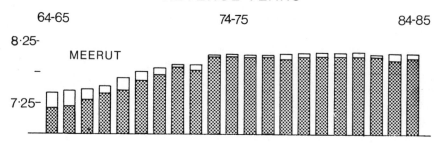

MEERUT

8·25-

7·25-

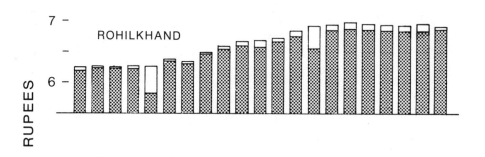

ROHILKHAND

7 -

6 -

RUPEES

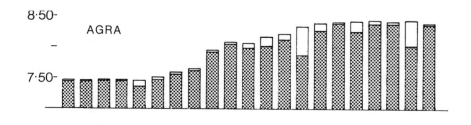

AGRA

8·50-

7·50-

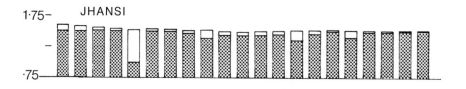

JHANSI

1·75-

·75-

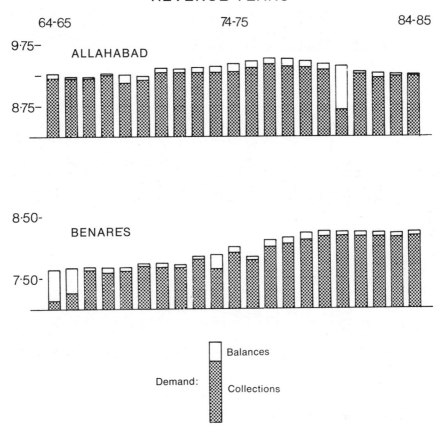

FIGURE 7. NWP. Land Revenue: Demand—Collections and Balances—by Divisions, 1864-65 to 1884-85 (in millions of rupees). Source: *NWP Revenue Administration Reports*.

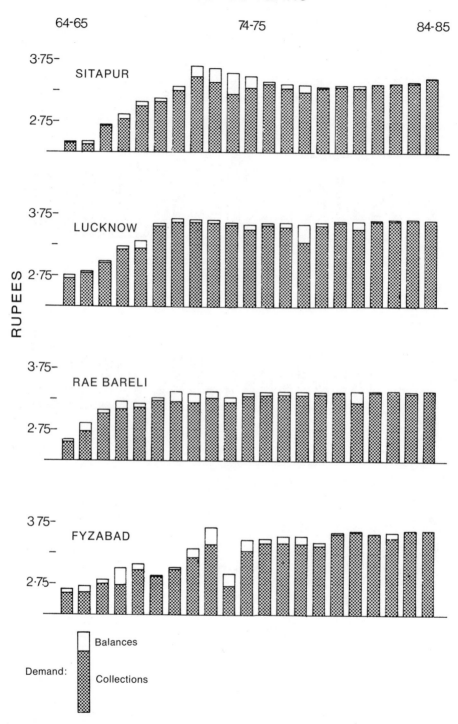

FIGURE 8. Oudh. Land Revenue: Demand—Collections and Balances—by Divisions, 1864-65 to 1884-85 (in millions of rupees). Source: *Oudh Revenue Administration Reports.*

REVENUE YEARS

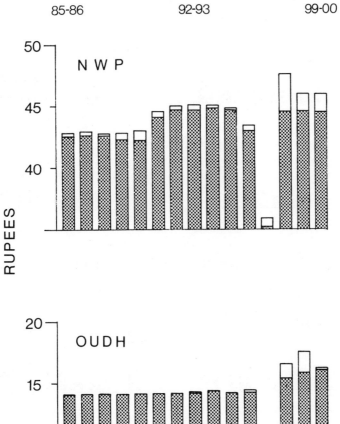

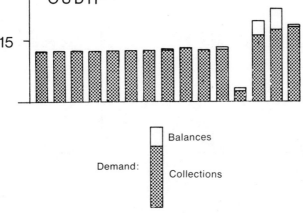

FIGURE 9. NWP and Oudh. Land Revenue: Demand—Collections and Balances—1885-86 to 1899-1900 (in millions of rupees). Source: *NWP and Oudh Revenue Administration Reports.*

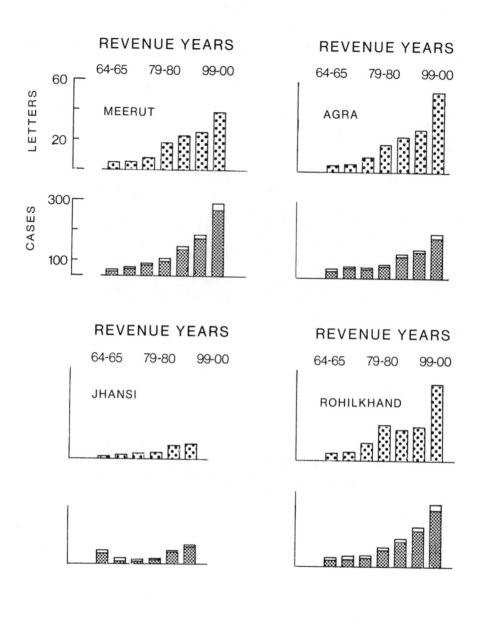

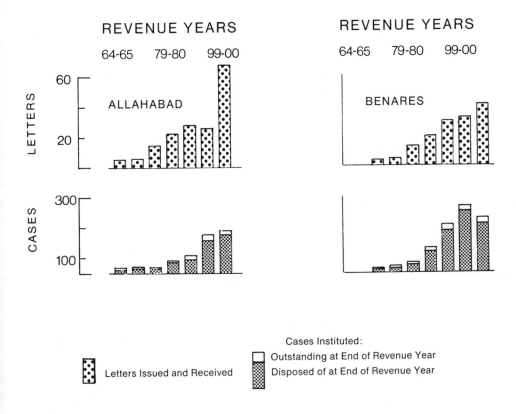

FIGURE 10. NWP. The Collector's Business by Divisions, 1864-65 to 1899-1900 (in thousands of letters and cases). Source: *NWP Revenue Administration Reports.*

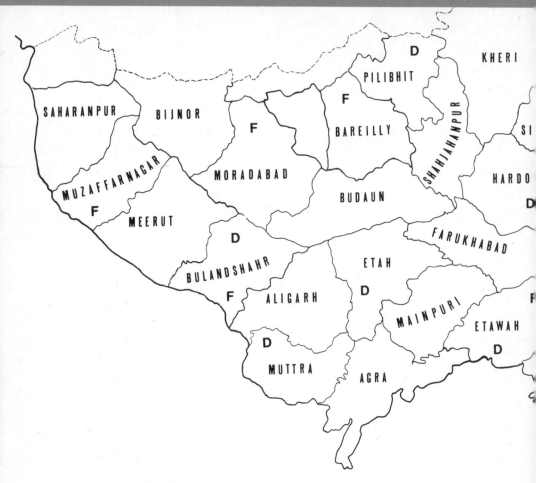

NWP AND **OUDH: ADMINISTRATIVE DISTRICTS**